CHRISTIANITY
The Pursuit of Divine Truth

CHRISTIANITY

The Pursuit of Divine Truth

Donald W. Ekstrand

Christianity: The Pursuit of Divine Truth
by Donald W. Ekstrand

Dr. Donald W. Ekstrand
P.O. Box 20784
Phoenix, AZ 85036

Printed in the United States of America

ISBN 978-1-60477-929-5

Library of Congress Cataloging-in-Publication Data
Ekstrand, Donald W.
Christianity: The Pursuit of Divine Truth
Includes bibliographical references, glossary and index
Library of Congress catalogue number – this number is pending.
1. Intro to Christianity. I. Title.

Unless otherwise indicated, Scripture references are the author's own paraphrased translation.

For more information about the author and this book, visit his web site:

http://www.introtochristianity.com

Book Cover: Stained-glass window at San Camillo Church in Milano, Italy

www.xulonpress.com

Table of Contents

List of Figures

List of Tables

List of Maps

PREFACE

This book is for the general reader or the college student who wants to understand the key beliefs and practices of Christianity. The students who attend my classes generally are not that knowledgeable about the Christian faith. Though 80 to 90 percent of them identify Christianity as their "religion of preference," most of them have mixed into their faith many of the cultural norms, standards, and values of our society. Because the majority are so lacking in biblical knowledge, it is important to begin with foundational principles.

The Goal of the Book

I write as a Christian who is committed to teaching and education. My goal is to make the information in this book clear, accurate, and readable. I have included diagrams and charts to illustrate key concepts, time-lines to give perspective, a glossary of terms to explain unfamiliar words and ideas, and a detailed index. In addition, I have placed the "scripture references" in footnotes at the end of the book to make for easier reading. *Christianity: The Pursuit of Divine Truth* does not attempt to cover every topic in depth; there are a number of excellent resources available to supplement your study should you desire greater clarification.

For those who have never before delved into religious ideology and history, the study of religion and the cosmos can be a daunting task. There are foreign concepts to be learned, belief systems to be evaluated, and spiritual mysteries to be apprehended. Such a study is challenging; it can enlighten the simplest and most obtuse minds, yet confound and astonish the most adept and sophisticated minds. Many believe God would have it no other way.

The Scope of the Book

Christianity: The Pursuit of Divine Truth presents Christianity from a number of different perspectives so that the reader can appreciate the substance and diversity of the Christian faith without being overwhelmed by its wide differences of opinion and practice. Within Christianity, as in all other religions, there are numerous subdivisions. Christians are extraordinarily diverse in their beliefs and practices, but they also share many common understandings.

Generally speaking, this book introduces Christianity from a thoughtful, orthodox position of faith. Though I have tried to be as objective as possible, like everyone, my own religious background and convictions may at times color my approach. A book like this is bound to be somewhat controversial no matter how hard one tries to be fair-minded and judicious in selecting material, examples, and topics. I encourage readers who spot any significant gaps in interpretation or historical understanding to further explore the topics that interest them through supplementary reading.

The Nuances of the Book

When speaking about God, I use the *masculine* pronoun throughout. To avoid it would involve using ungainly expressions like "Godself," which is not only awkward but also theologically problematic, because it undermines the biblical notion that God is a person. In addition, the masculine pronoun is called for since the Scriptures repeatedly use the terms Father and Son. I have also *capitalized* all of the pronouns used to represent God in order to highlight His distinctiveness from human beings, and to express His divine character with all due reverence.

For dates, I have employed the calendar designations that have been used in the West for the past 1,500 years. BC refers to the time "Before Christ," while AD refers to the time "Since the Birth of Christ." The initials AD stand for the Latin *Anno Domini,* which means "in the year of our Lord." Only since the latter part of the twentieth century have secular calendar designations been used: CE for "Common Era," and BCE for "Before the Common Era." The numerical dates are the same for both calendars; it is only the before and after designations that differ.

The Purpose of the Book

Religion is at the center of the vast majority of people's lives in the world today, and ever increasingly in the West, individuals are living side by side with people of radically different backgrounds and cultures. Sometimes people manage to adapt their ways to accommodate each other, while at other times they strive to maintain their ancient heritages despite the pressure to surrender them. The cross-cultural encounters that occur inevitably include religion. Because of the different religions in our communities it is paramount that we learn to live in a world of religious plurality. For many this will prove to be a difficult task. My hope is that this book will not only give readers a greater understanding of the Christian faith, but will also help them identify with the frailties and struggles that are common to all human beings.

INTRODUCTION

Christianity, like any religion, can be looked at either from the inside or the outside. When viewed from the *inside,* one gets a believer's perspective; when viewed from the *outside,* one gets a nonbeliever's perspective. I have attempted to incorporate both perspectives, though obviously within limits. Augustine held the conviction that, "one cannot fully understand a religion unless one believes it."[1] The truth of the matter is, it's impossible to describe Christianity without having experienced it, because to be a genuine Christian is to experience the living Christ inside of you. This spiritual reality is difficult for believers to explain to those who have not had the experience. In a sense it would be like trying to describe the experience of weightlessness in space without having been in space, or the experience of gravity on the moon without having been there. Yet, even these physical realities are relatively easy to communicate when compared to significantly deeper spiritual realities.

Over the years, many people have died for what they have believed. Many Christians have been martyred for their faith. When one attempts to teach about a system of beliefs that is a life or death matter to people, one will fail miserably unless he himself embraces that reality. For instance, a teacher might be able to explain the United States Constitution on a fairly sophisticated level, but he or she will not be able to match the spirit of those who labored over its formation, because they were willing to die for the freedom they were trying to protect. The more distant one is from the reality he is teaching about, the more sterile will his words be. Conversely, if someone teaches a subject about which he cares deeply, he will communicate far more effectively. As a practicing Christian, I trust I have presented the material in this book in a way that will help readers come to an understanding of a reality that transcends the physical.

The Need for Intellectual Honesty

Intellectual honesty is critical to the process of learning, especially when one is engaged in a quest for truth and is seriously seeking to maximize his or her potential in life. But being intellectually honest is not easy. It can be extremely difficult when new ideas and belief systems come into conflict with present ideas and beliefs. Most people are fairly passionate about what they already believe, and any challenge to those beliefs generally serves to make them defensive and uncomfortable. Over the years a lot of information has been written down on the chalkboards of our minds; though much of it may be accurate and helpful, some of it undoubtedly is erroneous and hurtful. It would be wonderful if each of us had a mind eraser to remove all of the pain and misinformation that we have accumulated on the chalkboards of our minds—but life is not that easy.

The famous American statesman Daniel Webster was a man of great wisdom and insight into the makeup of human beings. He believed getting a *new idea* into someone's mind was one of the most difficult things in the world, but he felt it was even more difficult to get an *old idea* out of someone's mind. Generally speaking, once people adopt a set of values and beliefs, two things happen: First, they continue to add to their paradigm, accepting any evidence that supports their position; and second, they begin to reject any evidence that runs contrary to their position. So, when we wed ourselves to a particular concept, it becomes difficult to divorce ourselves from it. Therefore, we should examine a concept very carefully before we adopt it as our position, because the end result is that this prejudiced position will now control our reasoning. It is sobering to think that there is enough information in the world to support one's *ignorance* on any subject. Let me explain. Probably three of the most sensitive issues in any society are politics, religion, and race. I believe there is enough information circulating in society to support one's hating any *political party* in our country—whether it be the Democrats, the Republicans, or the Green Party—if all you do is "selectively process" certain pieces of information. That's why we find so many people vigorously opposing each political party. It certainly does not help matters when self-serving politicians lace their campaigns with venomous attacks and half-truths about their opponents. Is it any wonder our citizenry is so partisan in its politics, so juvenile in its behavior, and so adolescent in its ability to work through differences and misunderstandings?

Let's look at another issue. There is enough on the information highway to support one's hating a particular *race*—whether it be Whites, Blacks, Asians, Hispanics, Native Americans, or whatever—if you selectively choose to believe only certain pieces of information. Likewise, one could apply this concept to hating a particular *religious group*. There is an abundance of information (selectively chosen) to hate Jews, Christians, Muslims, Hindus, and Buddhists. It is simply a matter of choosing to believe the information that leads to hatred, and rejecting the information that leads to acceptance. Some people even attempt to justify their hatred by pointing out how many people agree with them! Just because you can get a million people to agree with you does not make a particular position right; it only shows how extensive the problem of ignorance really is—it's universal!

Every year millions of people are murdered worldwide because people can find no other way to satisfy their hate, and America's statistics are some of the worst. Think about it—*millions* are murdered every year! Professor Thomas Schirrmacher was quoted by the German news agency *IDEA* that 43,000,000 Christians have been killed for their faith since the time of Christ.[2] That's an extraordinary number. There have been millions upon millions of Jews, Muslims, Hindus, and members of other religious groups who have been killed for their faith as well. And it's all due to the incredible power of hate! What kind of intellectual dementia moves people to such barbarism? Do we really live in a *value-free* universe? Is hate value-free?

In the following chapters, the information presented may or may not coincide with your belief system. I do not ask you to abandon your present beliefs, whatever they may be. I merely ask that you be willing to use your mind to the fullest. Education takes place where open dialogue and investigation occur through the uncovering and exploring of new ideas and concepts.[3] I invite you to join me on this journey as we look at the transcendent spiritual realities of the cosmos.

CHAPTER 1

THE WORLD OF RELIGION

What is the meaning of human life? To answer this question
at all implies a religion...the man who regards his own life
and that of his fellow-creatures as meaningless is not merely
unfortunate but almost disqualified for life.
— *ALBERT EINSTEIN* [1]

There are more than six billion people living in the world today,
80 percent of whom are associated with one of the world's five largest religions—Christianity, Islam, Hinduism, Buddhism, and Chinese traditional
religion. Six percent are affiliated with Primal-Indigenous or other religions,
and 14 percent claim no religious affiliation.[2] (See Figure 1.) Although 86
percent of the world's population are affiliated with a religion, the vast majority
of them are ignorant about the basic beliefs of their religion.[3] Therefore the
percentage of individuals in the world who claim to be religious adherents
is somewhat misleading. Though many individuals do identify themselves
as being highly committed to their religious beliefs, the vast majority appear
to have a fairly low level of commitment.

Figure 1 gives us a good idea of the percentages of people worldwide who
at least minimally identify with a particular religion. Obviously, the levels
of participation vary within each group. It should be noted that nearly every
country in the world has a single numerically dominant religion; that is, a
majority of the population in almost all countries are adherents of the same
religion. Because Christianity and Islam represent 55 percent of the world's
population, the predominant religion in the majority of countries around

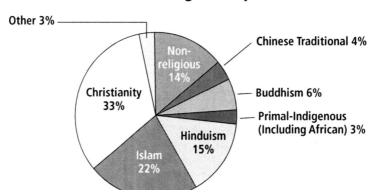

Figure 1. The approximate sizes are estimates derived from the Adherents.com database.

the world is one of these two religions, with Christianity being predominant in 171 countries, and Islam in 45 countries. The reason Christianity's total is significantly higher is due to the fact many of the so-called Christian nations have small populations. It should also be noted that the term "Primal-Indigenous" does not refer to a single religion but to members of traditional preliterate cultures. Some identify these religions as native or tribal. In the past, words such as pagan or animistic have been applied to these groups, but such identifications have gone out of favor and may be less accurate.

What Is Religion?

The religion practiced by an increasingly large number of Americans seems to be a syncretistic blend of Christianity, popular psychology, and personal superstition. Since antiquity the word religion has been used to signify the activity whereby a person gives proper reverence to God specifically through divine worship. In our modern secular state, however, the term *religio* is used in a more general sense, to describe systems of belief to which a person gives assent.[4] Because secularization lessens the influence of religious institutions in society, it promotes a "practical atheism" rather than a theoretical one. Coupled with the fact that secular ideology now dominates Western academia, the impact of America's religious institutions on society has been steadily decreasing in recent years, and with that decline we have seen a decay in the spiritual and moral fabric of society as a whole.[5] Traditionally when people wanted answers to life's ultimate questions, such as Why are we here? What is the purpose of life? What are we supposed to do? they looked to their ancestral myths or their sacred texts. But today we live in a different world. Since the eighteenth century people have increasingly turned to science for answers. The problem with expecting science to answer the ultimate questions of life is that its methodology is inadequate to answer such questions. What does interact with such questions is… *RELIGION.*

When most people think of religion, they think about the worship of a god or gods, and rightly so, since the worship of deities is at the heart of most religions. But due to the fact that not every religion in the world worships a deity, it's extremely difficult to come up with an all-inclusive definition of religion. Some get around this dilemma by categorizing the godless religions of this world as philosophies rather than religions. Having wrestled with a number of different definitions, two have become prominent in my mind. The first is by the great American philosopher William James in his book *The Varieties of Religious Experience.* James says that religion in the broadest sense, "consists of the belief that there is an *unseen order* [italics mine], and that our supreme good lies in harmoniously adjusting ourselves thereto."[6] Here, James differentiates between the world we see and the world we do not see. Religion transcends the physical realities that dominate postmodern thinking in the West, and ventures into a "spiritual realm" identified by religionists as the ultimate reality. In addition, James says the "supreme good" of man is not found in the visible world, but in the invisible world. And then he ends his definition by saying that the goal of human existence is to live in harmony with the unseen order; hence, all religions believe there is a right and a wrong way in which to live.

Another definition of religion that provides a good starting point is by Winfried Corduan in his book *Neighboring Faiths*: "A religion is a system of beliefs and practices that provides values to give life meaning and coherence by directing a person toward *transcendence* [italics mine]."[7] This brief definition has five basic elements:

1. Religion is a *system of beliefs and practices;* that is, it involves a number of ideas, doctrines, and ritual behaviors that the believer affirms to be true.

2. These beliefs and practices determine the *values* a person adopts for his or her life.

3. These values give *meaning* to one's life; that is, they give definition, understanding, and purpose to one's life.

4. These values give life *coherence;* that is, they make life a unified whole rather than a series of fragmented experiences.

5. It directs a person toward *transcendence;* to something beyond and much greater than himself. It is this directing of oneself beyond the mundane routine of everyday existence that we call transcendence.

For an individual to reach out beyond himself to a "Transcendent Reality" means two things: First, the realization that fulfillment in life is found in something greater than oneself; and second, the understanding that we are neither self-existent or self-sufficient. Christianity identifies this attitude as humility. Whereas the proud foolishly march on in ignorance, the humble realize their true condition and acknowledge their need for outside guidance.

So genuine religion implies that the ultimate meaning of life lies beyond the physical world in which we live. As the Greek philosopher Socrates put it, "the unexamined life is not worth living." Though theologians would agree with Socrates, religion (unlike philosophy) points to a Transcendent Reality beyond the natural order.[8] Whereas philosophy uses *reason* in its quest to understand reality, religion uses *reason and revelation.* C. S. Lewis said that philosophy is the mind's own study of itself in action by the method of reflection.[9] Philosophy therefore depends solely on the use of unaided human rational thinking to arrive at truth, whereas religion includes revelations given either in a sacred text or directly by God through a prophet. Religion and philosophy have in common their search for what is true about life. Though most philosophers today do not incorporate God into their reasoning, historically this has not always been the case. Aristotle and Plato both believed they could actually prove the existence of God. So human reason and belief in God are not antithetical. It was not until the sixteenth century that God was no longer the focal point of philosophical thought;[10] so it is important to realize that being religious is not the same as being *irrational,* any more than being philosophical implies being *irreligious.* The difference between the two disciplines is that philosophy only involves *thinking,* whereas religion involves both *thinking and belief.*

Nearly every religion has in its belief system an explanation of how the universe came into being, how it is structured, and how it operates. With an understanding of the meaning of life, each religion gives a corresponding definition to the ways in which people are to act and live. Because religions regard people as being both responsible and accountable, human lives are understood to be moving toward some ultimate reckoning or judgment; thus all religions imagine some form of life after death. Despite their diversity, most religions believe that meaning in life is found through a Transcendent Reality. Since religions recognize the superiority of the Transcendent, it logically follows that religious adherents honor the Supernatural with an attitude of submission, adoration, and reverence. Thus, human beings serve and worship the Supernatural in religion.[11]

The Origin of Religion

How did religion originate? Most modern scholars of religion simply accept the existence of religion as a given part of our humanity, because wherever we find humanity we find religion.[12] Religious institutions have been found to exist in every culture in the world. And just as there is a universal belief in religion, there is a universal belief in spiritual beings.[13] To account for this phenomenon, scholars today generally approach the origin of religion in one of three ways. First, some reason that the origin of religion simply *lies within us,* that a religious disposition is inherent in every person. They say all people have a feeling of absolute dependence, and this feeling demands that there is something to depend on; the feeling is expressed in terms of depending on an Absolute, which we call God. Those who hold to this position conclude that subjectivity is the exhaustive explanation for all religion; thus, all religion is rooted in subjectivity.[14]

The second approach reasons that man is a product of evolution, and therefore religion must be of human origin. Since the advent of evolutionary thinking in the eighteenth century, many have understood religion to be just another ever-evolving facet of human culture. When Western European scholars encountered a number of cultures that they considered primitive, they concluded, without any scientific proof, that these lower forms of culture were indicative of humanity in its earlier evolutionary stages. As such, they theorized that religion must have begun with a "basic feeling"; that is, a general awareness of a spiritual force in the world.[15] So the evolutionary model is very similar in one respect to the subjective model—they both present religion as something that humans created with reference to themselves rather than to a God who exists objectively and independently of them.

The biggest problem with the evolutionary model is that the kind of development it describes has never been observed anywhere in the world. Anthropologists today are discovering that the so-called *primitive* people groups are far more advanced than they ever imagined; thus they no longer refer to such people as primitive or pagan—they are now referred to as *preliterate.*

Though many of the preliterate people groups may not be as technologically advanced as the so-called civilized world is today, in many respects they exceed civilized man. For instance, the average person in America has a vocabulary of about 10,000 words.[16] In contrast, the Eskimos and the Zulus speak languages that are far more complicated than English, and their vocabularies are two to three times that of the average American.[17] During my years of graduate study in theology, I had the privilege of being a classmate of a young black man who had been raised in one of the most "primitive" tribes in Africa. His body bore the scars of numerous rituals that had been performed on him. He not only graduated faster than all of the other 150 students in my class—many of whom were exceptional scholars—but he took courses at such an accelerated rate that he had to receive a special dispensation from the school's administration to exceed the permissible number of courses one could take in a given semester; he took over 100 semester units of graduate study in a little under two years. You're probably wondering what his grades were like—his lowest grade was an "A." Today, Tokunboh Adeyemo is one of the top religious leaders on the continent of Africa.

The third approach to the origin of religion states that religion had its *beginning in God.* The argument goes like this: Since God existed prior to the human awareness of God (God created humans, therefore He existed prior to them), and people responded to God's self-disclosure, religion came into existence through God.[18] Most scholars credit German anthropologist Wilhelm Schmidt with this theory of Divine authorship. To summarize his research in numerous contexts around the world—be it Africa, America, Australia, Asia, or Europe—he found people everywhere believed in a God located in the sky (or on a high mountain) and almost always referred to Him with masculine language.[19] Schmidt visited some of the most primitive cultures in the world, including African, Filipino Pygmies, Australian Aborigines, and a few Native tribes in North America, and found that each tribe strongly believed in a Creator God and practiced little or no animism or magic.[20] Thus he concluded that scientific evidence clearly supports Divine authorship; that religion is not the result of some outside influence or missionary endeavor.

Functions of Religion

Religion serves a number of functions. It is through religion we see ourselves as we really are, we see the world as it really is, and we see the cosmos as it really is. As Robert E. Hume says, "Religion gives to a person what he can obtain from no other source—a confidence in the outcome of life's struggles through a personal connection with the superior power or powers in the world."[21] Hume also says that religion outlines the principles of an ideal society, and helps that society in which it exists.[22] So religion gives meaning to the lives of its adherents, instructs them in the path of life, and sustains them with hope in the face of suffering and loss.

Nearly all of the religions of the world hold that life has meaning and purpose, and ultimately, that meaning is grounded in relationships.[23] Most religions consider a *preoccupation with human happiness* to be self-centered and self-defeating; therefore, they enjoin their followers to give up three things: 1) a self-centered attitude to life; 2) the passion to possess material things; and 3) the need to exercise power over other people.[24] If people weren't so self-centered and preoccupied with themselves, they would discover genuine fulfillment in living and the wisdom of the spiritual maxim, that happiness is not the product of *selfish* living, but the by-product of *selfless* living.[25]

Religion offers answers to the four biggest mysteries of life: Why we're here; how we should live; what happens when we die; and why evil exists. Since religious life rests upon the various claims it makes about the nature of reality, and how meaning and value can be realized, let's examine these four big questions in more detail.

1. *Why are we here?* What is the meaning of human existence? Are we alive for some purpose? All religions agree that we are here for a reason, that our lives have some purpose, and they invite us to embark on a spiritual journey that can help us realize that purpose. As a whole, religions reject the idea that human beings are just material beings living in a purely material world; they teach that we each have souls and that there is a greater reality beyond the visible world. By accepting these beliefs, followers find deeper meaning and purpose in their lives.[26]

2. *How should we live?* Though the beliefs promoted by the world's religions differ greatly, the ethics they teach are almost identical. They all advocate compassion, mercy, and good works, and condemn murder, theft, and injuring others. Because the focus of religion in large part is on how we treat other people, each religion exhorts its followers to *think of others* and get beyond selfishness and self-absorption; to *practice charity,* because all we possess has been given to us by God to help those in need; to *forgive others* when we are wronged even if we do not feel like it; and to *build community,* because people reach their highest potential as spiritual beings when they live in communion with others.[27]

3. **What happens after we die?** All religions teach that a state of non-existence does not follow death, that life continues in some form after we die. Religions help people overcome the fear of death by letting them know what to expect when they die. Though most religions have a different answer as to exactly what transpires, they all insist that death is not the end.[28]

4. **Why does evil exist?** The problem of evil is one of the most perplexing issues that people face. For some, it is the reason they doubt or even deny the existence of God; for others it is the reason they have an intense hatred for God; for others it is the reason they question God's power or His goodness; and yet others accept the teaching their religion offers. Because religions differ so significantly on this issue, there is not one final answer that they offer collectively. However, there appears to be a number of unsatisfying answers: *Hindus* believe evil is just an illusion, that it really does not exist; *Christian Scientists* claim evil is all in the mind, that it's simply a matter of bad thinking; *Buddhists* believe it is one of those realities a person must accept until they can completely overcome their attachment to worldly things. *Atheists* find themselves passively accepting evil, because to them there is no God, hence there is no problem of evil; people must simply accept its reality and resign themselves to the pain and suffering evil brings, because no hope exists for a resolution.[29] *Christianity* maintains that God's plan for this evil-plagued world ends with the ultimate triumph of His greatness and goodness over all evil, and that it will ultimately be destroyed forever.[30] For a more extensive discussion on evil, be sure to read chapters seven and eleven.

Elements of Religion

Nearly all of the world's different religions include in their superstructure the same basic elements. Though they differ significantly in the beliefs that they promote, there are at least ten structural elements they all hold in common. These common elements are as follows:

- *Object of worship*—whether it be a God, gods, venerated beings, or spirits

- *Worldview*—each has a philosophy of how the universe operates: God, gods, dao, karma

- *Spirit World*—demons, angels, devil, ancestor spirits, nature spirits

- *Rules of Conduct*—belief in a moral universe with good/evil, right/wrong

- *Forms of Worship*—rituals, temples, shrines, liturgies, chants, sacred places, icons

- *Prayer or Divination*—for guidance, wisdom, forgiveness, blessing, assistance

- *Sacred Text*—sacred writings for literate societies, stories for preliterate societies

- *Spiritual Leaders*—prophets, priests, pastors, monks, shamans, medicine men

- *Time of Judgment*—by God or karma, it includes punishment and rewards

- *Future Life*—heaven or hell, nirvana or reincarnation

Understanding the various elements that make up the superstructure of the various religious belief systems makes it easier to navigate through the complexities of their beliefs and doctrines.

CHAPTER 2

RELIGION AND THE COSMOS

Religion is man's attempt to get into touch with an absolute
spiritual Reality behind the phenomena of the universe, and,
having made contact with It, to live in harmony with It.
— *Arnold J. Toynbee*[1]

Every religion gives a definition of the cosmos that helps its
adherents understand the bigger picture of reality. These definitions are often
referred to as worldviews. A worldview is simply how we view this world,
this universe, in which we live. Therefore religion is a way of understanding
the world. The philosophical systems developed by the Greek thinkers Plato
and Aristotle were worldviews. Every mature rational human being has a
worldview, whether or not he is fully aware of it. Becoming fully aware of
one's worldview is probably the most significant thing a person can do to
enhance self-understanding. We each have a deep-seated need to understand
reality in a way that is meaningful to us.[2] Every religion attempts to explain
one's thirst for the truth, one's need for significance, the problem of pain,
the question of evil, and the inevitability of death. Each endeavors to apply
the design of the cosmos to our lives individually. Every religious system
attempts to give meaning to existence, to explain that there is more to life
than meets the eye—that there is a Transcendent Reality. From the very
beginning, human beings have understood that there is a mysterious depth
to life that extends beyond the five senses. And alongside this recognition of

a Transcendent mysterious reality, there has been the conviction that human beings can contact it and be in relationship with it.

Types of Religion

Today, there are about six billion people living on our planet, and each of us uses our own set of glasses (worldviews) to make sense of the cosmos. No worldview is merely a theoretical philosophy; they are each intensely practical and affect the way people live their lives. The system of beliefs we embrace will include the most basic beliefs about God, the world, humanity, values and truth; and no human being is ever neutral with regard to God.[3] When someone looks at the world of reality from the perspective of a wrong worldview, the world will not make sense. In times of difficulty and uncertainty, a wrong worldview will leave the adherent bewildered and depressed.[4] If we adopt a false worldview, inevitably we will find ourselves going against the grain of the universe, and subsequently experience consequences we will not want to live with. If, however, we order our lives in accord with reality, we will not only find meaning and purpose, but also discover that our lives are healthier and more fulfilled.[5]

All human beings can differentiate between good and evil, right and wrong. Most humans who practice or believe in a religion act out of the primary conviction that the Transcendent Reality demands a certain kind of living from them. They often hope by their actions to achieve blessings in the next life as well as this one; therefore they follow prescribed behaviors in order to acquire these benefits. Humans also believe they have a responsibility for the quality of their lives.[6] Transcendence inspires and persuades people to worship and serve, and service usually has a strong ethical component. It involves showing kindness to others, which in turn brings stability and well-being to our communities.

There are thousands of religions in the world today, yet 94 percent of the world's population admit to being adherents to only seven of them—Judaism, Christianity, Islam, Hinduism, Buddhism, Naturalism, and Chinese traditional religion.[7] Though every religion has a very different idea about how God (Ultimate Reality) interacts with the world, all religions can basically be divided up into four groups: Monotheism, Polytheism, Pantheism, and Naturalism. Therefore everyone in the world essentially embraces one of four worldviews. In order to get a good picture of how many people embrace each of these worldviews, the world's population can be divided into seven parts. *Monotheism* accounts for four of those parts, while *Polytheism, Pantheism,* and *Naturalism* account for one part each. (See Figure 2).

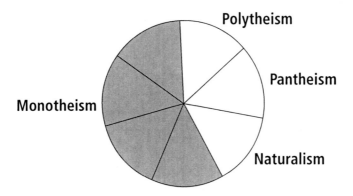

Figure 2. Types of Religion

Monotheism

Monotheism literally means God *(theos)* is one *(mono)*. The central tenet of monotheism, as the two words suggest, is that there is only "one God" in the universe. This Ultimate Reality is viewed as the eternal, infinite, personal Creator of the cosmos, who created both the material and the immaterial worlds out of nothing, and created humanity in His own image. Broadly speaking, monotheists believe this omnipotent, omniscient God oversees and intervenes in human events, and as a beneficent and holy being, is the source of all that is good. Thus the universe has a purpose for its existence, it is not just an accident in the cosmos; hence, the universe itself is not eternal or self-sufficient. God also designed and created not only the *physical laws* which run the universe, but the *moral laws* as well; as such, monotheism teaches that we live in a moral universe. Human beings live with the sense that they have significance and value, that life has a purpose, and that morality has meaning. The world's three monotheistic religions are Judaism, Christianity, and Islam.

The God of monotheism is described as being *transcendent*—that is, He transcends creation, He exists outside of it, He is beyond it; nevertheless, He is actively involved in it. God's involvement in our world is referred to as the *immanence* of God. Figure 3 shows the relationship between the transcendent God and the cosmos. The cosmos represents everything that exists in this orderly, harmonious, complex, systematic universe, both the material and the immaterial worlds, the seen and the unseen worlds.

As the diagram shows, God transcends the entire created order. As big and impressive as the cosmos is, it is infinitesimally smaller than God; that

God

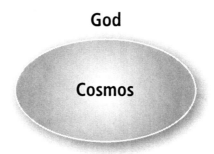

Figure 3. The Concept of Transcendence

is, it is so much smaller, it cannot even be measured. By looking at the circle on this page, it's easy to get the idea that both the cosmos and God are measurable, but that would be a gross misunderstanding. The God of creation, according to monotheism, continues ad infinitum (without end). Because God *created* the cosmos, He is neither to be identified as the cosmos, nor is He to be seen as dependent on the cosmos.[8]

When monotheists think of creation, they think of God's creation of the *space-time continuum;* some include *mass* in the equation, but such an addition is somewhat redundant since space and mass are essentially the same thing. The diagram above focuses on the *space* dimension of God's creation, but we also need to focus on the *time* dimension. Because God created time, He transcends time; that is, He is not bound by the constraints or the limits of time. Therefore, God is *eternal.* He cannot be placed within the parameters of the space-time continuum. To do so would humanize God and make Him out to be significantly less than He really is. Every monotheistic religion understands God as that Ultimate Reality which transcends the space-time continuum (the cosmos). Because God is eternal, His attributes are eternal, whereas all of ours are temporal and therefore vastly inferior. The prophet Isaiah puts it this way: "God's thoughts are not our thoughts, and God's ways are not our ways."[9] Therefore, if we try to define God in such a way that we can wrap our minds around Him completely, we reduce God to something far less than He really is. He then becomes the product of our imagination, rather than the Transcendent Creator of the universe. The God of creation is infinitely greater than all creation.

There are differences between the God of the three monotheistic religions, Christianity, Judaism, and Islam. All three religions strongly believe in a transcendent God, but the God of Christianity is more *personal,* more *immanent,* than the God of Judaism and Islam. Because Christianity gives greater focus to God's personal involvement in one's life, it gives greater emphasis to the fact that God is loving, good, merciful, and compassionate. Though God does judge absolutely, as Islam affirms, the God of the Bible also lovingly awaits the return of His wayward children and graciously and joyfully accepts them back when they renounce their sin and turn to Him.[10] In the Bible, God is portrayed as a *real person* who gives Himself in reciprocal relationship to human beings. Though God transcends creation, Christianity sees Him as actively involved in it. Christianity speaks about God as *personal* because it makes God less mysterious and theoretical, and more accessible and approachable.[11]

Monotheistic religions ascribe a unique value to humanity when compared to the value of the rest of creation. Christianity, Judaism, and Islam all believe human beings were created in the "image of God";[12] that they are the crown of God's creation. Among the *pantheistic* religions there is less of a sense that humanity is unique and of special value, because they see humanity differing from the rest of nature only in degree, not in essence.[13]

With regard to life after death, monotheistic religions maintain that people continue to exist as conscious individuals after death, either in God's presence (heaven) or in His absence (hell). All monotheistic religions define salvation as entering a state of eternal communion with God, which ultimately results in the individual being perfected. However, Christianity, Judaism, and Islam differ greatly on the way a person is saved. According to Judaism and Islam, salvation is attained by performing good deeds and following the moral law. According to Christianity, human beings are not capable of performing deeds that are good enough to merit salvation; therefore, they rely completely on the *merit of the work of Christ* on their behalf. (A complete explanation of Christian salvation is given in chapters ten and eleven.)

Monotheistic religions offer a way to understand the cosmological realities, and a way to live in line with those realities. All three religions would say the major task in life for human beings is that of discovering what is true and then living in step with that truth. Christianity helps people to make sense of the world in which they live, so they can order their lives more rationally and avoid behavior that will likely bring suffering, even when that behavior is not condemned by society as vigorously as it should be. Adultery, for instance, is often portrayed as glamorous by the entertainment industry, but it invariably produces anger, jealousy, broken relationships, and even violence. Christianity, like nearly every religion in the world, teaches that the transgression of moral law does not come without painful consequences. Therefore, if people want to live healthy, well-balanced lives, they must seek

MONOTHEISM

GOD / HEAVEN
Creator – Eternal – Personal

PEOPLE / EARTH
(Created in the image of God)

HELL
Eternal Separation from God

Note the three levels of existence in this graphic depiction of monotheism—heaven, earth (that sphere in which we live), and hell. All monotheistic religions believe the "goal" of life is to spend eternity with God in heaven, and they each believe this goal (salvation) is achieved by "works"; that is, something must be "done" in order to spend eternity with God in heaven. The key difference between Christianity and other monotheistic religions, is that the "work of salvation" is done by Christ Himself, not the individual. The individual must simply trust in the meritorious work of Christ on the cross for salvation. This central tenet of the Christian faith is explained in far greater detail in chapters nine, ten, and eleven.

to align their lives with the laws by which God has structured the world.[14] Because God determines the consequences of human behavior, human beings are encouraged to live life as God intended it.[15] To understand the moral laws of the universe is called wisdom in the Bible, and to be a person of wisdom is to live your life accordingly.[16]

About 55 percent of the world's population today embraces either Christianity, Judaism or Islam. Christianity is by far the largest with 33 percent of the world's population; Islam is next with 22 percent; and Judaism has a little less than one-half of one percent.[17] Monotheism differs from *polytheism* in its affirmation that there is only one God;[18] it parts company with *pantheism* by insisting that God is personal and must not be confused with the world that He has created; and it is the antithesis of *naturalism* in that it maintains that there is a God who transcends the created order, and is the source of its existence.

Polytheism

Polytheistic religions believe there are many *(poly)* gods and goddesses in the universe (i.e., millions of gods), each with its own specific significance.

It is commonly understood that each of these gods exercises dominion or authority over specific areas of life and the cosmos, and, as such, has a limited sphere of influence. The vast majority of these gods may be dominated by a supreme god or by a small group of more powerful gods. These gods are also transcendent beings who can reveal themselves in nearly unlimited ways—they are what they choose to be. Many of these gods are active in the world and can bring about either healing or harm. Another important element in polytheism, is that the gods worshipped are simply *intermediaries* to the ultimate reality, which is impersonal, not a being;[19] therefore the gods people worship are not ultimate reality. Polytheism attributes superiority to *nature* as the cause of the gods. This makes nature ultimate and not the gods, so nature, in a sense, becomes a substitute for God. Polytheists also believe that the world (nature) is eternal, which runs contrary to the scientific facts that the universe is *expanding* and *dying out*—therefore, the universe must have had a beginning.[20] We will discuss this in depth in chapter three.

Animism plays a significant role in polytheism. The word *anima* in Latin means "soul," so animists believe all physical objects possess soul. Hence, there are numerous nature gods in polytheism—sun gods, moon gods, earth gods, sea gods, rain gods, regional gods, and numerous others. An imposing mountain may be the home of a fearsome god; weather may be controlled by particular powerful deities; since fertility is crucial to survival in agricultural societies, a goddess of fertility is frequently held responsible for crop successes or failures.[21] In addition, polytheists personify abstract principles like love, war, marriage, wisdom, health and longevity. They see them as being inhabited by powerful spirits or gods. Since gods are seen as more powerful than spirits, they acknowledge their superiority and submit to them.[22] The sum total of all the gods and goddesses within a particular religion is referred to as its pantheon.

All natural disasters—floods, earthquakes, hurricanes, fires, drought, famine, etc.—are seen as *divine punishment.* As a result polytheists seek to appease the gods by satisfying their demands through sacrifices, prayers, and rituals. In Hinduism, millions of gods are thought to be responsible for certain events, such as creation, war, and preservation. People petition the gods for their favor, but the outcome ultimately rests with the will of the gods. About 15 percent of the world's population is polytheistic. Such a belief system is found in some forms of Buddhism, Hinduism, Chinese Traditional Religions, and various Primal-Indigenous Religions.

Polytheism also includes a belief in *ancestor spirits*. These are the spirits of deceased family members who have gone on to the spirit world. They

POLYTHEISM

ULTIMATE REALITY
Nature – Eternal – Impersonal

MANY GODS / SPIRIT REALM
The gods and spirits have limited degree of influence;
collectively they control the world.
There are thousands of levels of existence in this realm.

PEOPLE / EARTH

Note the three levels of reality in this graphic depiction of polytheism—impersonal ultimate reality, the spirit realm, and the earthly realm where human beings live.

are highly revered and treated with utmost respect. In polytheistic cultures each community has a spiritual leader called a "diviner"; such an individual is adept at communicating with the spirit world and getting the spirits to cooperate. These spiritual leaders are referred to as medicine men, witch doctors, or shamans. Because spirits have some powers that humans do not have, human beings are very conscientious about their duties to them. The spirits can come and go unseen, and can bring good and bad fortune to people's lives, but their powers are limited. Therefore, the relationship between human beings and their ancestor spirits is an interesting one. The living make sacrifices to benefit their ancestor spirits, who in turn bestow good fortune on the living. Thus this reciprocal relationship is beneficial for both the living and the spirit of the deceased. Each needs the other's assistance to experience good fortune in their sphere of existence. In the final analysis, if ancestor spirits refuse to bestow good fortune on their living descendants, the living only have themselves to blame. The common assumption is that the living must have offended the ancestor spirit in some way. Either they failed to honor them in some decision they were making, or they failed to carry out their ritual duties on their behalf. Polytheistic cultures often promote their most distinguished ancestor spirits to divine status.[23]

Pantheism

Pantheism literally means God *(theos)* is all *(pan)*, and all is God; therefore it maintains that the universe is God and that there is nothing in existence separate or distinct from God—as such, there is no difference between the creator and the created. All things are thought to be both a manifestation of God and an integral part of that which is divine. Broadly speaking, the central idea of pantheism is that everything constitutes a "unity" and this all-incompassing unity is in some sense divine. Albert Einstein was a pantheist of sorts. He believed in a God who reveals himself in the orderly harmony of what exists, not in a person who concerns himself with the fates and actions of human beings.[24] Pantheists see this divine substance as an *impersonal god* who is not concerned with, and cannot relate to, the suffering of people; therefore they avoid this problem altogether by denying that suffering even exists. Many pantheists believe that everything one experiences in life is illusory, that it is not real; only that which is lasting is real. Due to the fact that pantheism understands God to be impersonal, it is unfortunate that they refer to this reality as God, because Western thinking connotes God with personhood or a divine being. The impersonal god of pantheism is a difficult concept for most Western minds to grasp, because they assume God to be a person. But pantheism equates God with the *impersonal universe,* and in doing so, in contrast to Christianity, deifies the universe itself.

Regarding salvation, pantheists believe people are basically ignorant of their divine [impersonal] nature; thus they are encouraged to realize it through meditation, through which some may achieve the goal of *enlightenment.*[25] Therefore, the ultimate goal of pantheistic religions is to discover one's inner divine [impersonal] nature. This impersonal force can be tapped like an electric current. It's a matter of learning how to get hold of it and make it do things for you. Remember, this is not a god to be obeyed, but a force to be manipulated through meditation, spells, and incantations.

Some Eastern religions, such as Buddhism, insist that the goal of human existence is to merge into unity with the universe and eventually become one with the impersonal Ultimate Reality.[26] For most Eastern religions, liberation leads to the extinction of any *personal* existence. With regard to life after death, the goal for individuals is to lose their individuality by merging into the impersonal oneness of Ultimate Reality. Most pantheists believe life involves a series of reincarnations that are determined by the law of karma (that which judges your past life and determines your next life). They believe to live means to "suffer" (disease, pain, and death); therefore, to be reborn is a threat of continuing misery. The idea of reincarnation in Eastern religions is a *negative* concept; the desire is to be liberated from the birth-death-rebirth process. Pantheists see being liberated from the birth-death-rebirth process as the *ultimate goal* that will result in their being united with the Ultimate Reality. It is also commonly understood that this experience can take hundreds, thousands, or even millions of lifetimes to achieve. About 15 percent of the world's population is pantheistic—such a belief system is found in some forms of Buddhism, Hinduism, and in New Age thought.[27]

New Age Spirituality is an adaptation of Eastern pantheism in Western culture. It tries to get rid of Eastern pessimism and its seemingly endless lives of suffering, and replace it with an optimistic view of eternal progression of the self towards superior levels of existence. Many adherents of Eastern religion do not view their Western New Age counterparts very favorably; they feel offended at the way their religion has been perverted in the West. The Western form of pantheism is more correctly referred to as panentheism, and holds that god is "in" everything, not that god "is" everything. With this understanding, the New Age movement urges its followers to develop the [impersonal] god who is "in" them, because the divine nature of man has to

PANTHEISM

ULTIMATE REALITY
Impersonal – Nirvana

~~~~~~

PEOPLE / ANIMALS / SLUGS
Reincarnation / Law of Karma
(To live means to suffer)
Thousands of levels of existence

Note the two levels of realtity in this graphic depiction of pantheism—impersonal ultimate reality, and the earthly realm where all animal life exists. Every living being (human or animal) continually experiences reincarnation until it becomes one with ultimate reality. It is the Law of Karma that judges one's past life and determines the level of existence for the next life. The goal is to experience "nirvana"—becoming one with ultimate reality, no longer existing in the realm of the living.

be discovered inside oneself. A key discipline for them is to fan the flames of the impersonal *god-spark* within so as to become more and more like god.

Almost every facet of the New Age movement is based on features of Eastern religions; it borrows from them such modern religious practices as Transcendentalism, Spiritualism, Christian Science, Meditation, the use of Crystals, the search for physical and/or psychic Healing, and it even incorporates some of the language generally associated with Christianity.

The New Age experience is said to include deliverance from negative aspects of life, including "oppressive orthodox creeds or modes of thought (traditional Western religion), dysfunctional exploitative relationships, poverty, illness, boredom, purposelessness, and/or hopelessness."[28] The New Age goal is a way of life that leads to personal transformation, not simply throughout an entire lifetime, but over the whole course of a spirit's existence, which is believed to encompass numerous incarnations.[29] Therefore a common belief in reincarnation and karma provides a long-term framework in which to view individual spiritual progression.

Naturalism

The first premise of naturalism is that God does not exist; it sees the universe as all there is. By definition, naturalism excludes supernatural agency or activity; thus it is essentially an *atheistic* worldview.[30] It is a philosophical paradigm whereby everything can be explained in terms of natural causes. Naturalism's basic presupposition is that the material universe is the sum total of reality, that the universe in which we live contains no transcendent reality; as such, it is an *impersonal* universe. A naturalistic worldview assumes that the material which makes up the universe has never been created, but has always existed. It believes this always-existing matter just evolved into the present ordered universe by a blind, timeless process of chance. Thus humanity, as one part of the natural universe, is also the result of matter, time, and chance.[31]

Naturalism is most often referred to in the West as an *evolutionary* or *scientific worldview*. It frequently states that evolution is a "fact," which means the evolutionary worldview is the only acceptable description of reality. In our modern Western culture, it has become common for naturalists to claim that the Transcendent dimension to religion is simply a "fantasy" of ancient, less sophisticated people who knew less about reality than we know today.[32] Probably the most famous critique of religion in the nineteenth century was by the German social and political theorist, Karl Marx (1818–1883). He held that religious life was simply a symptom

Karl Marx (1818–1883), a German revolutionary socialist who is known as the "father of communism." His most famous work is *Communist Manifesto* (1848).

of unfulfilled human existence, that it was a medium for people to possess in fantasy what they did not possess in reality: affirmation, hope, love, faith in the future, and so on. In 1844, Marx wrote that religion was "the opium of the people."[33] For Marx, religion had become an oppressive structure supported by the governing classes who believed they were placed there by divine will.[34] As history records, Marx became the father of communism, which has been virulently antireligious.

The distinguished Harvard scholar Samuel Huntington has argued that the world is not divided so much by geographic boundaries as it is by the deeply held beliefs that people hold—their worldviews.[35] One of the major conflicts of our day is between two antithetical philosophies, theism and naturalism. Theism, as already mentioned, is the belief that there is a Transcendent Reality that created the universe; Naturalism believes that natural causes alone explain everything that exists. Therefore, ultimate reality is either *God* or the *cosmos*; either there is a supernatural realm, or nature is all that exists; either our lives have purpose, or we are simply cosmic accidents that emerged from the slime.[36] Obviously these two major worldviews are exact opposites.

It is interesting to note that there is *no evidence* to support a naturalistic worldview. Those who choose to believe in evolutionary naturalism do so not because the facts of science require it, but because this is the philosophical thought-structure they desire. Both the theistic and evolutionary worldviews require *faith*—the faith to believe that there is a Transcendent Reality in the cosmos or the faith to believe there is not. So, in one respect, both worldviews are religions. The theist worships a Transcendent Being and the naturalist worships (gives worth to) nature, himself, and science. The diagrams in Figure 4 illustrate the two competing worldviews.[37]

The diagram on the left illustrates the fact that in a theistic worldview, God exists outside the box, to which we might add two more important elements: God created the box and acts causally within the box. Thus, theism denies that nature always existed, and teaches that the natural order

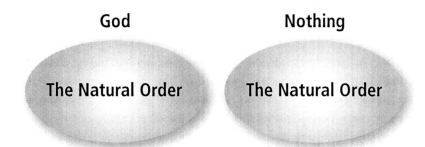

Figure 4. The Two Competing Worldviews

depends on God for both its existence and its order. In addition, all laws that operate within the natural order owe their existence to God's creative activity.[38] The diagram on the right illustrates the naturalist's worldview: man and nature are seen as completely autonomous; they act independently of any outside source.

One of the dominant views espoused in Western culture today is the belief that "this life" is all there is, and that nature is all that is needed to explain the cosmos. This naturalistic worldview believes life is simply the product of chemical and physical processes, without any outside intelligence involved. This is the worldview that is taught in our public schools and the textbooks.[39] As a result, students have been taught that science is in the only objective truth about the world in which they live. Because people understandably admire the scientific community, they are naturally inclined to accept whatever worldview *appears* to command scientific respectability,[40] and that view today is the naturalistic worldview. In chapters three and four we will examine some of the objective evidence from the world of science, as well as a number of statements by some of the world's leading scientists.

The question of morality often comes up when discussing naturalism. For the naturalist, morality results in *relativism*. If nature is all there is, then there is no transcendent source of moral truth; therefore we are left to construct a morality of our own. So the naturalist responds to the issue of moral decision-making by declaring it to be a matter of "personal preference." Such a position carries with it, however, a number of difficulties. Naturalists need to give a justification for behaviors that they choose. Why would one choose to live a good life as opposed to a bad life? Is there such a thing as good and bad? Was there something inherently wrong with the behavior of the Nazis? Was the Holocaust only horrible because a person "feels" it was horrible? Or was it "actually" horrible? The naturalist's *theory* precludes any appeal to the kinds of values that theists find central to a truly human existence; but the naturalist's *practice* shows that he does something quite different. When it comes to moral standards, the naturalist nearly always borrows from theistic worldviews. Once again the question is, why does he feel compelled to borrow? Obviously, naturalism and theism are polar opposites in the world of ideas—their views are discordant and in conflict—therefore, if one of them is true, the other by definition must be false.[41]

Naturalistic scientists try to give the impression that they are fair minded and objective, implying that theists are subjective and biased in favor of their personal beliefs. But naturalism is as much a "personal belief system" as is any religion. Naturalism begins with premises that cannot be tested empirically, such as the assumption that nature is "all that is, or ever was, or ever will be," as astronomer Carl Sagan said repeatedly on his popular science program *Cosmos*.[42] Clearly this is not a scientific statement, because it cannot be tested. Essentially it is a philosophy that is the foundation of the entire evolutionary model.[43] Sagan himself frequently claimed to be an atheist whose deity was the cosmos. He maintained that an infinitely old universe "requires no Creator."[44] In order to support his naturalistic worldview, he did what all evolutionists do. He injected into the evolutionary model such an enormous amount of time that one could conceivably allow for the "possibility" that anything is possible. That is precisely the hope on which this model rests. Contrary to popular opinion, however, the insertion of time into an evolutionary equation has never altered the laws of physics.

In spite of a lack of evidence, religion in the West is increasingly being displaced by secularism and scientism as the primary answers for humanity's hopes. The Englishman James Hung (1833–1869) stated that the secular disciplines are not value-free in the assertions they make; in fact "they can be just as obnoxious and domineering in their claims as religion; and just as destructive, if not more so."[45] About 14 percent of the world's population is naturalistic. Most of them are found in communist or former communist countries, such as the former Soviet bloc, and in Western Europe and North America.

Secularism and Pluralism

Sri Lankan scholar Dr. Vinoth Ramachandra writes about modern Western culture in his book *Faiths in Conflict*. He describes it as "the dominant global culture of our time" and identifies it as a "secularized culture."[46] He defines *secular* as a process whereby religious beliefs cease to be widely accepted and religious institutions cease to have much social or political influence. As a result, modern institutions displace traditional beliefs and engender a secular

(Western) sensibility; therefore the more secular a society becomes, the more *irreligious* it becomes.[47] Dr. Ramachandra believes the kind of religion that is practiced by most Americans is an eclectic synthesis of Christianity, popular psychology, *Reader's Digest* folklore, and personal superstitions.[48] What has happened in the West is that our secular values have strongly influenced many of our religious traditions, and this syncretism has resulted in a number of secular hybrids—religions of human invention that actually have no God at all.

The most fundamental tenet of secularism is that it denies the existence of the supernatural, and declares, like naturalism, that the physical universe is all that there is. Secularists see most religions as being restrictive and escapist, and contend that religion does nothing more than assuage the fears of ignorant people. Therefore they strive to free people from the shackles of religion.[49] Rather than promoting a theoretical atheism, secularism promotes a *practical atheism*, in which individuals function as atheists and live their lives completely indifferent to God's existence. So secularism begins and ends with humanity. It believes human beings have the ability to solve their own problems simply by looking within themselves, and by using reason and science.[50] By reducing the world to an object of technological research, secularism strips it bare of mystery and leaves humanity as the commander of its own destiny.[51]

Professor Allan Bloom says in his book *The Closing of the American Mind*, "There is one thing a professor can be absolutely sure of: almost every student entering the university believes, or says he believes, that *truth is relative* [italics mine]."[52] The philosophical idea that there are no absolute or universal truths, values, morals, or beliefs is at the heart of relativism. It is the idea that what is true or false, right or wrong, varies from time to time and person to person. The problem with *absolute relativism* is that for a society to be able to function there has to be some *consensus*; people cannot simply do as they please.[53] Imagine living in a world without rules where there is no right or wrong, no true or false. Who or what would you trust? The doctor? The mechanic? The salesman? The traffic? The water? The food? The electricity? The gas? Your money? Your parents? Your spouse? Your boss? Your friend? The list goes on infinitum. Why is it that truth must be relative when everything in life suggests it is not?

Pluralism and relativism maintain that there may or may not be a God, a heaven or hell, that people need to be open and tolerant of all views, because "all views are valid" for those who hold them. Pluralism says no religion can claim to be superior to all others. Such thinking is well entrenched in the academic world and is widely accepted on a popular level. Pluralism seems to capture nicely the spirit of this age. This approach at first glance feels very tolerant, but ultimately, it may be the least tolerant position of all, since the underlying belief of this system is that every other position's claim to legitimacy is bogus. The only ones who really have it right are the pluralists and the relativists, which is an exclusivism all its own.[54] It is important to recognize that even tolerance has *limits*, for how can we be tolerant of intolerance? The so-called "open mind" frequently does not seem to be much more than an empty mind.

Postmodernism

We live today in what is referred to as a postmodern world. We have just exited the *modern* world which was exclusively dependent on "reason" to obtain a knowledge of the cosmos. People living in America are now living in postmodernity, the time after modernity. Postmodernism is a term that has been widely used since the 1970s to denote a form of cultural philosophical change that makes a break with the era of modernism. Postmodernism is characterized by its rejection of the modernist ideals of rationality and individualism.[55]

Over the years, attempts have been made to divide history into different eras. Some have seen history like a book with as many as twenty chapters, while others have compressed it down to just a few. Table 1 shows history as being made up of five distinct periods:

Prehistoric World	Ancient World	Medieval World	Modern World	Postmodern World
2500+ BC	2500 BC	AD 500	AD 1500	AD 2000

Table 1. Five Periods of Human History

The *prehistoric world* was the era before man could write; the *ancient world* began with the ability to write history; the *medieval world* was the period that saw the collapse of the Roman Empire and of feudalism; the *modern world* was the age of reason and science; and the *postmodern world* means to have experienced the modern world and to have been changed by the experience—changed to such a degree that one is no longer modern.[56] Let me explain. Modernity was an era of conquest and control, the age of machines and analysis, secular science and objectivity. It was a critical age, the age of organization, individualism, institutional religion, consumerism. By contrast, postmodernity has become an era *postconquest* and *post* all of the other items as well; in short, postmodernity means culture has now moved beyond modernity.[57]

So postmodernity is a new era that is emerging out of the collapse of modernity. Postmoderns argue that *all knowledge* is subjective and personal, not objective and absolute. Therefore they say, "You have your truth, and I have mine; do not be arrogant and say that your truth is the only truth for me."[58] The postmodernist rejects the superiority of the present over the past; it gives priority to emotions, intuition, and both personal and mystical experience; it focuses on the self and the now; and it is deeply suspicious of reason. It sees reason as the basis of modernity and Western society. Postmodernists accuse the modernists of favoring the head over the heart, the mechanical over the spiritual, the impersonal over the personal.[59]

Modernism was a revolt against religion. It emphasized logic, rationalism, science, technology, and empiricism (the belief that knowledge and truth are derived from experience and observation, especially as used in the scientific method). In modernism, reality was seen as that which was material. No God was needed; it was essentially an atheistic system. Postmodernism has taken this a step further and has rigidly rejected the idea that there is a "norm" for everyone by which all cultures should be judged. Postmodernists insist that there is not only no norm for everyone, but that each individual has a right to his own norm. Therefore self becomes the ultimate, and is divinized. Before long, however, postmodernists lose sight of overall meaning, and the self becomes fragmented; as a result they define themselves by the community around them.[60]

Postmoderns live with the illusion that they are self-sufficient. In a culture in which people do not believe in a Transcendent Reality, they quickly become pessimistic about life and prisoners to themselves. Many postmoderns have had unhappy experiences early in life and have been deeply wounded; most are conscious of the pain and the psychological and emotional injury they have suffered.[61] Postmodernity is a lonely place—hence there is an intense need for community to bring wholeness to the fragmented self.[62]

Evaluation of Religion

Each of the various worldviews discussed above rests on specific claims about the nature of reality, about how meaning and value are to be achieved, and about what is the desired *telos* or end for human beings. For each religious tradition there is a fundamental or vital core of beliefs, and it is these core beliefs that render the worldviews incompatible with each other.[63] Every religion or worldview is exclusive in its own way; that is, if we take the orthodox position of each religion, we discover that they all teach that their religious goals can only be met by following their religion alone. Hence each religion is a "one and only"; each claims to be the only way for its kind of salvation.[64] Therefore each religion makes "conflicting truth claims" that contradict the truth claims of other religions. And based on the *law of noncontradiction,* they cannot all be right.[65] The law of noncontradiction states that two contradictory opposites cannot be right. For example, if someone comes to you and says there is a red Corvette locked up in your garage, and you insist there is not, only one of you can be right—either there "is" or there "is not" a red Corvette locked up in your garage. Truth-claims lie at the heart of every religion and ideology. Because each of them makes claims that conflict with those of other belief systems, they cannot all be true. So what are our options? Do we just accept the truth-claims of one particular belief system and hope it's the right one? Or do we evaluate these claims prior to embracing its system of beliefs? It seems logical that we should carefully examine any truth-claim before we own it for ourselves.[66] If God has indeed given us minds with which to think, then we honor Him when we use our minds. To passively surrender our minds to just any idea is dangerous and seriously contradicts the design of the Creator. As human beings we have the ability to evaluate and make sense of truth-claims. If we are able to test them, we are then able to reach a reasonable judgment in light of our findings, as to whether we want to embrace a particular belief system. But how do we objectively examine a belief system's truth-claims? How do we know if a particular worldview is right? Here are four questions a person should seek to answer when examining and evaluating a belief system:

1. *Is the belief system coherent and sensible?* That is, does the belief system correspond with reality? Does it agree with what we know about the world and ourselves? Is it rational? No one can be expected to believe something that is irrational.[67] It is only right for a person to object to a worldview when its truth-claims conflict with what we know to be true of the physical universe. For instance, if a worldview claims that the world is "flat" or that it is the "center" of the universe, we have a right to reject that worldview because it clearly disagrees with what we know to be true. We have a right to expect a worldview to concur with our experience of the outside world. A worldview should help us understand what we perceive and should fit with what we know about ourselves—the fact that as human beings we think, hope, and believe; we experience pleasure and pain; we're conscious of right and wrong; we feel guilty when we fail to do what is right.[68] Does the worldview under consideration

agree with our experience? If its truth-claims do not make sense or are contradictory, then the belief system should be judged as false.[69]

2. *Is the belief system practical and livable?* Does it bring understanding to reality on a day-to-day basis? If it does not, it is useless. One must expect a truthful worldview to be functional and work in the real world.

3. *Is the belief system all-encompassing and comprehensive?* If it ignores the tough questions of life, such as the nature of God, the problem of evil and suffering, the issues of morality, or the world in which we live, it is inadequate and should be rejected.[70]

4. *Is the belief system effective and pragmatic?* When you look at the adherents of a particular worldview, does it appear that the belief system has positively affected their lives? Has the belief system changed them for the better? Have its adherents positively impacted the world around them? If they have had a negative influence on their world, and they haven't served to increase the well-being of their community, their belief system should be rejected.

The goal of each religion is that its objective truth-claims become "subjectively real" in the lives of its adherents; that is, what a religion's adherents believe should become a part of who they are and radically affect the whole of their lives.[71] Ultimately, what really determines the credibility of a religion or belief system is the underlying foundation upon which it is built. Just as a building's stability can only be as dependable as the foundation upon which it is constructed, so a belief system is only as reliable as the foundation upon which it is based.[72] Christianity's truth-claims *vastly exceed* those of any other religion; that is, Christianity makes far more truth-claims than any other religion. As such, it provides people with a significant number of claims that can be evaluated, thus making it *far easier* to eliminate Christianity as true—if one can prove a single truth-claim to be false.[73] In the following chapters you will be exposed to a number of Christianity's truth-claims.

CHAPTER 3

THE ORIGIN OF THE UNIVERSE

The scientist is possessed by the sense of universal causation…
His religious feeling takes the form of a rapturous amazement
at the harmony of natural law, which reveals an intelligence
of such superiority that, compared with it, all the systematic
thinking and acting of human beings is an utterly insignificant
reflection.
— *ALBERT EINSTEIN*[1]

Naturalism and secularism believe the universe and life came
into existence by the operation of *natural processes*. Theism, on the other hand,
believes the cosmos came into existence by a direct act of a *Supernatural
Being*. Philosophers, theologians, and scientists have long wrestled with the
issue of the existence of a Supreme Being. Throughout history religions have
claimed that the universe is a creation of a Transcendent Reality outside the
universe. Today, many people believe that science provides the best explanation for the physical universe, thus eliminating the need for a God. Modern
physics says that the universe in which we live came into existence at some
point in the past, yet the *cause* of its origin is completely unknown to science.
Cosmologists have pondered all kinds of possibilities: Is our world unique
in the universe? Are we just the lucky result of a single spontaneous explosion? Are there other life-permitting worlds out there that have miraculously
sprung into existence against extraordinary odds? Or is our universe the
product of a brilliant Creator?[2]

The Problem of Bias

When a person discusses the subject of origins, one's beginning point always constitutes a bias. Everyone is biased. Scientists and theologians and philosophers are all biased. Anyone who thinks logically is biased. Everyone begins a topic of study with a biased reference point. The issue each of us must resolve is whether or not our bias conforms to reality.[3] This means being intellectually honest with the evidence, not intentionally steering it in one particular direction, but letting it give substantial definition to the outcome. Because we each begin with bias, it is important for us to understand how *limited* our knowledge really is. In Figure 5, the larger circle represents all of the available knowledge in the universe; the smaller circle represents the sum total of all that humans know.

Sum total of all available knowledge in the universe

Sum total of all human knowledge

Figure 5. The Sum Total of All Human Knowledge

In reality, humanity knows very little in comparison with all there is to know in the universe. As humbling as it may be, the little circle is actually a gross exaggeration of what we really know. So contrary to what some might believe, there are no cerebral giants living on planet earth. Regardless of how much knowledge we may have on a given subject, we all have a starting point that we believe is correct, and we base our starting point on what we know or have assumed to be true. This is our bias. Therefore, each of us believes in the correctness of our starting point based on our bias. As human beings with extremely limited knowledge, this bias is the best we can offer.[4]

In the Introduction to this book, I stated that there is enough information in the world to support one's ignorance on any subject. If this is true, the question we must ask ourselves is this: Are we *selectively choosing* information that only agrees with our bias, or are we being objective in our willingness to consider information that does not agree with our bias? If all we do is *selectively embrace* information that corresponds to our bias, then, invariably we will reject any information that runs contrary to it. When we wed ourselves to a particular concept, it becomes very difficult for us to divorce ourselves from it. Therefore, we should examine all aspects of a position before we embrace it as our own.

The examination of scientific data is like scrutinizing pieces of a jigsaw puzzle. The goal is to assemble the pieces in such a way that we obtain a full picture. When we assemble a puzzle, we use logic and experimentation to decide how particular pieces fit. Similarly, we use this methodology when constructing ideological positions. Scientists also employ this methodology to see how their scientific observation fits a particular paradigm.[5]

When it comes to developing a position on the origin of the universe, all scientists, regardless of the conclusions they make, are looking at the *same data*. The problem is not with the data itself, but with the *interpretation* of the data. Dr. Phillip E. Johnson, a professor of law at the University of California at Berkeley, and a specialist in logic, says evolutionists do not think their position is a philosophical one; they actually believe they are peering directly into reality.[6] To ask the naturalist if naturalism is true is like asking him if truth is true. He simply cannot imagine it not being true, he just *presupposes* that it is.[7] As a result, naturalists use the filter of an evolutionary mindset to test all ideas for truth content. They insist their view is the only scientific view, that supernatural creation is nothing more than a subjective religious view. But since evolutionary claims are not grounded in science, these naturalists are actually doing a disservice to science. Essentially their science becomes nothing more than quasi-science that intellectually bullies those who hold views contrary to theirs.

By selectively choosing to believe certain pieces of information and reject other pieces, a person can end up being either a *quasi-science evolutionist* or an *anti-science creationist*. Both positions lack integrity. Remember, there is a lot of information in the world to support both the theory of evolution and the theory of creationism; the key is to carefully consider that information and decipher whether it is true or false. One must not reject information just because it contradicts a particular position; if a given piece of information is proven to be true and is contrary to what you understand to be reality, intellectual integrity demands that you modify your position so that it conforms to that which is genuinely true. Pure authentic science can only lead one to a greater understanding of reality. It can never prove falsehood to be true, or truth to be falsehood; by definition, truth can only be proven to be true, and falsehood can only be proven to be false. All reputable science recognizes the problem is hardly ever with the data, it's almost always with how one interprets the data. This is why objectivity plays such a crucial role in science; to play fast and loose with the data only misleads people and does a disservice to science.

The Perspectives of Science and Religion

During the twentieth century the relationship between scientists and theologians was often confrontational. Since both tended to claim a comprehensive view of reality, they each ignored the other. The scientific community, however, has become increasingly aware in the last few years that reality is far more complex than they previously understood. So we are now beginning to hear a more common refrain from both scientists and theologians, that science and religion simply look at reality from two different perspectives. Science gives us insight into the *physical workings* of empirical reality, while religion gives us an *overall picture* of reality; whereas science deals with the *micro* perspective, theology deals with the *macro* perspective.[8] Science is about *problems*, and religion is about *mysteries*. Science is driven by the need to understand how the world *works*, and religion is driven by the need to understand what the world *means*.[9]

According to naturalists, evolution is based on *facts*, and theology is based on *faith*. Such thinking, however, is restrictive and fails to recognize the possibility of realities that exist beyond the physical. Sir John Templeton says in his book, *The Humble Approach: Scientists Discover God,* "Materialists overlook the spiritual realities because they get trapped in the purely physical."[10] Though theology and science both seek to make sense of the world in which we live, they use *different knowledge systems* because they ask different questions; that is, they employ different methods of analysis and draw conclusions that are distinctively characteristic. The truth is, we need different knowledge systems to examine the world around us.[11] We need theology to understand the *meaning and significance* of the cosmos; we need science to help us understand the *construction and operation* of the cosmos. For integration to take place, the knowledge systems must be complementary; that is, they must understand the limitations of their knowledge systems, and they must be intellectually honest with the data, and reject any outside bias that is not merited by the evidence. In economic terms, this means not playing with the numbers. It requires an openness to the world of ideas, and a commitment to neither diminish nor embellish the findings of science.

Dogmatism occurs when *theory* is equated to or confused with *fact*. Theory is an interpretation of factual observations and not the facts themselves. Let me illustrate this point with two statements that have been widely published in recent years. In a recent *Life* magazine article, an evolution-scientist responded to a creation-scientist with these words: "Evolution is a fact as much as the idea that the earth is shaped like a ball."[12] Likewise, evolutionary biologist Ernst Mayr stated in *Scientific American*, July 2000, that "No educated person any longer questions the validity of the so-called theory of evolution, which we now know to be a simple fact."[13] The problem with these statements is that evolution is *not a fact*; it is only a *theory*. So such statements are examples of the abuse of scientific theory. Essentially they are dogmatism, because theory is equated to or confused with fact.[14] Those who oppose the evolutionary model are not the narrow-minded fundamentalists or rabid religious fanatics they are often labeled to be by evolution-scientists; the truth is, the opponents of evolution simply are not offering the "politically correct" view, so their arguments are automatically dismissed or devalued.

Creationism is the idea that the universe came into existence by a Transcendent Reality. Evolution is the idea that the universe came into existence by the operation of natural processes. Clearly, creation and evolution are opposing philosophies; one is supernatural, the other is natural. They are both *interpretive schemes* for explaining scientific facts. Furthermore, since they are philosophical opposites, they are antithetical. If one is true, the other is false. They cannot both be true at the same time.[15] What is important in the world of science is that evidence must always be presented in an unadulterated form—pure and untouched—that genuine science might be served. To contaminate or misrepresent scientific findings serves no noble cause; it only does a disservice to the scientific community.

The Development of Science

Early scientists were known for placing a great emphasis on *truth*. They were committed to discovering the truth about the universe. To them, a scientific explanation was a true explanation, one that reflected reality.[16] Modern natural science was largely influenced by early European scientists who believed in a supernatural creation of the universe. The early scientists believed the natural world to be one of law and order. They expected to discover the laws of nature that helped run the universe, and they ran up an impressive record of discovering those laws.[17] Early science was so successful that people began to think of science as the ultimate guide to truth. With the astonishing developments of science and some amazing scientific discoveries, the public came to value science and nature more than the Transcendent Reality who brought it all into existence. This gave rise to scientism, or the worship of science.[18] But the worship of science was an inappropriate response. Science did not originate the way nature behaves; it simply observed it and described it. Laws did not become realities because science came into existence; science existed because the physical universe was seen to behave in a predictable way.

In the past, religion and science were far more compatible with each other than they are today. Originally the view of origins among scientists was that of supernatural creation; today creationism has been relabeled *religion* and naturalism is called *science*. Thus there developed a conflict between science and religion.[19] Up until the sixteenth century, it was the philosophers and theologians who were the scientists of their day.[20] Well-known scientist J. Robert Oppenheimer, who was not a Christian, said the early scientists were Christians who believed "there is a reasonable God, who has created a reasonable universe, and thus man, by use of his reason, could find out the universe's form."[21] Some of the creation-scientists who laid the foundation principles of modern science are:[22]

- *Nicolaus Copernicus* (1500s)—founder of modern astronomy

- *Johannes Kepler* (1600s)—barometer, celestial mechanics, and physical astronomy

- *Galilei Galileo* (1600s)—astronomy and physics

- *Blaise Pascal* (1600s)—mathematics and hydrostatics

- *Robert Boyle* (1600s)—chemistry and gas laws

- *Isaac Newton* (1700s)—calculus and dynamics

- *Michael Faraday* (1800s)—magnetic theory and electric generator

- *Louis Agassiz* (1800s)—glacial geology and ichthyology

- *James Simpson* (1800s)—gynecology

- *Gregor Mendel* (1800s)—genetics

- *Louis Pasteur* (1800s)—bacteriology, vaccination, and immunization

- *William Thomson (Lord Kelvin)* (1800s)—energetics and thermo-dynamics

- *Joseph Lister* (1800s)—antiseptic surgery

- *James Maxwell* (1800s)—electrodynamics and statistical thermo-dynamics

- *William Ramsay* (1800s)—isotopic chemistry

Though the vast majority of scientists today are proponents of evolutionary thinking, a number of the world's most distinguished scientists have begun to rethink the credibility of the evolutionary model. The renowned French scientist, Pierre P. Grasse, who wrote the book *Evolution of Living Organisms*, closed it by stating that biology is powerless to explain the origin of living things, that it may have to yield to metaphysics, or possibly to the concept of supernatural creation of some kind.[23] He argued that the "explanatory doctrines of biological evolution do not stand up to an objective in-depth criticism; they proved

Sir Isaac Newton (1642–1727), famed English physicist, astronomer, and mathematician.

to be either in conflict with reality, or else incapable of solving the major problem involved."[24] French scientist Louis Bounour, former president of the Biological Society of Strasbourg, and more recently director of research at the French National Center of Scientific Research, startled many of his scientific colleagues when he declared that "Evolution is a fairy tale for grown-ups. This theory has helped nothing in the progress of science. It is useless."[25] That's a pretty harsh indictment coming from one of the world's most respected scientists.

In spite of these statements, we still see a deep-seated bitterness on behalf of many in the scientific community toward the idea of supernatural creation. Why do evolution scientists have such an animus against religion? Why do they argue so vehemently in defense of evolution? In 1981, the British Museum of Natural History in London opened a new exhibit on evolution to mark its one hundredth anniversary. One of the world's leading scientific journals, *Nature*, ran a critical editorial in response to the museum's suggestion that evolution by natural selection was only one of a number of possible explanations. Two weeks later, twenty-two members of the museum's distinguished staff of biologists wrote the following letter to the editor of the journal.[26]

> Sir, as working biologists at the British Museum of Natural History we were astonished to read your editorial.... How is it that a journal such as yours that is devoted to science and

its practice can advocate that *theory* be presented as *fact?* [italics mine]. This is the stuff of prejudice, not science, and as scientists our basic concern is to keep an open mind on the unknowable.... Are we to take it that evolution is a fact, proven to the limits of scientific rigor? If that is the inference then we must disagree most strongly. We have no absolute proof of the theory of evolution.[27]

One must at least be open to the possibility that there are both physical and spiritual realities in the universe. Theists believe the material universe is not all there is. They believe there is both a *seen* and an *unseen* world, both a *physical* and a *spiritual* world. Theists may have been on the defensive for many years in their battle of ideas with scientists, but in recent years thousands of scientists have abandoned their convictions about the evolutionary theory of life, and the number continues to rise.

Stephen Hawking is one of the world's most respected cosmologists. He holds the position at Cambridge University once held by Sir Isaac Newton, and has been hailed by *Time* magazine as "an equal of Einstein." When addressing the subject of origins Hawking said, "I think there are clearly religious implications whenever you start to discuss the origins of the universe.... But I think most scientists prefer to stay away from the religious side of it.... The odds against a universe that has produced life like ours are immense."[28]

Albert Einstein, perhaps the greatest scientist of the twentieth century, developed the famous equation $E=mc^2$, which states that energy resides in mass (objects), and that mass is a form of energy.[29] A number of years later this theory was confirmed by experiment. Einstein's work was astonishing to scientists all over the world, and his theory of energy became a foundation stone in the development of nuclear energy.[30] He worked without providing footnotes, and was ignorant to a large extent of the work being done by other scientists, but with seeming effortless simplicity he worked out equations that he said brought humanity "closer to the secrets of the Old One [God]."[31] When commenting on quantum mechanics, he responded to his friend, Max Born: "Quantum mechanics is certainly imposing. But an inner voice tells me it is not yet the real thing. The theory says a lot, but does not really bring us any closer to the secret of the 'Old One.' I, at any rate, am convinced that He [God] is not playing dice."[32] Einstein's scientific inspiration was rooted in the fact that he believed the cosmos was the product of a supernatural Transcendent Reality.

To be sure, supernatural creation and evolution are conflicting philosophies. They each constitute a belief system about the past, and as such, they are both "philosophical" systems. Creationism and the theory of evolution both begin with assumptions and try to explain the data from those assumptions.[33] No one has ever logically or scientifically disproved supernatural creation; it is only *disbelieved*. Scientists, like all of us, are human. Consequently, they are not totally objective. They do not become something different from the rest of us just because they are scientists or because they put on a white smock and enter a laboratory. Their preconceived bias too often influences the outcome of their work.

Albert Einstein (1879–1955), famed German-born mathematician and theoretical physicist, is best known for his theory of relativity and his theory of mass-energy equivalence, $E=mc^2$.

Some years ago there was a scientific debate about the canals on Mars, which some astronomers claimed they saw. This caused a number of scientists to suggest that intelligent beings must have designed the canals, perhaps for water irrigation. If this were so, there must be some type of intelligent life on Mars—Martians! The public, of course, was fascinated by the debate. Recent Mars explorations, however, have laid the idea of Martians to rest. The point is that many of the scientists were not totally objective in their scientific declarations; what they assumed to be the case did not match the evidence.[34] This same lack of objectivity is also seen in the highly emotional debate going on between evolution-scientists and creation-scientists.

The only way to answer the question of the origin of the universe is to examine the evidence. If our universe was designed by a brilliant Master Designer, then we should expect it to demonstrate the *evidence of brilliant design*. On the other hand, if our universe evolved by purely natural processes from simple forms of life to more sophisticated forms, then the natural laws of the universe should demonstrate the *evidence of such processes*. Let's examine some of the evidence.

The Laws of Science

The two most universal and quintessential of all scientific laws are referred to as the Laws of Thermodynamics. Thermodynamics is a compound term that is built on two Greek words: *therme* (heat) and *dunamis* (power). It is the science that refers to the power or energy contained in heat, and its conversion to other forms of energy. Everything that exists in the universe is some form of energy, and everything that happens is some form of energy conversion.[35] In modern science the words *energy* and *work* are synonymous; something that has energy has the capacity to do work. If you were to push a wheelbarrow full of dirt up a small incline, you would be exerting energy over distance. All processes in the physical universe are fundamentally *energy conversion processes*.[36] No physical activity occurs in the universe that does not abide by the Two Laws of Thermodynamics. Let's look at these laws in more detail.

The *First Law of Thermodynamics* tells us that no matter what physical changes take place in the universe, the total amount of energy in the universe remains constant; thus, nothing can happen to increase or decrease the amount of energy that is in the universe. There are constant changes taking place in the universe, but the sum total of all its energy never fluctuates. In short, this First Law states that nothing that exists can be uncreated, that is, go out of existence; it may change form (a burning log will change into other forms) but the amount of energy will remain constant.[37] Physicist Isaac Asimov identifies the First Law as "the most powerful and most fundamental generalization about the universe that scientists have ever been able to make."[38] Before we examine the impact of this law, let's look at the Second Law.

The *Second Law of Thermodynamics* maintains that every change that takes place in the universe naturally goes from a state of order to one of disorder; that is, there is a downward directional change, but never an upward change. Another way of stating this law is that the universe is constantly getting more disorderly. This law is also referred to as the law of entropy or the law of decay, meaning that everything in the universe is running down and is in a process of gradual disintegration.[39] Entropy means that things tend to move from a state of order to disorder when left alone. Therefore, things decay over time. Stars burn out, springs unwind, heat dissipates, materials deteriorate. You do not have to do anything to cause these things to happen; they happen automatically. The Laws of Thermodynamics are as universal and certain as any that exist in science. In every case, without exception, when these Two Laws of Physics have been subjected to tests they have consistently been validated.[40] So what do these two laws have to do with the origin of the universe? The answer is twofold.

1. Evolution teaches that the development of life is the result of "natural processes." To help test this hypothesis, take a large container and mix in equal amounts of salt and pepper until the container is about half full; then put a lid on it and begin shaking the container in an effort to "unmix" the two. Living cells are like the pattern of the salt and pepper being separated, except that the patterns in living cells are *millions of times* more complex. To believe that the information contained in a complex living cell came from random, gradual evolutionary processes of nature is to have faith in processes for which there is absolutely no evidence—that's why it is called a theory.[41] Furthermore, such natural processes would in fact transgress the Second Law of Thermodynamics, which tells us that everything in the universe progresses in a downward direction (disorder), never in an upward direction (order).

Evolutionists are able to convince people of their argument simply because they employ such exceedingly *great amounts of time* in their equations. This leads people to unwittingly open the door to the possibility that with an almost endless amount of time anything must be possible. Essentially, however, all the evolutionist has done is muddy the waters of thoughtful human analysis. There is absolutely *no evidence* whatsoever that the Second Law of Thermodynamics could ever be rendered ineffective or reversed. As science grows in its understanding of how nature works, it is increasingly realizing that the intricate complexities and the phenomenal designs of nature far exceed anything they ever imagined. The more progress science makes, the stronger the case becomes for the involvement of a Master Designer.[42]

On November 5, 1981, Dr. Colin Patterson, the senior paleontologist of the British Museum of Natural History, addressed a group of fellow evolutionists at the American Museum of Natural History in New York City. He surprised them with the following announcement:

> One of the reasons I started taking this anti-evolutionary view was… it struck me that I had been working on this stuff for 20 years and there was not one thing I knew about it. That's quite a shock to learn that one can be so misled so long.… So for the last few weeks I've tried putting a simple question to various people and groups of people. Question is: Can you tell me anything you know about evolution, any one thing that is true? I tried that question on the geology staff at the Field Museum of Natural History and the only answer I got was silence. I tried it on the members of the Evolutionary Morphology Seminar in the University of Chicago, a very prestigious body of evolutionists, and all I got there was silence.…[43]

The theory of evolution is heavily based on the assumption that genetic mutations (accidental copying mistakes) can *improve* the genetic code of an organism. But the evidence for genetic improvement is nonexistent. Real-world experience demonstrates that believing accidental copying mistakes can generate the information required to create complex structures like wings and eyes is the stuff of fantasy, not science. Nevertheless, because creatures have the limited ability to adapt to changing environments, most evolutionists use these *adaptations* to show that "evolution happens." But the truth of the matter is that these adaptations are only evidence of *microevolution* (evolutionary changes within a species), not *macroevolution* (evolutionary changes from one species to a different species). Adaptations that occur within a species cannot be used as supporting evidence for the theory of evolution, in which one species is believed to have evolved into another species. Science has repeatedly demonstrated that all changes are either *genetically neutral* or *genetically inferior*, being losses of information instead of the gains the theory of evolution requires. Despite these facts, many evolution-scientists continue to hang on to their evolutionary model, though there is not one instance where the fossil record shows "a clear vector of progress" as dogmatically described in textbooks.[44]

It should be noted that all scientists—both creationists and evolutionists—agree that *microevolution* occurs; minor changes within species have been observed numerous times since history began. A common example of microevolution is the breeding of dogs for certain traits. This results in changes in size, color, shape, and various minor genetic alterations, but this does not represent *macroevolution*, which evolutionists claim has happened millions of times in the evolution of bacteria into man. The theory of macroevolution claims that beneficial change in complexity occurs naturally, and results in new genetic information. Microevolution, on the other hand, does not involve increasing complexity; it involves changes only in size, shape, color, or minor genetic alterations caused by a few mutations.[45]

Macroevolution has *never* been observed, as many of the world's most prominent evolution-scientists have attested. Note the following statements by some of the world's most prominent scientists: *Steven M. Stanley:* "No human has ever seen a new species form in nature... in fact, the fossil record does not convincingly document a single transition from one species to another."[46] *Pierre-Paul Grasse:* "No matter how numerous they may be, mutations do not produce any kind of evolution."[47] *David B. Kitts:* "Evolution requires intermediate forms between species and paleontology does not provide them."[48] *Lynn Margulis:* "I have seen no evidence whatsoever that these [evolutionary] changes can occur through the acccumulation of gradual mutations."[49] *David S. Woodruff:* "Fossil species remain unchanged throughout most of their history and the [fossil] record fails to contain a single example of a significant transition."[50] Though macroevolution is not substantiated by the facts, we still find a majority of scientists embracing Darwin's evolutionary model.

Ardent evolutionist Dr. Colin Patterson recently admitted to his colleagues that evolution was simply "a faith," and that for years he had been "duped into taking evolutionism as *revealed truth* in some way." He also has declared that evolution not only conveys no knowledge, but that it somehow seems to convey "anti-knowledge"; that is, knowledge that is actually harmful to systematics (the science of classifying different forms of life).[51] Even though large numbers of scientists still embrace evolutionary theory, we should remember that not too many centuries ago, the vast majority of scientists believed the sun revolved around the earth. It is important to remember that reality is not determined by a democratic majority.

2. Evolution teaches that the universe is "eternal." The late Carl Sagan, noted professor of astronomy from Cornell, and outspoken atheist, embodied the evolutionist's position when he said that nature is "all that is or ever was or ever will be."[52] This statement is basically the foundation for the evolutionary model. The Second Law of Thermodynamics, the law of decay, implies that the universe is in a process of gradual disintegration—it is steadily moving toward final darkness and decay. The best possible explanation of this fact is that the universe must have been created with a lot of usable energy, and though the amount is extremely large, it is limited. When all of the usable energy in the cosmos is ultimately consumed, the universe will experience what scientists call *heat death*—that point in time when everything will finally run out of energy and die. Lincoln Barnett in his book *The Universe and Dr. Einstein* puts it this way: "the inescapable inference is that every-thing had a beginning: somehow and sometime the cosmic processes were started, the stellar fires ignited, and the whole vast pageant of the universe brought into being."[53]

From a purely scientific standpoint, it is easy to demonstrate that matter cannot be eternal in nature. The various lines of evidence came together in the 1960s and led to the formulation of the *Big Bang* theory, which asserts that the universe began with a cosmic explosion.[54] It was the discovery that the universe is *expanding* that led the scientific community to conclude that the cosmos had a beginning. This means science can trace events back in time only to a certain point. At the moment of the Big Bang, science reaches an absolute barrier. When the theory was first proposed, a large number of scientists resisted it for that very reason. The great physicist Arthur Eddington summed up the feelings of many of his colleagues when he stated that the idea of a beginning is "philosophically repugnant." Astronomer Robert Jastrow, an agnostic, maintains that science has reached its limit, and that it will never be able to discover how the universe came into existence. The most common strategy among scientists and educators today is simply to *ignore* the startling implications of the Big Bang. Concerning oneself with the "ultimate cause" behind the Big Bang is dismissed as *philosophy* and is given no place in the science classroom; consequently, educators claim only to deal with science.[55]

The amount of hydrogen in the universe also demonstrates that matter cannot be eternal in nature. Hydrogen is the basic fuel of the cosmos, powering all stars and other energy sources in space. Obviously there is an enormous amount of hydrogen in the universe. The evidence is that the cosmic gas gauge, while moving toward empty, is still a long way from being there, but at some distant point in the future on the cosmological time clock it will be exhausted altogether. Additionally, the First Law of Thermodynamics implies that matter cannot just pop into existence by itself, so the universe cannot be self-caused. Nothing can create itself, because it would need to exist before it came into existence, which is a logical absurdity.[56] Since the universe had a beginning, then something external to the universe must have caused it to come into existence—something, or someone, that transcends the natural world. As a result, the idea of supernatural creation is no longer merely a matter of religious faith; it is a conclusion based on the most straightforward reading of scientific evidence.[57] British physicist Paul Davies, though not a Christian, says the Big Bang is "the one place in the universe where there is room, even for the most hard-nosed materialists, to admit God."[58]

The Fossil Record

If life did originate through natural processes, the laws of science would have been negated *millions of times* to account for the thousands upon thousands of transitional forms demanded by evolution, and the historical fossil record would give unequivocal evidence that this did occur. (Fossils are the remains of plants and animals that were once alive.) If invertebrate gave rise to vertebrate, if fish gave rise to amphibia, if amphibia gave rise to reptile, and if reptile gave rise to bird and mammals (each transformation requiring millions of years and involving innumerable transitional forms), then the fossil record undoubtedly would produce millions of these transitional types.[59] What the available data indicates, however, is a *complete absence* of any intermediate forms required by the theory. Noted Harvard paleontologist Stephen Jay Gould, an outspoken evolutionist, writes:

> The extreme rarity of transitional forms in the fossil record persists as the trade secret of paleontology. The evolutionary trees that adorn our textbooks have data only at the tips and nodes of their branches; the rest is inference, however reasonable, not the evidence of fossils. He continues: We fancy ourselves as the only true students of life's history, yet to preserve our favored account of evolution by natural selection we view our data as so bad that we never see the very process we profess to study.... [And surprisingly], new species almost always appeared suddenly in the fossil record with no intermediate links to ancestors in older rocks of the same region.[60]

While natural selection may account for *minor changes* in creatures observed in the fossil record (which no one contests), Gould clearly acknowledged that "the absence of fossil evidence for intermediary stages between *major transitions* in organic design... has been a persistent and nagging problem for gradualistic accounts of evolution."[61] In addition, Dr. Niles Eldredge, an invertebrate paleontologist at the American Museum of Natural History stated that "the smooth transition from one form of life to another, which is implied in the theory... is not borne out by the facts.... No one has yet found any evidence of such transitional creatures.... In the last decade, geologists have found rock layers of all divisions of the last 500 million years and *no transitional forms* were contained in them. It is not the fossil record which is incomplete," states Eldredge, "[therefore] it must be the theory."[62]

The outstanding characteristic of the fossil record is that it does not support the idea of slow, gradual change espoused by evolutionists; therefore, fossil evidence provides no support whatsoever for macroevolution (the idea that one type of animal has changed into another type of animal). Due to a complete lack of any evidence for gradual change, many evolutionists are now claiming that transitional fossils are missing because "relatively rapid evolutionary jumps" must have occurred over these gaps; but no evolutionist has even been able to explain how such large jumps could have happened. To complicate their position even further, evolutionists admit that these rapid evolutionary jumps would have had to occur thousands upon thousands of times.

The problem of the lack of fossil evidence that would support the theory of evolution goes back to Charles Darwin. Darwin expected *millions* of transitional fossils to be found, but only a very few *highly disputed ones* were. Darwin recognized this discrepancy and wrote in *On The Origin of Species*, "Why is not every geological formation and every stratum full of intermediate links? This is the most obvious and gravest objection which can be urged against my theory."[63] Nearly 150 years after Darwin, this "obvious and grave objection" can still be made. When evolutionist Dr. Colin Patterson of the British Museum of Natural History responded to a written question asking why he failed to include illustrations of "transitional forms" in a book he wrote on evolution. He commented:

> I fully agree with your comments on the lack of direct illustration of evolutionary transitions in my book. If I knew of any, fossil or living, I would certainly have included them. You suggest that an artist should be used to visualize such transformations, but where would he get the information from? I could not, honestly, provide it, and if I were to leave it to artistic license, would that not mislead the reader?.... You say that I should at least "show a photo of the fossil from which each type of organism was derived." I will lay it on the line—there is not one such fossil for which one could make a watertight argument.[64]

Charles Darwin (1809–1882), famed for his theory of evolution based upon natural selection. He explains it in his book *On the Origin of Species* (1859).

Patterson also made other surprising statements about transitional fossils: "[Stephan Jay] Gould and the American Museum people are hard to contradict when they say there are no transitional fossils.... [Let me reiterate]—there is not one such fossil for which one could make a watertight argument.... It is easy to make up stories of how one form gave rise to another.... But such stories are not part of science, for there is no way of putting them to the test."[65]

In the century and a half since Darwin wrote, paleontologists have not discovered one single fossil that would lend credibility to the theory of evolution. As a result, leading evolutionists now maintain the following: 1) Most species *do not change* at all during their existence on earth; they appear in the fossil record looking very similar to when they disappeared; and 2) Species *do not develop* gradually from more primitive ancestral forms; they appear "fully formed," all at once.[66] Discoveries reveal that animals appear as fully functional creatures and not in transition as evolutionists claim. These preserved fossils appear suddenly within the geological column and are not spread out over extended periods of time. The conclusion is unavoidable: There is no indication whatsoever that one form of life transforms into a completely different form.[67]

During the nineteenth century, long before modern science, the living cell was thought to be quite simple, and it was easy enough for the early proponents of evolution to propose that life just arose by chance. Darwin thought the cell was a simple blob of protoplasm, and he postulated that it evolved in a "warm little pond."[68] But as science began uncovering the intricate complexities of the cell, it became increasingly difficult to hold on to theories of chance. Unwilling to renounce their theory, biologists typically took refuge in the idea of *eons of time*. Given enough time, they argued, anything can happen. Over millions of years, "the unlikely becomes likely," they claimed, and the improbable is transformed into the inevitable. Was there any evidence for such conjecture? None whatsoever. Nevertheless, biologists got away with this kind of reasoning for a while, simply because the amount of time invoked was so immense that no one was capable of conceptualizing what that kind of time scale really meant. But when the computer revolution came along, it put an end to any "chance theory" of life's origin. Beginning in the 1960s, mathematicians began to write computer programs simulating every process imaginable, and before long they ventured into the sacred arena of evolutionary theory. Using their high-speed computers, they simulated the trial-and-error processes of neo-Darwinian evolution over the equivalent of billions of years. The outcome jolted the evolutionists: the computers showed that the probability of evolutionary chance processes is essentially *zero,* no matter how long the time scale.[69]

The Australian microbiologist, Michael Denton, wrote *Evolution: A Theory in Crisis,* about the actual fossil evidence that has been discovered. Although he claims not to believe in creationism, he has the intellectual honesty to examine how well naturalism matches the real world as revealed in biology and paleontology. He concludes that there is a "remarkable lack of any direct evidence for major evolutionary transformations in the fossil record."[70] This is amazing, because the total number of known *fossil species* in existence now exceeds 250,000.[71]

Despite this extraordinary lack of evidence, many students today are reluctant to believe that evolution is not a scientifically proven fact. They have been taught since childhood that science has proven that life began in a spontaneous way from nonliving chemicals by purely natural processes, and that this process took several billion years. Yet, today, it is common to hear prominent scientists scoff at the idea that life arose by chance. The famous astronomer Sir Fred Hoyle compares it to lining up "10" to the "50th" power (that's ten with fifty zeros after it) blind people, giving each of them a scrambled Rubik's Cube, and finding that they all solve the cube at the same moment![72] Dean Kenyon of San Francisco State University, coauthor of the book *Biochemical Predestination*, has repudiated his own theory that there must have been some "force" within matter itself that caused life to emerge under just the most perfect of circumstances; he has since accepted the idea of an Intelligent Designer as the answer to the origin of life.[73]

Recent evidence from *genetics* seems to have put the final nail in evolution's coffin and its claim that life originated from nonliving chemicals. Research with mitochondrial DNA and genetics connects mankind's lineage back to one woman and one man,[74] and has conclusively demonstrated that life-forms only reproduce after their kind (i.e., their own species); they do not merge with other species. So the evolutionary model is completely devoid of factual scientific data for its support. Well-known scientist Robert Jastrow, an agnostic, has come to the conclusion that there is no concrete evidence to support the hypothesis of the evolutionary origin of life.[75]

The *geological* record also argues against the evolutionary model. Evolutionists have dated cells capable of photosynthesis (discovered in rock from South Africa) at more than 3.1 billion years old. They have also dated five different kinds of cells in Australian rock at 3.5 billion years old. And there also appears to be evidence of living cells in rock from Greenland dated 3.8 billion years ago. But if the age of the earth is about 4.6 billion years, and life seems to be abundant, complex, and diverse by 3.5 billion years, that allows only 170 million years "after the earth cooled" for evolution to take place.[76] This is considerably less than the 2 billion years the evolutionary theory demands. Just to complicate matters further, there is growing evidence that the early earth was rich in oxygen but low in nitrogen, which is just the opposite of what evolution needs.[77]

The scientific method is limited to a process defined by that which is measurable and repeatable. So by definition, it cannot speak to issues of ultimate origin, meaning, or morality. For answers to such questions, science is dependent on the systems of knowledge that work with such matters.

Science has great potential for both good and evil. It can be used to make vaccines or poisons; nuclear power plants or nuclear weapons; it can be used to clean up the environment or pollute it; it can be used to argue for God or against Him. Science, by definition, can offer no moral guidance to govern our lives. All science can do is show us how natural law works, while telling us nothing about its origins.

The Cave Man

Evolutionists have long advocated that the Cave Man, or *Neanderthal Man* as he is more accurately known, is supposed to have been primitive man who lived in a pre-civilized culture and used crude implements. He is popularly portrayed as having stooped posture, carrying a club and dragging a woman by her hair. How accurate is this portrayal? Recent discoveries have shown that Neanderthal man and Cro-Magnon man were not primitive at all, but were simply "de-cultured" men. These cave dwellers were actually quite capable intellectually, but they had suffered cultural loss and as a result were improperly identified as primitive or aboriginal by those who believed that man had evolved from animals; their sophisticated "life-like" cave art is just one hint of their extensive mental capabilities.[78] Modern artists would be challenged to duplicate their three-dimensional effect.

For years many anthropologists held that Neanderthal man had disappeared from the earth about 35,000 years ago; but C. Loring Brace, curator of the physical anthropology division at the University of Michigan's Museum of Anthropology, says "the fact is, the Western European Neanderthals are today's Western Europeans.… the only difference between [them] and modern man is the indication of generally greater ruggedness in Neanderthal joints and muscles."[79] Both Cro-Magnon man and Neanderthal man possessed larger cranial capacities than modern man, once again contradicting the evolutionary model which suggests that the brain becomes larger as man evolves. Interestingly, the fossil record indicates that man's brain has actually been *degenerating* since "cave man" times, causing some to believe that primitive man may have had greater intellectual capacity than modern man.[80]

On December 13, 1996, evolutionary scientists were shocked when *Science* magazine reported the redating of the Java Solo *homo erectus* fossil skulls. These alleged evolutionary ancestors of modern humans were assumed to have existed long before modern humans. The new data, however, strongly supports the idea that *homo erectus* coexisted with modern humans (*homo sapiens*) long after *homo erectus* was supposed to have been extinct. These findings seriously challenge the concept of human evolution.[81]

Evolutionists have been eager to believe in ape-men discoveries, because they want to conclusively show the world that there is a "genetic connection" between the animal kingdom and human beings. According to evolutionists, such a find would be the crowning proof that their thinking is right. These discoveries, however, are simply cases of fraud, mistaken identity, or pure fantasy. The following is an update on the evidence of seven prime "jewels" in the evolutionary crown: [82]

- The *Piltdown Man* found in 1912 was proved to be a fake.

- The *Nebraska Man's* tooth found in 1922 was shown to belong to a rare pig.

- The evidence for *Peking Man* has disappeared since 1941.

- The *Java Man* found in 1891 was determined to be either human or ape, but not both.

- The teeth and jawbones of *Ramapithecus* found in 1932 were discovered to be that of an ape.

- The *Neanderthal Man* was found to be a hunched man who had a vitamin D deficiency.

Yet another example is that of the Lucy remains. In 1978, when Dr. Donald Johanson announced his discovery of Lucy to the world at the Nobel Symposium on Early Man, every major newspaper in the world picked up the story. Lucy was supposed to be the earliest ancestor of human beings. Evolutionists identified her as an almost complete skeleton of a creature that walked upright like humans. She was dated at about 3 million years old. There are some additional facts, however, that you should know. Lucy is really a demonstration of how imaginative people can be when playing with the rules of science. For example, her knee comes from a location over a mile away from one of her leg bones, and some 200 feet lower in rock formations. Lucy was actually assembled from materials discovered in two different locations separated by several miles! Strangely enough, all of the bones from one of the locations provide her with human-like characteristics, while all of the bones gathered from the other location provide her with ape-like characteristics. [83] Sound a little suspicious? When scientists insist on making *rash judgments* without positive evidence, they discredit not only themselves but also the scientific community. The three primary concerns of every scientist must be an objective presentation of all the facts, a clear differentiation between theory and fact, and a commitment to not let one's bias undermine the integrity of scientific discovery. For years evolutionists pointed to the "stooped posture" of the Neanderthal as a prime evidence of primitive man. Recent discoveries, however, have confirmed that this condition was due to a deficiency of vitamin D, resulting in a bone disease known as rickets. The deficiency in these cave dwellers was traced to a lack of exposure to direct sunshine. Sunshine on the skin produces vitamin D, and sunny weather was infrequent during the cloudy, rainy Ice Age.[84] Thus the fossil record continues to be an embarrassment to evolutionists, because discovery after discovery refutes the evolutionary model and supports supernatural creation.[85]

CHAPTER 4

THE EVIDENCE OF SCIENCE

The vast mysteries of the universe should only confirm our belief in the certainty of its Creator. I find it as difficult to understand a scientist who does not acknowledge the presence of a superior rationality behind the existence of the universe as it is to comprehend a theologian who would deny the advances of science.
— WERNER VON BRAUN, *THE FATHER OF SPACE SCIENCE[1]*

The science of determining the age of something is one of the most fascinating of all sciences, but it is also one of the most inaccurate. Often when a particular rock is dated by more than one method, it will yield "different ages." Even when the same rock is dated more than once by the same method, it will often produce a different result. Albert Einstein once defined insanity as "doing the same thing over and over and expecting a different result." Apparently, that's what some scientists do—they test something repeatedly until they get the result they want. Different crystals in the same rock will frequently yield different ages. Obviously, scientific dating methods are not very accurate; only by reporting *selected results* do they appear to work. There are numerous instances that indicate the untrustworthiness of scientific dating methods. Rocks from a recent volcano that we know erupted long after the Grand Canyon was formed were tested by four different dating methods. The results ranged from 10,000 years to over 2,600,000,000 years. In 1995, some of the minerals from rock which formed at the eruption of Mount St. Helens in 1980 were dated at 2,800,000 years, when, clearly, they were only 15 years old! And then there is the volcanic rock that just recently was formed in the eruptions of Hawaiian volcanoes.

It was dated at 30,000,000 years old! Scores of other faulty dating attempts can be cited.[2]

Radioactive Dating Methods

The two most popular radioactive dating methods are *radiocarbon* dating and *radioisotope* dating. Radiocarbon dating is generally referred to as *carbon-14 dating,* and is only used when the object being tested is less than 50,000 years old. Here's how the carbon clock works: Carbon has unique properties that are essential for all life on earth. Carbon-14 is unstable and slowly decays, changing back into nitrogen and releasing energy. This instability makes it *radioactive.* Carbon-14 gets cycled through the cells of plants and animals, and as soon as they die, the carbon-14 atoms which decay are no longer replaced, so the amount of carbon-14 is such that half of it will convert back to nitrogen in roughly 5,730 years. This is referred to as the "half-life" of carbon-14. So in "two" half-lives—about 11,460 years—only one-quarter of the carbon-14 will be left. Theoretically, once something is over 50,000 years old, there should no longer be any detectable carbon-14. Therefore, if a sample contains carbon-14, it is good evidence that the item being tested is not millions of years old.[3]

As simple as this dating method sounds, there are a number of complicating factors. First, plants take up less carbon-14 than would be expected, so they test older than they really are; second, the amount of cosmic rays penetrating the earth's atmosphere varies with the sun's activity, and this affects the amount of carbon-14 produced, which in turn changes the results; and third, the energy of the earth's magnetic field has been decreasing, so more carbon-14 is being produced now than in the past, which will make old things look *older* than they really are.[4]

Carbon dating in many cases embarrasses evolutionists because it yields ages that are significantly less than those expected from their evolutionary model. An item that is older than 50,000 years should have no detectable level of carbon-14. Laboratories that measure carbon-14 often request a source of organic material with *zero* carbon-14 to use as a "blank," thus insuring that their lab procedures are not adding carbon-14. Coal should be an obvious candidate because the youngest coal on our planet is supposed to be millions of years old, and most of it should be tens or hundreds of millions of years old. Obviously such coal should be completely devoid of carbon-14, but it is not. And not one single source of coal has been found that completely lacks carbon-14.[5] It is a total mystery to evolutionists as to why coal has carbon-14 in it, or why a piece of wood supposedly many millions of years old still has carbon-14 present; but it makes perfect sense to scientific creationists, because they do not believe the earth is billions of years old.[6]

The second radioactive dating method is referred to as *radioisotope* or *radiometric* dating. Radioisotope dating methods are used today to give ages of millions or billions of years for rocks. Uranium is the most well-known radioactive atom, and it occurs in several different forms or *isotopes*. One of these isotopes, *uranium 238*, decays into thorium 234, which itself is unstable and decays into a smaller atom which is also unstable. This radioactive atom continues to decay until it finally changes into *lead 206*, which no longer decays. In this case the uranium is referred to as the *parent* atom, and the lead is called the *daughter* atom.[7] Radioisotope dating is often applied to igneous rocks (rock formed from a molten state), and is used to identify how long ago the rock was solidified. For any dating method to be accurate, certain conditions must be met to get an accurate reading: 1) the *starting conditions* must be known; 2) the *decay rates* must have always been constant; and 3) the *isotope atoms* must have remained the same over time, without any being added or lost.[8] So, the problem with calculating the age of a piece of rock is that assumptions must be made about the past that cannot be proved.

The question that naturally surfaces is this: "What if something happened over the entire history of a piece of rock under examination that produced a *change* in that rock?" There are a number of ways in which either parent or daughter atoms can be added to or subtracted from a rock. One of the most significant elements would be the presence of water. Geologist John D. Morris says, "Water can dissolve either uranium or lead atoms, and transport them elsewhere, and if it has done so, the calculated date would be in error. It is also extremely unlikely that a rock would remain totally isolated for long periods of time, especially if major flooding took place."[9]

Since rock dating is potentially so full of errors, are there better ways to date the earth? Fortunately there are a number of ways to date the earth, as well as its oceans and its atmosphere, and these methods appear to be more accurate than dating an individual piece of rock. For example, the *ocean* contains a number of chemicals that have been dissolved in it, and rivers continue to bring more chemicals to the ocean every day. Scientists are able to measure the rate at which chemicals are added, and because they know the present quantity of chemicals in the ocean, they can calculate how long it took for the various chemicals to build up at the current rate of addition; this calculation will reveal the apparent age of the ocean.[10] For example, we know what the content level of salt is in the ocean, so if we add up all the possible ways salt can be added or removed from the ocean, we can determine its age. By doing so, scientists have calculated that the ocean could not possibly be any more than 62 million years old; therefore this is the *maximum* age of the ocean according to this method of dating.[11]

It is interesting to note that evolutionary theories assume that the oceans have been "salty" for at least 3 billion years. However, if the oceans are actually that old, and have continued to increase in salt at the present rate, they would contain so much salt no life would be able to survive in them (imagine the oceans containing "50 times" more salt than the present level!). Therefore, the oceans simply cannot be that old. In addition, if the oceans were to have contained some salt at the start, or if some major flood had resulted in enormous salt deposits being made at one time, then their maximum age would be even less. Science has conducted tests using this method on dozens of other chemicals that are continually being added to the ocean, and the results of these studies yield very similar dates.[12]

Another oceanographic study focused on measuring the total volume of *sediments* found on the ocean floor. By calculating the speed at which sediments are deposited on the ocean floor, present-day river flow would take only 14 million years to reach present levels. Therefore, according to this study, the *maximum* age of the oceans is only 14 million years. If, however, a major flood occurred at some point in the past, resulting in sediment deposits being made to the ocean at higher rates than what we're presently experiencing, then the maximum age would be much less. Once again, evolutionary theory assumes that the oceans are at least 3 billion years old.[13]

Scientists are also able to conduct dating studies on the *atmosphere*. They are able to measure how much of the lightweight gas helium exists in our atmosphere. They can measure its present level as well as the rate at which it enters the atmosphere from the crust of the earth. In addition, they also know how much helium is leaving the atmosphere and is drifting into space. At the present rate of accumulation, all of the helium that is now in the atmosphere would have gotten there in less than 2 million years. Again, if a major flood occurred at some point, a large amount of helium would have been released from the earth's crust, reducing the maximum age significantly.[14]

The earth's *magnetic field* has also been the subject of a large amount of scientific research. The magnetic field is produced by currents of electricity in the metallic outer core of the earth. This field of energy has served to protect the earth from harmful cosmic rays, and is the reason why our compass needles point north. Since the 1840s, scientists have accurately measured the strength of the earth's magnetic field, and they have discovered it is continually *declining;* at its present rate of decline, it will soon become too weak to provide any beneficial protection for living things.[15] If the magnetic field has always declined at the present rate, it would have been "too strong for life to exist" just 10,000 years ago. Science has discovered evidence that indicates the magnetic field has actually reversed in the past, with compass needles pointing south; most scientists believe this "flip-flop" in the magnetic field is due to rapid movement of the metallic minerals in the outer core. What effect would a flip-flop have on the magnetic field? It would cause it to decay even *more rapidly*.[16]

So, of all the methods that have been used to estimate the age of the earth, 90 percent point to an age far less than the billions of years asserted by evolutionists. And numerous other scientific discoveries point to a far younger earth than that claimed by evolutionists.[17] Another piece of scientific evidence that is particularly interesting involves our *moon*. The moon is slowly distancing itself from earth at about one inch per year, and most scientists believe this rate would have been even greater in the past. Nevertheless, if the moon has receded at only one inch per year, it would have taken only 1.37 billion years to reach its present distance from the earth, if it had actually been in contact with the earth when it was first formed. This *maximum age* for the moon is far too young for the evolutionary model, which claims the moon is 4.6 billion years old. It is also much younger than the radiometric "dates" that have been assigned to moon rocks.[18]

Creation-scientists cannot prove the age of the earth using a particular scientific method any more than evolution-scientists can. At best all science is tentative because it does not possess all the data necessary to be certain in its assertions, especially when dealing with events of the past.[19] Noted evolutionary scientist William D. Stansfield states, "There is no absolutely reliable long-term radiological clock."[20] So all dating methods, including those that point to a young earth rely on *unprovable assumptions*. Therefore, it is vital for science to be intellectually honest and not draw *absolute conclusions* from evidence provided by using such methods, since the methods, obviously, are not reliable. Wanting something to be true, and proving it to be true, are two different things.

Evidence for a Worldwide Flood

The single most significant physical phenomenon purported by nearly every religion on earth is that of a *worldwide flood*—not a local flood, but a worldwide flood. Traditions of such a flood are found among people groups all over the world, and these traditions, taken as a whole, strongly agree with the monotheistic account found in the book of Genesis (the first book in the Bible). The Bible *claims* to be completely true and trustworthy, and it would not appear to be that difficult a task to prove its account of a cataclysmic worldwide flood either true or untrue. Such a worldwide phenomenon could not have happened without leaving its "fingerprint" all over the globe. It seems logical that all of the evidence either unequivocally *substantiates* this claim or unquestionably *refutes* it. It is simply a matter of honestly evaluating all the evidence.

1. Historical Evidence. The story of the Flood is found in nearly every culture and geographical area in the world: North and South America, South Sea Islands, Australia, Papua New Guinea, Japan, China, India, the Middle East, Europe, and Africa. Researchers have gathered hundreds of such stories from across the globe,[21] and the basic story is the same: God (or the gods) tell a man to build a boat and take animals aboard, because he/they are going to flood the world. After the Flood, the boat is said to have come to rest on a high mountain peak, where the man exited the boat and offered a sacrifice to God or the gods; who responded by making a covenant with him. These core events all point to a historical basis for the Flood.[22]

The biblical character Noah is referred to as *Ziusudra* by the Sumerians, and *Utnapishtim* by the Babylonians. The Genesis account tells us that God destroyed the world with a Flood because corruption and violence were rampant on the earth, and that only Noah and his family would be saved because he alone had honored God by the way in which he lived.[23] The Flood is referred to numerous times throughout the Bible, and it is recorded that Jesus Christ Himself not only accepted it as a fact of history, but declared that it was worldwide in scope and effect.[24]

One ancient account tells of a list of Sumerian kings who treated the Flood as a real event. After naming eight kings who lived extraordinarily long lives (tens of thousands of years), the following statement interrupts the list: "[Then] the Flood swept over [the earth] and when kingship was lowered [again] from heaven, kingship was [first] in Kish."[25] Many ancient versions of the Flood contain *elaborations,* which suggest that their accounts had become distorted with the passing of time, thus lacking authenticity. Scientists agree that the cubical Babylonian ship would not have been a seaworthy vessel, and the fact that the Babylonians report that the waters, which covered the entire earth, subsided in "one day" is not reasonable either. In many of the versions the "hero" (Noah) is granted immortality and is exalted, but the Genesis account describes *Noah's sin.* It would seem that only a version that is extremely sensitive to the truth would include this realistic admission.[26] It should also be noted that only in Genesis is the year of the Flood given, as well as the dates for the whole chronology relative to Noah's life. The fact that the Genesis account is more realistic and less mythological than other ancient versions is a strong indication of its authenticity.

2. Logistical Evidence. The Genesis account describes Noah's ark as being 300 cubits long, 50 cubits wide, and 30 cubits deep. The length of a cubit in the most ancient times was about two feet, whereas more recently it is said to have been about one and one-half feet. So the ark was upwards of 600 feet long, 100 feet wide, and 60 feet deep. Scientists suggest these dimensions are the *most ideal* measurements for an ocean liner, and would prove to be a very seaworthy vessel. A vessel with these dimensions would have the capacity of about 2,000 cattle cars, each of which could carry up to 20 cattle, 80 hogs, or 100 sheep.[27] Many people wonder how many different kinds of animals exist in the world today. At the present time there are only *290 main species* of land animals larger than a sheep; *757 more species* ranging in size from a sheep to a rat; and *1358 species* smaller than a rat.[28] The Genesis account says that "two of every species" were taken into the ark[29] to repopulate the earth.[30] Researchers have concluded that two of every species would fit "very comfortably" into the 2,000 cattle cars, with plenty of room for fodder.[31]

3. Greenhouse Evidence. It is believed the Flood (often referred to as the "Deluge") completely altered the world that had been created. Many believe the pre-flood world was much like a "greenhouse" with tropical temperatures extending from the North Pole to the South Pole. The Genesis account says the original creation had what it called a "firmament in the midst of the waters."[32] This is understood by creation-scientists to be a *space* between the bodies of water on the ground and a body of water (vapor) above the atmosphere where birds fly.[33] Scientists have speculated that if there were about three feet of water surrounding the globe in vapor form (compared to the two inches we have today[34]), it would have had the effect of making the earth a giant terrarium, and tropical temperatures would indeed have extended from the North Pole to the South Pole. Incidentally, water vapor is clear, unlike clouds or steam. A sun-warmed "water canopy" would generate heat, thus producing a *greenhouse* effect over the entire globe. Though there is not enough water in the atmosphere today to yield worldwide greenhouse conditions, the two inches do provide us with enough temperature control to make the world habitable, and also protects us from vast amounts of harmful cosmic radiation from space. So the relatively small vapor blanket that exists in our present atmosphere is the very thing that makes life possible on earth today. If these radiations were not at least partially screened out before reaching the earth, they would quickly destroy all life.[35]

Therefore, with a water vapor canopy encircling the globe, the atmospheric conditions would have been radically different from what we have on earth today. Such a vapor canopy would have been invisible, and would have prevented extremes of heat and cold, resulting in a uniformly warm, probably subtropical climate, all over the earth. Winds and storms would not have been possible since they result basically from temperature differences, and heavy rains never would have occurred. The Genesis account tells us that it did not "rain" in the originally created state. Instead, a "morning mist" watered the earth[36] through the processes of evaporation, transpiration, and condensation.[37] This daily mist would have kept the entire earth in a comfortable state of humidity, and together with the artesian-spring fed rivers and water table, would have provided enough moisture to sustain lush vegetation and abundant animal life everywhere. The warm waters of the shallow network of seas everywhere[38] would likewise have sustained a thriving complex of marine life all over the world.[39]

Is there any proof that greenhouse warmth once surrounded our globe? Let's look at some of the evidence. Palm tree fossils have been found in Alaska and broad leaf ferns in the Arctic. Evolution-scientists have postulated that these trees and plants traveled there on the tectonic plate (earth crust) movement over millions of years. The problem with this theory is that these trees are not millions of years old. Creation-scientists do not have such a problem, because they believe they grew in the polar regions in the tropical world before the Flood, and that these trees were buried during the Flood of Noah's day, resulting in their fossilization.[40]

Scientists have found tropical forests and coal deposits in Antarctica. Plum trees which were quick-frozen and over ninety feet tall with green leaves have been found in the New Siberian islands where, today, only one-inch high willows grow.[41] In these frigid zones many trees, some fossilized and some quick-frozen, have been found with rings, signifying rapid, warm temperature growth. A number of excavations have revealed tropical plant life in some of the coldest arctic regions of the world. The evolutionist has no answer for how they got there; the creation-scientist believes they grew there before the Flood.[42]

4. Water Evidence. During the Flood, according to the Genesis account, "the windows of heaven poured forth rain (water canopy)," and "the fountains of the deep burst open" for forty days and forty nights.[43] It has only been in modern times that science has discovered that there are vast cavernous springs in the ocean bottom.[44] How could the writers of Genesis have known that these springs existed 6,000–9,000 years ago, unless it was revealed to them? Many have wondered how the entire globe could have been covered with water. If one were to make all of the earth's hard surfaces a completely smooth sphere without any oceans or mountains, there would be enough water in the oceans to cover the entire globe at a depth of over 1.5 miles (8,500 feet). The water in the oceans today covers over two-thirds of the globe.[45] It is thought that when the floodwaters began to recede, there must have been a deepening and widening of the oceans' basins into which waters flowed, while the continents themselves were appearing and mountain chains were being formed. This is why we find ocean fossils near the top of Mount Everest, the highest point on earth at over 29,000 feet.[46] In addition, the worldwide distribution of many geological features and rock types is very consistent with a global flood.[47]

Once the floodwaters subsided, life on earth would have been radically different. It probably took several hundred years for the earth to settle back down into the equilibrium we enjoy today. The centuries to follow would have been marked by massive storms, violent earthquakes, and volcanic eruptions. Estimates are that the world's oceans were substantially warmer than our present-day oceans. The excessive moisture contained in the warm air would have condensed and fallen as snow on the colder areas, particularly towards the Polar Regions. The snow in the Polar Regions would have packed down into ice and then spread out as large continental glaciers. This condition would have continued until the oceans surrendered their excess heat. The Ice Age probably lasted 600–1,000 years, approximately between the time of Noah and the biblical patriarch Abraham. Incidentally, the polar ice caps today are much smaller than they were during the Ice Age, and they are decreasing in size every year.[48]

5. Worldwide Flood Evidence. Evolutionists reject the biblical account of a worldwide flood, obviously because of the "religious overtones" associated with it. The evolutionary history of the earth interprets the fossils under our feet as the sequential history of the appearance of life over vast periods of time. The issue is whether or not the *evidence* supports the occurrence of a worldwide flood. What evidence should we expect from a global flood that drowned all the animals, birds, and people that were not on the ark? All around the world, in rock layer after rock layer, we find billions of dead things that have been buried in water-carried mud and sand. Their state of preservation frequently tells of rapid burial and fossilization, just like one would expect in a flood the magnitude of that described in Genesis. There is abundant evidence that many of the rock strata were laid down very quickly, one after the other, without significant time breaks between them. Polystrate fossils (ones which traverse *many* strata) speak of very quick deposition of the strata. The scarcity of erosion, soil formation, and roots between layers of strata also shows they must have been deposited in quick succession.[49]

Perhaps some of the most striking evidence of the violence of a global flood are the enormous numbers of animals whose violently separated bones have recently been discovered in several deep fissures excavated both in Europe and North America.[50] Since no skeleton is complete, scientists are fairly certain that none of these animals (mammoths, bears, wolves, hyenas, rhinoceroses, aurochs, deer, and many smaller mammals) fell into these fissures alive, nor were they dumped there by streams.[51] The calcite cementing of these bones together indicates that they must necessarily have been deposited there under water. Such fissures have been discovered by the Black Sea, the island of Kythera, the island of Malta, the Rock of Gibraltar, and at Agate Springs, Nebraska.[52]

Since fossils are the remains of plants and animals, an important question is how these remains could have been *preserved* for a long time. Scavengers and other animals and insects eat dead bodies, and tiny bacteria cause what is not eaten to *decompose*. Where bacteria are absent, oxygen and other chemicals in the air cause dead matter to totally *deteriorate*. Material that was once alive seldom lasts very long under normal circumstances after it dies. Yet we have multiplied *trillions* of fossils that have been preserved. Fish and other marine creatures are often fossilized in enormous numbers, some of them in the process of giving birth.[53] It's almost like a still snapshot of their life. How could this have happened?

In some places, hundreds of thousands of dinosaur bones are buried and fossilized, comprising entire hillsides. The great majority of fossils, however, are creatures with hard parts, like clams or coral, which lived on the ocean bottom. These are preserved by the trillions. It is important to realize, that under today's normal circumstances, *no fossils* are being formed. What happened in the past to cause them to be preserved in such large numbers? There are a number of different conditions under which it could happen, but the main requirement is that the organism must be buried rapidly. It must be protected from scavengers, which would eat it, and it must be where bacteria and chemicals cannot decompose it. Once it is protected, then the agents of fossilization can take over and turn it into a fossil.[54]

The record found in the geologic strata provides some of the best *physical evidence* for a worldwide flood. The fact that there is so much sedimentary rock on the earth's surface indicates that the entire world was under water at some time in the past. And the fact that most of the fossils, including those of human beings, are found in the geologic strata is good evidence that the sedimentary rock is the result of a worldwide catastrophic flood which occured during *human* history. Further, the idea that the different layers of sedimentary rock and the fossils they contain represent millions of years of gradual accumulation, during which the stages of evolution took place, is not consistent with the facts, because "lower life fossils" are *frequently* found above "higher life fossils" throughout the geologic strata; and often fossils of "lower" and "higher" forms of life of all kinds are found mixed and buried together in what are called fossil graveyards.[55] Such findings are not only incongruent with evolutionary theory, but strong supportive evidence of a worldwide flood.

6. Dinosaur Evidence. The theory of evolution does not have an answer to the question of why the dinosaurs were so big. Creation-scientists believe they were simply enlarged reptiles; reptiles do not have a built-in growth-inhibiting factor like other animals and humans. The dinosaurs would have continued growing as long as they lived; hence, the older they got, the bigger they grew. Reptiles function best as cold-blooded animals in warm temperature climates.[56] The pre-flood atmospheric conditions and the lush vegetation would have permitted them to live for an extremely long time and grow to immense sizes.

The Genesis account indicates all animals ate plants, *not flesh,* before the Flood.[57] Even Tyrannosaurus rex ate plants, not animals or dinosaurs, before the Flood. The illustrations often found in textbooks of this great dinosaur eating another reptile are *not* based on scientific method and are not supported with factual information.[58] The five- to eight-inch-long teeth of the Tyrannosaurus rex have roots that are not long enough to support a meat-tearing, bone-crunching diet, but they would have been extremely effective in stripping leaves from plants. After the Flood, these reptiles would not have grown to be as large. The *lighter* atmosphere, the *cooler* average temperature, and the presence of predators would have prevented long life and massive size.[59]

Evolutionists are also puzzled by ancient giant flying reptiles with 40 to 50 foot wingspans. To be able to fly they would have needed a much a heavier atmosphere than that which exists today. This is no problem for the creation-scientist, but it's a nightmare for the evolution-scientist. Gigantism would have been common during the heavy pre-flood atmosphere. Fossil dragonflies with a 32-inch wingspan have been discovered, and hornless rhinoceroses grew to a height of 17 feet and were nearly 30 feet long. In addition, giant saber-toothed tigers, mastodons, and woolly mammoths roamed the earth side-by-side with great dinosaurs.[60]

Contrary to what the evolutionary model claims, human beings lived during the age of the dinosaurs. Most textbooks claim that the dinosaurs became extinct about 60–70 million years before man stepped onto the scene.[61] But in cretaceous rock strata of Paluxy River bottom near Glen Rose, Texas, *numerous* human and dinosaur footprints have been found *crisscrossing each other*. Much has been said about these footprints because, if authentic, they prove in solid rock that man and dinosaur lived at the same time. If they are genuine, they deal a fatal blow "in rock" to evolution.[62] A group of evolutionists must have felt threatened by this discovery and actually tried to *destroy* it. But two scientists, Dr. Carl Baugh and Dr. Don Patton, were able to stop them and preserve the find.[63] Why would someone be so upset at discovering something that contradicted his or her philosophical model? Why would a person seek to destroy a discovery in an effort to make their position more tenable? Such behavior only does a disservice to the scientific community. For science to be credible, it must give preeminence to the truth, whatever the cost. Another piece of evidence that supports the theory that people and dinosaurs lived at the same time in history are the *cave paintings* of dinosaurs. How could a "prehistoric" man or woman paint a picture of a dinosaur if he or she had never seen one?[64]

7. Longevity of Life Evidence. Another result of the water (vapor) being above the firmament in which the birds flew would be the *shielding effect* from cosmic radiation. Scientists have conducted studies which measure how much solar radiation is filtered out by "water." Their conclusions have been reported by Dr. Joseph Dillow in his book, *The Waters Above: Earth's Pre-Flood Water Vapor Canopy.* The atmospheric system which existed prior to the flood would have permitted people to live much longer than in our present system. Some scientists maintain that one of the primary aging factors is solar radiation.[65] By filtering out the harmful radiation (as a water canopy would do), it is thought that humans might be able to live close to 1,000 years. The Bible reports that Adam died at 930 years of age, and Methuselah lived longer than any other man—969 years.[66] Some present-day researchers who study longevity believe humans could live that long again if they were sheltered from the harmful effects of solar radiation and our polluted air.[67] With a reduction in the amount of water vapor in the atmosphere following the flood, the human life span dropped off drastically to an average of 70 to 80 years.[68]

8. Carbon-14 Evidence. Solar shielding by a water canopy would have had a radical effect on dating techniques. Significantly less carbon-14 would

have formed *before* the flood than happens today; therefore carbon-14 dating techniques are worthless when dating objects effected by the flood of
6,000–9,000 years ago.[69] Dr. Willard F. Libby, who discovered the carbon-
14 dating technique, noticed a problem when he developed it. He believed
that if the earth is older than 30,000 years, carbon-14 and carbon-12 would
have to be in a steady state of *equilibrium* with each other. The problem is
they are not. In fact, there is more than a 25 percent discrepancy between
carbon-14 and carbon-12, meaning that the earth and its atmosphere must
be less than 30,000 years old.[70] This is another piece of evidence that frus-
trates the evolutionist.

    9. Quick-Frozen Animal Evidence. Evolutionary science has no answer
for the existence of numerous quick-frozen animals found in various places
around the globe. What is a quick-frozen rhinoceros doing in Siberia? Perhaps
he was on a summer vacation and lost track of time, and before long he got
snowed in? No! The truth of the matter is there were tropical animals living
in Siberia before the Flood of Noah's day. The evolutionists maintain that it
was a *slow-moving ice age* that caught up to these animals, but the animals'
remains are such that they were caught and permanently frozen (they are still
frozen today) with such incredible speed that undigested plants remained in
their mouths and in their stomach's digestive juices. Giant nine-ton mammoths have been discovered with undigested buttercups in their mouths
and in their stomachs, which are still identifiable as to genus and species of
the plant.[71]

    Science has also discovered that the skin of these pre-flood mammoths
contained no "oil glands," and this is also extremely surprising to evolutionary scientists. Why? Because cold temperature animals have a plentiful
supply of oil glands to oil their hair and fur. Wolves, seals, and polar bears
have such oily fur that frigid water rolls off and does not penetrate to the
skin. Cold temperature animals need a lot of oil to protect them from cold
wet weather. A mammoth, no matter how large, could not last very long in
a frigid climate without oil in its hair. Therefore, these ancient mammoths
were warm-temperature animals, eating warm-temperature plants, and were
caught suddenly and frozen quickly and permanently in the distant past.
Evolutionists have no explanation for this. But a cataclysmic event such as
the collapse of the *water canopy* at the Flood provides the answer and the
evidence.[72]

    This sudden and permanent temperature change in the earth's atmosphere,
from pole-to-pole greenhouse warm to the present permafrost or permanent
ice condition at and near the poles, could have happened during the collapse

WHAT WOULD IT TAKE TO "QUICK-FREEZE" A NINE-TON MAMMOTH?

What would it take to quick-freeze a happy, healthy nine-ton mammoth grazing on buttercups, and several hundred other identifiable plants which no longer grow in the frigid climate where the frozen mammoths are found? A group of scientists went to a major food-freezing company and posed this question. They were told it would take a temperature of –175 degrees Fahrenheit (the coldest temperature ever recorded on earth is –128 degrees Fahrenheit), and a wind-chill factor of a 200–400 mph wind over a time frame of about four hours (eight hours at the outside limit). The problem with these extreme conditions is that there is nothing on today's earth that approaches them, and yet the animals are frozen! To preserve the meat and undigested plants, drastic conditions not known on our present earth would have been necessary. One thing is certain, the freezing of these ancient plants and animals was not caused by a slowly creeping ice age. Many textbooks will show an artist's fanciful picture of a mammoth standing in a blizzard as a slowly creeping glacier moves up from behind. This is the stuff of fantasy and imagination, not reality. The mammoths were warm-temperature animals, eating warm-temperature plants, in a warm-temperature climate that suddenly, in a matter of hours, became permanently frozen. These mammoths, and many other animals, were frozen so quickly that their meat can still be eaten today![73] How does one account for this phenomenon?

of the water canopy at the Flood-judgment of God in the days of Noah.[74] The Bible does not tell us if there was some antecedent physical cause that triggered the bursting of the earth's crust and the precipitation of the canopy, but there are numerous theories as to how it could have happened. It could have been caused by a large meteor hitting the earth, and tipping it 23.5 degrees off dead center during impact. It could have been caused by the simultaneous eruption of numerous volcanoes all over the world, with the dust particles causing the vapor to condense into rain. Or possibly all of these cataclysmic events happened at the same time.[75] However it happened—it happened. The evolutionary model that denies the worldwide flood is an empty deception, and more and more people are realizing it. Today there are thousands of scientists all over the world who maintain that belief in God and in the truth of the events recorded in the Bible, including the Flood, is compatible with all we know about our universe and ourselves, and that it contradicts no known facts.

Three Reasons Why Life Did Not Evolve by Natural Processes

The central tenet of evolutionism is that all living things developed or evolved by purely *natural processes* from simple life-forms and advanced to

BIBLICAL ARGUMENTS FOR A WORLDWIDE FLOOD vs. A LOCAL FLOOD

In spite of all the foregoing evidence that supports a worldwide flood, there are some even in the Christian community who do not accept the concept of a worldwide flood. Their thinking parallels the prevailing scientific view which does not allow for a universal flood as recorded in the Bible. These individuals believe the flood must have been a relatively small and localized event in the region of ancient Mesopotamia, but this position does not do justice to the biblical data. The Genesis account says that "all of the high mountains everywhere under the heavens" were covered with water, "all flesh that moved on the earth perished," and "only Noah and his family were spared because they were in the ark."[76] Furthermore, to interpret the Genesis story as a description of a local event given in relative terms overlooks a number of obvious problems in the account and raises numerous other questions, such as: "What was the purpose of building such an *enormous ark* if the flood was simply a local flood?[77] Could not God have simply warned Noah and his family to escape from the coming judgment by fleeing to another region? "Why was there such concern for all the *birds* and *animals* if this was a local flood?[78] Could they not have just escaped to an unflooded region?" "How could the tops of the *mountains* be under 22 feet of water if this were a local flood?[79] Does not water seek its own level across the entire surface of the globe?" "Why did God open up the *fountains of the deep*[80] in the bottoms of the oceans if this was just a local flood?" "Why did the waters on the earth take so long to recede if it was simply a local flood? Why were the tops of the mountains not seen until seven months had passed, and why did it take one year and ten days to dry up the floodwaters enough[81] so Noah and his family could leave the ark?" "What about God's promise that He would never again destroy the earth with a flood? Does not the Bible say in a parallel account that the next time God destroys the world He will do so with fire?"[82] "How do you explain the fact that other Scriptures speak of a worldwide flood, and that both Jesus and Peter referred to it?"[83]

more sophisticated life-forms. In other words, the theory of evolution states that the universe arose from nothing without a cause. There are several reasons why life did not emerge simply by natural causes and nonliving material:[84]

1. *Life never results from nonlife.* It has been scientifically demonstrated that life cannot come into existence where there is no life. World-renowned scientist Louis Pasteur (1822–1895) showed the scientific community that life never emerges from a nonliving environment.

2. *Intelligent life requires an intelligent cause.* Just as a dictionary did not simply evolve by an explosion in a paper mill, and the faces on Mount Rushmore did not emerge as the result of erosion, neither did intelligent life develop through natural processes.

3. *The idea that life evolved by chance is unscientific.* Science prides itself on its methodology of observation and experimentation, not on reasoning founded on chance. Furthermore, the odds of life beginning by chance are basically zero. Some mathematicians have calculated the chance (assuming it's possible) to be 1 in 10 to the 40,000th power; that's 10 with 40,000 zeros after it! Just to give you an idea how large that number is—there are not that many *atoms* in the entire universe! It takes far more faith to believe in evolution than it does to believe in supernatural creation.

Three Reasons Why Many Scientists Accept Evolution as Fact

Nearly all textbooks and magazine articles on the subject portray evolution as an undisputed fact concerning the origins and the development of life. The three main reasons why many secular academicians accept it as fact are these:[85]

1. *Some scientists overestimate the evidence for evolution.* In their desire to find clues that prove the credibility of evolution, some scientists simply overlook the problems with the evidence itself.

2. *Some teachers present evolution as fact and their students accept it as true.* Most students rarely question evidence that is labeled scientific, and they do not know enough to object to educational bias. In addition, the explanation for the origin of life is almost always one-sided. Rarely is the evidence questioned or refuted; and even more rarely is a rational justification given for supernatural creation. Consequently, this inaccurate view is adopted by the student without ever being satisfactorily investigated or critically examined.

3. *Some people believe evolution is fact because the media proclaims it as fact.* Television and radio shows present evolution as an indisputable fact that every "reasonable" person believes. Nearly all public communications and entertainment media consistently indoctrinate the public in evolutionary philosophy, and as a result it is quickly accepted as true.

The theory of evolution has been widely accepted by secular colleges and universities. The primary reason for this is that religion has basically been ruled out of the public arena in the Western world. Whether religion is true or not is irrelevant; it has been ruled out of bounds in the public arena. The evidence notwithstanding, science is *in* and religion is *out*. It is simply one of the sober realities of Western culture. Nevertheless, truth is derived from established evidence, not majority vote. The evidence for creationism far outweighs the highly questionable evidence for evolution. Evolutionism does not fit with reality. It does not fit the fossil record; it does not fit modern studies in molecular biology; it does not fit the study of human artifacts, and it does not fit with historical evidence. Ironically, agnostic scientist Robert Jastrow accurately assesses the scientific pursuit: "For the scientist who has lived by his faith in the power of reason, the story ends like a bad dream. He has scaled the mountains of ignorance; he is about to conquer the highest peak; as he pulls himself over the final rock, he is greeted by a band of theologians who have been sitting there for centuries."[86]

CHAPTER 5

THE EXISTENCE OF GOD

In my most extreme fluctuations I have never been an atheist
in the sense of denying the existence of God.
— *CHARLES DARWIN*[1]

Philosophers, theologians, and scientists have long wrestled with
the age-old questions, Does God exist? Who or what made this world? Was
it made at all? If it was not made, how did it get here? Can humans know
that God exists? Such questions have perplexed humanity since the beginning of human history. The philosophy of religion invites us to explore the
questions of divine existence *epistemologically*. Epistemology is that branch of
philosophy that concerns itself with knowledge theory—how we can know
things, and how we can know we know them. Throughout the centuries the
world's most eminent thinkers have carefully crafted arguments that have
come to be known as the classical arguments for the existence of God. The
three most popular arguments are: 1) The argument of *cause*; 2) The argument of *design*; and 3) The argument of *morality*.

The Argument of "Cause"

The mere existence of the world is a fact that demands explanation.
Providing this explanation is the task of what is referred to as the *cosmo-
logical* argument. Cosmology is the study of the cosmos and its processes.
Cosmological arguments reason back from the existence of the world to a

Transcendent Reality that explains the world. This Reality is usually called the *First Cause* or the *Prime Mover*,[2] the latter a term coined by the Greek philosopher Aristotle. When one thinks of the cosmos, it is only natural to wonder how it came into existence. Did it always exist or did something or someone cause it to exist? Essentially there are only two possible explanations. Either the cosmos had a beginning or it did not. Until recently, most modern-day scientists believed the universe was *eternal,* that it had no beginning. However, new scientific information indicates the universe must have had a beginning. Astronomer Edwin Hubble stunned the scientific community when he discovered that the universe is *expanding;* all known galaxies are moving away from the earth at a high rate of speed. This means the universe is not simply in a holding pattern, but is actually getting larger and larger with each passing day. It appears that all of the galaxies are moving outward as if from a central point of origin, and that these cosmic bodies actually moved faster in the past then they do today.[3]

This profound discovery of an expanding universe has caused the vast majority of scientists to reject the earlier view that the universe is eternal in favor of the belief that the universe exploded into existence. As we saw in chapter three, it is now believed that this explosion—commonly referred to as the *Big Bang*—was the beginning point from which the entire universe came into being. The Big Bang theory maintains that if one were to put an expanding universe in reverse, it would lead back to the point where the universe would get smaller and smaller until it vanished into nothing. Therefore, the universe, at some point in the distant past, came into being out of *nothing*.[4] The discovery of an expanding universe forged a consensus within the scientific community that the universe came into being in a sudden and cataclysmic way.

The *Second Law of Thermodynamics* also supports the fact that the universe had a beginning. This law basically says that the universe is wearing down and running out of usable energy; that is, it is growing old and deteriorating like an old automobile or an old building. Our solar system's sun is a tremendous source of power, but its energy will gradually be dispersed through space; the same is true for all of the other suns in the universe. This means the universe eventually will die a *heat death,* with all of its power uniformly scattered as low-level heat throughout the universe. The energy will still exist, but it will no longer be available to keep things going; therefore, the universe will die. Due to the fact that the universe has not yet died, it must not be infinitely old, and it must have had a beginning.[5]

Another argument that supports the idea that the universe had a beginning is seen in the energy sources that fuel the cosmos. The sun, like all stars, generates its energy by a process known as *thermonuclear fusion*. Every single second the sun compresses 564 million tons of hydrogen into 560 million tons of helium, with 4 million tons of matter released as energy. Because this happens more than 31 million times every year, the total amount of hydrogen compressed *annually* by our sun is unfathomable— 17,000,000,000,000,000 (quadrillion) tons, and in the process it produces more than 124,000,000,000,000 (trillion) tons of matter released as energy. In spite of this enormous consumption of fuel, the sun has only used up 2 percent of the hydrogen it had the day it came into existence.[6] By the way, this incredible thermonuclear furnace is not a process that is confined to our sun. Every one of the 70 sextillion stars *(that's billions of trillions!)* in the universe generates its energy in identically the same way, thereby reducing the total amount of hydrogen in the cosmos by an amount that is almost incalculable. In case you're wondering how big 70 sextillion is—it's a "seven" with 22 zeros after it: 70,000,000,000,000,000,000,000! That means there are far more stars in the sky than there are grains of sand and specks of dirt on the entire Earth. A group of astronomers led by an Australian, Simon Driver, made this calculation in 2003 using the Isaac Newton Telescope in Spain and the Anglo-Australian Telescope in New South Wales.[7]

Though the human mind is not able to comprehend such figures, we can consider the impact of thermonuclear fusion on our universe. If all of the hydrogen everywhere in the cosmos is being consumed, and if this process has been going on *forever,* how much hydrogen should be left? If the answer is not clear, think of it this way: If you were to fill up your automobile with gas and start driving on a trip across country, what will eventually happen? You will run out of gas. Therefore, if the cosmos has been here *forever,* we would have run out of hydrogen a long time ago.[8] But as mentioned above, the sun still has 98 percent of its original hydrogen, so it's going to keep producing energy and heat for awhile; but the day will eventually come when the energy supply of hydrogen in the universe will be fully expended.

Given all these facts, it is clear that if we were to go backwards in time to the beginning, we would arrive at that moment our universe exploded into existence. The question is, what precipitated the Big Bang? It must have had a cause. Everything in the cosmos has been *caused* to exist by something that existed before it. Science is based on causality; every event has a cause; things do not come into existence by themselves. The scientific law that gives defini- tion to this concept is called the *principle of causality*. It states that every effect must have a cause. We see the effects of this principle in our everyday life. Buildings, watches, paintings, airplanes, computers, television, newspapers, and automobiles all had a beginning; therefore, they all had a cause. The world of causation demands a beginning, a moment when some *force*, some *being*, some *thing* began the series of events that eventually led to the present. Ultimately, this force, or being, or thing that caused everything to start must have had *no cause itself.* In a nutshell, something had to begin the chain of events that led to the present, or we could not have arrived at this moment. It does not matter how far back in time the first moment was; the point is that everything came into existence through a *First Cause.* And it is this first-cause proof which demonstrates that our universe is not eternal.[9]

Scientists and logicians think in terms of cause-and-effect relationships. Nothing happens in and of itself alone; all events are invariably the effects of one or more causes. In science, causality is a basic assumption. In fact, this assumption is so obviously true to all observation and experience that it is called the *Law of Cause and Effect.* Every observed phenomenon is an effect, and its originating cause must be adequate to produce it; therefore, no effect can be greater than its cause.[10] This is the essence of science; the scientist states that a particular process or situation is a function of one or several variables, which affect its behavior. Thus each effect has a cause adequate to produce it. Ultimately, logic compels us to one of two conclusions: either the chain of causes is infinite, with no beginning at all, or else it all began with a *First Cause,* which itself was eternally uncaused.[11]

Classic evolutionists assert that the world is *uncaused.* But even the great eighteenth-century Scottish philosopher and skeptic David Hume said, "I never asserted so absurd a proposition as that anything might arise without a cause."[12] Yet this absurd proposition is accepted by many who make their living by the law of causality—evolutionary scientists. Unfortunately, this view is still being taught by those who have not kept up with the latest discoveries in the study of the universe. Interestingly enough, Carl Sagan, one of the proponents of the notion that the universe is causeless, also believed that a "single message" from outer space would confirm his belief in extraterrestrial life. In other words, some very common behaviors, such as communication, require an *intelligent cause.* This type of intelligent order is known as *specified complexity.* It is more than just simplistic design or order; it is order of a complex nature that has a clear and specific function. For example, a chain of random polymers may be *complex,* but it does not suggest any specific function or message; the polymers might appear like this: DLVKIWMJQWCTHWNVPTNBX. On the other hand, *specified complexity* has order that communicates function, such as the following: THIS SENTENCE CARRIES A MESSAGE.[13]

It is obvious that wherever we see a clear and distinct message (a complex design with a specified function), we can be confident that it was caused by some *intelligent intervention*. Specified complexity, however, should not be confused with natural phenomena that are orderly and awe inspiring. Thrilling sights like the Grand Canyon or Niagara Falls were shaped by the forces of wind and water; but the same cannot be said for the four faces on Mount Rushmore or a hydroelectric plant. In these cases there is clearly a specified message or function. For such phenomena we know there must have been intelligent intervention. Whether it be a novel or a poem, a sculpture of human anatomy, or a television set, we immediately understand that it took some smarts to create it; that it did not happen by itself. Every bit of our experience confirms this to us.[14] It is completely reasonable for science to look for intelligent causes that show signs of intelligence. Archaeologists do it all the time. When they find pottery or arrowheads, they rightly conclude some intelligent being produced them.

In the thirteenth century, Thomas Aquinas described the principle of causality as such: "Everything that happens has a cause, and this cause in turn has a cause, and so on in a series. A *starting point,* itself independent of other causes, must exist. This point is God."[15] The Judeo-Christian notion of creation includes more than the idea that the world had a *beginning* in time;[16] it also includes the notion that the *continued* existence of the world is ontologically dependent on God.[17] This idea is captured in the following equations:

God minus the world equals God.
The world minus God equals nothing.[18]

God's creative activity not only brought the world into existence out of nothing; He also continually sustains the world in its existence. So to describe God as First Cause is to say more than that He was the efficient cause that *started* the world; it is also to recognize that God is the ultimate ground without which the world could not *continue* to exist.[19]

A great deal of evidence now supports the belief that the universe had a beginning. Avowed agnostic, Robert Jastrow, founder and former director of NASA's Goddard Institute for Space Studies, has summarized the evidence in his book, *God and the Astronomers*. He writes, "Three lines of evidence—the motion of the galaxies, the laws of thermodynamics, and the life story of the stars—point to one conclusion: the universe had a beginning."[20] Logically, if we are looking for a cause which existed before the universe existed, we must look for a *supernatural cause*. Even Jastrow has said as much: "That there are what I or anyone would call supernatural forces at work is now, I think, a scientifically proven fact."[21]

If we know the cosmos had a beginning, we are faced with another question. Was it caused or not caused? Theists tell us the cause was God. Atheists tell us that there was no cause. If the cosmos had a beginning and yet was uncaused, philosophers tell us one must logically maintain that something would have had to come into existence out of nothing. From empty space with no force, no matter, no energy, and no intelligence, matter would have had to come into existence. For the sake of argument, even if this could have happened by some strange process unknown to science, there is a logical problem. In order for matter to come out of nothing, one would have to discard all known laws and principles of science. No reasonable person is going to nullify all known laws simply to maintain a personal atheistic position.[22]

The atheist tries to convince us that we are the product of "chance." Evolutionary biologist Julian Huxley once said: "We are as much a product of blind forces as is the falling of a stone to earth or the ebb and flow of the [ocean] tides. We have just happened, and man was made flesh by a long series of singularly beneficial accidents."[23] However, such a position is now untenable. A principle of modern science emerged in the 1980s that is known as *the anthropic principle*, according to which chance is simply not a valid explanation of the origin of life. Therefore, we are constrained to reject Huxley's claim and to realize that we are the product of an intelligent Transcendent Being.[24]

In contrast to Huxley, Einstein recognized there was an intelligent creative transcendent force through which the universe came into existence. He defined it as "the illimitable superior reasoning power which is revealed in the incomprehensible universe.... I see at the beginning of the cosmic road—not eternal energy or matter, not 'inscrutable fate,' not a 'fortuitous conflux of primordial elements,' not 'the great Unknown'—but the Lord God Almighty."[25]

The Argument of "Design"

All theists believe the universe is a result of supernatural creation, that it is not self-existent, but was intentionally brought into being by a Transcendent Reality that exists outside of creation, which itself is self-existent. Most scientists believe the universe will go on *expanding* until it runs out of fuel and comes to a frozen standstill. Whatever happens, one thing is clear, this physical universe in the distant future, barring supernatural intervention, will cease to exist in its present form. So the universe as we know it had a *beginning*, and is ultimately destined to come to an end.[26]

The vast majority of scientists also agree that our universe does not exist in a chaotic state. On the contrary, it works in conjunction with consistent principles and laws, which are elegant and extremely beautiful, and it comprises an astounding complexity and intelligibility that is indescribable and beyond human understanding.[27] Thus the cosmos can easily be seen as the product of an immensely brilliant mind. Most cosmologists refer to the intricate design in nature as the *teleological proof* for the existence of God. Teleology is the study of design or purpose in nature. One of the best ways to explain a teleological proof is to imagine that you are walking along a beach when you suddenly see something shiny in the sand. You pick it up and discover that it's a watch. Here's the question: Are you *certain* that someone made the watch? Obviously, the answer is yes. You know with absolute certainty that somebody made the watch. Watches show design, purposefulness, and function, and they do not just "poof" into existence. Even if you never find out the watchmaker's name, you still know he exists because that watch could not exist without him. Such knowledge is not an assumption or something you believe because you were told to believe it. It is a fact. In the same way, the universe is like a watch in that it shows design and purpose; it is extremely complex and intricate. Everything works according to plan. Flowers do not bloom in the winter, and birds do not fly north in the fall. In addition, the design of the human body shows far more complexity, purpose, and structure than anything ever imagined by science. In the next chapter we will consider eight incredible features of the human body. Just look at all the other designs and patterns in the universe—how could they have arisen from any source other than an intelligent Creator?[28]

In 1963, the American philosopher Richard Taylor presented a compelling teleological argument in his book *Metaphysics*. He introduced his argument with an interesting story that asked his reader to imagine himself in a coach on a British train. Looking out the window, the passenger sees a number of large "white stones" on a hillside lying in a pattern that spells out the letters: THE BRITISH RAILWAYS WELCOMES YOU TO WALES. How implausible is it that such an arrangement of stones could be a purely accidental happening? We must admit that such a thing is logically possible, though the odds are astronomically high. Taylor states that there are at least two explanations for the arrangement of the stones: a natural, nonpurposive explanation, and an explanation in terms of the intentions of at least one intelligent being.[29] If the passenger infers that the stones communicate a true message, it would be quite inconsistent for him also to assume that the positioning of the stones was an accident. Once you conclude that the stones do convey an intelligible message, Taylor continues,

> You would, in fact, be presupposing that they were arranged that way by an intelligent and purposeful being or beings for the purpose of conveying a certain message having nothing to do with the stones themselves.... It would be irrational for you to regard the arrangement of the stones as evidence that you were entering Wales, and at the same time to suppose that they might have come to have that arrangement accidentally... the result of the ordinary interactions of natural or physical forces.[30]

Another scientist who argues in favor of design is Dr. Werhner von Braun, who is considered one of the twentieth-century's greatest scientists. After pioneering work in rocketry, Dr. von Braun developed the Saturn V rocket that successfully powered the first manned moon landing. In 1972 this great scientist was asked to comment on the case for design as a scientific theory for the origin of the universe. He wrote:

> For me, the idea of a creation is not conceivable without invoking the necessity of design. One cannot be exposed to the law and order of the universe without concluding that there must be design and purpose.... While the admission of a design for the universe ultimately raises the question of a Designer (a subject outside of science), the scientific method does not allow us to exclude data which lead to the conclusion that the universe, life and man are based on design.[31]

Design in creation, ultimately, points to a *designer*. Anytime we see something with complex design, we know by previous experience that it came from the mind of a designer. Ordered, intelligent designs such as research papers, buildings, presidential faces sculpted on Mount Rushmore, and computer programs came from the minds of designers. Intelligent design does not emerge by random chance any more than *Webster's Dictionary* could be composed by an explosion in a print shop. Design informs us that a designer is responsible.[32] The seventeenth-century English philosopher and mathematician, Isaac Newton, concurs with this when he says, "The existence of a Being endowed with intelligence and wisdom is a necessary inference from a study of celestial mechanics."[33] So also writes the Greek philosopher, Plato, in his work *Delegibus*: "The earth, the sun and stars, and the universe itself; and the charming variety of the seasons, demonstrate the existence of a Divinity."[34]

The design in the universe is extremely intricate and complex, and far exceeds a human's ability to understand. The universe is an incredibly intricate system of forces that work together for the mutual benefit of the whole. For example, a single-cell animal (invisible to the naked eye) contains far more information than a dozen sets of the *Encyclopedia Britannica*. Isn't it reasonable to assume that an encyclopedia found in the forest had an intelligent cause? Isn't it reasonable to believe that computers, cameras, and sophisticated machinery need intelligent causes like humans to create them? Why, then, do some find it hard to believe that human beings need an intelligent cause?[35] Some people still object to this argument on the basis of "chance." They claim that when the dice are rolled any combination could happen. However, this is not very convincing for several reasons, but let's just consider the following: One scientist figured the odds of a "one-cell" animal coming forth naturally by pure chance at 1 in 10 to the 40,000th power. That's a "ten" with 40,000 zeros after it! Let me remind you—those are the odds for an invisible *one-cell* animal. Now consider what the odds would be for an *infinitely* more complex human being to emerge by chance. Scientists tell us that the odds are so astronomical they cannot even be calculated.[36] It takes far more faith to believe life can develop by chance than it does to believe it requires an intelligent cause.

Scientists have discovered a large number of coincidences in the universe that allow life to exist on this planet. The odds that the universe could have become "life permitting" merely through the operation of chance are beyond human calculation; the number is incomprehensible! The universe appears to have been created specifically for the existence of life on earth. It is important to realize that life can only exist in an extremely limited environment; if any one of the limiting factors is altered just slightly, life would cease to exist. Consider just the following seven examples:[37]

1. *If the earth was located only slightly farther away from the sun* (just 2 percent) it would freeze like the planet Mars; if it was only slightly closer, it would burn up in heat like the 860-degree F temperature on Venus.[38]

2. *It the earth did not revolve at its regular rate,* the day- and nighttime temperatures would be radically altered, and vegetation would be greatly effected. If it did not revolve at all, one side would be uninhabitable ice, and the other would be an uninhabitable desert.

3. *If the earth were not tilted at 23 degrees*, it would not have the seasonal variation that produces the abundance of crops that feed the planet's huge population. Without this tilt, less than half of the present land that's used for cultivation of crops would grow vegetables.

4. *If the earth was only a small percentage smaller*, the reduced gravity would be incapable of holding the atmosphere that is essential for breathing.

5. *If the planet earth was twice as large as it is*, the effect of increased gravity would make everything on the planet weigh eight times what it weighs today. This increase in weight would destroy many forms of animal and all human life.

6. *A much thinner atmosphere would provide no protection* from the 25,000 meteors that burn up over the earth every day. A thinner atmosphere would also be incapable of retaining the higher temperatures required for the existence of human and animal life.

7. *If the atmosphere were not 78 percent nitrogen and 22 percent oxygen and other gases*, breathing would be impossible.

The world we live in is clearly the product of transcendent brilliance. The earth is just the right size; its rotation is within certain limits; its tilt must be correct to cause the seasons; the human biological structure is very fragile—a little too much heat or cold and we die; we need light, but not too much ultraviolet; we need heat, but not too much infrared.[39] Everything we find in nature points to harmony, design, purpose, and intelligence, and is consistent with the Judeo-Christian presupposition that God exists and also provides supporting evidence for it.

Given these conditions, every religious or philosophical thinker is faced with a choice. Either the universe is a product of design, or all these features developed by chance. If we believe in the God described in Scripture, we should expect to find that the world is law-like and exhibits signs of purpose and design; we should expect to discover that our sensory organs give us reliable information about the world; we should expect to find that our rational faculties enable us to draw sound inferences and discover truth. The innumerable signs of purpose in the universe are clues that should not be ignored or explained away.[40]

The English philosopher William Paley (1743–1803) argued that the universe is like an exceedingly complex mechanism. When one takes stock of the whole range of data—nature, creation, and human moral, cognitive, and aesthetic experience—God's existence becomes more probable than not. If God created the world, we can reasonably expect that the created natural order would show His workmanship.[41] Obviously, no one can "prove" to a skeptic that God exists, because God is a *spirit being*, and as such is invisible. The created dimension human beings experience does not include the world of reality beyond space, mass, and time. Science only deals with the *physical world*, and you do not find God by looking into the heavens with a telescope. So if God transcends space, mass, and time, how can one prove His existence? One can only examine the *evidence* that is an integral part of His creation, and the sum total of this evidence clearly demonstrates that He exists.

The Bible confirms this when it says God's invisible attributes can be seen and understood through what He has made;[42] thus suggesting that the intricate design and delicate balance of the universe is like a message from God. The created order speaks of His genius, wisdom, power, creativity, excellence, majesty, character, beauty, providence, and His skill. Of all the arguments for the existence of God, none overwhelms the mind so completely as the teleological argument from design. In the next chapter we will look at just a fraction of the illimitable genius exercised in the creation of the human body.

Theists believe the process of creation culminated in beings who are capable of consciously knowing the Creator, and whose task it is to care for the earth and its other life-forms. The core belief of monotheism is that there is a Creator who is gradually working out His purposes in the universe, and invites human beings to play an important role in that purpose.[43] Dr. Arthur H. Compton, Nobel Prize Winner in Physics, states his case for believing in the existence of God:

> For myself, faith begins with the realization that a supreme intelligence brought the universe into being and created man. It is not difficult for me to have this faith, for it is incontrovertible that where there is a plan there is intelligence—an orderly, unfolding universe testifies to the truth of the most majestic statement ever uttered—"In the beginning God!"[44]

The Argument of "Morality"

The moral argument begins with an understanding of the fact that of all the various types of life on earth, *only human beings* can choose between good and evil. As far as science can tell, no life-forms other than human beings have free will and make moral choices. Lions do not choose to kill antelopes;

they're driven to do so by instinct. All animals obey the laws and compulsions of nature. They mate with whomever they want; they excrete waste wherever they want; they eat whatever they want; and they kill whenever they want. Only human beings can resist animal-like urges for the sake of some higher moral good. But where does the human capacity for making moral choices come from? Obviously it does not come from nature, because nothing else in nature demonstrates this capacity. Therefore, it must come from some force beyond nature, from that which made nature, but which is not a part of nature. Thus, a Transcendent Reality[45] must exist in order to explain the existence of morality in human beings.[46]

Due to the fact that every person has a built-in moral compass, a sense of right and wrong, there must be a corresponding Moral Lawgiver (God).[47] Some people, however, ask the question, "How do we know all human beings know the difference between right and wrong?" There are two answers to this question. First, all humans seem to agree that certain behaviors are *always* wrong. People everywhere at all times know that murder, rape, betrayal, theft, lying, and molestation are wrong; they carry this sense of moral awareness within them, and it is accompanied by a sense of guilt, shame, and embarrassment.[48] Likewise, everyone desires to be treated with fairness, respect, and dignity. If there were no consistent moral law implanted in the minds and hearts of people, one would expect far greater diversity in the behaviors people judge to be wrong. Instead what we see in societies all over the world is virtually a *universal agreement* on what is right and wrong. This strongly suggests that there is a standard that exists in every person's conscience, the source of which must be a morally good God.[49]

Second, we find that even those who deny having such a moral compass live their lives as though they do have one.[50] Therefore, such common behavior excludes the possibility that social convention is at the root of moral law. Those who claim that morality is strictly subjective make strong objective statements in opposition to moral law; but in the very act of trying to deny its existence, their reasoning implies that there is a moral law. Even those who say that there is no moral law *expect* to be treated with fairness, equity, and respect. If such a person should argue with us concerning moral law, and we were intolerantly to say "Shut up! Who cares what you think?" we would quickly find that they do believe in some moral "oughts." Everyone expects people to follow certain moral codes; even those who try to deny them. In short, moral law is an undeniable fact.[51]

The knowledge of "ought" is universal. Every human being and every society has a system of morals—actions and behaviors humans feel they ought and ought not to do. This sense of moral obligation very frequently runs *contrary* to plain self-interest and may even lead to self-destruction. Where does it come from? It is hard to explain unless one accepts that it must have been imposed from without; in other words, it requires a Transcendent Reality as its cause.[52] It is also interesting to note that every society has established a complex system of justice to deal with those unacceptable behaviors that run counter to their system of morals.

Immanuel Kant (1724–1804), German philospher who is regarded as one of the most influential thinkers of modern Europe, and the end of the Enlightenment. His most famous work, *Critique of Pure Reason,* is now recognized as one of the most significant works in the history of philosophy.

The eighteenth-century philosopher Immanuel Kant wrote in his *Critique of Pure Reason,* "Two things fill the mind with... admiration and awe... the starry heavens above and the moral law within." This moral sense within human beings is not merely the result of the mores or customs of their cultures; rather, it is an innate capacity to know right and wrong. That humans have this capacity can hardly be explained unless there is a moral governor of the universe.[53] Only God could have implanted this "moral code" deep inside of every human being. Our consciences and feelings of guilt give evidence to our moral nature; therefore, our *source* must be both moral and personal, for impersonal natural forces do not have moral sensibilities. In other words, since there is a moral law binding on all of us, there must be a Moral Lawgiver.[54]

C. S. Lewis, the English essayist from Oxford University, was an atheist or agnostic in his earlier years, but eventually he came to believe in the existence of God and the validity of the Christian religion. In his work *Mere Christianity,* he presented the moral nature of man as a major argument for the existence of a moral Creator behind the universe. He states:

> Everyone has heard people quarrelling. Sometimes it sounds funny and sometimes it sounds merely unpleasant; but however it sounds, I believe we can learn something very important from listening to the kind of things they say. They say things like this: "How would you like it if someone did the same to

you?" "That's my seat; I was there first." "Leave him alone; he is not doing you any harm." "Why should you [butt] in line first?" People say things like that every day, educated people as well as uneducated, and children as well as grownups.... [Man] appeals to some kind of standard of behavior which he expects the other man to know about.... Nearly always he tries to [justify] that what he has been doing does not really go against the standard, or that if it does there is some special excuse.... It looks, in fact, very much as if both parties had in mind some kind of Law or Rule of fair play... about which they really agreed. And they have. If they had not, they might, of course, fight like animals, but they could not quarrel in the human sense of the word. Quarrelling means trying to show that the other man is wrong. And there would be no sense in trying to do that unless you and he had some sort of agreement as to what Right and Wrong are....

I know that some people say the idea of... decent behavior known to all men is unsound, because different civilizations and different ages have had quite different moralities. But this is not true. There have been differences between their moralities, but these have never amounted to anything like a total difference. If anyone will take the trouble to compare the moral teaching of, say, the ancient Egyptians, Babylonians, Hindus, Chinese, Greeks and Romans, what will really strike him will be how very like they are to each other and to our own.... Think of a country where people were admired for running away in battle, or where a man felt proud of double-crossing all the people who had been kindest to him.... Selfishness has never been admired. Men have differed as to whether you should have one wife or four; but they have always agreed that you must not simply have any woman you liked....[55]

Lewis' argument was designed to demonstrate that if there is a sense of *moral oughtness* within human beings, there must be some kind of moral or ethical Being behind the universe. Humans cannot, if they are moral beings, be simply accidental concourses of atoms.

The fact that men are creatures of choice, and the further fact that their choices are made in terms of some awareness of moral and ethical principles, are firm evidences that they originated from a source that also had the capacity of making moral and ethical judgments. The atheist has a severe burden of proof at this point. In order for his position to be accepted, he must demonstrate how a morally responsible being could come from a purely *materialistic* source. Particularly impressive is the fact that man does not always follow his strongest instincts; he often acts in a different way altogether. As C. S. Lewis put it, there is something within man that judges between his instincts and that decides which should be encouraged. Often it is the *weaker instinct* on which man acts, because it is ethically and morally superior to the other stronger instinct. This unique quality in man demands a moral architect and designer.[56]

Related to the fact that every human being possesses a moral compass is the idea that every human being seems to have an *innate sense of God,* a sense they are born with. It is the reason people are *religious at heart;* it's the reason they go to church, synagogue, mosque, practice the art of self-denial, or, like New Agers, try to stir up the "God spark" that is within them.[57] Every culture in the world has some kind of religion, and all of them answer the question, "What is the meaning of life?" Anthropologists have not found a single people group anywhere that does not believe in a transcendent reality; every people group in the world is religious. Contrary to those who would have us believe that the idea of God or religion was first "taught," there is no evidence whatsoever for this conclusion.[58] The Scriptures tell us that God has given everyone an *awareness* of who He is both through the physical universe He created as well as through their conscience.[59]

Furthermore, denying the existence of God does not dispel the mysteries of life. Attempts to exclude God from the language of civil life does not eliminate the persistent longing for more than this life has to offer.[60] There is something about truth, beauty, and love that make us hunger for these things. Strangely enough, even in our anger with a God who would permit injustice and pain, we draw upon a *moral conscience* to argue that life is not as it ought to be.[61] Unwittingly, we are drawn to something that is more, rather than less, than ourselves, because within all of us there is a longing for something beyond us.

While secularists might say publicly that they accept death as being the final end, there is nevertheless, in many cases, a *private doubt* that lingers. For example, atheist philosopher Bertrand Russell expressed some hesitation concerning the idea that this life is all there is: "It is odd, is it not? I care passionately for this world and many things and people in it, and yet... what is it all? There must be something more important, one feels, though

I do not believe there is."[62] What would be the *source* of our yearning for an existence beyond? Perhaps the universe has played a cosmic joke on us, or our yearning is a mistake of evolution. Or perhaps the experience simply points to that which is real and true.[63]

Conclusion

Philosophical objections can be raised against each of these standard arguments for God; nevertheless, when the phenomena which they explain in terms of God are tested in terms of other philosophical systems—atheism, polytheism, pantheism, naturalism—the theistic explanation emerges in far better light than the others. Though these arguments do not prove the existence of God, they do provide *strong evidence* when considered as a whole and when compared with other systems.[64]

The obstacle or barrier that keeps people from seeing beyond the surface is a lack of faith. The classic illustration of "seeing and not seeing" is found in the biblical book *Exodus*. Some 3,500 years ago, the children of Israel were enslaved in Egypt, and God appointed Moses to take His people out of the land. The problem was that the leader of Egypt, Pharaoh, was not about to let this large free labor force leave. So God sent a series of "ten plagues" upon the land of Egypt through His servant Moses, but each of these plagues only served to harden Pharaoh's heart. Pharaoh saw the evidence, but he never saw beyond the surface. Moses and Pharaoh observed the same events, yet they each saw things differently. Whereas Moses saw God at work, Pharaoh chose not to.[65] When you stand at the edge of the ocean on a *massive rocky shoreline,* you can either see the evidence of God's work, or you can just see ocean. When you stand looking over the *jagged mountain peaks* in the Rocky Mountains, you can either see God's work, or you can just see mountains. When you look at a *beautiful sunset* that spreads across the sky, you can either see God's hand at work, or you can just see sky.[66]

The theory of evolution is based on *faith* just as much as creationism is, but evolutionists move from the observable to the theoretical in a way that is not warranted by the evidence. They observe, for example, that minor changes occur within species *(microevolution),* but they extrapolate from those observations the theory that such changes eventually add up to the formation of entirely new species *(macroevolution).* While microevolution is empirically verifiable, the extrapolation to macroevolution is only a "theory" that has never been observed; therefore, evolution is a matter of faith that is *not* justified by the evidence.[67]

Belief in creationism is a *reasonable* inference, and as such is a highly defendable alternative to evolution. After all, one of the principles of science is that every effect has a sufficient cause. Creationism posits a *sufficient cause* for our existence as persons: a personal God who is perfect, eternal, virtuous, intelligent, and self-existent. Evolution, on the other hand, posits what appears to be an *insufficient cause* in that the complex (human life) comes out of the simple (nonlife). In other words, the theory of evolution says that the universe arose from nothing, without a cause. Such reasoning is *not* reasonable.[68]

In spite of the evidence given for the existence of God, many are still not convinced. The data input is not the problem—the problem lies with how we process the data we have. Human nature is such that we consistently read the data and draw the wrong conclusions. People worship something or someone other than God; they trace their origin to evolution or aliens instead of God; they acknowledge luck rather than God for the good things they experience; and they push away the moral law of God and set their own standards in its place. All this is done without the slightest bit of substantive evidence. That is why people desperately need an intelligible word from the Creator Himself, so that they can overcome human error and gain a right perspective on life. It is for this reason God has given to us a blueprint whereby we can understand His eternal purposes. This blueprint is His Written Word.[69]

Consider for a moment the following questions. What evidence would *prove* to you that God really exists? If God is "spirit" and He did create the world, what else could He have created that would have convinced you that He exists? What could He have created that would have eliminated your skepticism? Consider the beauty of creation, the magnitude of creation, the order of creation, the complexity of creation, the miracle of life, and the provisions of God in creation: food, warmth, clothing, and health. It is possible just to see the physical evidence of these things without acknowledging their Creator, but that is such a limited view. Perhaps it's just a matter of *focus*—looking past the obvious and what's on the surface—in order to see the Ultimate Reality.

Christianity clearly proclaims that God has revealed information about Himself to the world. The skeptic, however, chooses to believe that divine revelation is not possible, and that creationism cannot be demonstrated. But skepticism self-destructs when skeptics make the claim that ultimate knowledge is unattainable. In doing so they make an affirmation that is a *contradiction*. While they hold that no one can know anything, they are quite certain that they themselves *know* that no one can know anything. The world of philosophy describes such positions as absurd and nonsensical.[70] Much postmodern thought, with its own certainties and forceful rejection of all fixed worldviews, manifests a secular mindset when it says truth cannot be known. The paradox of such thinking should be easy to detect. How can a belief in no absolute truths be so absolutely certain of anything?[71]

Assuming that a Master Designer (God) did create the universe and life on earth, is it possible to know who this God is? The world's religions differ significantly in their descriptions of God, and they each make varying and contrasting claims regarding many other issues as well.[72] To evaluate the claims of any one particular religion or belief system, we must test it in areas that it *can* be tested in. That means examining its claims concerning matters of history and science. If some of these claims *fail* to withstand objective scrutiny, i.e., they prove to be false or contradict other known facts, this would tend to lessen the credibility of a particular belief system. On the other hand, if these claims are *corroborated* by history and archaeology and other such disciplines, and they successfully withstand objective scrutiny, this would tend to strengthen the authority and credibility of that religion.[73]

By employing the foregoing strategy, we can conclude that the Bible possesses a remarkable integrity in that it has been able to withstand every counter-argument presented against it. The Bible has surprised many in the scientific community with some of its scientific accuracy and detail. Some biblical statements appear to reveal an exceptional knowledge of scientific matters that only recently have been discovered and proven by scientific observation. Under close scrutiny, the Bible has been found to not make any false scientific statements, and this applies even to positions that were *popularly held* when the text was written.[74]

The seventeenth-century Dutch philosopher, Baruch Spinoza, had this to say when questioned about the existence of God: "No cause or reason can be given which prevents [God] from existing, or which rules out His existence."[75] Yet, strangely enough, many people still rule Him out. Someone put it this way: "To ask one to *prove* the existence of God is like asking one to prove the existence of beauty." Some people, apparently, are too preoccupied with what is ugly.

CHAPTER 6

THE INCREDIBLE HUMAN BODY

Wonders are many, and none is more wonderful than man.
— SOPHOCLES[1]

Perhaps the most astounding of all the intricate complexities of design in creation are those of the human body. What is a human being? Dr. Werner Gitt, Director of the Federal Institute for Physics and Technology in Braunschweig, Germany, describes in his book, *The Wonder of Man*, how one scientist answered this question:

> [A human being] is a wonderful, inconceivably complex being... [who possesses] a chemical factory, an electrical network, climate control, a filtration plant—all these controlled centrally by the brain, a thinking computer with the additional ability of loving and hating. [The human body] keeps itself alive for several decades, and through various control mechanisms, operates almost without friction. [It] consists of 100 trillion microscopic parts, all of which are fantastically fine-tuned to, and co-operatively integrated with each other. When healthy, these parts are continuously rejuvenated and can even repair themselves....[2]

Whose plans and ideas resulted in the body's remarkable construction? Who made us? There are essentially only two possible answers: Either we were the result of blind physical and chemical processes planned by *nobody*, or we were made by an incredibly brilliant *Creator*.

As we have seen, evolution is based on a theory referred to as "spontaneous generation," a hypothetical process by which living organisms develop from nonliving matter. This concept was disproved by Louis Pasteur, whose contributions have been hailed as some of the most valuable in the history of science. Pasteur proved through a number of experiments that all life comes from life, never from nonlife.[3] Another scientist, Ian Macreadie, a winner of several scientific awards for outstanding contributions to molecular biological research, confirms Pasteur's observation. Discussing the possibility of new genetic information being added by evolution, he affirms that "all you see in the lab is either gene duplications, reshuffling of existing genes, or defective genes (with a loss of information).… But you *never* see any new information arising in a cell… we just do not observe it happening. It's hard to see how any serious scientist could believe that real information can arise just by itself, from nothing."[4] Nevertheless, the evolutionist and Nobel Prize winner George Wald demonstrates the *inconsistency* to which evolutionists are driven when he says, "Spontaneous generation of a living organism is impossible. Yet here we [human beings] are, as a result, I believe, of spontaneous generation."[5] So regardless of the evidence, many scientists still continue to embrace the theory of evolution.

What are the odds against the spontaneous generation of life? Scientist Sir Frederick Hoyle, a renowned mathematician from Cambridge, England, who is known for many popular science works, has calculated the odds of the *accidental formation* of a simple living cell to be roughly comparable to the odds of rolling "double-sixes" 50,000 times in a row with unloaded dice![6] Nobel Prize winner Francis Crick, codiscoverer of the molecular structure of DNA—an accomplishment which became a cornerstone of genetics and is one of the most important discoveries of twentieth-century biology—also arrived at the theory that life could never have evolved by *chance* on planet earth. His conclusion is particularly noteworthy because he is an atheist.[7]

The more that is discovered about the detailed and complex architecture of living things, the stronger the evidence becomes for the involvement of a Master Designer. It is for this reason many famed scientists, such as the codiscoverer of DNA, have begun to abandon their faith in chance alone.[8]

To help us answer the question of how we came into existence, let's look at some of the extraordinary complexities involved in the construction of the human body.

The Eye

The eye is our window to the outside world. It is one of the most important sense organs we have, since well over half of all the information we take in about the world comes to us through the eye. Because of our ability to perceive light, we are able to read letters, newspapers, and books, marvel at the colors of a blossom as well as a beautiful landscape, admire the beauty of a dress, or the appeal of a painting. But most of all, we can see those people we care most deeply about, and those we encounter in our daily lives. We evaluate and understand our world mostly from being able to see it.[9]

The eye, basically, has two functional parts: the physical mechanism through which we look, and the receptor area of the retina where the light triggers processes in nerve cells. The *retina* is located inside the back of the eyeball and makes up the innermost layer of the wall of the eyeball. This thin layer of nerve tissue is about one-thirteenth of an inch thick (a little thinner than a dime), and is as fragile as a piece of wet tissue paper. Light-sensitive cells in the retina translate the incoming light rays into electrical signals, and send them on to the brain. The two kinds of light cells are called *rods* and *cones*; they are so named for their shape. The retina of each eye has about 120 million rods and about 6 million cones.[10] That means one square millimeter (approximately one-twenty-fifth of an inch, roughly the size of a grain of table salt) of the retina contains approximately 400,000 optical sensors, far too small to be seen with the naked eye.[11]

Amazingly, each of these light-sensitive cells has the ability to translate the impulse of light it receives into the language of the nervous system. This says nothing about the ability of the eye to focus on objects, adapt to light and dark conditions, perceive colors, or protect itself. To perceive color, the rods and cones contain extremely tiny pieces of colored pigment that enable us to distinguish more than 200 colors. The information received by the light cells is communicated to the brain through the nerve fibers that are attached to each of the rods and cones. These fibers join at the center of the retina and form the *optic nerve*, which itself consists of about one million fibers. The optic nerve serves as a flexible cable that connects the eyeball to the brain, and is the vehicle through which the electrical signals are passed.[12] Incredibly, the eye can send one billion impulses to the brain in a second, and the brain then chooses significant details of that which is seen.[13] The evolutionist would say this remarkable process involving 126 million microscopic light-sensitive cells "just happened by accident."

Listen to what Darwin said about the eye in his book *On The Origin of Species:* "To suppose that the eye with all its inimitable contrivances for adjusting the focus to different distances, for admitting different amounts of light, and for the correction of spherical and chromatic aberration, could have been formed by natural selection, seems, I freely confess, absurd in the highest degree."[14] And he had no idea how intricate and complex the human eye really is. As modern scientists began uncovering the intricate complexities of the living cell, it became increasingly difficult for them to hold on to their chance theories. The simple little cell is not the little blob of protoplasm it was once thought to be; thus, the scientific community is being humbled by life's quintessence.

The Ear

The ear is our highest-precision sense organ, and the process of hearing is one of the most complicated in the human body. Sound consists of "air vibrations" that travel in waves. These sound waves enter the ear where they are converted to electrical impulses, which in turn are sent to the brain. The brain then identifies these signals as information. Imagine, if you will, the process of hearing that you experience when you listen to someone speak. Their words are actually sound vibrations that travel through the air to the *outer canal* of your ear, and then to your *eardrum.* From there, these vibrations are sent to your *liquid-filled middle ear.* Three tiny bones then transmit the vibrations to your *air-filled inner ear.* At that point the sound vibrations are detected in two very small spiral-shaped bones that have some *15,000 sensory hair cells,* each of which are sensitive to different sound frequencies. These sensory hairs then pass on electric nerve impulses to your *brain,* through a thick cable of nerve fibers. Your brain then *evaluates* what is being said to you! The human ear is a detection device, which utilizes a level of technology that no science has as yet been able to attain or in many aspects even understand.[15]

The Nose

The nose is our chemical sense detector; smelling and tasting are chemical senses. It is the nose that makes eating and drinking a pleasurable experience. Through our nose we can detect danger, and also enjoy the fragrances of food, flowers, trees, spices, and perfumes. Inside the nasal cavity there are over 20 million "receptor cells" covering an area of about two square inches.

These cells are invisible to the naked eye and are *continually* being renewed, because they only have a half-life of about ten days (that's the amount of time for half of the atoms in a cell to fully disintegrate).[16] That means every 20 days every one of these receptor cells is replaced with a brand new cell. That is 40,000 new receptor cells every hour!

The invisible molecules which cause "odors" are captured by the receptor cells in the mucous membrane of the nose. Each cell then converts this information into electrical impulses which are transmitted to the brain. The process used by the brain to decode this information is one of the most difficult unsolved problems in neuro-physiology. With the nose, human beings can distinguish over 10,000 different scents.[17] Both nasal passages have a lining of soft, moist mucous membrane, covered with microscopic hairlike projections called *cilia*. The cilia wave back and forth constantly, moving dust, bacteria, and fluids from the nose to the throat for swallowing. Each nasal passage also has three large bones called *turbinates*, which serve to warm the air before it enters the lungs.[18] Since the lungs prefer damp, warm, clear air, it is moistened and warmed by its long passage over the mucous membranes of the nose. Most of the coarser, harmful particles in the air are trapped by the nose's fine hairs or its thick mucus to keep them from passing into the lungs.[19] Once again, the genius of creation is clearly visible.

The Heart

The heart is a powerful muscular organ, which pumps blood through the body's distribution system known as the cardiovascular, or circulatory system. With each contraction the heart pumps a little more than two ounces of blood; at a rate of 70 beats per minute, that amounts to about five to six quarts a minute. The human heart beats approximately 100,000 times a day; therefore over the course of seventy years the heart will beat about 2.5 billion times and pump about 45 million gallons of blood—enough to fill a huge skyscraper![20] Every day this mighty little muscle, about the size of a clenched fist and weighing just over half a pound, pumps nearly 2,000 gallons of blood through the 60,000 miles of arteries, veins, and capillaries in our body to bring nourishment to our 100 trillion cells. The daily amount of blood pumped through our veins is enough to fill 40 bathtubs with 50 gallons each! Night and day, and every moment of our lives, the heart pumps blood through the body's miles of blood vessels, continually adjusting its output to the body's differing demands.[21] The volume of blood pumped per minute by one chamber can increase from 1.5 gallons to more than 8 gallons during strenuous activity.

The arteries carry the blood *from the heart* to the cells, and the veins carry the blood *from the cells* back to the heart. Before each circuit is repeated, the blood passes through the lungs, where, by the process of exhaling and inhaling, the waste material is removed, and the bloodstream is recharged with a fresh supply of oxygen. The lungs receive all of the oxygen-depleted blood; they in turn oxygenate the blood and return it to the heart, where the arteries then deliver it to the various parts of the body. The flow of blood through the vessels is very rapid, making the journey through the lungs in about 15 seconds and through the entire body in about 60 seconds. By this perpetual steady operation of the heart, life is sustained.[22] The larger blood vessels are the "main highways" which deliver the blood, and the body's 1.2 billion capillaries are the "side streets" that provide the actual nourishment.[23]

The Blood

The blood is the life-stream of the human body; it is the physical carrier of life itself. Some 3,500 years ago the prophet Moses said, "The life of all flesh is in the blood."[24] Today's biologists know this is true, but it could not have been known 3,500 years ago unless it was revealed by a transcendent source. Until recent times physicians *leeched blood* out of their patients in an attempt to save their lives.[25] Every minute the body's five quarts of blood are circulated through the entire circulatory system so that every cell in the body is cleansed and supplied with nutrients; therefore the blood is the great transport medium of the body. While circulating, this liquid performs several important functions.

1. Respiration. The blood carries *oxygen* from the lungs to each of the body's 100 trillion cells for them to utilize, and at the same time it carries *carbon dioxide* from the tissues back to the lungs where it is exhaled.[26] All of the living cells in our body continually absorb oxygen and give off carbon dioxide. The cells use oxygen to produce energy, and this process creates carbon dioxide. Most of the carbon dioxide passes from the cells through the capillary walls, and is carried in the bloodstream by the red blood cells to the lungs. When it reaches the capillaries in our lungs, it is exhaled.[27]

2. Nourishment. The cells of the body continually require energy and raw materials, and it is the blood that transports these nutrients to each cell. The cells use nutrients to produce the energy needed for cell growth, reproduction, and other functions.[28] The products resulting from digestion of food are absorbed by the blood from the *small intestine*. The length of the small intestine is anywhere from 16 to 23 feet. If all the parts that protrude from it were to be ironed out flat, its total surface area would be about the size of a tennis court![29] Nutrients dissolved in water are collected by the blood from the small intestine and carried to the body's largest internal organ, *the liver.* The basic metabolism of the body takes place in the liver. Employing extremely complex processes, the cells chemically convert sugar, fats, proteins, and other nutrients. The products are either stored, reused or released. About 30 percent of the blood leaving the heart passes through the liver, and from there the nutrients are distributed throughout the body.[30]

Like nutrients, wastes enter the bloodstream through the capillary walls, and are transported to the liver. The liver filters wastes and other harmful substances from the blood. It converts some wastes into a compound called *urea.* The blood carries urea to the kidneys, which in turn removes it in urine.[31] The liver is truly a remarkable organ. It performs at least nineteen different functions. It affords protection from disease, supplies sugar to meet the need of muscle tissues, turns waste nitrogen into urea for disposal, regulates the clotting of the blood, plays a key role in the digestive process, and produces and distributes bile, which aids in the absorption of fats into the body and serves as a medium for excreting harmful substances which the liver removes from the blood. And when damaged, the liver can immediately regenerate its own tissue.[32]

The *digestive system* is the most wonderful chemical laboratory known to science. It converts plant and animal substances, such as vegetables of various kinds, cereals, fruits, and nuts, and the flesh of different animals, birds, and fish, which man consumes as food, into human flesh and blood, bones and muscles, nerve and brain matter, and into the hair of the head, and the nails of fingers and toes. In doing so it sustains life, creates energy, and engenders the required heat for the well-being of the body.[33] Miraculously, the digestive system does most of its work automatically.

The life process of the body is maintained within the cell. The miracle of the constant repairing and rebuilding of the living cell is performed by the digestive system. As food enters our mouths, the saliva glands start the process of digestion. Food is taken into the body and is crushed and ground into pulp by our teeth; the well-masticated food is then transported down to the stomach by an ingenious muscular action we call swallowing, and while it is in the stomach it is dissolved and separated into its constituent elements.[34] Each person's stomach has at least 35 million glands that secrete various fluids and acids. These fluids not only aid in the digestion of food but also dissolve insoluable minerals and kill large numbers of bacteria that enter with the food. After the food is churned for several hours to break it

up and mix it with the secretions, the stomach valve opens at intervals and
the food continues its journey on through the small intestine.[35] There it is
absorbed into the bloodstream and is carried to every part of the body where
it is assimilated to form body substances. This process is automatic and
operates day and night, whether we are awake or asleep, without our being
conscious of the miraculous work that is being performed.[36]

3. Excretion. The end products of cellular metabolism that cannot be used
by the body are transported by the blood to the various excretory organs,
where they are eliminated mainly through the bowels, urine, and sweat.[37]
Food that is not digested in the small intestine continues on to the large
intestine where it is disposed. So the various ways in which waste products
are disposed by the body are the large intestine, the kidneys, the liver, the
lungs, and the skin.[38]

4. Temperature control. While the digestive system maintains the
proper chemical balance in the body and repairs or rebuilds the living cells,
it also produces bodily energy and the required *body heat* to make normal
life possible. The cells in our body can function optimally only when the
temperature of the body is close to 98.6 degrees F. If it sinks below or rises
above that figure, that's a sign there may be serious trouble. The amazing
thing about the body's automatic thermostat is that it keeps the body at the
same temperature at all times; whether the climate is hot or cold, it operates
in the same way in all races of men everywhere in the world. The body temperature of the fur-clad Eskimo in Alaska is the same as that of the naked
Indian in the Amazon Basin.[39]

All cell activities produce heat. But some cells, particularly those in muscles
and glands, create more heat than others. The heat enters your bloodstream
and travels throughout your body; the main component of blood, water, has
a high capacity for heat. If blood did not distribute heat, some body areas
would become extremely hot while others would remain extremely cold.
Thus, blood circulation helps keep your body temperature steady and safe.[40]
Since the blood flows continually, the transfer of heat is much faster than
in the case of non-moving liquid. So the blood absorbs all excess heat from
the body and lets it either escape through your skin and your lungs, or uses
it to give warmth where it is needed.[41]

5. Transporting hormones. The body produces various hormones in certain
tissues or glands. They in turn are taken up by the blood and transported
to other tissues or organs. When a hormone reaches a part of the body it
regulates, it may promote growth, affect the reproductive processes, control
how the body uses food, control heat and metabolism, cause blood vessels

to contract, control blood pressure, control the processing of glucose, and control the immune response.[42]

6. Coagulation. The human body would bleed to death from a small cut if our blood did not clot, so blood coagulation affords a vitally important protection against loss of blood. An injured blood vessel causes plasma proteins to stick to the damaged surface and to one another, forming a "plug." These proteins normally circulate in an inactive form in the blood, but if a blood vessel is damaged, the injured vessel gives off chemicals that react with the proteins, creating a mesh over the area. We refer to clots on the skin surface as scabs. Incidentally, blood also contains substances that dissolve blood clots as well as produce them. These substances circulate in an inactive form until clotting occurs, and are then activated to control the extent and duration of the clotting.[43]

7. Defense. The purpose of *white blood cells* is to protect the body against the invasion of germs, disease, toxins, and intruding microorganisms, and defend it to the death.[44] They literally die by the millions wherever there is a point of entry for infection. The white corpuscle army is an impressive regiment of specialists. While half of them are patrolling within the blood, the other half is on external duty guarding the tissues. Bacteria, viruses, fungi, and parasites continually enter our bodies through breaches of the skin, through the air we breathe, and through food in the digestive tract. When they are identified as enemies, they are located and the army goes into action.[45] Their manufacture is greatly stepped up when an invasion is reported. A host of them race to the danger spot to kill the invading germs; they fire chemical weapons at them, surround them, absorb them, and then digest them. After the battle is over, these same handy little fellas clean up the battlefield and build new tissue (cells).[46] Remarkably, this secret army is able to clearly distinguish between friend and enemy, and between the body's own materials and foreign substance.[47] Obviously, the blood carries out vitally important functions. It supplies each of the body's 100 trillion cells with fuel obtained from the nutrients we ingest, with *oxygen, vitamins, hormones*, and *warmth*, and the metabolic products and excess heat are carried away from every one of these cells.[48] And the evolutionist claims it all "just happened by accident." Let's take a closer look at the blood cells themselves.

The most numerous of the cell types in the body are the *red blood cells*. There are 25 trillion red blood cells in the body. These blood cells carry the fuel of fresh oxygen to every cell (tissues). In addition, they pick up the waste products from these cells and carry them to the organs of elimination such as the kidneys, bowels, and lungs. One *drop* of blood contains 250 million red cells.[49] Just to give you an idea how many 250 million is—if you were to place 250 million pennies in a 1,500 square foot home, the entire house would be covered with more than *four feet* of pennies! Remember, that's how many cells are in just *one drop* of blood! If you're wondering how much room it would take to contain 25 trillion pennies—you could fill 100,000 homes of the same size with more than four feet of pennies!

During the "120-day life span" of each one of these highly specialized red blood cells, they each perform two extremely important tasks. They absorb oxygen and discharge carbon dioxide 175,000 times. It should be noted that just under 1 percent of all the red blood cells in your body are renewed *every day,* because every 120 days they are all renewed. The production rate of red blood cells is 160 million *per minute,* or 230 billion *per day;* this amounts to 2.7 million *per second.* That's an astounding rate![50] The core of human bones is filled with a substance called *marrow.* In adults, the red bone marrow produces millions of blood cells per second. Two body organs, the liver and the spleen, remove worn out red blood cells from the bloodstream and break them down.[51]

In comparison with 25 trillion red blood cells, there are only 35 billion *white blood cells* in the human body. So for every 35 white blood cells, there are 25,000 red blood cells. The number of white blood cells in your body increases after a meal or after physical activity. As mentioned above, their purpose is to defend the body against germs and disease and to defend it to the death. Whereas *red blood cells* live about 120 days, and platelets about 10 days, the life span of *white blood cells* varies greatly. For example, neutrophils (the most numerous white blood cells) live only a few hours, dying soon after they engulf foreign material. But some lymphocytes (they constitute 20–30 percent of all white cells) live many years, thus providing long-term immunity against certain diseases.[52]

The Kidneys

The human kidney is a complex physio-chemical factory that is essential for *purifying* the blood. All of the blood in the body passes through the kidneys continually and is cleansed and filtered by them of waste material that would become deadly poison if it were not removed. They maintain the chemical balance in the blood, help in the production of red blood cells, and regulate the water supply in the body. They perform so many functions for the health and well-being of the body that life would not last very long if they failed to function.[53] The kidneys control the fluid balance of the body and keep constant the composition and volume of the extra-cellular liquid in which all the cells of the body are *bathed*. In this way the functioning of all the cells of the body is optimized. The kidneys control the water and salt content of the blood and excrete the waste products; when there is too much liquid or too much dissolved substances, the kidneys ensure that excesses are eliminated.[54]

This pair of organs weighs only five ounces, and each of the kidneys' arteries ends in a blood-filtration unit called a *nephron* or *tubule*. Two healthy kidneys contain about 2 million nephrons. If stretched in one long line, they would measure more than 70 miles. Substances that are not absorbed in these filtration units are wastes that the body cannot use. These nephrons filter some 500 gallons of blood every day.[55] That's more than twenty times a human being's entire body weight. Therefore all of the blood in the human body is processed through the kidneys 340 times every day, which means that all of the blood in the circulatory system is purified every four minutes! The recovery ratio by this incredible filtration system is about 100:1. Thus the body only eliminates one to two quarts of urine each day, depending on the quantity of ingested liquid and other water losses, such as sweat.[56]

The Brain

The brain is the master control center of the human body. It constantly receives information from all of the senses about conditions both outside and inside the body. The brain analyzes this information almost instantly and then sends out messages that control all of the body's activities and actions.[57] Although the brain weighs only three pounds, its work and capacity is far more complex than the world's entire telephone system. The human brain directs the activity of the entire body through over one billion nerve cells. The brain also remembers the past, plans for the future, makes decisions, and carries them out. In addition, the brain is the source of thoughts, dreams, moods, and emotions; it is quizzical, inventive, logical, and creative, and is capable of holding more information than the entire nine million volumes in the Library of Congress![58]

The human brain has been called the most complex physical structure in the universe, and practically nothing is known about the way it processes information. Nobody knows how the information is derived from the incoming electrical signals. We do know where certain activities originate in the brain, but we have very little understanding of how things happen. The only real knowledge we have of the brain is on the statistical level.[59]

The brain works both like a computer and a chemical factory. Brain cells produce electrical signals and send them to various *cells* through a network of circuits, where the information is received, processed, stored, and retrieved. But unlike a computer, the brain creates its electrical signals by chemical means. For the brain to function properly, it is dependent upon a number of complicated chemical substances that are produced by brain cells. Scientists do not yet understand how physical and chemical processes in the brain produce much of the brain's activity. This field of study is referred to as *neuroscience.*[60]

The brain is made up of about 100 billion nerve cells. The term *neurons* is used as a synonym for nerve cells. In addition to this immense number of neurons, there are also 100 billion other kinds of cells in the brain that provide metabolic functions and structural support. Amazingly, every neuron is connected to thousands of other cells by means of *synapses.* Even though nerve cells are not in direct contact with other nerve cells, they are all indirectly linked with each other via intermediate connections. Therefore it follows that the number of possible pathways linking the nerve cells in every human brain is *extremely large*—five sextillion (that's a five with 21 zeros after it!). With between ten and fifty thousand connections *per nerve cell,* the entire system forms an immeasurably complex branched network. If it were possible to describe it as a circuit diagram, it would be *several hundred times more complex* than the entire global telephone network. And all of this resides in your three-pound brain! It confounds logic how a scientist can be aware of some of the intricate complexities of the human brain, and still believe that it just evolved in a random, chance fashion. By the way, it would require 40 printed pages simply to list the number of "direct connections" of a *single neuron.* And one mathematician has calculated that it would take 500 libraries the size of the Library of Congress in Washington, D.C., simply to list all of the *direct connections* in the human brain![61]

The brain's incredibly dense network of neurons can process signals at an extremely high rate. It can do *one quintillion* (that's a one with 18 zeros after it!) computations in a second, which is 100 million times as fast as the *fastest supercomputer* in existence.[62] Remember, this is just a three-pound brain! A network of blood vessels supplies the brain with the large quantities of oxygen and nutrients that it requires. Though the brain makes up only 2 percent of a human being's total body weight, it demands about 20 percent of the body's blood supply and oxygen, both day and night. The brain has a very limited capacity to store energy, yet it is critically dependent upon oxygen; it cannot go without oxygen for more than three to five minutes without causing severe brain damage.[63]

One of the amazing facets of the brain is that it has a *blood-brain barrier* that safeguards the brain's tissues from damage by prohibiting certain molecules from coming in contact with it. Generally, substances in the blood reach body tissues by passing through the thin capillary walls. In brain capillaries, the cells are packed together far more tightly than in other parts of the body; therefore, the passage of substances from blood to brain cells is more restrictive. Incredibly, however, the brain does require some kinds of large molecules for nutrition. So the capillary walls contain certain enzymes and other properties that enable only particular molecules to pass through to the brain.[64] Many medications, for example, are incapable of passing through the blood-brain barrier into the brain.[65]

Given all this astonishing complexity of the brain, it is not surprising that Professors Robert Ornstein (University of California at Berkeley) and Richard F. Thompson (Stanford University) both of whom have done extensive studies on the brain, comment: "After thousands of scientists have studied the brain for centuries, the only adequate way to describe it is as a *miracle*."[66] Regardless of the evidence, the evolutionist still continues to beat his primitive drum.

The Cell's DNA

The body's most precious substance—DNA / *deoxyribonucleic acid*—is stored deep inside each of the body's 100 trillion cells in the tiny nucleus. This substance is known as the *genome*, the genetic information. DNA is a thin, chainlike molecule that directs the construction, growth, and reproduction of all cells and organisms. The genome is the entire set of genetic instructions that oversees the extraordinary transformation from a relatively simple single cell (fertilized egg) into a stunningly complex adult, comprised of 100 trillion cells.[67] The human body's 100,000 *genes* provide exact instructions to each cell for manufacturing everything required for it to carry out the role for which it is *programmed*—whether hormones, enzymes, mucus, sebum, the weapons of the immune system, or the impulses in the nerve cells of the central nervous system. Our genes ensure that we become human beings rather than animals. Our gender, the color of our eyes, our skin and hair, and to a large extent our size, intelligence, and unique personalities are all determined by our personal genome.[68]

The amount of genetic information in a single human cell is staggering. Dr. George W. Beadle, former chancellor of the University of Chicago and a DNA authority, says that if the coded DNA instructions of a "single human cell" were put into English, they would fill a 1,000-volume encyclopedia![69] Keep in mind this information is inside *every single cell* in the human body, all of which are *invisible* to the naked eye! From measurements of the amount of DNA in a single cell, science has been able to estimate that the human genome (inherited material) contains some 3.1 billion base pairs of genetic information.[70] And every one of the human body's 100 trillion cells carries all of this genetic information, regardless of its locality; the different types of cells simply access and process different sections of the available information according to how each cell is programmed.[71] Therefore *each cell* must have a computer capability of processing at least a 1,000-volume encyclopedia!

Scientists from all over the world instigated an ambitious "15-year project" to chart the human genetic code and to decipher it letter by letter (known as sequencing). For this purpose the *Human Genome Organization,* which has some 900 members in 40 countries, was officially established on October 1, 1990. The effort required to determine the letter sequence of human DNA was originally estimated as many thousands of "man-years." But with present-day computers, the job was completed in 10 years. With all the enormous information in the entire sequence, it is assumed that only 3 percent of this huge amount of information represents the approximately 100,000 human genes, distributed among 23 chromosomes. The purpose of the other 97 percent is still largely unknown.[72]

Most people are fascinated by the information that is emerging concerning human DNA. A recent science article in the *Arizona Republic* reported that a strand of DNA from a single human cell would be about six feet long if you straightened it out (obviously it would be invisible). It then stated that if you were to uncoil a "half a gram of DNA" (that's about one-thousandth of a pound, or the size of a kernel of corn), it would stretch from the earth to the sun![73] It is difficult to imagine a tiny little ball of thread-like substance the size of a kernel of corn stretching 93 million miles, but that is the reality! By the way, if you were to take all of the body's 100 trillion cells of DNA, it would amount to just over a pound, and would become a strand 110 billion miles long—that's 1,200 times the distance of the earth to the sun!

Science is now confronted with the staggering amount of information contained in a DNA molecule. Since DNA contains *information,* the case can best be stated in terms of information theory. Using a computer to create a message that contains millions of letters grouped into words amounting to 1,000 volumes of a large textbook—without programming it to do so—and have the message make perfect sense, is not possible under any set of circumstances, no matter how many eons of time the experiment continues. It just *cannot happen* by "chance." It would be like storing a line-o-type machine in Yankee Stadium, filling the place with blank paper, somehow hermetically sealing it shut, and then returning a trillion years later to discover the

THE CONCEPT OF INFINITY

To the human mind it does not seem possible that all of the DNA in a human body is 110 billion miles long. Perhaps a discussion of infinity would be helpful. Most of us have entertained the idea of something that is *infinitely large*, like outer space. The universe is frequently said to not have an end; that is, it is believed to just go on and on, forever and ever, never ending. Our finite minds cannot conceive of such a concept, simply because they cannot envision that which is infinite. Some have postulated that the universe ultimately does come to an end. But if that is the case, then what is on the other side of it? Again, such thinking exhausts the limited dimensions of human thinking. Though many have thought of something *infinitely large*, few seem to have ever thought of something that is *infinitesimally small*. The idea here is that things can always be smaller no matter how small you make them. Years ago, Darwin thought he had discovered nature's smallest building block, the living cell. He thought it was simply a *blob of protoplasm*.[74] A few years later, scientists were astonished when they discovered this little blob was, in fact, a world all of its own.

Apparently this new understanding so impressed the scientific community that they thought they had discovered "the ultimate!" As time passed, science began to discover that the tiny living cell was immeasurably greater than they had ever imagined. If the truth be known, the smallest building block known to science can be reduced *ad infinitum!* There is nothing so small that it cannot be divided by trillions and trillions time and time again, without end. Once again, a human being simply cannot wrap his mind around such a concept.

The infinite God of this universe is *eternal*. He has no beginning and He has no end. His power is without limits. His size knows no boundaries. His wisdom is endless, and as incredible as it seems, even creation itself reflects His eternality. The most astute scientific minds are overwhelmed by the *boundless* magnitude of the heavens, and the *limitless* realities of the subatomic world. So rather than boasting of the small achievements of science, humanity should be humbled by the *infinite realities* of the created order.

world's largest library of beautifully bound books fully stacked in alphabetical order! The conclusion is undeniable. Only an intelligent cause could create the information contained in the DNA molecule. *Empirical evidence* has clearly determined that natural forces do not produce structures with high information content. Holding on to the hope that some natural process will one day be found to explain DNA transcends rational thinking. When it comes to the origin of life, the evidence of science is unquestionably on the side of creation by an Intelligent Agent.[75]

Consider yet another point. Scientists have been aggressively doing research with mitochondrial DNA and genetics, and they recently discovered that all human beings can trace their lineage back to just "one woman and one man"; needless to say, evolutionists are not very comfortable with this idea, because that is exactly what the Bible says when it teaches that Adam and

Eve were the first human beings God created.[76] After tracing man's origin back to one woman, the question arose: How long ago did *mitochondrial Eve* live on earth? In a 1988 *Newsweek* article, it was reported that she lived 200,000 years ago.[77] According to the evolutionary model, however, humans existed *at least a million years ago.* So evolutionists then had the problem of compressing the evolutionary process into a much shorter time span.[78] Since this discovery in 1988, subsequent investigations have produced even more astonishing results. The mitochondrial DNA clock was calibrated using actually *observed data* rather than the *speculative data* provided by evolutionists. The result has revealed that the DNA clock ticks *much faster* than originally expected. Using the new clock, Eve was dated to have lived just *6,000 years ago.*[79] Such a late date is strikingly close to the Bible's time scale, and is even more disturbing to evolutionists.

Ultimately, genuine science can only substantiate the truth. It can never prove something to be true that does not conform with reality. If the cosmos really came into existence by *supernatural creation,* the evidence cannot suggest otherwise; conversely, if the cosmos really came into existence by *natural processes,* the evidence cannot help but substantiate this to be the case. Regardless of how the universe came into existence, the evidence must be allowed to stand on its own without the infusion of unfounded biased speculation.

Conclusion

The human body, indeed, is a miraculous wonder. It consists of thousands of individual parts, large, small, and microscopic; but all are joined together in such a way that they function as a perfect, synchronized organism. This organism consists of 100 trillion individual cells, and every cell is a distinct unit that functions in perfect harmony with every other cell.[80] There are 206 bones in the human body, and over 400 different muscles that aid the various movements in and of our bodies. Many of these muscles work voluntarily, performing vital tasks for us constantly without any conscious effort on our part.[81] The bones are hollow to give them greater strength and are joined together in an ingenious ball-and-socket device, which is lined with a smooth, cartilaginous substance to eliminate all possible friction. The joints are supplied with an automatic lubrication system, which functions throughout life, and the body itself manufactures this lubricant.[82]

Human beings have the capacity to adapt themselves to some of the most diverse conditions on earth. Yet in many ways we are less prepared to cope with our environment than most of the world's other creatures. We do not have fur to protect us, and we are not endowed with many of the instincts that enable the animal kingdom to survive. Our God-given mechanism for survival is *intelligence*. We are equipped with the wit and the will to not only adapt ourselves, but also adapt our environment. Unlike animals, we do not require a specialized habitat like animals, yet we can survive in conditions so hostile that other creatures would perish. Almost every corner of the world is inhabited by human beings. We have lived in the frigid polar world, probed the depths of the ocean, and walked on the moon. We create our own protective dwellings, grow crops in barren places by managing the water supply, disperse the darkness by flipping a switch, and drive away the cold by making fire. And unlike any other creature, we nourish our bodies with an extensive menu of foods.[83] The human being, indeed, is a miraculous wonder.[84]

CHAPTER 7

GOD'S PERSPECTIVE OF ANCIENT HISTORY

God governs the world; the actual working of His government
(the carrying out of His plan) is the History of the World.
— GEORG WILHELM HEGEL[1]

Both Jews and Christians give primacy to the Bible in worship because they believe it puts them in touch with God's actions in human history.[2] They believe the Bible is God's *inspired* word, that God directed its writing. Scores of passages throughout the Bible allude to its inspiration; that's why the Bible is referred to as "God's Word."[3] These ancient Scriptures tell of the formative experiences and sacred history of the people of Israel, and her experience of God as the Lord of history.[4] The God Christians worship is the same God who called the universe into existence by *divine fiat,* and made known His purposes to Abraham and Moses. Christianity also teaches that God disclosed Himself conclusively to the world in the person of Jesus Christ; that Jesus is the very incarnation of the creative Word uttered in the beginning.[5] Throughout the Bible God is revealed in history as holy, gracious, generous, and compassionate, and eager to deliver people from bondage and draw them into close relationship with Himself. He makes agreements (covenants) with people and wants them to respond with trust and obedience.[6] The purpose of this chapter is to recount the story of creation and the subsequent events of human history, through which God chose to reveal Himself so that people might come to understand who He is and how they might live.

Creation and the Fall—Beginning to 4000 BC

The Creation of Humanity

The Bible begins with the story of creation. The very first verse says, "In the beginning God created the heavens and the earth."[7] According to the Bible, God is not only the *creative source* of all that exists—including space, mass and time—but He is also the *sustaining reality* that holds everything together.[8] Therefore, the universe is not only dependent upon God for its creation, it is also dependent upon Him for its continued existence.[9] According to the biblical record, human beings were the final objects of His creation, and it says they were created in "God's image."[10] So, what does it mean that they were created in the image of God? Most theologians do not believe the image of God refers to *physical* qualities, since God is spirit and does not have a physical body, but rather to the qualities of who He is as a *person*. Therefore, according to Christian tradition, the following five themes reflect the essence of God's likeness:

1. *Spiritual likeness.* Humans are not only physical beings, they are also spiritual beings,[11] and it is our spirit that is our primary link to God. We relate and connect with God spiritually, hence our worship is described as a spiritual experience.[12] Therefore, since God is spirit, it is our spirit that reflects His likeness.[13]

2. *Moral likeness.* God has given human beings an inner sense of what is right and wrong,[14] and it is this conscience that prompts us to act in such a way that we reflect God's moral character.[15] The Bible teaches that God's character is loving, good, joyful, peaceful, patient, kind, and trustworthy.[16]

3. *Intellectual likeness.* Human beings have the ability to reason and think logically and to learn in ways that set them apart from the animal kingdom. Only humans contemplate the future, study history, create music, write literature, value artistic expression, make scientific discoveries, and make advances in technology. In this sense, only human beings reflect the image of God.[17]

4. *Volitional likeness.* When God created human beings He gave them freedom to make their own choices; He did not create them in such a way that they were programmed like robots. He wanted them to respond to Him freely, not by force. This gift of freedom was put to a test. God

told them they could eat the fruit of every tree in the garden except one: the tree of the knowledge of good and evil. According to the Bible, the people failed the test, and used their freedom to become autonomous creatures. Ever since the fall, human beings have sought to live autonomously, independent of their Creator.[18]

5. *Social likeness.* God is a relational or social being. Christianity teaches that God is a Trinity, that is, there is one God eternally existing in three coeternal and coequal persons (God the Father, God the Son, and God the Holy Spirit); therefore it takes all three members of the Trinity to make up the Godhead. Each member of the Trinity lives in perfect communion and relationship with the other members of the Trinity. (The concept of the Trinity will be dealt with at length in chapter ten.) As Max Anders states, it takes both male and female to make up humanity, and it is this male-female combination that gives us a more complete picture of the Trinity. In Genesis we read, "God created man in His own image; in the image of God He created him; *male and female* He created them."[19] Therefore, together in our maleness and femaleness, humanity reflects the image of God.[20]

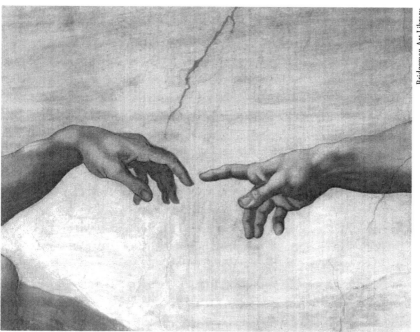

Bridgeman Art Library

Michelangelo's "Hands of God and Man" is taken from his work, *The Creation of Adam,* that was painted in 1511 on the ceiling of the Sistine Chapel at the Vatican, in Rome, Italy.

When God said, "Let us make man in our image,"[21] His primary focus was not on just making a person who could think and talk and act and create like He could; rather it was to make a *relational being* who could experience the same kind of dynamic relationship He enjoyed with the Godhead. Therefore, when God created humanity, His desire was that the human community would be characterized by loving, friendly, caring relationships.[22] The single most important commandment God gave to the human family was that they "love God and love other people."[23] According to the Bible, nothing is more important for a human being than to love.

Obviously there are other ways in which humanity could be said to reflect the image of God, but these are five of the main ones, and they help give significant understanding to this important truth. The Bible tells us that of all the creatures God created, only humans were uniquely made in the "image of God." The songwriter, David, asks the question, "What is man that God is mindful of him... and has made him ruler over the works of His hands?"[24] David recognizes that human life is sacred in a way that the animal kingdom and nature are not. Commissioned by the Creator, humans are given the responsibility of caring for the animal world, as well as cultivating and maintaining the Garden of Eden.[25] Responsible, purposive work was given by the Creator as a uniquely human capacity.[26]

According to the Bible, God gave human beings everything they could possibly want in terms of comfort and power, and He even gave them *freedom.* The only restriction on their freedom was that they were not to eat of the "tree of the knowledge of good and evil."[27] As a prohibition, this commandment set forth a boundary that was not to be overstepped; thus, God established a situation in which the *human will* would be in juxtaposition to the *divine will.* The issue at stake in the garden narrative was whether or not Adam and Eve would choose to remain obedient and loyal to their Creator; hence, the business of life is the business of making right choices. The Bible teaches that human beings fell from their original condition because they chose to disobey God.[28]

The Fall of Humanity

When Adam and Eve sinned against God, they brought death, decay, and destruction upon all creation.[29] The created order, which was beautiful, perfect, and pure, would no longer remain so. Something happened to the *paradise* in which they lived because of their disobedience. They would no longer live in a beautiful garden; painful realities would enter their lives; work would now be frustrating, fruitless, and difficult; childbirth would be painful; sickness and death would become a part of the human experience;

people would become wicked, aggressive, selfish, and never satisfied; and the relationship they would have with their Creator, formerly one of intimacy and closeness, would become more distant.[30]

Professor Josef H. Reichholf, a German scholar, comments on the difficulties of human birth in the German magazine *Natur*.[31] He points out that animals basically give birth "without pain." The *giraffe*, he said, falls from a height of six feet or more, but the entire birth proceeds in quite a relaxed fashion and with very little drama. The *cow* gives birth to a large well-developed calf, without a hint of pain or complaint. The *seal* gives birth rapidly and easily, and the process, which lasts only a few seconds, involves neither pain nor difficulty. Reichholf states, "Wherever we observe the birth of mammals, it seems to be relatively effortless and appropriate to their way of life." But when we come to human beings, he says, "only humans do not fit this pattern; usually only one baby is born, and it involves a lot of pain." He then asks the question, "Why is it so hard for humans, of all creatures, to come into the world?" He responds: "One has the impression that something must have gone wrong, something important, during man's evolutionary descent. This is the logical conclusion when comparing human beings to the other higher mammals."[32] Incredible as it may seem, no biologist or gynecologist can really explain why human childbirth is so difficult and painful. The Bible alone provides the answer. God told Eve, "Because of your sin I will greatly increase your pain in childbirth."[33]

Eve's sin brought forth pain in childbirth. Why? Sinful people beget children tainted by *sin*, therefore it is only fitting that the process of bringing them to birth be a *painful* one. Living in this world is *painful* because it is *sinful*. Adam's punishment also fits the crime. Prior to the fall, he enjoyed the benefits of paradise without expending any effort, but after he ate the forbidden fruit that God had commanded him to abstain from, his sin brought an end to the free bounty of the Garden of Eden. From this point forward, Adam and his progeny would have to till the soil for a living.

Though God intented that His creation would remain perfect, it did not do so because Adam and Eve disobeyed Him, and as a result all creation was subjected to death. Plants were cursed, animals were cursed, humanity was cursed, the entire earth was cursed.[34] Because of humanity's primal sin, everything decays and eventually dies, and this includes the inanimate universe itself. The sun is burning out, the moon's orbit is decaying, and even the atoms themselves are unstable. Science has observed that in every process in the universe all components deteriorate; this is the *Second Law of Thermodynamics*. Amazingly, the two great laws of science are attested to in

---

HOW EVIL ORIGINATED

The Bible tells us that evil came about as a result of an *angel* (Lucifer/Satan) exercising his free will against God's will; therefore evil did not have its origin in God.[38] Scripture tells us that Satan, one of the most powerful and exalted angels in heaven, became filled with pride and rebelled against God. As a result, God cast him and his followers out of heaven.[39] Many people wonder how an all-good and all-powerful God could allow evil to exist. The answer is that God created angels and humans with *freedom of choice*, and Adam and Eve, in addition to Satan, chose to disobey God. At that point evil emerged on earth as a by-product of human decision. Evil is the result of free will. The ability to choose is extremely important. It is "choice" that makes love meaningful; humans have not been programmed like robots to love.[40]

The first sin in the human family occurred when Satan (the adversary) planted a *seed of doubt* in the minds of Adam and Eve. He did this by appealing to their freedom of choice.[41] Satan broached the subject, but it was the man and the woman's decision to eat of the prohibited fruit that is at issue. Furthermore, their decision was a *free and uncoerced* act of disobedience.[42] Satan influenced Adam and Eve, but they exercised their own free will by choosing to disobey.

For some reason, only known to God, humanity was placed on the "grand stage" of the entire universe to participate in the final battle between good and evil. As a result of the first sin, all of humanity has been imbued with a tendency to rebel against God.[43] Therefore, sin is universal, and has affected the entire human race.[44]

---

the two greatest events of early history—Creation and the Fall. The *first law of science* tells us that nothing can now be created; the Scriptures say that God is the Creator of everything and that after He made everything He "rested" from all His work (creation).[35] The *second law of science* says that everything is subject to decay, deterioration, and death; the Scriptures tell us that death came into the world as a result of sin and disobedience.[36] Though the balance of nature maintains the earth's systems to a remarkable degree, everything in the universe is nonetheless in the process of wearing down.[37]

The corruption of humanity that was caused by man's disobedience was total. He was corrupted spiritually, physically, emotionally, intellectually, socially, and in every other way.[45] The entire story of history tells of an endless succession of civilizations that rise on good principles and then fall due to corruption. From ancient Egypt to Israel, Babylon, Persia, ancient Greece and Rome, Spain, France, Turkey, Britain, and countless other nations, history is the tale of the rise of great civilizations and empires and their fall because of moral, social, and cultural degeneration.[46] These are all problems that we cannot solve because they are problems of the *human heart*. Politics and armies cannot change the heart. We have had nearly 5,000 years of recorded history, and it all suggests that while there is some good in humanity, nevertheless it is inherently and fatally flawed by sin.

When human beings disobeyed God, they destroyed their relationship with God. No longer did they enjoy the intimacy and closeness of perfect love. There was, and is now, estrangement between them. The *image of God* is no longer reflected in them, and only God can restore it. That's the central message of Christianity. God is in the business of transforming sinful human beings back into the *image of God*.[47] Human beings were *created* perfect in God's image,[48] but sin destroyed their perfect state, and now God is *re-creating* sinful human beings into His likeness.[49]

Though the story of creation teaches us something about *God as Creator*— He is a God of transcendent wisdom, power, and goodness, who wants His people to enjoy an intimate relationship with each other and with Him—it also teaches us about the *reality of sin;* all people are susceptible to it, and it damages and pulls people away from God. Oftentimes in Scripture, sin is explained in terms of direction. People turn away from God or go astray, or follow the wrong leaders or false gods. Repentance implies a *change of direction,* a move back toward God.[50] Over and over again the Old Testament prophets told the children of Israel to remember the covenant God made with them, and pleaded with them to turn back to Him.[51] In the New Testament, Jesus called people to repentance, which involves a change of direction, a turning away from sin, and turning to God.[52]

The Scriptures teach that people can either move *closer* to God or move *further away* from God. Each individual can have his sins forgiven and be given a new direction in life. The Bible thus divides the entire human race into two groups, those who know God and those who do not know God; those who love God and those who oppose God; those who seek to move closer to God and those who seek to avoid God. According to the Scriptures, no one is neutral toward God; people either open up to God or they run away from Him.[53] Fallen man wants to run his own life, and he interprets all reality and experience independent of God. Such a person *does not believe* the things of God; he actually thinks such things are "foolishness."[54] Therefore, instead of recognizing that the material universe was created by God, he assumes it to possess an existence independent from God; as a result, everything is reducible to chemistry and physics, including life itself.[55]

When Adam and Eve disobeyed, they were driven out of the Garden of Eden, and from that point on they had to make a living through agriculture and animal husbandry. The Book of Genesis tells us that in just seven generations from Adam, the human race developed a number of significant technologies,

GOD INSTITUTED A "BLOOD SACRIFICE" FOR SIN

When Adam and Eve disobeyed God in the Garden of Eden by eating from the tree of the knowledge of good and evil, they realized they were no longer pure and innocent. They were now naked and ashamed. The Genesis narrative tells us that Adam and Eve, in response to their nakedness, "sewed fig leaves together" in an attempt to cover themselves.[58] When God came to visit them the day they sinned, "they hid themselves because they were afraid."[59] God found them and discussed the consequences of their sin with them, and then He told them that He would provide "garments of skin for them to wear";[60] thus the covering for sin that God provided involved a *blood sacrifice.* An innocent animal paid the price for their sin, and God clothed them in the skin of that animal to cover their shame and to be a reminder of that fact.[61] This is the first blood sacrifice recorded in the Bible, and it was offered by God Himself on behalf of sinful man.[62] This blood sacrifice predated the sacrificial system instituted under the Mosaic Law by thousands of years.

Throughout the ages *blood* has been the symbol of life,[63] and its shedding, the medium through which God conveys *forgiveness.*[64] The Old Testament provided for the offering of certain animals whose blood was shed vicariously for the sins of those who *repented* and trusted in God's covenant love. Though the death of the animal itself did not take away one's guilt, the required sacrifice was a "sign" that demonstrated one's repentance; God's requirement for forgiving sin has always been *repentance.* Such sacrifices were graphic reminders of the true cost and consequences of sin—*death.*[65] It was possible, however, for someone to sacrifice the animal without having repented in their heart; this behavior was referred to as "hypocrisy" in scripture.[66]

The main idea behind a blood sacrifice was that of *substitution.* The sacrificial blood was shed on behalf of the guilty; the life of the sacrifice is in the blood. The clear teaching of scripture is that each individual must bear the responsibility for his own disobedience.[67] In the Old Testament, when individuals made blood sacrifices, they were acknowledging not only their own sinfulness, but also their need to satisfy God's divine justice for sin,[68] and their need to depend upon Him for mercy. By laying one's hands on the animal to be sacrificed, it was understood that the worshipper was transferring his own sin to the victim.[69]

The practice of *animal sacrifice* was a primary characteristic of early religion. God was perfect and holy, and sinful beings could not approach Him because they were impure. This view is also reflected in the ancient literature of the Greeks, Egyptians, Chinese, and Hindus, and the traditions of many races agree that the first human beings brought animals to represent them and be their substitute in their worship of God.[70]

The *sacrificial system* in the Old Testament was established for the purpose of awakening one's consciousness of sin, and impressing upon the worshipper the possibility of obtaining God's forgiveness and being made right before Him. The basis upon which a sacrificial offering was made was that of a Divine command: "No one shall appear before Me empty-handed."[71] The underlying premise behind any sacrifice is that it is a *gift,* and any gift given to God was to be given with a *grateful heart* as a joyful expression for the privilege of being able to participate in the benefits and blessings of His Covenant love.[72]

—*THE BIBLICAL RECORD FOR CREATION AND THE FALL: GENESIS 1–5* including organized agriculture, animal husbandry, the domestication of animals, stringed and wind instruments, metallurgy (including brass and iron and alloys of base metals), smelting and refining technologies, and science and the arts.[56] If man actually evolved through a long series of evolutionary changes then it would logically follow that the further back one went in time, the more primitive humans would be, and the more primitive their artifacts would be. But the findings of science and archaeology reveal just the opposite.[57]

The Rebellion of Early Man—About 3000 BC

With the passing of time, Adam and Eve's offspring multiplied into the millions, and a fallen progeny filled the earth with violence.[73] When evil became rampant on the earth, God told Noah that "He would not strive with man forever"; that because of man's rebellion He was going to "destroy the world by a flood."[74] He preserved Noah and his immediate family by having them *build an ark* and placing in it two of every land creature on the face of the earth.[75] After the floodwaters submerged the entire world, the waters began to subside, and the ark then came to rest on the mountains of Ararat[76] (the eastern border of present-day Turkey). It was there that Noah and his family disembarked the ark with the animals, and the earth began to be repopulated.

It was not long, however, until corruption and sin began to impact this select family. Once again, humanity challenged God and refused to submit to Him in worship. Instead of carrying out God's command to inhabit the whole earth,[77] the people drew together and planned to *build a tower* around which they would center their civilization.[78] This time when God looked down and saw their stubborn hearts, He frustrated their project by causing the people to speak different languages. Thus everyone's speech sounded like "babble" to those around them.[79] (The name "Babylon" is a derivation of this term.) Therefore, from the *Tower of Babel*, the different people groups were scattered in different directions because of their inability to communicate; the inevitable result was social isolation. The Book of Genesis lists the various groups and locations where they migrated and settled.[80] One of the world's greatest archaeologists, William F. Albright, called this list "an astonishingly accurate document." It lists the descendents of Noah's three sons and indicates regions in which they settled and the nations that developed from those first tribal settlements.[81] Modern scientific studies on the origins of languages give strong support for the Genesis account.[82]

What is remarkable is that there are no traces of evolution in these settlements from the simple to the sophisticated.[83] It is interesting to note that cultures all around the world appear to have originated at about the same time—roughly 5,000 years ago—which would be the time of the *Flood* and the *Tower of Babel* (about 3000 BC) and that they appear with an already high level of technical development. An article in *Omni* magazine notes, "The unprecedented explosion of knowledge 5,000 years ago... may have been foreshadowed by an earlier society whose cultural remnants have long since vanished."[84] Once again, the integrity of the biblical record is supported.

With regard to the issue of "race," in the biblical sense, there really is no such thing. We're all members of only one race, the human race. The physical features usually associated with race, such as the shape of the eye, hair texture, and the color of the skin are not mentioned. The truth is all human beings are of the same color; that is, everyone has the same chemical coloring agent—*melanin*. Individuals whose inherited genetic structure gives their skin the capability of producing higher amounts of melanin are *black*; individuals whose skin produces moderate amounts are *middle brown*; and those who produce limited amounts are *white*. The facts learned from scientific studies on genetics fit very well with the biblical view of creation and our origin from *one* common genetic source.[85]

—THE BIBLICAL RECORD FOR THE REBELLION OF EARLY MAN: GENESIS 6–11

The Descendants of Abraham—About 2000 BC

The Bible shows that evil continued to increase after the great Flood. During this period people worshiped many gods,[86] and immorality was rampant. So God instituted a plan to save humanity by starting with one family, "through whom all the families of the earth would be blessed."[87] The father of that family was *Abraham*. He lived in Babylon (present-day Iraq) in a culture that worshiped a moon god, but he himself worshiped the Creator God.[88] The Lord said to Abraham: "Leave your country and go to the land which I will show you, and I will make you into a great nation and will bless you. And all the families of the earth will be blessed through you."[89] Abraham did as God instructed. He and his wife Sarah migrated to the land of Canaan (present-day Israel), where they founded a clan that worshiped God alone. The nation born out of Abraham was *Israel*, and it was through this family that God promised to make Himself known among the nations and correct the misunderstandings people had of the one true God.[90]

God promised to give Abraham a son, whose descendants would become the nation of Israel. At first Abraham believed what God said, but when God did not give him a son as soon as he expected, he had a son by his wife's servant girl *Hagar*. Though the ancient world accepted this means of securing an heir, it violated God's law for marriage,[91] and Abraham suffered greatly because of this sin. His firstborn son *Ishmael* turned against the child God had promised to Abraham, *Isaac*, who was born 13 years later to Sarah. Because of the hostile relationship that existed between Sarah and Hagar, Abraham sent Hagar and Ishmael away into the wilderness south of Canaan.[92] As Hagar journeyed, God told her He would make her son Ishmael the father of a great nation as well.[93] Most scholars today regard the *Arab* world as the descendants of Ishmael.[94] As the years passed, Abraham came to trust God more completely.

Abraham had a grandson through *Isaac* whose name was *Jacob*. His name would later be changed to *Israel*, and he would become the father of twelve sons, who would become leaders of the twelve tribes of Jacob (or Israel). When a severe famine occurred in Canaan, the entire household of Jacob went to live in Egypt. One of Jacob's sons, *Joseph*, had become the Pharaoh's most respected leader, so the descendents of Israel prospered and enjoyed great prominence in that land. Over a period of 400 years, the children of Israel grew into a great nation, But with the passing of time there arose a Pharaoh in Egypt who did not know of the greatness of Joseph. Because the descendants of Jacob[95] were multiplying so rapidly, the pharaoh feared they would overpower the Egyptians. So this new pharaoh made them all slaves and treated them harshly. Finally,

---

THE GOD OF ISRAEL

The emergence of the people of Israel in the Bible is set against the depressing narrative of humanity's rebellion against God. The God of the Bible is portrayed as the God of history, and He brings that history to its goal—salvation—through the particular history of a particular people, the Jews. The Jews knew this God by the name *Yahweh* or *Jehovah*—the Creator and Sustainer of the entire universe.[96] According to the Bible, Yahweh is not Israel's private possession, but the God of the entire earth, and is actively involved in the histories of nations other than Israel. The Bible is clear that God is *one*, that His name is *Yahweh*, and there is *no other* God but Yahweh.[97] This is the heart of the monotheism of Israel.[98]

Israel had been entrusted with the responsibility of bearing witness to Yahweh's uniqueness as the living God.[99] Israel only existed as a nation because of Yahweh's intention to bring salvation to all nations. While Yahweh works in all nations, He has chosen to work uniquely only through Israel. As a nation, Israel was given the responsibility and privilege of demonstrating what Yahweh was like to the rest of the nations, by living out the requirements of the Law.[100] The Bible, however, testifies to the fact that on numerous occasions Israel *abandoned* this global vision and calling. The *great temptation*, to which Israel repeatedly succumbed, was thinking of Yahweh as simply another tribal deity who could be worshiped any way they chose, thus betraying the revelation God entrusted to them for the sake of all nations.[101]

in response to their cries for deliverance, God raised up *Moses* to lead them out of Egypt and back to the promised land of Canaan.

—*THE BIBLICAL RECORD FOR ABRAHAM AND
HIS DESCENDANTS: GENESIS 12–50*

The Leadership of Moses—About 1500 BC

During the 400 years the Hebrew people were in Egypt, most of them had forgotten about the one God and had adopted pagan religious practices.[102] In the fifteenth century BC, Moses reintroduced them to the worship of God and led them out of Egypt to reestablish them in the monotheistic faith of Abraham. Three crucial events happened in connection with their exodus out of Egypt, which would later play a significant role in the history of Judaism. The first happened when Pharaoh refused to let the Israelites leave Egypt. God sent ten devastating "plagues" on Egypt to make him change his mind; but because of the hardness of his heart, he refused.[103] The last plague involved the death of the firstborn son of every home throughout the land of Egypt.[104] God instructed all of the people of Israel through Moses to choose an unblemished male sheep and eat it as part of a feast to the Lord. He further instructed them to smear the blood of the lamb on the two doorposts and on the lintel of their houses.[105] That evening the "death angel" would pass through the land, killing the first born of every household, but the Lord said, "When I see the blood, I will *pass over* you and will spare you and your home."[106] Hence this annual Jewish celebration is called the *Passover*. Once again, we are reminded that the way of salvation is through the "blood."[107]

The result of the slaughter carried out by the death angel was that Pharaoh gave in to Moses' demand to "let my people go."[108] But as soon as the Israelites left, Pharaoh changed his mind and sent his army to bring them back. God had directed the Israelites to the Red Sea, where He parted the waters in front of them and miraculously let them cross over on dry ground. When the pursuing Egyptian army followed them into the sea, God proceeded to drown the entire army.[109] The Bible tells us that

Bridgeman Art Library

Marble sculpture of the head of Moses by Michelangelo (1513–1516), located at the tomb of Pope Julius II (1453–1513).

there were 600,000 Hebrew men involved in the exodus.[110] Most scholars estimate that the total number of Hebrews, including women and children, would have been at least 2 million.[111]

The crossing of the Red Sea on dry land was the second major event in connection with the exodus. It became Israel's "defining moment" as God's redeemed people.[112] The third major event occurred just a few weeks later at Mount Sinai, where *God revealed to Moses a system of law* that would govern His people in the Promised Land.[113] This system of law came to be known as the *Mosaic Law*, and included the following elements:[114]

1. *Ten Commandments*—the Commandments defined the Israelites' relationships with God and other people

2. *Legal Code*—covered social relationships, as well as criminal and civil matters

3. *Instructions for Building the Tabernacle*—the Tabernacle was to be the central place of worship

4. *Guidelines for the Priesthood*—priests were to be selected from the tribe of Levi

5. *System of Sacrifices*—sacrifices were to be administered exclusively by the priests

6. *Code of Ritual Purity*—included religious practices, hygienic precautions, dietary laws

God instituted the Mosaic Law as a covenant with His people after He delivered them from their oppressors. Israel was required to obey God and live according to the law in order that its people might have a right relationship with Him.[115] The portable *Tabernacle* (and later the permanent *Temple* in Jerusalem) was the place where sacrifices were to be offered in order that the people might be absolved of their guilt when they would sin or break God's Law. The Tabernacle also served to *remind* them of their total dependence on God. The demands of the Mosaic Law were a constant reminder that any sin demanded a specific sacrifice, in order that God could forgive the sinner. Through the sacrifice performed by the priest, it was clearly shaped in the mind of the sinner that his sins were forgiven because the *blood* of an innocent animal was shed. The animal became *man's substitute* to fulfill God's justice.[116]

When the Israelites were given the opportunity to enter the land of Canaan, they saw that it was inhabited by seven powerful nations.[117] As a result they

---

THE CHILDREN OF ISRAEL FREQUENTLY DISOBEYED GOD'S LAW

The Old Testament tells us that the children of Israel transgressed the Mosaic Law often and seriously, especially when they worshiped other gods, an act forbidden by the very *first* command, "You shall have *no other gods* before Me."[119] As you will see in the next chapter, even the function of the Temple itself was perverted; those who worshiped there were condemned for offering sacrifices and performing empty rituals aimed at securing God's favor, and by practicing the idolatrous patterns of other religions, without any desire to obey God's Law.[120] As a result of this attitude, God sent the Israelites into captivity at the hands of the Babylonians in 586 BC (see Psalm 78:52–61). All their sacrifices failed to produce a change of attitude in the people's hearts.[121]

---

became *fearful* and refused to trust the Lord, even though God promised them victory.[118] Because they were unwilling to trust the Lord, that generation was not permitted to enter the land; they would have to wander in the Sinai wilderness for 40 years until the distrustful generation died, and then the Lord would allow them to enter the land. Moses would not be permitted to enter the land either, because at one point he became so angry at the constant complaining of his fellow countrymen that he disobeyed God's instructions about how he was to respond in front of them. Therefore, just prior to their entering the land, God took Moses up on Mount Nebo to show him the land that His people would enter. There the Lord took his life and buried him.[122]

—THE BIBLICAL RECORD FOR MOSES AND THE EXODUS:
EXODUS, LEVITICUS, NUMBERS, AND DEUTERONOMY

The Rule of Judges—About 1450 BC to 1050 BC

After the death of Moses, God chose His faithful servant *Joshua* to go into the land and complete the wars of conquest. Under Joshua's leadership the Israelites took possession of the land of Canaan by conquering 31 kings.[123] Following this conquest, Joshua divided the land among each of the twelve tribes according to God's directions.[124] When Joshua died, the nation of Israel had no strong central government; they were simply a confederacy of twelve independent tribes. Their form of government was referred to as a *Theocracy*—that is, God Himself was to be the Ruler of the nation. But the people did not take God seriously and were continually falling into idolatry.[125] During the 400-year period after the death of Joshua, the nation was ruled intermittently by *Judges*. The difference between a judge and a king is that a kingship is a hereditary position. A king gives his throne to his son, but

THE CONQUEST OF THE LAND OF CANAAN

The seven nations living in the land of Canaan during the exodus worshiped many gods and demons. They understood worship as a matter of placating the gods with offerings and sacrifices in order to gain their favor. Ultimately, their offerings became more substantial in an effort to manipulate their gods, and this ultimately resulted in their offering their own children as *human sacrifices*,[127] a not uncommon practice in many of these pagan societies. The Old Testament gives a scathing indictment of the inhabitants of the land. They were grotesquely evil and immoral, and their religion was odious and obnoxious.[128] In 1928, ancient clay texts were discovered in northern Syria that confirmed the Bible's portrayal of this immoral practice.[129] So when Moses led the children of Israel out of the land of Egypt, God presented him with various rules of conquest for the land of Canaan. The Lord said to him:

> I will send an angel before you to the Promised Land to help you drive out its inhabitants. They are not to live in the land, lest they influence you to sin against Me; if you serve their gods, it will surely be a snare to you. You are to make no treaties with them; you're to destroy their idols; and you're not to intermingle or intermarry with them. You are to serve the LORD your God only, because I have chosen you to be a people for My own possession.[130]

When the Israelites entered the land, they could have followed four courses of action regarding the Canaanites. They could have *killed* them, *expelled* them, made *slaves* of them, or *coexisted* with them. Except in actual battle situations, the Israelites chose the last two options, for the Canaanites continued to live in the land long after Joshua's death. Because Israel did not obey God's command to remove them from the land, they ended up making treaties with them, intermarrying with them, and even embracing their idolatrous practices, just as God had warned.[131] The Bible says the Canaanites constituted a *moral cancer* that would even bring about the destruction of Israel if she were not careful to exorcise it from their midst.[132] The loathsome sin of idolatry would later become the downfall of a number of Israel's leaders in different periods throughout her history. At one point God would allow the nation to be defeated "because of their sacrifices" to pagan idols.[133] God told the prophet Isaiah, "I will not share My glory with another, nor My praise with carved images."[134] Scripture describes the worship of something *created* with human hands, rather than the *Creator* Himself, as sheer folly.[135]

a judge is someone who is raised up in a time of crisis and endowed with special gifts from God to meet the needs of the people.[126]

During the 400-year period of the Judges, the nation of Israel repeatedly lapsed into recurring cycles of *apostasy* (abandoning the faith), *judgment* (bondage to foreign powers), *pleading* (to God for deliverance), and *deliverance* (by a judge whom God would raise up, and who would then rule over them for a time).[136] The book of Judges recounts the oppression Israel experienced at the hands of captors because of her failure to obey God. It also tells the stories of 14 faithful judges whom God raised up to deliver His people from their enemies, and to administer divine justice, wisdom, and leadership.

The last of the judges to rule over the nation of Israel was *Samuel*, who also served as a prophet and a priest.[137] During the period of the Judges, the Israelites lived with an unstructured form of government. Whenever a problem would arise, the Lord would raise up a judge to give them divine guidance and direction. After 400 years of being ruled by judges, however, the people of Israel demanded that Samuel give them a king as their ruler, so that they could be like other nations; they didn't like being different from the rest of the world. Samuel was grieved by the request of his fellow countrymen; nevertheless, the Lord told him to grant their request. The truth was, it was God, not Samuel, the people were rejecting. So Samuel reluctantly complied with their request, and the Lord directed him to appoint *Saul* as the first human king over Israel, thus establishing a monarchy for the Hebrew people.[138]

—THE BIBLICAL RECORD FOR CONQUERING CANAAN AND
THE RULE OF JUDGES: JOSHUA, JUDGES.

CHAPTER 8

THE RISE AND FALL OF THE KINGDOM OF ISRAEL

Israel was made to be a "holy people."
This is the essence of its dignity and the essence of its merit.
— *ABRAHAM J. HESCHEL[1]*

It was God's original intention that He himself would be the King of Israel. His people were to be a holy people, unlike any other nation. But the people of Israel did not want to be different; they wanted a king like other nations. So the Lord instructed Samuel to appoint a man named Saul king over Israel.[2]

The Kingdom of Israel—About 1050 BC

During the first 120 years of the monarchy, Israel had three famous kings each of whom reigned for forty years: Saul, David, and Solomon. *Saul* was a man of impressive stature; he was handsome, and stood head and shoulders above his fellow countrymen. When he was appointed king the people were ecstatic. In his early years, Saul appeared as a man of humility and self-control, but over the years his character changed. He became a man of immorality, self-will, disobedience to God, jealousy, hatred, and superstition.[3] His jealousy of David, a young warrior who had killed the giant Goliath and who served as his court musician, turned to anger because David became more popular than he was.[4] Little did Saul know that God had already chosen *David* to be the next king of Israel.[5]

David had the kind of qualities that were needed as a leader: military skill, political savvy, and a keen sense of religious duty. During his reign, David made the nation stronger and more secure than it had ever been,[6] and Jerusalem became established as the religious and political center of the nation.[7] The first part of David's life as king of Israel was magnificent, but then in the very prime of life and at the height of his glory, he turned aside from the will of God and became soft, indulgent, and lustful like other Middle Eastern kings. He committed adultery and then tried to conceal it by murdering the woman's husband. God punished both David and Israel because of his sin.[8] The punishment not only brought tremendous harm to David, but it brought shame upon His God before the nations, and David's reputation would never be the same. But when David admitted his sin and grieved over his actions, God forgave him and even chose him to be that line through whom His own Son (Jesus Christ) would one day be born.[9]

After David died, his son *Solomon* took the throne.[10] The Lord told Solomon, "If you will obey Me as your father David did, I will establish your throne forever; but if you turn away from following Me and serve other gods, I will tear the kingdom from you."[11] He warned Solomon to "not associate with foreign women, because they would turn his heart away after their gods."[12] The Bible tells us that Solomon took 700 wives for himself and 300 concubines from all kinds of nations, and as the Lord predicted, "they turned his *heart* away from the Lord to serve their gods."[13] As a result of his sin, God divided his kingdom after he died.[14]

Solomon began his reign with much glory and triumph, but despite his legendary wisdom, he did not always live that way, because his foreign wives "turned his heart" away from God. But though he failed miserably later in his reign, early on God used him to construct the great Temple in Jerusalem (circa 950 BC), which became the focal point of religious life and ritual for the nation of Israel[16] (see Figure 6). *Jerusalem* is a city that is built on seven hills, and for Jews and Christians it is the holiest place on earth. The name Jerusalem comes from two words that mean "City of

Marble sculpture of the head of David by Michelangelo (1504), located in Florence, Italy.

THE PROBLEM OF THE "HEART"

Both the Old and New Testaments place a primary emphasis not on outward behavior or ritual but on the "heart." God focuses on the individual's innermost being; rather than looking on the outside of a person, He looks on the inside. When human beings have beauty contests, they mainly focus on what is seen, not on what is unseen. The problem with human beings is they are not able to see what people are really like on the inside, but God can and does see, and this is the primary area in which He operates. It is interesting to note that external beauty lasts only a few years, no matter how attractive one might be; yet the primary concern for many people is the "shell" that houses their real person. It is tragic that for many people, beauty is only skin deep. Consider what the Bible teaches:

- 1 Samuel 16:7—"Man looks at the outward appearance, God looks at the *heart.*"
- Psalm 24:3-4—"Only those with a *pure heart* can stand before the Lord."
- Psalm 51:10—David prayed, "Create in me a *clean heart,* O God."
- Psalm 51:17—"The true sacrifices of God are a broken spirit and contrite *heart.*"
- Psalm 78:37—"Their *hearts* were not loyal or faithful to His covenant."
- Proverbs 4:23—King Solomon said, "Watch over your *heart* with all diligence."
- Jeremiah 17:9—"The *heart* is deceitful above all else, who can understand it?"
- 1 Chronicles 28:9—"The Lord searches and understands the *hearts* of all people."
- Isaiah 29:13—"Though they worship Me with their words, their *hearts* are far off."
- Jeremiah 32:39—"I will give them a *heart* that they may fear Me and obey Me."
- Ezekiel 36:26—"I will give you a *new heart* and put a new spirit within you."
- Joel 2:12—"Return to Me with all your *heart,*" declares the Lord.
- Matthew 5:8—"Blessed are the pure in *heart,* for they alone shall see God."
- Matthew 5:28—"Sexual lust is tantamount to committing adultery in one's *heart.*"
- Matthew 6:21—Jesus said, "Where your treasure is, there your *heart* will be also."
- Matthew 22:37—Jesus said, "Love the Lord your God with all your *heart.*"
- Romans 10:9—"If you believe in your *heart*... you will be saved."
- Ephesians 3:17—"May Christ dwell in your *heart* through faith."
- Hebrews 4:12—"God's word is able to judge the intentions of your *heart.*"
- James 1:26—"If one thinks himself religious and does not control his speech, this man deceives his *heart,* and his religion is worthless."

The Bible says that society's real problems are problems of the "heart." In the age of information and technology, failures of character have scandalized institutions of family, government, science, industry, education, and the arts. The most technologically sophisticated society the world has ever known is marred by racial prejudice, sexual perversion, drug and alcohol addiction, abuse, divorce, and sexually transmitted disease. Sadly, many believe our problems are rooted in ignorance, diet, or government. But the root of the matter according to the Master Designer of the universe is the "heart." Jesus said, "Out of the heart proceed evil thoughts, murder, adultery, sexual perversion, theft, lying, deceit.... It is these things that defile a person."[15]

Generation after generation has hoped for the very best. They fought wars that they believed would end all wars. They developed educational theories that would produce enlightened, nonviolent children. They invented technologies that would deliver people from the oppressive slavery of work. Yet human beings are no closer today to a world of peace, harmony, and fulfillment than they have ever been.

Peace." The Temple that Solomon built was destroyed in 586 BC by King Nebuchadnezzar. Seventy years later the Jewish people returned from exile in Babylon and rebuilt the Temple, and then this Temple was desecrated in 168 BC by *Antiochus Epiphanes* of Syria. In 19 BC *King Herod* began to rebuild the Temple, and in AD 70 it was completely destroyed by *Titus* and the Roman Army. The only thing left of King Herod's Temple today is the Western Wall, which is known as the "Wailing Wall." This is the site where Jews from all over the world come to place small prayer notes in the cracks of the wall, to mourn and pray for the day when the Temple will be rebuilt for yet a fourth time.

The Temple that Solomon built is said to have had several courtyards and an inner sanctuary called the *Holy of Holies* where the Ark of the Covenant was kept. The ark was a chest-like piece of furniture that contained the tablets on which the Ten Commandments were inscribed. Only the high priest could enter the Holy of Holies, and he could enter only once a year on the Day of Atonement *(Yom Kippur)*, to sprinkle blood on the mercy seat for the forgiveness of his own sins and for those of all the people of Israel. When he would enter the Holy of Holies, his assistants would tie ropes to his ankles so that if he happened to die inside the inner chamber, they would be able to pull him out without entering the chamber themselves. Even today, Orthodox Jews never walk on the Temple Mount in Jerusalem, because nobody knows the precise location of the Holy of Holies; for them it would be a grave sin to even accidentally step on it, if they were not a true descendent of Aaron, the high priest.[17] Figure 6 is an artist's conception of what Solomon's Temple looked like.

InterVarsity Press — Leicester, UK

Figure 6. Rendering of Solomon's Temple showing the twin free-standing pillars, the entry chamber, and side storage chambers[18]

When Solomon died, his sons and generals fought for the throne, and Israel stumbled into a bloody civil war. *Rehoboam* had his father's blessing to be the new king; but his rival *Jeroboam* wielded more influence among the military chiefs of the land. In the end, Rehoboam took the southern half of the country and called it *Judah* (the name of its largest tribe), and Jeroboam set up his own government in the northern half and retained the name of *Israel*.

—*The biblical record for the United Kingdom of Israel: Ruth, 1 & 2 Samuel, 1 Kings 1–11, 1 Chronicles, 2 Chronicles 1–9. In addition, the five books of poetry: Job, Psalms, Proverbs, Ecclesiastes, Song of Solomon.*

The Divided Kingdom—About 931 BC

After the death of Solomon, the nation of Israel rebelled against God and His laws, and as a result God divided the kingdom in two. During this period there was apostasy of every kind in both kingdoms; people turned away from God to idolatrous practices. The northern kingdom of *Israel* was the more wicked, but the southern kingdom of *Judah* did not fare much better. Over the first 200 years of division, the northern kingdom of Israel was ruled by 19 kings, none of whom obeyed and served Yahweh (see Table 2). The main problem with the people of the northern kingdom was their attitude toward Yahweh, their neglect of His laws, and their adherence to heathen worship. Israel's final overthrow and her captivity were the result of God's judgment.[19]

The kings of the southern kingdom of Judah were classified into two groups. The majority were condemned because "they walked in the way of the kings of Israel and did evil in God's sight,"[20] while the rest were commended for doing what "was right in the eyes of the Lord." For most of those who did right, this was a qualified commendation because they fell short of the biblical ideal;[21]—they failed to completely eradicate all forms of heathen worship.[22] Only two kings received an unqualified commendation from the Lord—Hezekiah and Josiah. They alone abolished all forms of heathen worship and conducted worship in the Temple as God required.[23] For a period of 350 years only eight of Judah's 20 kings were commended for a degree of faithfulness.[24] (See Table 2.)

The kingship of Israel never became self-sufficient; therefore it frequently required monitoring by *prophets* instructed by God.[25] Two important prophets emerged during the early years of the divided kingdom. The first was *Elijah*. He stands out as a uniquely bold and rugged character. He appeared before wicked King Ahab and declared that God would bring a disastrous drought upon the land because of the wickedness of the people. He told Ahab to summon all the prophets of the pagan god Baal, whom his wife Jezebel worshiped, and meet him on Mount Carmel. There Elijah challenged the prophets of Baal to a contest to prove whose god was stronger. Each of them would prepare to sacrifice a bull as a burnt offering to its god, and call on his god to answer by consuming it with fire. The prophets of Baal danced and prayed around their altar for an entire day but received not the slightest response. Elijah even poured water on his sacrifice, and when he asked God to send fire from heaven to consume it, He did. Elijah then had all of the 450 false prophets of Baal killed, and when he asked God to end the drought, the skies poured forth rain.[26]

Elijah confronted Ahab a second time because he and Jezebel had murdered a neighbor so they could have his vineyard for themselves. This time Elijah pronounced doom on the king and his wife.[27]

KINGS OF THE DIVIDED KINGDOM (931–586 BC)			
NAME	KINGDOM	YEARS OF REIGN	REFERENCE
Jeroboam I	Israel	22	1 Kings 11:26–14:20
Rehoboam	Judah	17	1 Kings 11:42–14:31
Abijam	Judah	3	1 Kings 14:31–15:8
Asa	Judah	41	1 Kings 15:8–24
Nadab	Israel	2	1 Kings 15:25–28
Baasha	Israel	24	1 Kings 15:27–16:7
Elah	Israel	2	1 Kings 16:6–14
Zimri	Israel	7 days	1 Kings 16:9–20
Omri	Israel	12	1 Kings 16:15–28
Ahab	Israel	22	1 Kings 16:29–22:40
Jehoshaphat	Judah	25	1 Kings 22:41–50
Azariah	Israel	1	1 Kings 22:40–2 King 1:18
Jehoram (Joram)	Israel	11	2 Kings 3:1–9:25
Jehoram	Judah	8	2 Kings 8:16–24
Ahaziah	Judah	1	2 Kings 8:24–9:29
Jehu	Israel	28	2 Kings 9:1–10:36
Athaliah	Judah	6	2 Kings 11:1–20
Joash	Judah	40	2 Kings 11:1–12:21
Jehoahaz	Israel	16	2 Kings 13:1–9

NAME	KINGDOM	YEARS OF REIGN	REFERENCE
Jehoash (Joash)	Israel	16	2 Kings 13:10–14:16
Amaziah	Judah	29	2 Kings 14:1–20
Jeroboam II	Israel	40	2 Kings 14:23–29
Zechariah	Israel	6 months	2 Kings 14:29–15:12
Azariah (Uzziah)	Judah	52	2 Kings 15:1–7
Shallum	Israel	1 month	2 Kings 15:10–15
Menahem	Israel	10	2 Kings 15:14–22
Pekahiah	Israel	2	2 Kings 15:22–26
Pekah	Israel	20	2 Kings 15:27–31
Hoshea	*Israel Falls to Assyria*	9	2 Kings 15:30–17:6
Jotham	Judah	18	2 Kings 15:32–38
Ahaz	Judah	19	2 Kings 16:1–20
Hezekiah	Judah	29	2 Kings 18:1–20:21
Manasseh	Judah	55	2 Kings 21:1–18
Amon	Judah	2	2 Kings 21:19–26
Josiah	Judah	31	2 Kings 22:1–23:30
Jehoahaz	Judah	3 months	2 Kings 23:31–33
Jehoiakim	Judah	11	2 Kings 23:34–24:5
Jehoiachin	Judah	3 months	2 Kings 24:6–16
Zedekiah	*Judah Falls to Babylon*	11	2 Kings 24:17–25:30

Table 2. Kings of the Divided Kingdom

The second significant prophetic voice during these days was the prophet *Elisha*. He was like his teacher Elijah in a number of ways. Both men brought rain in times of drought, destroyed the enemies of God with supernatural power, performed extraordinary miracles including raising a person from the dead, and pronounced doom upon kings.[28] The Scriptures tell us that Elisha performed more miracles than any other Old Testament prophet.[29]

The Lord raised up *prophets* such as Elijah and Elisha to warn His people of impending judgment if they failed to turn from their wicked ways. The prophets were also sent to encourage the children of Israel to trust God even when their circumstances were difficult. God used these holy men as His spokesmen in this crucial time in Israel's history. Seventeen of these prophets have an Old Testament book that bears their name. In spite of repeated efforts by prophets to warn the people, their warnings were ignored and many of them were killed.[30] Finally, God let the pagan empires of Assyria and Babylon destroy both kingdoms and take the people into captivity. The Northern Kingdom of Israel was conquered by the *Assyrians* in 722 BC, and the Southern Kingdom of Judah was conquered by the *Babylonians* in 586 BC.

> —THE BIBLICAL RECORD FOR THE DIVIDED KINGDOM (931–586 BC):
> 1 KINGS 12–22, 2 KINGS, 2 CHRONICLES 10–36. THE PROPHETS
> IN CHRONOLOGICAL ORDER WERE: OBADIAH, JOEL, JONAH, AMOS,
> HOSEA, ISAIAH, MICAH, NAHUM, ZEPHANIAH, JEREMIAH, HABAKKUK
> (THE ORDER IN WHICH THEY APPEAR IN THE BOOKS OF THE KINGS).

The Exile and Return—About 586 BC

The period of the exile in Babylon cured the nation, once and for all, of the sin of idolatry. Historians tell us that since the Jews returned from Babylon, the monotheistic faith, along with a foundational commitment to the law, has never again been at risk in Jewish society;[31] though they continued to struggle in their allegiance to Yahweh, never again did they embrace idols.[32] In the days of the Babylonian captivity, Jeremiah prophesied in Jerusalem, while Ezekiel and Daniel comforted and strengthened the people of God in Babylon.[33] When the Persians under King Cyrus conquered the Babylonians in 539 BC, they decreed that the Jews living in captivity in Babylon could return to Jerusalem and rebuild it. Fifty thousand people returned (according to the Book of Ezra) under the leadership

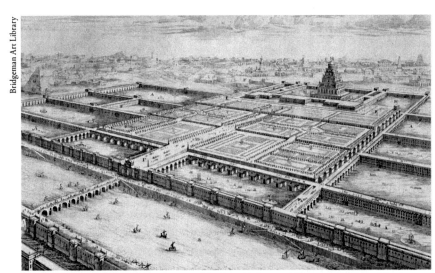

Bridgeman Art Library

This is an engraving of a panoramic view of the Royal Palace and Hanging Gardens of Ancient Babylon in the 6th century BC. In the foreground are the banks of the Euphrates River.

of three men—Zerubbabel, Ezra, and Nehemiah. They rebuilt the city, rebuilt the temple, and restored the public worship of God. (The story is told in the Book of Nehemiah).

The Hebrew people who were in captivity in Babylon (586 BC) were all from the southern kingdom of Judah. The northern kingdom of Israel had gone into captivity over a hundred years earlier (722 BC), and its people had been scattered among the nations to the north (under the control of Assyria). So the Hebrew people were now commonly identified as *Jews*, because they were from the region of *Judea*. Therefore, in the following chapters the Hebrew people will be referred to primarily as *Jews*.

The Jews who returned from exile in Babylon were encouraged by the prophets Haggai, Zechariah, and Malachi. Of the three, most theologians believe Zechariah was the greatest. He spoke much about the nation of Israel, the end of time, and the conversion of the Jewish people. Out of the pain of the Assyrian and Babylonian captivities came the prediction by the prophets of a Savior and King whom God would send to His people. More and more as the days went by, the great spiritual leaders of Israel and Judah began to describe the coming of one who would redeem His people from their sins and bring them everlasting hope. They referred to him as the promised Messiah. The term *Messiah* is a Hebrew word for "anointed one," meaning anointed of God. Its Greek equivalent is *Christos*, which is translated "Christ" in English. This messianic hope that was introduced by the prophets continued to grow as the centuries passed.[34]

The Babylonian exile brought certain changes to Jewish religious life. Because the Jews were no longer living in their land, and no longer had a Temple with its priestly functions, Judaism became a *nonsacrificial religion*. Sacrifices were no longer possible without a Temple. Therefore, the Jews began to meet in homes to read the scriptures and pray, and this became the impetus for the creation of the *Synagogue*, from which the Christian Church would later develop its pattern for worship. The *Scribes* at this point also became the priestly interpreters of the Torah.[35]

The historical record of the Hebrew Bible (Old Testament) ends at the time of Ezra, Nehemiah and Malachi, about 430 BC. The last prophetic word during the Old Testament period was uttered by Malachi. After this, the prophetic voice would be silent for four centuries.

—*The biblical record for the Exile and the Return: Ezra, Nehemiah, Esther. The Prophets in chronological order were: Daniel, Ezekiel, Lamentation, Haggai, Zechariah, Malachi.*

The Intertestamental Period—About 430 BC to 4 BC

The period of time between the Old Testament and the New Testament is known as the *Intertestamental Age*. During this 400-year period, Persia fell to the Greeks, and the Greeks fell to the Romans. Thus the Roman Empire was the world's ruling power when the promised Messiah was born and the New Testament was written.

The Period of the Persians (430 to 332 BC)

At the close of the period covered by the Old Testament, Judea was a province under Persian rule. Persia had been a world power for about 100 years, and it would continue to be so for another 100 years. During the 100-year period after the historical record of the Old Testament ends, not much is known of Jewish history. Persian rule, for the most part, was mild and tolerant,[36] but the kind rulership of the Persians gave way to the tyrannical reign of the Greeks.

The Period of the Greeks (331 to 167 BC)

Alexander the Great conquered Persia and the entire Middle East by 331 BC. He established Greek cities all over his conquered territories, and made the language, education, and culture of the Greeks the societal norms throughout the empire. This is often referred to as Hellenization. The Greek word *helenes*

Bridgeman Art Library

The Parthenon is a temple of the Greek goddess Athena Parthenos, built on the Acropolis of Athens in the 5th century BC, and is recognized as one of the world's great cultural monuments.

literally means "Greek," so to Hellenize a culture meant to Grecianize it, to give it a strong Greek influence. When Alexander the Great died his entire kingdom was divided up by his four generals, and his successor in the region of Israel (Seleucus) set out to further Hellenize the Jewish nation culturally and religiously. The last of Israel's Greek rulers was *Antiochus Epiphanes*, a man who violently hated the Jews and made a concerted effort to exterminate them and their religion.

In 168 BC Antiochus devastated Jerusalem and committed the ultimate blasphemy by sacrificing a *pig* to Zeus on the altar of the Jewish Temple. Additionally, he erected an altar to Jupiter, forbade the observance of the Jewish Sabbaths and festivals, deemed circumcision a capital offense, sold thousands of Jewish families into slavery, destroyed every copy of Scripture he could find and slaughtered anyone who was found in possession of one, and resorted to every conceivable torture to force Jews to renounce their religion.[37] During his reign, Antiochus killed over 100,000 Jews.

Until Antiochus began his barbaric rule, the Jewish people had been fairly compliant with their Greek occupiers. But in 164 BC, the high priest Hyrcanus and his five sons, led by the eldest, *Judas Maccabee*, instigated a successful revolt against Antiochus. Judas, a warrior of amazing military genius, won battle after battle against unbelievable odds. His feats have been described by historians as some of the most heroic in history.[38]

The Period of Independence (167 to 63 BC)

The Maccabean revolt ended with the purification and rededication of the Temple that had been desecrated by Antiochus, and the establishment of a newly unified kingdom that lasted approximately 100 years. This kingdom came to be known as the *Hasmonean Kingdom* after Hyrcanus' clan. The purification of the Temple is commemorated each year by Jews all around the world in a *Feast of Dedication*, more commonly known as Hanukkah. The New Testament tells us that Jesus celebrated the Feast of Dedication during His earthly ministry.[39] During the period of the Hasmonean Kingdom, political power resided with the priestly family rather than a royal monarchy.[40]

The Rule of the Romans (63 BC to Christ)

When the Romans conquered the Greeks, they extended their empire throughout Europe and the Middle East, and built upon the successes of Hellenism. In 63 BC, the land of Palestine was conquered by the Romans under Pompey, and they installed a series of rulers over the Jews. The most notable was *Herod the Great* (a non-Jew who was an Edomite). Herod worked

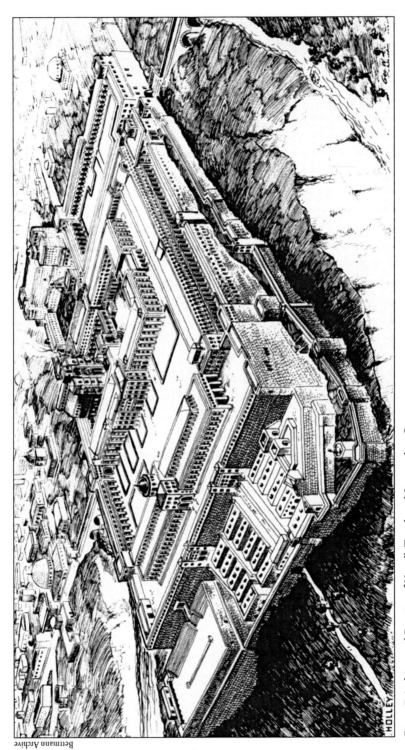

Figure 7. Architectural Drawing of Herod's Temple and Surrounding City

hard to obtain favor with the Jews, and he started a major reconstruction of the 400-year-old Temple that was built following the Babylonian captivity. The rebuilding began in 19 BC,[41] but was not completed until some 30 to 40 years after his death. The New Testament tells us that Jesus celebrated a Passover in Jerusalem in the forty-sixth year of its construction,[42] which would have been in AD 27.[43] The Temple has been described by historians as a magnificent feat of great splendor. An architectural drawing of the Temple and the surrounding city is shown in Figure 7.

The Temple was located inside a large 750-foot-square courtyard, and was built on a higher terrace; it was approximately 600 feet long and 200 feet wide. The *Women's Courtyard* was 200-foot square, and was located just to the east of the *Court of the Israelites* for men, which was 275 feet long and 200 feet wide. Inside this courtyard was the *Temple Proper* (the tallest building—150 feet long, 100 feet wide, 150 feet high), consisting of a *Holy Place* (60 feet long, 30 feet wide, 90 feet high), and a *Holy of Holies* (30 feet square, 90 feet high). The Holy Place was where the priests conducted daily rituals, and the Holy of Holies was where the High Priest would sprinkle the blood of sin offerings on the mercy seat once a year, on the Day of Atonement, to atone for his own sins and for the sins of all the people of Israel.[44] The Scriptures tell us that the entire Temple site was very impressive in appearance.[45]

When King Herod died, the Romans carved his kingdom up into several *tetrarchies*. The Judean province (tetrarch) was divided up into four parts, each with its own governor. But the relationship between the Romans and the Jews deteriorated until they came to full-blown war in the year AD 70.

Jewish life during the Roman occupation was characterized by devotion to God, messianic expectation, and party divisions.[46] The five most prominent groups in Judaism during the first century AD were the Sadducees, Pharisees, Zealots, Essenes, and the Common People.

1. **Sadducees.** The Sadducees, who numbered between 2,000 and 3,000, were the small, wealthy, aristocratic ruling class. They occupied the top of the social pyramid, and were the party of the priests.[47] Their position in society was legitimized by their priestly heritage. However, the description of the Sadducees by the first-century Jewish historian, Josephus, is rather unflattering. He defined them as elitists who have "the confidence of the wealthy alone, but no following among the populace," unlike the Pharisees who "have the support of the masses."[48] The administration of the Temple and the worship that took place there was under the direct control of the Sadducees. In addition, the high priest was a Sadducee, as was the leader of the Sanhedrin (Israel's highest court); in all likelihood

the Sadducees occupied the majority of the seats on the court. Because they were wealthy and represented the Jewish establishment, they tended to deal with the Romans in a polite and professional way. They were political collaborators and were willing to adapt to Roman rule because the status quo worked in their favor.[49] In addition, they were conservative both religiously and politically. A number of the scribes who copied the sacred texts were also Sadducees.

2. **Pharisees.** The Pharisees numbered about 6,000. They were made up of artisans and merchants,[50] and are the religious group most frequently referred to in the New Testament. In order to insure that the Jews remained faithful to the Law, the Pharisees were inclined to extend the Law to every phase of life and insist on perfect observance. They believed that every decision in life could be governed by the Torah, and they developed a system of elaborate interpretation, which later became known as the *Mishnah* and the *Talmud*.[51] By the second century BC, the Pharisees began to teach that the oral law carried the same authority as the written law of Moses.[52] They excluded "unclean" people such as tax collectors, the physically handicapped, or the emotionally disturbed from table fellowship; they rigorously observed Sabbath Law; they fasted and tithed meticulously; and they went to great lengths to occupy places of honor in the synagogues. From the time of the Maccabean revolt on, the Pharisees were the dominant political and religious force in Israel.[53] The rabbis and most of the scribes who copied the Scriptures were Pharisees.

3. **Zealots.** The Zealots were a small band of underground activists who expected the Messiah to be a warrior-king who would lead them in an uprising against Rome.[54] The awareness that the children of Israel were "God's chosen people," and that they were the benefactors of the Promised Land, was a vital ingredient in the faith of the Zealots. Since God gave Israel exclusive claim to the land, zealous Jews believed any occupation by the Romans or any other alien power violated God's design. To be illegitimately taxed by Rome for what was rightfully theirs made them embittered against the Romans. Such zeal naturally inspired a venomous hatred against those who advocated accommodation to foreign domination; thus, the priests and Sadducees were actively scorned by the Zealots. Many zealous Jews felt the Temple had been compromised, and it was their duty to defend and restore its sanctity, even if it cost them their lives.[55] They promoted independence from the Romans and carried out

terrorist activities against them. These attacks eventually led to war and the destruction of Jerusalem and the Temple in AD 70.[56]

4. ***Essenes.*** The Essenes, who numbered about 4,000, were disenchanted ascetics and apocalyptic visionaries who withdrew from general society to form communes in the wilderness near the Dead Sea at Qumran, where they waited for the Messiah and the destruction of the Romans. They believed the end of the world was near and that in the short time remaining their lives should be lived in perfect obedience to God. They believed God was about to establish His messianic kingdom on earth and would then form a new covenant with them.[57] At the onset of the war with Rome, between AD 66 and 70, the Essenes hid a vast number of canonical and non-canonical manuscripts in a series of caves on the northwest shore of the Dead Sea. When these manuscripts were discovered in 1947, the world gained a much greater understanding of first-century Judaism and early Christianity.[58] This momentous archaeological discovery is referred to as the *Dead Sea Scrolls.*

5. ***Common people.*** The vast majority of Israelites professed membership of none of the four major groups. They were called *am ha-aretz*, a Hebrew term for "people of the land." They were called such because they were not as scrupulous as some in observing many of the commandments, and were considered inferior and religiously impure by the rabbis (Pharisees). The Bible often alluded to *ordinary people* in its messianic passages, emphasizing God's concern for downtrodden people and the fact that the Messiah would eventually appear to them.[59] The *am ha-aretz* were the ordinary people the Messiah said were "like sheep without a shepherd."[60] David Rhodes, in his book *Israel in Revolution*, says the majority of the Jews in the first century were peasants who were "lukewarm about religion."[61] The Pharisees criticized some of Jesus' disciples because they ate with "unwashed hands," which made them ritually impure in the manner of the *am ha-aretz*. Jesus clearly took their side against the scribes and Pharisees,[62] and His association with lepers, the handicapped, and sinners suggests His concern for those *outside* the arena of traditional religious expression, or for those suffering exclusion and prejudice.[63]

The three most important institutions for understanding Jewish religious life in the first century were the Temple, the Synagogue, and the Scriptures. The *Temple* was the heart and soul of Jerusalem. Through the reenactment of the sacred acts God had done for the nation, both the Temple and its liturgy were made holy. The *Synagogue* was a vital force in the Hebrew religion of the first century. While full development of the synagogue did not come until after the destruction of the Temple in AD 70, the synagogue, as we read in the New Testament, provided a powerful social setting for studying the Torah, for prayer, for instruction, and for providing the people with guidance and consolation in their daily struggles and their search for salvation.[64] The Synagogue, both in Israel and in the Diaspora (a term that refers to Jews who had been scattered elsewhere throughout the world), was a vital community center. In addition to worship, the building often served as a hostel for Jewish travelers, a dining hall, a school, a cultural center, a place for the administration of community discipline or justice, and an assembly point for the elders. Social and political purposes were also served by the synagogue. The synagogue, then, had a multiple function—religious, social, and political.[65]

The *Scriptures* were central to the thought and life of every first-century Jewish community. They defined social roles, provided a moral code, and offered instruction, comfort, and encouragement. Weekly readings in the synagogues recalled Israel's story, and kept fresh the Jews' commitment to the covenant God of Israel. Knowledge of the Scriptures conferred status; the sage was deemed wise because he was learned in the Scriptures.[66] In the third century BC the Hellenized Jews of the Diaspora no longer understood Hebrew, so seventy Jewish scholars from Jerusalem went to Alexandria, Egypt (the intellectual center of the Western world) to translate the Bible into Greek; ultimately, this translation became known as the *Septuagint*—the Latin word for "seventy." The Septuagint made it possible for Greek-speaking Jews to study God's word in the vernacular of the day. On several occasions, Jesus quoted from the Septuagint.

In the first century AD, then, many roads were converging that would lead to the coming of the Messiah. The Old Testament prepares the way: with its colorful picture of God dealing with humanity; it is the story of how God raised up the Hebrew nation for the purpose of bringing into the world a Messiah (Christ) for *all* nations. Throughout history, God in His providence has been preparing the world for the coming of the Messiah. *Greece* united the civilizations of Asia, Europe, and Africa, and established one universal language; *Rome* made one empire of the whole world, and Roman roads made all parts of it accessible; and the *Diaspora* (the dispersion of the Jews among the nations) paved the way for the propagation of the good news of the coming of the Messiah in their Synagogues and their Scriptures.[67]

The term *Judaism* is often used to describe not only the faith of modern Jews, but also the Jewish faith described in the Old Testament. It is best, however, to use the term *Judaism* to refer to "the religion of the rabbis" that developed from about 200 BC and crystallized following the destruction of the Temple in AD 70. This form of Judaism should more correctly be labeled *rabbinic Judaism*. The destruction of the Temple resulted in the abolition of both sacrifices and the priesthood, so rather than being guided by priests, prophets, or kings, people accepted the *rabbis* as the authorities who established the laws and practices that had normative authority. Therefore, the office of the rabbi, as it existed during the time of Christ, did not exist during Old Testament times. Therefore Christianity should not be described as a daughter religion of Judaism, but more correctly as a sister religion. Judaism and Christianity both have their roots in the monotheistic faith of the Old Testament[68] (see Figure 8).

For centuries most devout Jews longed for the day when God would cleanse the land of foreign rulers who did not worship Him, and reestablish

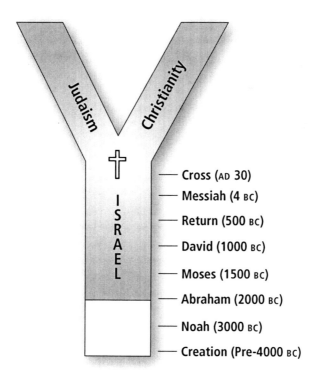

Figure 8. Common Root of Judaism and Christianity

His own rule (kingdom) through His own anointed priest or king, the Messiah.[69] This Messiah was not only to be a Savior to the Jews, but He was also to be a blessing to all people everywhere, according to God's promise to Abraham.[70] His exact identity was never given, but all through the Old Testament there were promises of a coming king who would establish God's kingdom on earth.[71] The Hebrew Bible taught that the Messiah would be a wise and ideal king who would establish justice over the entire earth, thus establishing Jewish political prestige throughout the world.[72] Bible scholars have identified nearly 100 prophecies in the Bible that give specific information about the Messiah: where He would be born, His family lineage, events of His life, His work and ministry, and the circumstances of His death.[73]

The popular Jewish expectation was that by remaining faithful to the Law, God would at some point act decisively in their behalf.[74] God had rescued them from the land of Egypt and had restored them to Israel after they were exiled in Babylon; therefore, they had reason to believe that God would continue to act for them. As the Jews became more threatened by events, especially in the first and second centuries BC, the expectation that God would perform something great was common. The "kingdom of God" became a slogan for what a new age might look like; the coming kingdom would mark the establishment of God's rule over the entire earth, a rule that would last forever.[75]

A SURVEY OF BIBLICAL HISTORY							
ADAM	NOAH	ABRAM	MOSES	DAVID	EZRA	JESUS	APOSTLES
Pre-4000 BC	3000 BC	2000 BC	1500 BC	1000 BC	500 BC	Born 6–4 BC	AD 30–90
The Early World		The Nation of Israel				The Messiah	The Early Church
Before The Flood	After The Flood	The People	The Land	The Kingdom	The Return	The Cross	The Church
Genesis			Exodus—Malachi			Matthew—John	Acts—Revelation

Table 3. A Survey of Biblical History

CHAPTER 9

THE COMING OF THE MESSIAH

My Servant will be despised and rejected by men.
He will be pierced for our transgressions.
The Lord will lay on Him the iniquity of us all,
and will be pleased to make His life a guilt offering,
in order that He may justify many.
— *ISAIAH*[1]

At the time of Jesus Judaism was enormously varied politically, religiously, and socially. It is tempting to think there was normative Judaism, very neat and tidy, and that Jesus was offering a clear alternative to it. But the truth is that there was no single Judaism at the time of Christ; people were divided on all sorts of issues, much like our country today.[2] Most Jews were loyal to the Temple, the Law, the festivals, the city of Jerusalem, and the idea of a holy land, but they differed sharply on theological issues.[3] This is the setting into which the Messiah was born.

The Birth of the Messiah—About 6 BC to 4 BC

The promised Messiah about whom the prophets spoke was born in Bethlehem of Judea around 4 BC.[4] The New Testament books of Matthew and Luke give us the most extensive accounts of the events surrounding the birth of the Messiah. We are told that the angel Gabriel went to a virgin named *Mary*, who was engaged to be married to a man named *Joseph*, and said to her:

> Greetings, Mary, you are highly favored by the Lord, and He
> is with you. His Spirit is going to come upon you, and you

will give birth to a son, and you shall call his name *Jesus,* for
He will save His people from their sins. He will be great and
will be called the Son of the Most High God, and will sit on
the throne of David forever.[5]

The name Jesus in Hebrew is *Yeshua,* meaning "Yahweh is the Savior."[6]
As was prophesied in the Old Testament, He was born of the family line of
Abraham and David.[7] When Jesus was a baby Joseph and Mary took Him
to Egypt for a brief time because King Herod, who had heard of His birth,
was trying to kill Him. After Herod's death, however, they moved to their
hometown in *Nazareth,* just west of the Sea of Galilee. There are few details
in Scripture regarding the childhood of Jesus, other than that when He was
12 or 13 years old, He conversed in the Temple with the religious leaders
and experts in the Law about the Jewish faith. The Scriptures tell us that
He showed an extraordinary understanding of the true God, and that His
answers amazed all those who heard Him.[8] So Jesus lived a normal childhood with other brothers and sisters, and was raised the son of a carpenter
in the northern region of Galilee.[9]

Most of what we know of Jesus comes from the gospels, but there are also
references to Him by other writers of the first century. The Jewish historian
Flavius Josephus, the Talmud, and other rabbinic literature all refer to Jesus.
Josephus also recounts the martyrdom of James, "the [blood] brother of Jesus
called the Christ," in AD 62.[10]

The Prophecies of the Messiah

There are nearly 100 prophecies concerning the Messiah in the Old
Testament, and many of them are very specific. When Jesus began His
earthly ministry, He not only claimed to be the long-awaited Messiah, but
He fulfilled each prophecy to the letter. No one ever accused Jesus of failing
to fulfill any of the Old Testament messianic prophecies. Unfortunately,
the religious leaders of Israel believed the Messiah would deliver them from
political oppression and establish a political kingdom. They failed to see that
the primary work of the Messiah was that He would *die for their sins,*[11] and
that He would build a *spiritual kingdom.* They were angry with Jesus because
He did not fit their idea of what their Messiah would accomplish. The result
was they crucified Him, which was exactly what was prophesied in the Old
Testament. Here are just a few of the messianic prophecies recorded in the
Old Testament:

- Born of a Virgin[12]

- Tribe of Judah[13]

- Suffer Rejection[14]

- Enter Jerusalem on a Donkey[15]

- Silent before Accusers[16]

- Beaten[17]

- Side Pierced[18]

- Bones not Broken[19]

- Cast Lots for Garments[20]

- Born in Bethlehem[21]

- Taken to Egypt[22]

- Betrayed by a Friend[23]

- Thirty Pieces of Silver[24]

- Mocked[25]

- Spit Upon[26]

- Crucified with Thieves[27]

- Buried in Rich Man's Tomb[28]

- Would Rise from the Dead[29]

The number of Old Testament passages regarded by Jews in pre-Christian times as prophetic of the Messiah is significantly larger than those commonly referred to by the Christian community. Some studies indicate that in the pre-Christian era, Jews believed the Hebrew Scriptures contained as many as 456 messianic prophecies; however, many of these could not be described as direct predictions.[30] Because the biblical scholars of ancient Israel viewed the Bible as having a strong prophetic emphasis that looked forward to the coming of the promised Messiah, they saw implicit prophetic implications in hundreds of passages. However, the Old Testament passages to which both Christians and Jews have generally attached special importance number at least 30.[31] One fascinating prophecy explicitly states that the Messiah must come from the tribe of Judah.[32] Since it was necessary that the prophecies of Scripture be verifiable (provable), then the Messiah must have been born prior to AD 70, because since that time no one would be able to *prove* that he came from the tribe of Judah. When Rome destroyed the Temple in AD 70, they destroyed all the records that identified each individual's tribe of origin. Being that no one could prove today he was of the tribe of Judah, this suggests that the Messiah must have already been born.

Bearing this in mind, if we thoroughly examine each claimant's history to determine who prophetically qualifies to be the Messiah, we find that no person in history—other than Jesus of the New Testament—has come *close* to fulfilling even a small portion of these prophecies, and Jesus fulfilled every one of them to the letter.

The Ministry of the Messiah—About AD 26 to AD 30

The writings of Matthew, Mark, Luke, and John tell us about the life and ministry of Jesus. Each of them primarily concentrates on who Jesus was as a *person*, what He *did*, and what He *said*. Their purpose was not to give us a daily diary of Jesus' activities.

When Jesus was about 30 years old, a prophet named *John the Baptist* was preaching in cities along the Jordan River, and he was urging people to prepare for the coming of the Messiah.[33] Isaiah and Malachi prophesied his mission as the "forerunner" of the Messiah;[34] that is, the scriptures foretold that there would be a prophet who would go *before* the Messiah to prepare the way for His coming.[35] This occurred in about AD 25, when John the Baptist came preaching a message of repentance, urging people to return to God and obey Him, because the "kingdom of heaven" was near.[36] His preaching attracted a great following from the entire region of Judea and the Jordan.[37]

At the age of 30 Jesus left Nazareth and went to the southern region of Judea, where John baptized Him, thus confirming John's ministry as His forerunner.[38] It was at this time that John identified Jesus as "the Lamb of God who takes away the sin of the world."[39] Jesus then began His public ministry as an itinerant preacher. After a short period of ministry in the south, He relocated north to the area around the Sea of Galilee, making Capernaum His home base; this small town was located on the north shore of the Sea of Galilee. Most of His three-year ministry was conducted while at Capernaum, though many significant events took place in the region around Galilee. Jesus gained a reputation for performing miracles, healing the sick, exorcising demons, and reaching out to the poor. He criticized and challenged the pride and legalism of the Pharisees; He astonished people by

His authoritative exposition of the Scriptures and His wisdom in piercing to the secrets of the heart; He taught forgiveness, compassion, humility, and lovingkindness to all without distinction of race or gender, a nonjudgmental attitude toward others, and a vivid hope for the rule of God in human life.

Soon, a faithful group of men began to follow Jesus and call him "teacher" or "rabbi." These men Jesus chose to become His *twelve disciples;*[40] a special group He would systematically teach and train to be His *apostles* (literally, "ones sent with a message"). They were common men from numerous walks of life—fishermen, businessmen, laborers, farmers, tax collectors, and tent makers. The twelve came to believe that Jesus was the designated Messiah of Israel, the One chosen by God to be King in a new Messianic age of peace, righteousness, and justice. They accompanied Him fulltime for three years, and during this time Jesus taught them how to serve and minister, because after His death, the work of ministry would be in their hands. As they listened to Jesus teach and preach, they began to grow in their faith, and before long Jesus gave greater focus to their training. Their commission was to call the people of Israel to *repentance*, and to tell them that the *kingdom of God* was at hand. Toward the end of His earthly ministry, Jesus revealed to them that He was the "Son of God,"[41] and that He was going to suffer a terrible death, but would be raised from the dead after three days. However, at the time, the disciples did not understand what He meant.[42] Only after Jesus was resurrected from the dead did they come to understand much of what He had taught them.[43]

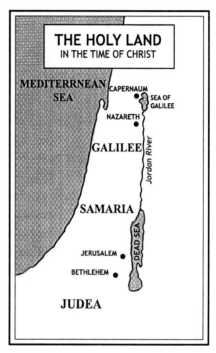

THE HOLY LAND
IN THE TIME OF CHRIST

MEDITERRNEAN SEA
CAPERNAUM
SEA OF GALILEE
NAZARETH
GALILEE
Jordan River
SAMARIA
DEAD SEA
JERUSALEM
BETHLEHEM
JUDEA

The Central Message of the Messiah

Jesus traveled from village to village teaching the truth of God's Word in private homes, on hillsides, and in synagogues, and He healed those who were hurting and suffering. He was renowned for His teaching, and for His power to perform miracles and heal the sick. Jesus taught largely through "parables" (short stories with spiritual meanings), and His teaching was revolutionary. It presupposed the universal realities that all people were basically sinful and rebellious towards God,[44] and that this produced a sickness of soul[45] that defiled the human personality.[46] Jesus therefore called everyone to *repentance,*[47] to change their heart and mind about their own sinfulness and the righteousness of God, and to submit their lives to His lordship and rule.[48] Jesus taught them to pray daily for forgiveness, and that humility and contrition were the only acceptable attitudes with which to approach God.[49]

In addition to the call for repentance, the central message the Messiah preached to the nation of Israel was of the coming of the *kingdom of God.* The expressions kingdom of God and *kingdom of heaven* are generally used synonymously, and describe the *rulership of God* on earth. A kingdom is a domain over which there is a ruler called a *king.* The Bible describes Satan as the *ruler of this world;*[50] that is, he rules over the *evil system* that governs this world, known as *worldliness.* This system is hostile toward the righteousness and rule of God. A prominent theme of the New Testament is the raging conflict between the cosmic forces of good and evil. *Hell below* has been reserved for the devil and all other enemies of righteousness,[51] and *heaven above* has been reserved for the community of the faithful.[52] Satan and his demonic spirits are in the world fighting the forces of righteousness;[53] but the good news of the Messiah is that His life, death, and resurrection has signaled the arrival of *God's rule in the world,* and the ultimate destruction of Satan and all the powers of darkness.[54]

When viewed prophetically, the kingdom of God also has reference to the establishment of a still future *kingdom of Israel* on earth that will be ruled by the Messiah; this kingdom is spoken of a number of times in the Old Testament.[55] Though it is still a future reality for the nation of Israel,[56] the Bible teaches that the rule of God exists today *within the heart* of every individual who trusts in the Messiah for his or her salvation.[57]

The Miracles of the Messiah

During the course of his four-year ministry, Jesus revealed His divine power over nature and the created order,[58] over physical and spiritual diseases,[59] over the world of spirits and demons,[60] and even over life and death.[61] Jesus also claimed to be the final authority over the eternal destiny of every human being, and He authoritatively proclaimed the laws of the kingdom of God.[62] While demonstrating that He was indeed the promised Messiah, Jesus also responded with love and compassion to those who suffered physically and spiritually.[63] He repeatedly declared that He had come to seek and to save those who were lost, and He exercised the divine prerogative of forgiving sins.[64]

As Jesus went throughout the land of Israel proclaiming the message that the kingdom of God was at hand, He performed *extraordinary miracles*. He turned water into wine,[65] cured people instantly of sickness,[66] multiplied a few fish and a few loaves of bread to feed a crowd of thousands,[67] walked on water,[68] instantly restored sight to a man born blind,[69] and even raised a man from the dead,[70] just to name a few. All of the biblical prophets *claimed* their messages were from God, but false prophets also made this claim. So God often gave His prophets *supernatural abilities* so their listeners would be able to distinguish them from false prophets. The ability to perform miracles was therefore a way of *confirming* a prophet's legitimacy;[71] that is, supernatural miracles were used by God to authenticate a messenger and substantiate His message. Interestingly enough, of all the world's religious leaders, only the Judeo-Christian prophets and apostles were *supernaturally confirmed* by genuine miracles of nature that could not possibly have been due to illusion or trickery.[72] When *Moses* was called by God, for example, he was given the power to perform miracles so that he could prove he spoke for God.[73] Likewise, *Elijah* on Mount Carmel was confirmed by fire from heaven to be a true prophet of God.[74]

Miracles were an earmark of Jesus' ministry. The Apostle John describes the first miracles Jesus performed, at a wedding at Cana in Galilee, and explains that "through them He revealed His glory, and His disciples came to *believe* and placed their faith in Him."[75] So the primary purpose of miracles is that they are *signs* that authenticate the messenger and substantiate His message. Why are miracles referred to as signs? A road sign on a metal post along the side of a highway may just be a flat metal surface with some design painted on it, but what it *means* is of far greater importance—it means what it points to. It is the same with a gift we may give to someone on a special occasion; more than just a physical object, the gift is an expression of our affection for that person. When Jesus was asked by John the Baptist if he was the Messiah, Jesus cited His miracles as *proof* of His identity. He said the following: "the blind see, the lame walk, the deaf hear, and the dead are raised to life."[76] *Nicodemus*, one of the religious leaders of Israel, acknowledged to Jesus, "Rabbi, we know you are a teacher who has come from God; for no one could perform the *miraculous signs* you are doing if God were not with him."[77] The gospel of John recounts many of the miracles that Jesus performed, and John concludes with these words: "Jesus did many other miraculous signs in the presence of His disciples, which are not recorded in this book. But these are written that you may *believe* that Jesus is the Messiah, the Son of God, and that by believing you may have life in His name."[78] The *purpose* of miracles was to authenticate the messenger and substantiate his message.

When Peter preached his first sermon after Jesus ascended into heaven, he said to his listeners: "Men of Israel, Jesus the Nazarene, a man *attested* to you by God with miracles, wonders and signs, which God did among you through Him, as you yourselves know… this Man you put to death by nailing Him to a cross, but God raised Him from the dead!"[79] That day "about 3,000 more people came to *believe* in the Messiah of Israel."[80] The apostle Paul declared that signs, wonders, and miracles were given to "*confirm* whether or not a person was a true apostle."[81] The apostles were given the ability to speak languages they had never learned;[82] to heal a man who had been crippled from birth;[83] and to raise a man from the dead.[84] Luke says the "apostles performed miraculous signs and wonders among the people."[85]

It is significant that Muhammad, the founder of the Muslim religion, acknowledged that the prophets before him were confirmed by miraculous signs,[86] yet when challenged by unbelievers, he refused to perform similar miracles.[87] Only the teachings of Scripture have been *supernaturally confirmed* to be the Word of God by special acts of God.[88] The Scriptures teach that God never asks people to believe something without any evidence. People are not supposed to blindly believe; they're to question and examine the evidence to determine whether a particular teaching is true or not.[89]

Though the Bible is very clear regarding the *purpose of miracles,* it is unfortunate that some unnecessary confusion still exists on this subject even in the Christian community. The key is to always keep in mind the *primary purpose* for which God gave miracles—if this purpose is ignored, one can come up with all kinds of spurious interpretations. For those who struggle with this teaching, it is important that they carefully read what the Scriptures have to say on this subject, rather than what some well-intentioned person might be saying. There are numerous passages in the Bible that clearly identify the *primary purpose* of miracles. I have identified more than 20 of them in this section and in the footnotes at the end of the book.[90]

The New Covenant of the Messiah

The Messiah taught His disciples about the "New Covenant" the prophets spoke of in the Old Testament;[91] God was now bringing His salvation to the world through His Son. He helped the disciples see that sin had destroyed man's intimacy with God, and as a result all of humanity was confined to a life of pain and futility. The purpose of the *New Covenant* was to restore people to an intimate relationship of forgiveness and love with God. The Old Covenant with its system of laws, and priests, and sacrifices was being supplanted by a new and better covenant. God instituted the conditional "Old Covenant"[92] to demonstrate that humanity was not capable of fulfilling the moral obligations of God's Law;[93] thus, it was preparatory for the New Covenant,[94] and actually acted as a child's tutor to lead them to the Messiah.[95] The scriptures clearly teach that obedience to God is only possible when the *heart* of man is made new and God's Spirit lives within him.[96]

The central idea behind a covenant is that it is a "promise." In 2000 BC God made a promise (covenant) to *Abraham* that He would make him a great nation.[97] Abraham's response was to "believe God," and God counted it as righteousness.[98] Some 500 years later, in fulfillment of His promise to Abraham, God confirmed His covenant with the children of Israel through *Moses*. God promised Moses He would deliver His people out of Egypt, that He would make them *His people*, and that He would be *their God*.[99] He told them He would *bless* them greatly if they obeyed Him,[100] but that He would *curse* them if they disobeyed Him.[101] The Bible teaches that *holiness* is an integral aspect of covenant blessing. If people obey God they experience blessing; if they disobey God they experience discipline. The only *conditional* aspect to the Mosaic Covenant were the blessings; the children of Israel would remain God's people even if they disobeyed Him, but they would not enjoy His blessings.[102] Salvation has always been *realized by faith* (i.e., believing God); and obedience has always been the *result of faith*. Even the New Covenant requires obedience to enjoy its blessings,[103] and discipline is always the result of disobedience.[104]

The advantage the New Covenant has over the Old Covenant is that God's mercy, love, and grace is revealed in its fullness. One of the greatest benefits of the New Covenant is that God by *His Spirit* takes up residence in the hearts of His children.[105] In doing so, He delivers them from the desire to sin;[106] He empowers them to live righteously;[107] and He transforms them into the image of Christ Himself.[108] The Holy Spirit lives *within* each believer to teach them the truth, to convict them of sin, to train them in righteousness, to empower them to live right, to comfort them when they are discouraged, to discipline them when they go astray, and to minister God's grace to them.[109] Under the Old Covenant, the believer did not have God's Spirit within him; therefore, the life of faith was a far more difficult challenge. In the Old Testament, God's Spirit only resided temporarily in the lives of a few individuals, and disobedience generally meant the withdrawal of His Spirit.[110]

The Messiah instituted the New Covenant when He celebrated the Passover with His disciples the night before He went to the cross. He said His blood was "the blood of the New Covenant" which would be shed for the forgiveness of sins, and that the cup of wine He drank with them at the Last Supper was "the New Covenant in His blood."[111] From the beginning God has required death when there has been disobedience.[112] He demonstrated through *blood sacrifice* that it was possible for another to die in the sinner's place, but that the sacrifices of innocent animals never took sin away—they only temporarily covered it.[113] Whereas the Old Covenant required repeated sacrifices year after year, the Messiah's death on the cross was a "once for all" sacrifice.[114] When the Messiah atoned for our sins through His death, the Old Testament system of animal sacrifice for sins was abolished.[115] The Messiah's blood permanently covered the believer's sins, resulting in complete forgiveness once and for all.[116] The New Testament is basically a proclamation of the *New Covenant*—God's promise of salvation through His Son—accomplished through His death on the cross.[117]

The Acceptance of the Messiah

The Apostle John wrote in his gospel that Jesus came to His own people (the Jews), but they did not *receive* Him as their Messiah[118]—the vast majority actually rejected Him—but those who did receive Him (i.e., those who *believed* in Him) He made them children of God.[119] The Bible teaches that *believing in the Messiah* (God's Son) is essential for salvation;[120] conversely, the Bible also teaches that it is impossible to please God if one chooses *not to believe in Him*.[121] Scripture is very clear when it teaches that one becomes a child of God simply by believing in the Messiah—that's what it means to have *faith*—and that there is nothing a person can do to earn salvation.[122] The essence of faith is simply *believing* what God says in His Word about His Son, and what He accomplished on the cross. The result of such faith is a loving relationship with God.[123] Jesus taught that there are only two options—belief and unbelief;[124] either one believes in the Messiah, or one does not believe in Him. The Scriptures teach that it is the sin of *unbelief* that brings eternal judgment.[125] Consider what the following scriptures have to say about *faith*:

- Hebrews 11:6—"Without *faith*, it is impossible to please God."

- Romans 1:17—"The righteous shall live by *faith*."

- Romans 3:28—"One is made righteous by *faith*, not by observing the law."

- Romans 4:3—"Abraham *believed* God, and his *faith* made him righteous."

- John 3:16—"Whoever *believes* in the Messiah, God's Son, has eternal life."

- Ephesians 2:8—"God by His grace saves us through *faith*, not by works."

- Romans 10:17—"*Faith* comes by hearing the word of God."

- 2 Corinthians 5:7—"God's children are to walk by *faith*, not by sight."

The Bible teaches that a person experiences salvation when he *believes in his heart* that God raised His Son from the dead.[126] In the Bible the words *heart* and *mind* are frequently used interchangeably.[127] Believing in salvation is not just a matter of believing something intellectually—even Satan believes the facts about the Messiah[128]—it involves a *change of heart or attitude* toward God;[129] and it involves *humility of spirit* because God only gives spiritual wisdom and salvation to those who humble themselves before Him.[130] Conversely, it is the *proud unrepentant heart* that God opposes and judges.[131]

When a person genuinely comes to faith in the Messiah, he accepts Him as his Savior.[132] The Scriptures say such a person *repents*; that is, he *changes his outlook* on how he views life. No longer does he see himself as the ruler (god) of his own life, he now submits to the God of creation and His desire for his life. No longer is life all about satisfying his own desires, it is now about pleasing God. No longer is life about loving himself, it is now about loving God.[133] Incidentally, only when a person truly believes in the Messiah does he experience a genuine change in his life; because when one repents, *God Himself* makes that person a brand new person (a brand new creation) and gives him *His* peace, joy, contentment, and love.[134]

The Rejection of the Messiah

The authority with which the Messiah taught, and His refusal to be frightened by the religious leaders, caused Him to become tremendously popular among the masses of Galilee.[135] This popularity reached its peak in the miracle of the feeding of the 5,000,[136] when the masses wanted to make Him their King.[137] He denounced the religious leaders of His day because their faith was a sham. He challenged them to *repent* of their self-righteousness and hypocrisy, and realize that the Kingdom of God is rooted in service, compassion, and love. Jesus' teachings stirred people's hearts and created instability within the religious community, something the Jewish authorities feared.[138] As a result the opposition toward Him among the Jewish rulers and religious leaders steadily grew.[139] They used every possible method and scheme to try to break His continuing influence on the masses, and to find a reason to have Him handed over to the Roman authorities for execution.[140] Jesus' popularity was an obvious threat to them.

All of the Messiah's solemn warnings addressed to His enemies, all of His penetrating teaching aimed at producing a *change of heart*, all of His benevolent works of healing the sick and even raising the dead to life,[141] only inflamed the majority of the religious leaders with greater hatred against Him.[142] But the Messiah fearlessly and relentlessly continued to expose their hypocrisy[143] as He taught in the Temple court during His fateful final days.[144] The Messiah addressed these words to a large crowd:

> The teachers of the law and the Pharisees sit in Moses' seat, so you must obey them and do everything they tell you. But, do not do what they do, for they do not practice what they preach.... Woe to you teachers of the law and Pharisees, you are hypocrites!... You are like whitewashed tombs, which look beautiful on the outside but on the inside are full of dead men's bones and every form of wickedness.... You build tombs for the prophets and decorate the graves of the righteous. And you say, "If we had lived in the days of our forefathers, we would not have taken part with them in shedding the blood of the prophets." So you testify against yourselves that you are the descendants of those who murdered the prophets!... O Jerusalem, Jerusalem, you who kill the prophets and stone those sent to you, how often I have longed to gather your children together, as a hen gathers her chicks under her wings, but you were not willing![145]

Jeremiah was God's spokesman to His people during the last days prior to the destruction of Jerusalem by Babylon in 586 BC. Repeatedly Jeremiah warned the people of impending judgment and pleaded with them to turn from their evil ways, but they despised him! The Bible records these words, "When Jeremiah finished speaking all that the Lord had commanded him to speak, the priests and the prophets and all the people seized him, saying, 'You must die!' The priests and the prophets spoke to the officials saying, 'A death sentence for this man! For he has prophesied against this city!'"[146] Over and over again the religious leaders of Israel responded to God's prophets with disdain and contempt. Why would they respond any differently when *God's greater prophet*—the Messiah—arrived?

The Pharisees and other leaders failed to acknowledge their sinfulness, and failed to recognize their Messiah, just as the prophets predicted. They weren't satisfied with what God revealed to them in the Old Testament, so they kept adding to it and revising it. They believed that their own worked-over version of the scriptures gave them the only true religion.[147] The Messiah called them back to God's original words time after time, but in spite of His careful appeal to the Scriptures, they refused to change their minds. Jesus accurately diagnosed their condition when He said, "You seek to kill Me, because My word has no place in you."[148] When a person's heart is evil, so also will be his actions.[149]

The Crucifixion of the Messiah

Just as they had scorned so many of the prophets before him, the Jewish leaders would not find Jesus acceptable either. The religious leaders were outraged that Jesus claimed authority to speak for God in a way that was superior to their own authority.[150] Their antagonistic response to Jesus was both religiously and politically motivated. The Pharisees wanted to kill Him because He spoke as an authoritative interpreter of the law, assuming more authority than even Moses.[151] They accused Him of blasphemy for claiming to be God![152] The Sadducees were afraid of Jesus because any type of messianic revival among the people would bring in the Roman legions, and the Sadducees would lose their position as the Jewish aristocracy under Roman rule. Both groups were jealous of Jesus because the people listened to Him as a true prophet of God.[153] It is interesting that the enemies of Jesus never questioned His credentials, and they never attempted to disprove His worthiness of being the Messiah on the grounds that he did not fulfill any of the messianic prophecies.

At the end of Jesus' earthly ministry, one of His twelve disciples—Judas Iscariot—betrayed Him to the hostile religious leaders of Jerusalem for thirty pieces of silver.[154] Jesus stood trial first before religious authorities and then before civil authorities. The *religious trial* was illegally convened during the night and abounded in false testimony; the whole matter was a mockery of justice.[155] The *civil trial* occurred the following morning before

Pontius Pilate, the Roman Procurator of Judea. After a brief trial Pilate said to Jesus' accusers, "I find no guilt in this man," and declared himself innocent of His blood.[156] He then sent Jesus to King Herod who mocked Him and returned Him to Pilate.[157] Pilate then capitulated to the demands of the crowd that kept shouting, "Crucify Him! Crucify Him!" Yet in the midst of all the clamor, Jesus remained calm and silent.[158]

Jesus was then taken outside the walls of Jerusalem to the hill named Golgotha, where He was nailed to a wooden cross *(crucifixion)* to die among common criminals about 9 o'clock that morning.[159] Roman crucifixion was viewed with horror and disgust in the ancient world. This form of execution was considered the most humiliating death a man could suffer. It was the penalty reserved for most dangerous criminals of the lower classes. Crosses were set up at busy, crowded road junctions and these gory exhibits were intended to act as deterrents to the masses. It was Rome's way of preserving the imperial status quo.[160] It is difficult to imagine how the Messiah of God could suffer such a cruel death, but such was the extent of the intense hatred of the religious leaders of Israel.

Though many people even today are bitter toward the Jewish people for the crucifixion of the Messiah, such bitterness is *unwarranted*. To blame the Jews is to absolve the Romans of their guilt. It was the Romans who scourged and beat and mocked Him; they were the ones who hammered the nails through His hands and His feet; and they were the ones who conducted an unfair trial. Scripture cannot be used to justify anti-Semitism. Jesus clearly stated in John's gospel, "I lay down My life on My own initiative. *No one takes it from Me.* I have the authority to lay it down, and I have the authority to take it up again."[161] Jesus also said that He could call out to His Father if He wanted to, and "He would immediately put thousands of angels at His disposal" if that was what He wanted. "But," Jesus added, "How would the Scriptures be fulfilled if I did that?"[162]

Remember, the Messiah's manner of death was *prophesied* by the prophets,[163] hundreds of years before the Romans had even invented such a method of death. The cross was *God's will* for His Son. Jesus clearly saw the cross as His calling in life;[164] as the writer of the scriptural letter to the Hebrews wrote, "because of the joy God put before Him—the salvation of millions—Jesus endured the cross."[165] Remember, to Christians, it was the *death of Christ* that purchased their salvation, so if He had not gone to the cross, they would have had no salvation. Conversely, it was the sins of *all people* throughout all generations that put Jesus on the cross, not just the sins of a few Jews. Most anti-Semitic people fail to understand that all of biblical history is Jewish, and the reason it's Jewish is because God in His wisdom ordained it such. Like it or not, Jesus was a *Jew*, all the prophets were *Jews*, and salvation is of the *Jews*.[166] God has clearly given the Jews a *special place* in His divine economy, and He commands us to *bless* them, not curse them.[167] He did not ask us for our opinion;[168] He simply asked us to honor His choice. The fact is, God in His wisdom brought salvation to the rest of the world through the *Jews*.[169]

The Resurrection of the Messiah

Following the crucifixion, the disciples were in a state of fear, confusion, and bewilderment; the Man they had followed and grown to love and believe in had been brutally executed. They were now concerned about their own survival, and were so terrified they ran and hid from their enemies behind locked doors, fearful that they would be the next to die.[170] Jesus' death plunged them into deep despair. They would not even believe the women who told them that they had just *seen* Jesus;[171] and one of the twelve disciples, Thomas, refused to believe unless he could put his hand in Jesus' side.[172] Yet on Pentecost, just a few weeks later, these same fearful men boldly and publicly preached the Resurrection.[173] What happened to totally transform them? What changed their fear into courage? They encountered the resurrected Messiah! No longer afraid to die, nearly all of them would now be *martyred* for their faith![174]

The resurrection of Jesus Christ is the central event of the New Testament, and it is the most important message of the Christian faith, because without a living Christ, the price of sin is still not fully paid, and there is no eternal life. Christianity stands or falls with the resurrection of Christ. It is the very foundation upon which the Christian faith is built;[175] without the resurrection there would be no Christianity.[176] This event not only affirms what Jesus taught,[177] but who He is—the God of creation.[178] Jesus Himself said: "I am the resurrection and the life. He who believes in Me will live, even though he dies; and whoever lives and believes in Me will never die."[179]

One of the best proofs of the resurrection was provided by Christ's enemies themselves. Fearing that Christ's disciples would steal the body and then claim that He had been raised from the dead, they went before Pontius Pilate and had him seal the tomb and place a full guard around it.[180] The typical Roman Guard consisted of four Roman soldiers,[181] and like all Roman soldiers, they were responsible with their very lives if they failed to carry out their duties.

If the resurrection did occur as the New Testament states, what other evidence is given to substantiate that this event really occurred? The Bible focuses on the reliable reports of those who were eyewitnesses of the event. Consider the following four points:[182]

1. The authors of three of the four Gospels[183] claimed to have been eyewitnesses, and Luke claims to have gathered information by speaking with those who had seen the events.

2. There is no written evidence from anyone in the first century contradicting the Gospel reports of the Resurrection; many secular historians provide abundant testimony that matches the Gospel records of Jesus' life, death, and resurrection (see chapter twelve).

3. If the Gospel accounts were all untrue, how could the apostles have had such dramatic success in their Jerusalem ministry, when the religious leaders had just demonstrated how influential they were in crucifying those who disagreed with them? And if their accounts were all fictitious, why would they have bothered to go to the trouble of writing them down in the first place? And why would they have depicted themselves in such an unflattering light, as cowardly, ambitious, slow to understand what Jesus was teaching them, needing to be chided by Jesus for their behavior?[184] Individuals perpetuating a hoax do not respond with such truthfulness and honesty. If the resurrection was a hoax, the citizens of that area would have quickly exposed the disciples' lies. Finally, why would the disciples be willing to suffer martyrdom for something they knew was not true?

4. The resurrection of Christ was confirmed by numerous eyewitnesses who saw Him alive after He died and was buried. The witnesses in most cases were independent of one another, and these appearances occurred over a period of forty days.[185] This shows us that they were not conspiring together to lie about the resurrection. Note the following fourteen recorded appearances:[186]

- Mary Magdalene[187]
- Mary the mother of James[188]
- Salome and Joanna[189]
- Several other women from Galilee[190]
- The Apostle Peter[191]

- Cleopas and the other disciple on the road to Emmaus[192]

- Ten apostles in Jerusalem[193]

- Eleven disciples, when Thomas was present a week later[194]

- Seven disciples on the Sea of Galilee[195]

- Eleven disciples on the mountain in Galilee[196]

- Five hundred people at one time[197]

- James the blood-brother of Jesus[198]

- The disciples on the Mount of Olives[199]

- The Apostle Paul[200]

If one chooses to reject the eyewitness testimonies of Christ's resurrection, one must also reject the eyewitness testimonies of nearly all other ancient events. This is because there are far more eyewitness testimonies for the resurrection of Jesus than for any other event of ancient history.[201] It is also interesting that the kinsmen and brothers of Jesus initially *did not believe Him;* they were skeptical; they thought that Jesus must have *lost His senses.*[202] But following His resurrection, their skepticism passed away and they came to believe in Him.[203] The Bible says that Jesus appeared to His blood brother James,[204] and James became one of His apostles,[205] and one of the chief leaders in the Church of Jerusalem,[206] presiding over the first Church Council that was held there.[207] James also wrote the New Testament letter that bears his name.[208] When one examines the entire body of evidence for the resurrection, it becomes increasingly difficult to impugn the integrity of the biblical narrative.

—*THE BIBLICAL RECORD FOR THE LIFE OF CHRIST:*
MATTHEW, MARK, LUKE, JOHN

The Formation of the Church—The First Century AD

After Jesus' death and resurrection, He appeared to hundreds of His followers over a period of forty days, and gave them some final instructions concerning the *kingdom of God.*[209] He told them to return to Jerusalem and wait for God's Spirit to come upon them as He had promised.[210] Jesus then commissioned His disciples to take the new message of salvation throughout the entire world.[211] After His final words with them on the Mount of Olives, He ascended before them into heaven.[212] A few days later the disciples received the Holy Spirit, who would empower them to fulfill their worldwide task.[213]

One of Jesus' twelve disciples, *Peter*, became the foremost leader of the apostles, and it was his ministry that rallied the enthusiasm of the early church. An *apostle* was a man the Messiah had chosen for special training in ministry,[214] and it was the apostles who took the lead in the formation of the early church.[215] They were empowered by the Holy Spirit to perform supernatural miracles just like the Messiah had done; thus, God was authenticating them as His messengers and substantiating their message.[216] On the day the apostles received the Holy Spirit, Peter declared the salvation of the Messiah to a large crowd in Jerusalem, and about 3,000 people *believed* the message.[217] The Church maintained a close fellowship among its members. They shared meals in their homes; they worshiped together; and they shared their wealth with those in need.[218]

It is the Book of Acts that describes the ministry of the apostles in the early church, and brings the biblical narrative to a close. In this book we see how the Messiah's message of salvation spread from Jerusalem all the way to Rome, the center of the Western world, and how God used the persecution of the new Church to spread His message all over the Roman world. As the Church continued to grow, the authorities in Jerusalem began to persecute Christians openly. When they imprisoned Peter and some of the apostles, and ordered them to stop preaching about Jesus, the apostles refused, saying, "We must obey God rather than men."[219] So they continued to preach about the resurrected Messiah even though the religious leaders beat them and threw them into prison several times. As thousands of Jews came to believe in the resurrected Messiah, violent persecution erupted in Jerusalem, and a majority of the believers fled the city.[220]

One of the greatest persecutors of Christians was a Jew named *Saul of Tarsus*. Around AD 35, he obtained letters from the Jewish leaders in Jerusalem, authorizing him to proceed to Damascus to make sure that the Christians there were imprisoned and put to death. While Saul was on his way to Damascus, the Messiah blinded him and asked him, "Why are you persecuting Me?"[221] Saul's conversation with the resurrected Christ changed his life completely; God restored his sight and he immediately began to preach about the very Jesus whose followers he had persecuted so brutally, and the Jewish leaders of Damascus drove him out of town![222] Thus Paul began a new life in which he would use his Roman name, Paul, in place of his Jewish name, Saul, and he would later lead a missionary movement that would impact the entire Roman world.

Paul's *first missionary journey* covered the ancient territory of Asia Minor (present-day Turkey near the Mediterranean coast). He and his companion Barnabas would preach in the local synagogues, and before long persecution would erupt. A group of hostile Jews stirred up a crowd in the city of Lystra who stoned Paul and left him for dead.[223] But the Lord revived Him and He continued his work. On his *second missionary journey* Paul traveled with a man named Silas, and together they established a number of churches throughout the land of Greece.[224] His *third missionary journey* covered many of the cities he had visited on his second journey, but he established a number of churches in other cities as well.[225]

When Paul returned to Jerusalem, the Jewish religious leaders imprisoned him. As he was about to be taken away, he gave an impassioned speech in defense of his Christian faith.[226] Eventually the religious authorities sent him to Rome for trial, because Paul was a Roman citizen; all Roman citizens had a right to a Roman trial. The Book of Acts ends with Paul's activities in Rome. He was under house arrest for two years, and during that time he preached to the leading Jews in Rome, and any others who would visit him.[227] Though Paul died in Rome, he had effectively spread the message of the resurrected Messiah all over the Roman Empire. The Christian community began to separate itself from the Jewish synagogue and became a distinct organization.[228] Christian disciples were now firmly entrenched throughout the Mediterranean world, and the message not only lived on but also mushroomed into a major world religion.[229]

The New Testament contains twenty-one letters that had been written to Christian communities and Christian leaders throughout the Roman world; the Apostle Paul wrote at least nine of them. These letters reflect the life, questions, and conflicts that the early Christians experienced. The message of the resurrection was central to these letters, just as it was the primary tenet of the Christian faith. It was the resurrection that demonstrated to Jesus' followers that He was the Messiah and the Lord; His teachings and His miracles pointed not only to His power over death, but also to His divinity. Through the resurrection, God tells humanity that death is not the end of things, and that He calls people everywhere into an intimate relationship with Him even before death.[230] Not only is Jesus the cornerstone of Christianity, but the person of Jesus Christ—His life, death, and resurrection—is the centerpiece of human history.

CHAPTER 10

THE TRIUNE GODHEAD

In the opinion that there is a God, there are difficulties;
but in the contrary opinion there are absurdities.
— VOLTAIRE *(TRAITÉ DE MÉTAPHYSIQUE, CHP II, 1738)[1]*

The most fundamental teaching of the Bible and Christian theology is that God existed before the universe,[2] that He created it simply by speaking it into existence,[3] and that He is ultimately in control of it.[4] This is the foundation upon which all Christian theology is built. The opening passage of the Bible reveals God as Creator and the Sovereign of heaven and earth. Christianity teaches that God *transcends* creation, that He is detached from all that He has created, and is infinitely exalted above it. In a manner that exceeds our finite understanding, God exists in His own infinite realm as the transcendent Lord over all that has been created.[5] Because God created the world, He is not defined by it, nor is He dependent on it, and this is the reason God opposes idolatry, since idolatry is making a "god" out of something God created;[6] therefore idolatry confuses the created with the Creator.[7]

From the biblical viewpoint it is generally agreed that it is impossible to give a strict definition of the transcendent God of creation. Since the God of the Bible is unique and incomparable,[8] there is nothing to which he might be measured against. The monotheistic religions of Judaism and Christianity tell us that God is beyond any human concept: "My thoughts are not your thoughts, nor are your ways my ways."[9] Because the human mind is only capable of finite understanding, it cannot attain to infinite wisdom. In the fourth century Augustine stated the case well: "All things can be said of God, yet is nothing *worthily* said of God."[10] Though God cannot adequately be described,[11] in this chapter we will attempt to describe some of the attributes He possesses. According to the Scriptures, God is known only through His *self-revelation*. Apart from this self-disclosure man could not know anything about God. Human attempts to logically explain the likelihood of His existence do not attain to the knowledge of who He is or what He is like,[12] even though the evidence for His existence is compelling. Man is simply not capable of fashioning a definition without considering the two primary ways in which God has revealed Himself; creation and scripture.

To the extent that *human reason* yields a concept of God it is related to His general or natural revelation in creation.[13] The Bible says the intricate perfection of the universe is *like a message from God* that He exists and that he cares about humanity.[14] Man must simply observe all that God has made—the perfect order of things, the rain, the sun, the climate, plant life, fruit, vegetation, animals, fish, birds—to see how God provides for him.[15] Yet as amazing as creation is, and as much as it points to God's existence, human beings need more information. Therefore, God gave humanity an intelligible communication about Himself and the world to 40 divinely chosen individuals, and He inspired them to write His personal message to humankind. This message is contained in the Bible, which is why the Bible is known as the *Word of God.* (In chapter twelve we will examine the Bible in considerable detail.)

The Bible does not present a general definition of God, rather it describes Him as He has revealed Himself in His Word, through interactions with human beings, and through the many names by which He identifies Himself.[16] According to the biblical description, God is an invisible, personal, and living Spirit, and is distinguished from all other spirits, in that He is self-existent, eternal, unchanging, transcendent, all-powerful, all-knowing, loving, just and compassionate. He also detests evil. This definition defines God by His attributes or characteristics that make God what He is. In plain English, this means that God is absolutely and completely perfect. He knows everything, He can do anything (in keeping with His holiness), and He is absolutely good.

The Attributes of God

The essence of anything, simply put, equals its *being* (substance) plus its *attributes* (inherent qualities).[17] Christianity presents God as the self-existent, eternal, personal creator God who has revealed Himself to humanity. Different religions describe God as a force, a universal principle, or as a kind of superhuman cosmic grandfather who sits on a white throne somewhere, disengaged from His lowly subjects. This is not the God of orthodox Christianity. The term "orthodox" comes from two words meaning *right belief,* and is used to describe beliefs that are in agreement with the teachings of the Bible and historic Christianity. The orthodox teachings of Scripture characterize God as possessing the following ten primary attributes:

God is Eternal

God is not confined to time; He always was and He always will be.[18] Everything that exists has a cause, and the first cause of everything is God, who Himself has no cause. The Bible says, "In the beginning GOD created the heavens and the earth."[19] In order for that to happen, He had to exist before the beginning; hence, He *transcends* or exists outside of space and time. Implied in the eternal nature of God is the idea that He is not dependent on anything for His existence, that He is self-existent; therefore, He has no origins, He is self-sufficient, He has no needs, and He depends on no one.[20] Related to God's eternal nature is the fact that God is *spirit,* not material.[21] He reinforced this idea by commanding us not to make an "idol" (a physical image) of anything in heaven or on earth and employ it in worship.[22] God wants our worship to be an inward *spiritual* experience.[23] Physical objects frequently only serve to distract the worshiper from the invisible God, and cause him to focus on that which is not God. Using idols for worship seriously compromises God because it limits Him to our human imagination. It *reduces God* to something that is finite and easily identifiable.[24]

God is Holy

The idea of holiness means God is perfect in purity and righteousness. Of all God's attributes, the Scriptures tell us that this is His most prominent one. In the Old Testament language of Hebrew, if a word is repeated twice it is deemed emphatic. When Isaiah records an angel of the Lord saying, "Holy, Holy, Holy is the LORD of hosts"[25] (note the threefold repetition), it became the strongest pronouncement in all of Scripture. So, above everything else that is said about God in Scripture, God is "HOLY!" That means there is not the slightest contamination in Him; He is absolutely pure.[26] Related to God's holiness is the fact that He is *just and righteous.* In Him there is no evil whatsoever; therefore, He is never unfair, nor does He play favorites or show partiality.[27] God's standard of holiness, righteousness, and justice is what He expects from humanity; no other standard is acceptable to Him.[28]

God is Unchanging

God does not change; that is, He is not capricious or unpredictable. He is the same yesterday, today, and forever.[29] Because God is immutable, He can be trusted. His laws do not change from day to day. Gravity does not change, the laws of physics do not change, and neither does God change. His standards and His promises are eternal.[30]

God is Creator

All created things have come into being by God.[31] He is Creator of the universe. He designed it, made it, owns it, sustains it, and He rules over it. As Creator, God is not limited by the world in terms of time or space, or by what He can do. The created order gives evidence to the fact that God is *brilliant*—His wisdom is inscrutable; *orderly*—everything that exists possesses immaculate design; *powerful*—unfathomable and beyond description; *unchanging*—the laws which govern the universe never change; *good*—provision has been made for every need of His creation; *majestic*—the created order is beautiful beyond description; *infinite*—no two things in all creation are exactly the same, therefore the diversity of such illimitable possibilities is incomprehensible; *generous*—the abundance of all that is made is endless and incalculable; and *dynamic*—the fact that life exists can only be understood as a supernatural miraculous phenomenon, no other possibility is even plausible.

God is All-Powerful

God is all-powerful and is able to do anything that is consistent with His nature; nothing is too difficult for Him; therefore, nothing can conquer Him.[32] When God created the world, He created it out of nothing![33] He did not have to begin with a box of existing materials; not even a bag full of seeds to plant and grow trees.[34] He merely "spoke" all of the celestial bodies in the universe into existence. Such power is unfathomable! When the prophet Isaiah compared all of the world's powerful nations to God, he concluded, "They are like a *drop in a bucket* before Him; like a *speck of dust* on the scales."[35] God is frequently referred to in Scripture as "God Almighty." This Hebrew expression, *El Shaddai,* emphasizes the fact that "all power" is God's power.[36] There is no power anywhere else in the universe except God's power. He can choose to delegate some of it to whomever He wants, and He can choose to stop its exercise instantaneously. Scripture says, "He does all things after the counsel of His own will."[37]

God is All-Knowing

God knows everything about everything. He knows not only the past, but also the future, and He even knows the thoughts and intentions of every heart.[38] God is infinite in His knowledge and understanding. He knows even the numbers of the hairs on every head.[39] This was a statement Jesus made just to let people know the *depth* of His knowledge; He does not just know about the big things, but even the seemingly most insignificant things.[40] He knows how many stars there are and has even named them all.[41] Science just recently discovered that there are at least 70 sextillion stars in the universe (that's a seven with 22 zeros after it!),[42] and that's only what human instrumentation is capable of counting. By the way, Isaac Asimov in his book *Isaac Asimov's Book of Facts* tells us that there are 4,891,500,000,000,000,000,000,000 "atoms" in just *one pound* of iron—that's nearly five trillion trillion![43] God not only knows the exact location and composition of each of these atoms, but He knows the precise location and composition of every single atom in the universe! God is mindful of the most remote atom in the farthest corner of space. In addition, He knows everything about each one of us and everything that will ever happen to us. There is *nothing* hidden from God. Therefore, it is not even possible to keep something "secret" from Him.[44] God knows the end from the beginning, and He knows the day the world will end. There are no surprises with God. He is all-knowing, and His magnificent plan for this world is unfolding exactly as He planned it.[45] The argument from design in creation shows us that God not only has incredible power, but He also has unfathomable intelligence.

God is Ever-Present

God is present everywhere at all times, but He is not *in* everything, which would be pantheism; that is, God is not the universe. He exists apart from His creation, yet He is always present. That means God *transcends* this finite space-mass-time continuum that He created; there is no place anywhere where He is not present.[46]

God is Love

God's holiness and justice demands that He judge imperfection and sin, but His love motivates Him to reach out to sinners in their fallen condition (even when they reject Him), and pay their penalty of death for them.[47] The central message of Christianity is that God demonstrated His love for sinful humanity by sacrificing His Son on the cross.[48] God loves humans not because *they* are lovable—the fact is they are not—but because *He* is love. That means God's Love is *unconditional* by its very nature. If it were conditional human beings would somehow have to "measure up" to be worthy of His love, which would be impossible for fallen man, so salvation had to be achieved for him. That's where the Messiah entered the picture. Because He loves humanity, He went to the cross to pay the penalty for human sin.[49] When individuals accept the Messiah as their Savior—that's faith—God makes them His children;[50] hence, they become Christians or *Christ followers*.

God is Sovereign

God is the supreme ruler and lawgiver of the universe. He controls everything and is under no external restraint whatsoever. The very idea of "God" implies sovereignty,[51] and the fact that God rules supreme throughout the universe is abundantly clear in the Scriptures.[52] He is able to accomplish His good desires, carry out His decreed will, and keep His promises. Nothing can thwart His plan.[53] There is not a single entity in the universe that exists independently of God; everything owes its existence to Him. Because *all power* belongs to God, and He is the author of everything that exists, it is unreasonable to think that there could be another power that is a threat to Him. Though every form of existence is within the scope of His dominion, God's sovereignty does not frustrate the moral freedom of His creatures. In His infinite wisdom He has seen fit to create beings with the power of choice between good and evil, yet He reigns supreme over them with perfect wisdom, grace, and justice.[54]

God is Personal

God is personal. He did not create the universe like a clock maker makes a clock, winding it up, only to let it wind down on its own. God is not distant from His creation; rather He is personally involved in it and sustains it with His power.[55] The Bible says He is personally interested in every human life and is intimately acquainted with each one.[56] The belief that God is personal is seen in the fact that God possesses attributes such as goodness, love, and compassion.[57] The Scriptures portray Him as a real person who gives Himself in reciprocal relationship to human beings as a genuine transcendent "Thou" or "Other." In the creation narrative God is described as walking, speaking, working, and resting.[58] In the New Testament, Jesus addresses God as His "Father,"[59] and speaks of Him as one who cares for His creatures,[60] and the One to whom they can turn.[61] Though God is intimately concerned with all that goes on in our lives, His word teaches that He will not respond to those who walk in sin and refuse to trust Him.[62] Related to God's personal nature is the fact that He is involved in the world and is not separate from it. This is referred to as the *immanence* of God.[63] Foundational to the principle of prayer is believing that God is immanent. As we now proceed to examine the essence of God's nature, our understanding of Him will become more defined, in particular as we see how He relates to humanity.

The Triune Nature of God

The Trinity Defined

The Bible teaches without any equivocation that GOD IS ONE,[64] but equally crucial to the Christian faith is the doctrine of the Trinity, the belief in the Triune God. This doctrine does not teach that there are three gods who exist together to make up one God; rather it asserts that God is one in essence and substance, within whom there are three distinct, coequal persons: God the Father, God the Son, and God the Holy Spirit. Each of these persons shares one divine nature, and is equally, fully, and eternally God. So the Christian faith believes that God has a Trinitarian nature. Each Person is unique, yet they share a mysterious oneness. Because God is made up of three distinct coequal persons, theologians often refer to them collectively as the Godhead. The Triune Godhead can be briefly described as follows:

1. *God the Father.* The Father is the God of creation (the Creator). This is roughly equivalent to the God of Judaism. He is the invisible creator God who is all-powerful and supernatural and beyond human understanding. He is the Lawgiver, the all-knowing, all-powerful, benevolent God depicted in the Old Testament.

2. *God the Son.* The Son is God incarnate. He is fully man and fully God at the same time. He was sent to earth by the Father to die for the sins of every human being, that they might be forgiven and reconciled to God. The deity of Christ will be discussed later in this chapter.

3. *God the Holy Spirit.* The Holy Spirit is the indwelling presence of God in the life of every believer. He is subordinate to both the Father and the Son, yet the Spirit is the One through whom they operate and minister in this world. It is the Spirit who enlightens, guides, convicts, instructs, directs, empowers, encourages, and comforts human beings. This will be discussed in greater detail later in this chapter.

The unique relationship that exists within the Godhead is frequently referred to as the *Trinity.* Christians are to be baptized in the name of the

Father, the Son, and the Holy Spirit;[65] the apostle Paul invoked a divine blessing incorporating all three;[66] in his teaching he expounded on doctrinal issues mentioning all three;[67] and the apostle Peter made reference to all three in one of his salutations.[68] Though the Triune God is not a concept that is easily understood, it is the unequivocal teaching of Scripture.

The Trinity Misunderstood

The concept of the Triune Godhead admittedly is *difficult* to understand. The Scriptures teach that the Triune God is made up of three distinct persons who are united together in a *mysterious oneness*. The limited ability of human understanding makes this concept impossible to fully grasp. Therefore, objections to this doctrine come from a rationalism that insists on dissolving this mystery into human understanding, by thinking of the oneness and threeness in terms of mathematics and human personality.[69] In the Western world, when a person is unable to completely wrap his mind around a concept, red flags go up and he begins to proceed very cautiously. We all have a natural tendency to question and probe until our understanding is satisfied. We like answers to all of our questions. We even like answers to the perplexing questions of life, so that we can neatly package our *system of beliefs*. But trying to put the transcendent, infinite, eternal God of the universe into a nice little package just is not possible; certainly not with our small, finite, temporal minds. Human beings have a difficult time understanding themselves, so to insist on fully comprehending the God of creation is both unreasonable and inconsistent with the laws of logic. Though the biblical evidence for the Triune God is compelling, no amount of evidence will convince the skeptic who demands that He see, touch, and hear everything.

Non-Christians often accuse Christians of believing in three different, separate gods, but this is completely antithetical to what the Bible teaches on the doctrine of the Trinity. Some actually have propounded the teaching that God the Father and His goddess wife had a son whom they named Jesus. The founder of Islam, Muhammad, believed that Christianity was a perverse religion because "its god" (Jesus) was born when God the Father (Creator) had sexual relations with a human named Mary (the mother of Jesus). There are even a few highly unorthodox *Christian cults* that embrace similar teachings. But these are all *gross misunderstandings* of the Christian doctrine of the Trinity, at odds with the clear teaching of Scripture. Throughout the centuries erroneous doctrines would surface when heretical teachers would claim that *their new ideas* were the true teachings of Christianity. This would result in some Christians who were not grounded in the Scriptures becoming confused.[70] Historically the Christian Church handled such problems by calling their leaders together to *refute unbiblical teaching*. One such teaching denied the deity of Christ, so the church held a council at Necea (Turkey) in AD 325 that confirmed the biblical position that *Jesus* is of the same essence and substance as the Father. Later, another erroneous teaching arose that questioned the deity of the Holy Spirit. A church council was held at Constantinople (present-day Istanbul, in Turkey) in AD 381 which confirmed the biblical teaching that the *Holy Spirit* is of the same essence and substance as the Father.

The Trinity According to Scripture

Although the doctrine of the Trinity finds its clearest expression in the New Testament, the *plurality* of the Godhead is also found in the Old Testament. The most common name used for God in the Old Testament is the Hebrew word *Elohim,*[71] which emphasizes the fullness of divine power. *Elohim* is the plural form of the root word *El*, the Old Testament term that generally serves to contrast the human and the divine. In Scripture the word *Elohim* is always construed in the singular when it denotes the true God; in the Pentateuch (the first five books of the Bible) it signifies God as the transcendent being, the Creator of the universe.[72] In addition to the fact that the most common Old Testament name for God is plural, there are a number of instances in the Old Testament in which *plural pronouns* as well as *plural verbs* for God are used.[73] The use of such plural designations certainly suggests that God is a *plurality*, and points in a Trinitarian direction.[74] For example, in the creation narrative, God says, "Let *us* make man in *our* image, according to *our* likeness."[75] In addition, God frequently speaks of "His Spirit" in the Old Testament,[76] and the three persons of the Godhead is noted by the prophet Isaiah in a passage where the speaker is obviously God: "He *[Jesus Christ]* has been sent both by the Lord God *[the Father]* and by His Spirit *[the Holy Spirit]*."[77] Though the Old Testament is not as explicit as the New Testament on the doctrine of the Trinity, these references clearly point to it.

In the New Testament, the doctrine of the Triune God is clearly taught in numerous passages. In the gospel of John, Jesus says, "When the Helper *[the Holy Spirit]* comes, whom I *[Jesus]* will send to you from the Father, He *[the Holy Spirit]* will bear witness of Me *[Jesus]*."[78] It should be noted that each of the attributes of God, mentioned earlier in this chapter, apply equally to all three Persons of the Trinity (see Table 4).

COMMON ATTRIBUTES OF EACH PERSON OF THE TRINITY			
ATTRIBUTE	GOD THE FATHER	GOD THE SON	GOD THE SPIRIT
Eternal	John 5:26	John 17:5	Hebrews 9:14
Holy	Psalm 99:5	1 Peter 2:22	Romans 1:4
Unchangeable	James 1:17	Hebrews 13:8	John 14:16
Creator	Genesis 1:1	Colossians 1:16–18	Genesis 1:2
All-Powerful	Job 42:1–2	Matthew 28:20	Luke 1:35
All-Knowing	Psalm 139:6	John 2:24	1 Corinth. 2:10–11
Ever-Present	Jeremiah 23:24	Matthew 28:20	Psalm 139:7–10
Loving	Psalm 25:6	1 John 3:16	Romans 14:17
Sovereign	Psalm 103:19	1 Timothy 6:15	Acts 5:3–5
Personal	Psalm 139:1–4	Matthew 11:28	John 14:26

Table 4. Common Attributes of Each Person of the Trinity

The Trinity Illustrated

The concept of the Trinity is a tough one to grasp. Perhaps by looking at other "three-in-one" concepts, the idea will not seem so impossible. The universe in which we live in a sense is a TRI-UNIVERSE; it consists of *Space, Time* and *Matter*. It's not part space, part time, and part matter—it is all space, all time, and all matter. The universe is not a triad of three distinct entities which, when added together, comprise the whole; so in that sense it is *not* like an egg that has a shell, a yolk, and egg white—three distinct parts making up the whole. The universe is a true trinity because each of the three are themselves the whole. Creation scientist Henry Morris compares the Trinity with the universe by pointing out that each of the three major elements of the universe is actually comprised of three components:[79]

1. **Time**. Time can be viewed as *Past, Present,* or *Future*; all three are distinctly different. The past is distinct from the present, which is distinct from the future, which is distinct from the past; yet they all share the same nature; they are all *time.*

2. **Space**. Space can be viewed dimensionally as *Height, Width,* or *Depth*; all three are distinctly different. Height is distinct from width, which is distinct from depth, which is distinct from height; yet they all share the same nature; they are all *space.*

3. **Matter**. Matter can be viewed as a *Solid,* a *Liquid,* or a *Gas*; all three are distinctly different. The solid is not the same as liquid, which is not

the same as gas, which is not the same as solid; yet they all share the same nature; they are all *matter.* It should be noted that matter includes energy, and matter/energy permeates all space and time.[80]

Perhaps it would be helpful to contrast the Triune Godhead with the triune nature of a human being. Just as the Godhead involves the *Father,* the *Son,* and the *Holy Spirit,* a human being has a *Body,* a *Soul,* and a *Spirit.* Therefore, we can think of a human being as having three distinct elements, yet collectively the human being is one. In addition, people have three aspects to their being: *physical, psychological,* and *spiritual.* Though they possess all three aspects, they are one. Another way to view the human being is that he *thinks* and *feels* and *acts*; each of these features is distinct, yet they are one.

The most graphic way to illustrate the Trinity would be that of a *triangle* with three sides (see Figure 9). Just as there are three distinct corners in one triangle, so the Godhead consists of three distinct persons and one essence or nature. Though each corner of a triangle is distinct, they share one essence. The universe and humanity each demonstrate triune natures. That does not mean a person's truine nature can be directly correlated with that of the Triune God, but it might be fair to suggest that these trinitarian concepts are the "fingerprints" of God upon His creation.

Figure 9. An Illustration of the Trinity

The Trinity Differentiated

The idea that Jesus is the Son of God does not mean that He is *inferior* to God the Father. The biblical idea of the "Sonship" of God focuses on His position or role in relation to that of the Father. Jesus' position as the Son of God is a *relational* one and a *functional* one. He is equal to the Father in *deity,*[81] but He is lesser in His *role* or *function.*[82] The difference between *essence* and *function* is an important one.[83] The idea of *equality in nature* and *difference in function* is found in every institution of society. God designed society in such a way that for it to operate optimally it would require authoritative positions and subordinate positions. Citizens are to be subordinate to government leaders; students are to be subordinate to teachers; children are to be subordinate to parents; employees are to be subordinate to employers; ballplayers are to be subordinate to coaches; workers are to be subordinate to supervisors; and so on. This is the way God meant societies to operate, with different people having different roles or functions. No one in society is always in the position of authority. Even the president of the United States has to accept the authority of a rookie police officer when driving on public streets. There are a number of things he cannot do without breaking the law. Nearly every adult is in some position where his role is authoritative, and some position where his role is subordinate. The subordinate functions or roles we occupy in society should not be seen as degrading or inferior, but as the way God designed society to operate; all human beings are *equal* in essence, but their roles and functions differ. If we all refused to be subordinate to anyone in society, the result would be anarchy. The reason people rebel against society's roles or functions is either they have been victimized in some way, or they have such an inordinate degree of pride that they are determined to fight the system.

Obviously in our fallen world there may be times when we either misuse our authority, or become a victim of its wrongful use by others. If we do become a victim, how are we to respond? Take the law into our own hands and become judge, jury, and executioner? No. The Bible tells us that God has established all authorities for our good, and to resist them is to oppose God.[84] When a person becomes a victim, he is to take his case to a higher authority; that's the way society was meant to function. The Scriptures teach us that life is not always fair, that sometimes we will be mistreated. The key is to respond in the right manner. God says in His Word, "Vengeance is Mine; I will repay."[85] God blesses those who do the right thing.[86]

Just as each of us have been given various roles in which we are to function, so also the Son of God is in a subordinate role to God the Father;[87] yet He is equally God even though the Father occupies a position or function that is greater than the Son's.[88]

The Deity of Christ

The gospel of John begins by declaring the deity of Christ. It reads, "In the beginning was the Word, and the Word was with God, and the *Word was God.* He was in the beginning with God. All things came into being through Him, and apart from Him nothing came into being that has come into being.... And the Word became flesh and dwelt among us, and we saw His glory, the glory of Him who came from the Father."[89] The term "Word" (*logos* in Greek) was widely used in the philosophical teaching of the Greeks and the Jews of the first century.[90] John here employs it as an appellation for the Messiah *(Christ)*. In this passage John says the Word *(Christ)* was in the beginning with God *(the Father)*; thus the Word *(Christ)* is eternal. John then says that the Word *(Christ)* was God, and the Word *(Christ)* created all things. According to the Scriptures the Word *(Christ)* was the agent of creation in conjunction with the Father and the Spirit.[91] It was the Word of Life *(Jesus Christ)* that the disciples saw and bore witness to,[92] and it was His salvation they proclaimed throughout the Roman world.[93]

The Claims of Christ

Jesus claimed to be "God in human form." He did not say He was *like* a god; He said that He *was* God.[94] The Bible tell us that Jesus claimed to be God on several occasions. He said:[95]

- To *know* Him was to know God.[96]

- To *see* Him was to see God.[97]

- To *believe* in Him was to believe in God.[98]

- To *hate* Him was to hate God.[99]

- To *receive* Him was to receive God.[100]

- To *honor* Him was to honor God.[101]

The night before Jesus went to the cross, He shared a special meal with His disciples, and told them He would be leaving them. This was troubling to them, so one of the apostles said to Jesus, "Lord show us the Father, and that will be enough for us." Jesus responded, "Philip, do not you know Me, even after I have been among you such a long time? Anyone who has seen *Me* has seen the *Father*. Do you not believe that I am in the Father, and that the Father is in Me?"[102] The mystery of the complex nature of the Godhead is not easily understood or grasped; even Jesus' disciples struggled to understand it, yet they came to trust Him fully.

It is interesting how many people deny the divinity of Christ, yet believe He may have been one of the most wonderful people who ever lived. The irony of such a position is perplexing, because one who is merely a good human being does not go around claiming to be God. Likewise, the actions of Christ are also inconsistent with the theory that He was simply a good man. For example, He allowed people to worship Him with a reverence that is only appropriately directed to God.[103] Additionally, Jesus claimed to have authority to forgive sins, and He even forgave people for sins they had committed against other people. This only makes sense if He really was the God whose laws were broken and whose love was wounded. Therefore, the view that Jesus was nothing more than a good man simply ignores the facts.[104] It is important to remember that Jesus worked within the context of a strict Jewish monotheism, a context in which people who understood His meaning sought to kill Him for blasphemy. The British author C. S. Lewis put it this way, "A man who was merely a man and said the sort of things Jesus said would not be a great moral teacher. He would either be a lunatic—on a level with the man who says he is a poached egg—or else he would be the Devil of Hell.... Either this man was, and is, the Son of God; or else a madman or something worse."[105]

The teachings of Christ have caused some to misrepresent and distort His teachings by implying that He meant something different from what He said. Some do so out of ignorance, but others do so because they reject what Christ taught. As a result they use all kinds of contrivances to make the text say what they want it to say. Interestingly enough, the people of the first century (the audience Jesus was addressing) knew exactly what He meant. His enemies also understood Him perfectly, and they sought to kill Him because of His claims.[106] Jesus' followers also understood Him; so much so that they were willing to die for Him. History tells us that all but one of the twelve apostles were martyred for their belief in the deity of Christ. They believed He was *God incarnate,* God in human form—in Latin *incarnate* literally means "in the flesh." And that is exactly what the Bible teaches: "God became *flesh* and dwelt among us, and we beheld His glory."[107] The New Testament writers repeatedly declared that Jesus indeed was God:

- "When Thomas saw Jesus' wounds, he cried out, *'My Lord and my God.'*"[108]

- "He is the *image* of the invisible God."[109]

- "In Christ the *fullness of God* lives in a human body."[110]

- "You [John] will go before the *Lord* [Jesus] to prepare His ways."[111]

- "Christ is the *exact representation* of His nature."[112]

- "Thy throne, *O God* is forever" it says of Jesus.[113]

- "Our great *God and Savior*, Christ Jesus."[114]

- "The righteousness of our *God and Savior*, Jesus Christ."[115]

- "Are You the Messiah?" Jesus responded, *"I am."*[116]

- "The *living God* (Jesus Christ) who is the Savior of all men."[117]

- "Jesus existed in the *very nature* of God."[118]

- "Jesus Christ is the *true God* and eternal life."[119]

According to scripture, Jesus was recognized as having a "divine nature" by a number of individuals and supernatural beings. *Angels*—at Christ's birth, the angel Gabriel told Mary she would give birth to the Son of God.[120] *God the Father*—when Jesus was baptized in the Jordan river, the Father declared, "This is My beloved Son."[121] *Satan and Demons*—knowing that Jesus was God's Son, the devil challenged Him to use His supernatural powers to bypass God the Father's plan; likewise, when the demons were confronted with Jesus they shrieked that He was the Son of God.[122] *Disciples*—when they saw Jesus walk on water in the midst of a storm, they worshiped Him and concluded He was the Son of God; and later Peter declared, "You are the Christ, the Son of the living God."[123] *Martha*—when Jesus raised Lazarus from the dead, his sister Martha said, "I believe that you are the Christ, the Son of God."[124]

The Appellations of Christ

The Bible shows that the exclusive names and titles that are applied to God the Father are also applied to Jesus. By applying these appellations to both the Father and Jesus, the Scriptures reveal their common identity as God. Jesus and the Father are both identified as:[125]

1. The Creator[126]

2. The First and the Last[127]

3. God[128]

4. The Savior[129]

5. The Shepherd[130]

6. The I AM[131]

7. The Forgiver of Sins[132]

8. Addressed in Prayer[133]

9. Confessed as Lord[134]

10. Worshiped by Angels[135]

11. Worshiped by Men[136]

12. Unchanging[137]

13. Eternal[138]

14. All-Knowing[139]

15. Present Everywhere[140]

16. All-Powerful[141]

The Miracles of Christ

Thousands of people saw Jesus' miraculous works, yet many still refused to believe in Him. The religious leaders of the day had seen many of His miracles, yet they were bent on killing Him because He did not conform to their system of religious thinking. Jesus offered several proofs of His divine nature to counter their unbelief. He performed incredible miracles that defied nature; He made sick people well; He made blind people see; He made deaf people hear; He made the lame people walk; and He even raised people from the dead.

On one occasion Jesus healed a man on the Sabbath who was born blind.[142] The Pharisees responded, "This man is not from God, because He does not keep the Sabbath." But others said, "How can a sinner perform such miraculous signs?" The Pharisees simply appealed to their own authority by saying that they "knew Jesus was a sinner." So they began questioning the man who was healed and he replied to them, "Whether He is a sinner or not, I do not know. But one thing I do know, I was blind and now I see." The healed man then began questioning the wisdom of the religious leaders, who in turn reviled and denigrated the man: "How dare you lecture us! You've been a sinner ever since you were born! Who do you think you are trying to teach us?" At this point it became clear that the religious leaders were losing some of their influence. The text goes on to say that when the Pharisees later confronted Jesus about what had happened, Jesus accused *them* of "being blind," which really infuriated them. So Jesus said to them, "If you were blind, you would have no sin; but *because you say you see*, your sin remains." The problem with this group of Pharisees was that they failed to acknowledge their blindness; they failed to admit that they *could not see* or that they did not understand. As a result, their *pride* was the impediment that kept them from recognizing Jesus as the Messiah.[143] If they would have admitted their blindness, Jesus would have *opened the eyes of their hearts*, and they would have seen and recognized the true Messiah.[144]

How Other Great Spiritual Leaders Compare with Christ

When we explore the great religious traditions of the world, we are introduced to a number of individuals who impressed their contemporaries with the *other-centeredness* of their way of life. They lived lives of remarkable courage, compassion, and sacrifice. *Gautama the Buddha* is an outstanding example from Asia. But such individuals make no grand claims for themselves, other than to point people to the truth. One noted authority on Buddhism observes that the Buddha saw himself as simply preaching the Dharma. Likewise, in Islam, *Muhammad* is simply a prophet, supposedly the final one, in a long tradition of prophets and messengers commissioned by God to turn people away from idols. Dr. Vinoth Ramachandra says in his book *Faiths in Conflict*, "In all these cases there is no call to personal allegiance, no claim to be communicating anything other than a word from God or an insight into ultimate reality."[145] *Jesus Christ*, however, did not just come to this world to tell people how to live a good life; He came to redeem sinful humanity and reconcile them to God.

The major difference between Jesus, Buddha, Confucius, Muhammad, and Hare Krishna is that Jesus substantiated through His miracles that everything He said and did was true. No other religious leader has ever substantiated His claims with supernatural miracles the way Jesus did.[146] In contrast to those spiritual teachers who lived moral lives and pointed people to the truth, are those who made *self-centered claims,* but these claims did not impress for very long. As Ramachandra remarks:

> Not only have the Caesars, the Hitlers, the Stalins, the Idi Amins, [and the Saddam Husseins] of the world disappeared into the mists of history, their megalomania led them into forms of brutality and self-aggrandizement which seemed to fit quite naturally with the claims they made for themselves. It is here also that Jesus stands out as unique. One may search all the religious traditions of humankind, and indeed all the great literature of humankind, and still fail to find one like Jesus, who makes seemingly the most arrogant claims

concerning Himself, and yet lives in the most humble and selfless manner conceivable. Jesus of Nazareth simply boggles our imaginations.[147]

The Holy Spirit

The Spirit of God Defined

The third person of the Trinity is referred to in Scripture as the Holy Spirit, God, the Spirit of God, the Spirit of Christ, the Spirit of the Lord, and most often just as the Spirit. The Scriptures explicitly ascribe a distinct personality to the Holy Spirit, just as it does to the Father and the Son.[148] The attributes of personality, self-consciousness, and freedom are ascribed to the Holy Spirit,[149] as are divine attributes such as knowledge, sovereignty, and eternity.[150] The divine works of creation and the new birth are also attributed to the Spirit,[151] and worship and homage are directed to Him.[152] The Holy Spirit is *subordinate* to both the Father and the Son, as He is sent from them, yet they operate through Him.[153]

The word for "spirit" in both the Old Testament language of Hebrew *(ruah)* and the New Testament language of Greek *(pneuma)* are similar. They both stem from words meaning "breath" or "wind"; therefore, ancient cultures connected the word "spirit" with *unseen spiritual forces*. Thus it is understandable that God's creative word[154] is closely akin to God's creative breath.[155] God's Spirit is the *life principle* of both men and animals.[156] The *personhood* of the Holy Spirit is emphasized throughout Scripture by its constant usage of the masculine pronoun;[157] the Spirit is never referred to as an impersonal "it" or "force."

The Spirit of God in the Old Testament

In the Old Testament the Holy Spirit was active in the creation of the universe.[158] He inspired the writing of the Scriptures,[159] and He is generally associated with carrying out the mighty acts and deeds of the Lord.[160] His primary function in the Old Testament was as the motivating force that inspired the prophets and revealed God's message. This was most often expressed by the prophets as, "Thus says the Lord."[161] The general implication in the Old Testament is that the Spirit of God inspired the prophets.

As we noted earlier in this chapter, the Holy Spirit possesses the same attributes as the Father and the Son. In addition, He performs the same actions as the other members of the Godhead;[162] the names of God are ascribed to

Him;[163] miracles are ascribed to Him;[164] and worship is required and ascribed to Him.[165] One of the most profound prophecies in the Old Testament was when the prophets foretold of a time when God would actually put "His Spirit" into the hearts of His people. Ezekiel wrote:

> Thus says the Lord, "It is not for your sake, O house of Israel, that I am going to act, but for the sake of My holy name, which you have profaned among the nations where you have gone.… I am going to take you out of those nations and bring you back to your own land. I will give you a new heart and put a new spirit in you; I will remove your heart of stone from you, and give you a heart of flesh. And I will put *My Spirit* in you and cause you to walk in My ways."[166]

Though the Holy Spirit was instrumental in carrying out the will of God in Old Testament times, it was not common for Him to take up residence *within* a person. There were occasions when He did, but these were rare, and His residency generally was not permanent.[167] The outpouring of God's Spirit prophesied by Isaiah, Ezekiel, and Joel was to be of a permanent nature, and this prophecy was fulfilled after the Messiah's New Testament ministry was completed.[168]

The Spirit of God in the New Testament

The prophet Joel prophesied that God would pour out His Spirit, not just on the house of Israel, but on "all mankind"[169]—on both Jews and Gentiles. No longer would religious leaders be permitted to use the law as a means of oppressing the ignorant and the disenfranchised of society;[170] Jesus would send His Spirit to live within them and guide them into all truth.[171] Jesus preached this good news to the poor, the captive, and the blind; He told them that the new law of life would henceforth be written on their hearts.[172] As a result, all of the abuses of Scripture could now cease, because of the presence and power of the indwelling Spirit.[173]

In the New Testament we are told that the Holy Spirit directed and governed the earthly ministry of the Messiah;[174] the Spirit of God came upon Him to bring the good news to the afflicted and the brokenhearted, and to proclaim the favorable year of the Lord.[175] Following His ascension into heaven, Jesus would send the Holy Spirit as a Comforter and Helper to His children by actually having Him *live within them.*[176] One of His primary functions would be to *guide believers* in their understanding of the truth,[177] and to confirm in their hearts who Jesus really is, that they might testify about Him to the world.[178] The Spirit was also sent to direct the mission of the church as it proclaims Christ to the world.[179]

The primary work of the Holy Spirit is set forth by the apostle John in his gospel. He writes: "When the Helper comes, whom I will send to you, that is the Spirit of truth, He will guide you into all the truth; for He will not speak on His own authority, but whatever He hears He will speak, and He will declare to you the things that are to come. He will glorify Me (Jesus), and He will bear witness of Me."[180] It is important to note that the Holy Spirit does not speak about Himself; He speaks about Jesus. The emphasis in Christianity is on the person of Jesus Christ, not on the Holy Spirit. That means any emphasis that detracts from the person of Christ is not of the Spirit, because the Spirit does not draw attention to Himself. As important as the Holy Spirit is, He is never to preempt the place of Christ in the mind of the Christian. On the other hand, wherever Jesus Christ is exalted, there God's Spirit is at work.[181] The ministry of the Holy Spirit, according to the New Testament, can be summarized as follows:

1. *He enlightens every believer*—Christians are given the responsibility of sharing the truth of Scripture with others, but it is the Holy Spirit who brings it to life in the listener; He illumines their minds that they might understand, and opens the eyes of their hearts that they might see.[182] This gift of God's grace is poured out upon those who are humble before Him.[183]

2. *He convicts of sin and righteousness and judgment*—It is only by the work of God's Spirit that a person is convinced of his own sinfulness and the dangers of continuing to live a life of sin. It is God's Spirit who convicts people of their faulty views of Jesus and His work of love on the cross.[184]

3. *He gives new life to every believer*—When a person believes in Christ, a spiritual transformation takes place. He is born again—born from above—and becomes a brand new creation. This rebirth is accomplished by the Holy Spirit and results in a believer becoming God's child.[185]

4. *He baptizes every believer into the body of Christ*—When a person comes to believe in Christ, God's Spirit baptizes (places) him into the body of Christ; that is, he becomes an actual member of God's family, the Church, and as such becomes a brother or sister in Christ, a member of the household of God.[186]

5. *He dwells within every believer*—When a person becomes a believer, God's Spirit takes up permanent residency within that person. The Bible says if the Spirit does not live within a person, he does not belong to Christ.[187] Sometimes the Bible refers to the Holy Spirit being in a person as Christ being in that person, because the Holy Spirit is the Spirit of Christ.[188] When God's Spirit takes up residency in a person's life, He confirms in that person's heart that he or she is truly a child of God.[189] So God dwells within every member of the mystical body of Christ, known as the Church. Thus the Church is the dwelling place of God on earth.[190]

6. *He instructs every believer*—When a person becomes a believer, God's Spirit teaches and guides him in the truth, teaches him about the person of Christ,[191] comforts and helps him during times of trial and difficulty,[192] and confirms the teachings of Scripture regarding those things which are still to come.[193]

7. *Every believer is sealed in Christ with the promised Holy Spirit*—The word "sealed" indicates security and permanence.[194] As soon as a person comes to believe in Christ, he is permanently sealed with the Holy Spirit.[195] The Holy Spirit is referred to as the down payment or the guarantee of the believer's future eternal inheritance;[196] thus suggesting there is much more to come.[197] In essence, the deposit of the Holy Spirit is a little bit of heaven here and now with a whole lot more to come later.[198]

8. *He empowers every believer to do God's will*—The prophet Ezekiel prophesied that God would give His people a new heart and would put His Spirit within them that they might "walk in His ways."[199] God knew that fallen humanity needed a new heart and the power of His indwelling Spirit if they were to live in a way that was pleasing to Him. If the believer follows the promptings of the Spirit in his heart, he will live a life of obedience to God rather than living by the dictates of his fallen nature.[200]

9. *He enables every believer to serve others by gifting them for this purpose*—All families have needs, and only when each person genuinely cares for the other members of the family, and is responsible in carrying out his or her own assigned duties, will that family be healthy and productive. In the body of Christ the Holy Spirit encourages each person to build up the others within the body (as opposed to tearing them down), that they might become mature in their faith and love.[201] The Spirit gives special abilities (gifts) to every believer that they might accomplish this task.[202]

10. *He produces fruit in the life of every believer*—As the believer obeys the leading of the Spirit in his life, God develops that person's character, making it like Christ's.[203] Human beings were created in the image of God,[204] but when they fell into sin they no longer reflected His image. It was God's purpose through the cross to forgive man's sinfulness and reconcile him back to God, thus reestablishing that lost image or likeness.[205] This transformation occurs as God's Spirit works in the believer's heart and mind through His Word.[206] When a believer lives according to the Spirit's leading, his life will bear the fruit of love, joy, peace, patience, kindness, goodness, faithfulness, gentleness, and self-control.[207]

As this chapter has demonstrated, the Trinitarian doctrine of God is central to orthodox Christianity and the teaching of Scripture. This doctrine developed out of the church's desire to safeguard the biblical truths of the transcendent God who entered human history to redeem and share Himself with His creatures.[208]

CHAPTER 11

CHRISTIAN BELIEFS AND PRACTICES

A person can do many things against his will;
but belief is possible only in one who is willing.
— ST. AUGUSTINE *(TRACTATE XXVI IN JOANN)*[1]

Whereas other religions are primarily *ritual-oriented,* Christianity is a *belief-oriented* religion; therefore, it tends to put more importance on proper belief than other religions. The term "orthodox" comes from two words meaning "right belief," and is used to describe beliefs that are in agreement with historical biblical Christianity. A Christian is someone who accepts the major orthodox beliefs of the Christian faith. The preeminent belief in Christianity is that Jesus is the Messiah—*God incarnate*—who came to this world to die for the sins of humanity. The Bible teaches that if a person does not believe this, he is not a Christian. This is unlike the relationship between Jews and Judaism. A person is Jewish by birth, regardless of what he or she might believe. Jews who do not believe in the subscriptions of Judaism are referred to as secular Jews, but there is no such thing as a secular Christian; if one does not believe that Jesus is the Messiah, that person is not a Christian,[2] even though he might claim to be one. According to orthodox Christianity, a Christian is one who believes in the Messiah and the work He did on the cross to reconcile him to God. So the heart of Christianity is not belief in an *idea,* but belief in the *person* of the Messiah Jesus.

Though orthodox Christianity is united in its belief about the Messiah, there is great diversity in its worship and leadership styles. For instance, there are two traditional ways in which believers proclaim the Christ of Christianity. First, there is *proclamation* through the *preaching of the Word*, which finds its expression both in evangelism and the practice of worship;[3] and second, there is the *memorializing* of these truths through the *ordinance of Communion.*[4] Reformed Christianity (Presbyterians, Baptists, Methodists, Evangelical Free, Assemblies of God, Congregational, et al.) places a stronger emphasis on the proclamation of the Word, with its insistence on the reading and preaching of scripture, evangelizing, and singing; whereas Eastern Orthodoxy and Roman Catholicism give greater emphasis to the Eucharist (Communion) because they place a greater emphasis on the sacrament, and their worship is more liturgical and iconic in nature. Some church bodies such as the Anglicans, Episcopalians, and Lutherans have strong roots in both traditions, and they attempt a *middle road* between the two emphases.[5] In spite of these differences, all Christian demoninations agree that Jesus the Messiah is the disclosure of God and the means of human reconciliation with Him. Following is a brief explanation of some of the major beliefs and practices of orthodox Christianity.

Salvation

Christianity believes salvation is only made possible by *God's grace;* that is, no one can do anything to deserve or merit God's favor.[6] Therefore, Christian orthodoxy teaches that salvation cannot be attained by performing rituals, good deeds, asceticism, or meditation. Salvation is only possible because God took the initiative to send His Son (the Messiah) to this world to pay the penalty *(death)* for the sins of humanity,[7] and according to the Scriptures, it was His love for humanity that motivated Him to do so.[8] The recognition of one's sinful state, followed by the acceptance of the Messiah's death on the cross as God's solution for salvation,[9] is known as *repentance.*[10] Therefore, repentance involves a total change in one's thinking. No longer does the individual see himself as worthy of salvation because of his own efforts, rather he now understands himself as an object of God's love and forgiveness because of the death of His Son on the cross.

Orthodox Christianity teaches that the "effort" man puts forward in order to be saved is that of *opening his heart* (humbling himself) and *receiving* God's free gift of salvation through faith.[11] Therefore, saving faith involves more than just knowing that God exists and believing that what He says is true, because even demons believe and shudder before God;[12] rather it means *trusting* in what the Messiah did on the cross for you personally. So saving faith in Scripture involves a belief that is accompanied by an action. For example, it is one thing to believe that a prescribed medicine can heal a person of a particular illness; but if the medicine is not *taken* it is not going to bring about healing, no matter how strongly the person may have believed the medicine had the ability to effect healing. In the same way, if a person does not *genuinely affirm in his heart*—that's faith—the truth that God's Son came to this world to pay the penalty for his sins, it is not going to result in salvation.

Christianity believes that human beings only live once in this physical world, and following this life there will be a day of judgment before God.[13] Christianity does not teach the doctrine of karma and reincarnation, whereby one continues to work his way up the ladder, so to speak, through multiple lives, in hopes of one day attaining communion or oneness with God.[14] The Scriptures teach that after death man either enters into an eternal, intimate communion with God *(heaven)* or an endless state of complete isolation from God *(hell)*, as a result of the choice he makes during his earthly existence.[15]

According to God's eternal wisdom, He chose humanity to be a participant in the cosmic battle between the forces of good and evil in the universe, and God has done everything He can to keep people out of hell—without denying them the freedom of choice. Orthodox Christianity teaches that God paid the ultimate price to redeem sinful man. He died a brutal death of crucifixion for man's sin. According to the Scripture, God's goal for man's eternal destiny is *not* the annihilation of his soul and personhood, but a state of perfect and eternal communion with Himself. Christianity believes God was so moved by man's desperate condition that He entered space and time in the person of His only Son, and suffered death on a cross as man's substitute,[16] and His supreme desire is that no one suffer eternal death and hell.[17]

If someone persists, however, in rebelling against God through indifference or a desire for independence, God does not force him to enter the kingdom of heaven, where he would have to worship God against his will. Because Christianity understands coercion to be an abuse of man's freedom, hell is seen as the result of *man's choice* to be independent from God and *reject* His offer. This is the essence of choosing not to believe.[18] Chuck Colson, who discovered Christianity as he served time in prison for his part in the Watergate scandal of the 1970s, writes: "In a sense, the concept of hell gives meaning to our lives. It tells us that the moral choices we make day by day have eternal significance, that our behavior has consequences lasting to eternity, that God Himself takes our choices seriously."[19] The message of Christianity is that forgiveness and eternal life can be found in Jesus Christ.

Christian Virtues

Christianity attempts to live out an ethic in the world that is based on self-less love, forgiveness of sins, caring for the poor and dispossessed of society, and nonviolence, all of which Jesus preached. The historical development of Christian caregiving institutions (orphanages, hospitals, leprosaria, schools for the poor) must be seen as a concerted effort on behalf of the Christian community to fulfill the command of Jesus to care for "the least of the brethren."[20] Many believe the early success of Christianity in the Roman Empire was due to the commitment of Christian communities to provide such assistance at a time when social services were rudimentary or nonexistent.[21] Following are ten virtues that lie at the heart of the Christian faith:

1. Love. According to Jesus the greatest commandment is "loving God with all your heart, soul and mind, and loving your neighbor as yourself."[22] No other command is greater than these. Hence, love is of preeminent importance in the Bible. The highest and noblest form of love presented in Scripture is a self-giving love that is not merited, it's a love that seeks the highest good of the other person (even though they're undeserving), and it's a love that does not desire to possess.[23] God in His essence is described as being love; that means the very substance and nature of God is love,[24] which is why God is capable of loving the undeserving. To say that God is love implies that *all of His activity is loving activity.* If He creates, He creates in love; if He judges, He judges in love; if He rules, He rules in love; everything God does is done in love.[25]

For man to understand love, he must first perceive that God loves him. The fact that God loves man is stated repeatedly throughout the Bible,[26] and its greatest expression was demonstrated at the cross.[27] God's love is a love that is unselfish and undeserved. Man in his fallen state is hostile toward God[28] and is deserving of His wrath, but his hateful heart is transformed into love because God loved man. He sent His only Son to this world to die for hostile, sinful human beings in order that He might reconcile them to Himself and make them His children.[29] It was God's love that motivated Him to go to the cross.[30] When a person realizes that God indeed loves him, he responds by embracing Him as his Savior *(salvation),* and God's love is then poured out upon him through the Holy Spirit,[31] thus making it possible for him to love unselfishly in return.[32] On the basis of God's love the believer is enjoined to love God *(who is deserving),* and to love his fellow man *(who is undeserving).*

Love is ordained by God to be the normal, ideal human relationship, and as such is given the sanction of divine law.[33] The night before Jesus went to the cross He told His disciples they were to love one another as He had loved them.[34] Thus, love for one another became the dominant theme of the early church,[35] and the primal evidence of the Christian's identity.[36] *Thomas Aquinas* (1225–1274), the Italian theologian and philosopher, considered love the foundation of all other Christian virtues. According to Christian theology, people do not give of themselves because the object of love is worthy; they give because, by giving, both the giver and the recipient are transformed.[37] Love therefore is the preeminent virtue of Christianity.[38]

2. Compassion. The biblical concept of compassion means that you can *feel others' pain;* literally it means "to suffer with." Compassion is both a divine and a human quality. The prophets were deeply aware of God's mercy to sinful men, and they taught that anyone who had experienced His mercy would feel it was his duty to be compassionate toward others, especially the fatherless, the widow, and the stranger.[39] Jesus made it clear to His followers that they are to show compassion to anyone who needs their help.[40] In Christianity, showing compassion to others is how believers imitate the kindness and mercy that God has showered upon them through His Son.

3. Gratitude. Christianity teaches that gratitude comes from the understanding that everything we have—our lives, abilities, possessions, and experiences—are all gifts from God.[41] As a virtue, gratitude is expressed in rituals like giving thanks for food, celebrating the Lord's Supper, and commemorating various life-cycle events. In God's divine economy for the Christian, He says they are to "give thanks for *everything,* that this is *His will* for them in Christ Jesus."[42] Therefore, the Christian is to find a reason to be grateful in all things. Christians are to see Jesus' suffering as a model for living;[43] even in their own struggles and pain, they can still have the joy of knowing that God is with them,[44] that nothing is happening to them that will not ultimately work out for their very best,[45] that God will use the pain to produce in them a quality of character that is like Christ,[46] and that He will see them through all of their trials.[47] Knowing this, the Christian can even be *joyful* in the midst of pain, because God is using the difficulties he experiences to completely transform his life.[48]

4. Joy. Joy is a delight in one's thinking that arises as a result of considering a present or certain future good. When a person's desires are limited by his possessions he may experience *contentment*; when one's highest desires are accomplished it brings *satisfaction*; when undesirable opposition is eliminated it is called *triumph*. All of these experiences can be referred to as natural joy.[49] There is also a moral joy that arises from the performance of any good actions, and a *spiritual joy* that has God as its focus. Spiritual joy is one of the central themes of the book of Psalms. The various uses of joy in the psalms connect it to an appreciation of God's love and care, a trust in His salvation, and the hope that the promise of tomorrow will wipe away the burdens of the present. Note the following:

- Let all who take refuge in You rejoice; let them *sing for joy*.[50]

- You will show me the path of life; in Your presence is *fullness of joy*.[51]

- Weeping may remain for a night, but *rejoicing* comes in the morning.[52]

- My soul will *rejoice* in the Lord and *delight* in His salvation.[53]

- David prayed, "Restore to me the *joy* of Your salvation."[54]

- My lips will *shout for joy* when I sing praise to You.[55]

- Those who sow in tears will reap with *songs of joy*.[56]

In the New Testament, joy comes from knowing that God loves you.[57] The Apostle Paul tells us that joy is a gift from God and is a response to His offer of salvation and love;[58] therefore, the death and resurrection of Christ brings the joy of salvation to the Christian.[59]

5. Patience. The Christian faith requires the virtues of patience, diligence, and perseverance because its rewards are not immediate, and it does not promise a life without struggle or pain.[60] The primary example of patience as a virtue is found in the Bible in the person of Job.[61] Job was an innocent man who refused to curse God despite his sufferings.[62] The New Testament word for patience is often translated "longsuffering," and is characteristic of God's dealings with sinful men, who are fully deserving of His wrath.[63] Christians are to demonstrate the same kind of godly character to others.[64]

6. Humility. A humble spirit shows a respect for God and an awareness that all blessings flow from Him; therefore, it involves seeing yourself for who you really are, in the light of who God really is, and leaves no room for arrogance. Christianity provides the classic religious statement of humility in the Sermon on the Mount: "Blessed are the *meek* for they shall inherit the earth."[65] Jesus' point here is that the secular world recognizes and rewards power and wealth, but those who are truly righteous lift up the ones whom the world has passed over and crushed.[66] Therefore humility is the antithesis of that value that the nonreligious world prizes. Humility is so highly regarded by God that He bestows a *greater grace* upon all those who exhibit it.[67] Occasionally a political leader emerges who understands the virtue of

humility. President Abraham Lincoln, in his proclamation of a National Day
of Prayer wrote these words:

> We have been recipients of the choicest bounties of Heaven.
> We have been preserved, these many years, in peace and
> prosperity. We have grown in numbers, wealth and power, as
> no other nation has ever grown. But we have forgotten God.
> We have forgotten the gracious hand which preserved us in
> peace, and multiplied and enriched and strengthened us; and
> we have vainly imagined, in the deceitfulness of our hearts,
> that all these blessings were produced by some superior wisdom
> and virtue of our own. Intoxicated with unbroken success, we
> have become too self-sufficient to feel the necessity of redeem-
> ing and preserving grace, too proud to pray to the God that
> made us! It behooves us, then to humble ourselves before the
> offended Power, to confess our national sins, and to pray for
> clemency and forgiveness.[68]

What was Lincoln's point? The U.S. Civil War was God's punishment
for a proud and arrogant nation.[69] The Scriptures tell us that "righteousness
exalts a nation, but sin (pride) is a disgrace to any people."[70]

7. Hope. In Christianity the three cardinal virtues are love, faith, and
hope. Christian hope cannot be separated from faith in God. Because of
what God has done in the past and is doing today, the Christian dares to
expect future blessings that are presently invisible.[71] The believer's hope is
buoyed as he reflects on the activities of God in Scripture;[72] the goodness of
God for the believer is never exhausted; the best is yet to come.[73] Hope for
the Christian is not a pipe dream at the mercy of changing conditions, but
rather an anchor of the soul that penetrates deep into the invisible eternal
world.[74] Because of his faith the Christian has a deep inward assurance,
produced in his heart by the Holy Spirit, that the things he hopes for are
real and not just imagined.[75]

As a result of the resurrection, the Christian is saved from the miserable
condition of having his hope in Christ limited only to this world.[76] His
hope is inseparably linked to what comes after death—the return of Jesus
Christ and eternal life in Heaven. The reality of this hope in the heart of the
believer makes it impossible for him to be satisfied with momentary joys;[77] it
also acts as a stimulus to purity of life;[78] and it enables him to suffer joyfully,
when conditions in and of themselves do not warrant it;[79] thus this virtue is

radically different from stoic endurance. Faith, hope, and love are the three inseparable cardinal virtues of the Christian faith. Hope cannot exist apart from faith, and love is the supreme expression of faith. Together these three comprise the Christian way of life.

8. Purity. The striving for purity within Christianity is really a way of coping with our physical and spiritual urges. We have the physical urge to eat, for example, but we can eat to excess and gain weight. We have the need to procreate and enjoy sex, but that can lead to sexual promiscuity. So spiritual purity involves abstaining from those sinful desires that naturally wage war against the soul.[80] One of the most powerful intoxicants in the world is sex, so it's not surprising that all of the world's great religions have something to say about avoiding or moderating it. Human sexuality is a gift from God and is to be used in the way God intended. Nearly every religion teaches that it is acceptable only in the marriage union of a man and a woman; it is impermissible in any other context.[81] Therefore one way to keep sexual urges within the bounds of acceptable religious expression is to promote marriage.[82] Christianity teaches that moral purity involves both one's *thoughts* as well as one's *actions*,[83] that God's Spirit provides the strength to win the battle with impurity,[84] and that He blesses those who are pure in heart.[85] Modest dress is to be the norm, because dressing provocatively can easily arouse sexual desire in another person and cause them to stumble.[86] Some churches actually require modest attire, as does Hasidic Judaism and a number of Islamic sects.[87]

9. Forgiveness. The natural response of many people when they get hurt is to get even, to return hurt for hurt. For that reason, forgiveness is one of the central virtues of the Christian faith.[88] When people practice this virtue, they actively seek reconciliation with those whom they've harmed or who have harmed them.[89] Christianity teaches that people are to seek forgiveness face to face with the person they've hurt. When believers refuse to forgive a person because they have wronged them, they do not lose their salvation,[90] but they forfeit the peace and the joy of God's ruling presence in their life,[91] and God chastens them until they come to a point where they are willing to forgive.[92] Once moral failings occur, they're impossible to take back, and you may have to live with the consequences of your failure the rest of your life. For example, if you have a child born out of wedlock, you'll have to live with that the rest of your life. If you commit a crime, you'll have to live with a criminal record and possibly being incarcerated. Nevertheless, when you bring your sin before God with a penitent spirit, *God in His grace* is able to forgive you and remove the shame, the pain, and the guilt of your sin, and restore you to Himself in perfect righteousness.[93] That's the miracle of grace in the life of the Christian. It is not because the Christian merits forgiveness that grace is bestowed; God graciously responds with love and mercy simply because His child comes before Him with a broken and contrite spirit.[94]

In Christianity, the command to forgive comes from the belief that because God has forgiven the believer of his sins,[95] he must forgive others of theirs.[96] A person may have been wrongfully accused and even suffered a great injustice; they may have been the victim of abuse and suffered terribly because of it, and as a result, they may feel completely justified in their unforgiving anger. From a human perspective they may have every right to not forgive, but God's Word tells us that *we are to forgive those who have committed an offense against us, no matter how wrong or ugly their offense.* God says, "Vengeance is Mine; I will repay,"[97] which means vengeance and vindication belong to God. The Scriptures teach that He will judge the guilty, and full justice will be meted out as the sin deserves.[98]

The question many Christians ask is, "How does one forgive what seemingly is unforgivable?" First, the believer must recognize that forgiveness is a journey or a process that God takes His children on when they are prepared to begin it. The journey is ultimately completed as one spends time in God's Word and in prayer before Him, *asking God for the grace to forgive,* just as he himself has been forgiven by God. Forgiveness then is made possible by the atoning work of Christ on the cross, and as such it is an act of sheer grace.[99] Only as one experiences the grace of God's forgiveness for his own sins can he extend grace to others and truly forgive them.[100] The believer's capacity to forgive does not come from his own strength, but from the indwelling presence of God's Spirit.[101] Jesus exemplified the fullness of forgiveness by forgiving those who unjustly and brutally murdered Him.[102]

10. Obedience. Perhaps the most difficult of all virtues is that of obedience. People weren't created by God just to do what they feel like doing; they were created to reflect God's holiness and walk in obedience before Him. Virtues like compassion and love are hard to argue against, but most people struggle to see the virtue of obedience. Why? Well, the central idea behind obedience is that of yielding or submitting to authority, and that goes against the grain of modern thinking, especially in the West where we prize individualism, freedom, and self-determination; but obedience to authority is a cornerstone of Christian ideology.[103] According to Scripture, God demands that His revelation be taken as a rule for life. The virtue of obedience in the Old Testament began with a covenant between God and the Jewish people. This covenant called for the people to obey God. In return He would greatly

THE LIBERATING EFFECTS OF OBEDIENCE

The Christian faith teaches that salvation through Christ sets a person free to be the person God created him to be.[121] God did not create people to live as slaves of sin; He created them to live as free moral agents of goodness. Some people, however, have a very distorted understanding of freedom. They think true freedom means you can do whatever you want; but such freedom would obviously be disastrous to any society or individual. Let's take a look at how freedom functions in accordance with the law of gravity. Either you honor it when contemplating walking off a cliff, or you'll find yourself experiencing an unpleasant rapid decrease in elevation. Conversely, in a society that values freedom, there are *limits* to that freedom. You are not permitted to yell "fire!" in a movie theatre when there is no fire. You do not disregard stop lights when driving. You do not show up to work or school whenever you want. You do not write checks for money you do not have in your bank account. God gives His children freedom, but the freedom He gives has limits and conditions.

The freedom the believer experiences can be equated to a locomotive on a train. For it to run properly it must stay on the *train tracks* for which it was designed. If one were to decide he did not like the tracks, conceivably he could take his little engine off the tracks and see how wonderfully it would operate without them. The train tracks are not meant to *inhibit the little locomotive's freedom;* on the contrary, they're meant to *enhance its freedom.* Just like a train was meant to run on tracks, and boats are designed to operate in water, so humanity was designed to live according to the rules authored by its Maker.

God has given human beings all kinds of tracks to run on in life. There are *dietary tracks*—if you eat rocks and dirt you're going to notice your body does not function too well; there are *exercise tracks*—if you fail to move around and exercise your muscles, you're going to discover your body mass will start to deteriorate; there are *work ethic tracks*—if you fail to produce at normal levels, you're going to find that you are no longer receiving a weekly paycheck; there are *relational tracks*—if you treat people poorly, you're going to find yourself the recipient of derisive acts; there are *behavioral tracks*—if you act strangely and abnormally, you're going to find that people avoid you; there are also *moral tracks*—if you do not act in a morally acceptable fashion, not only will people question your character, but God is not going to be too highly thrilled with your behavior either. The truth of the matter is, whenever you violate the laws God designed for human beings to live by, you're removing yourself from the tracks of life, and you're going to suffer the consequences of your actions.[122] Common sense should tell us there is nothing wrong with the laws themselves; problems arise only when those laws are violated.

The reason parents erect *fences* around their swimming pools is not to make life miserable for their children, but to enhance their safety. Conversely, *crash helmets* are not worn by motorcyclists to mess up their hair, but to protect their heads. In the same light, God's laws are not arbitrarily established without any thought given to the benefits derived from them; they are divinely prescribed directives that help us live fulfilling and meaningful lives. When Christians live within the constraints of God's laws, they come to understand the truth of divine wisdom, and the results are "liberating."[123] It's as liberating as running a locomotive on train tracks, compared with trying to run one on sand and dirt.

bless them.[104] If they chose to disobey Him, however, they would experience His wrath rather than His blessing.[105] Though perfect obedience was the goal for humanity, the imperfect results of man's most strenuous efforts revealed the need for God to be merciful and gracious. God then promised to establish a *New Covenant* with man. He would place His Spirit within him and cause him to walk in His ways and obey Him.[106] Hence, obedience became a *gift of His grace* through Jesus the Messiah.[107]

Believing in Jesus the Messiah is an act of obedience[108] because God commands it;[109] conversely, *disbelieving* is an act of disobedience.[110] A life of obedience to God is the result of *faith* in Christ. Christian obedience springs from gratitude to God for His love and grace and forgiveness,[111] not from the desire to gain God's favor, or to justify oneself before Him.[112] Christians are justified because they have placed their faith in Jesus the Messiah.[113]

The Christian's obedience to God is reflected in his obedience to the family,[114] to the church,[115] and to the state.[116] Jesus Himself said, "Give to Caesar what is Caesar's, and to God what is God's."[117] Without some authority, society would collapse into chaos; thus, even if the state is not right all the time, as long as it is basically just, God has obligated people to obey its laws.[118] This does not mean that Christianity requires blind obedience to secular laws. When the law of the land is immoral, obedience to that law is also immoral. When claims clash, the believer must be ready to disobey men in order not to disobey God.[119] In this way, the practice of one's faith can be *a force for positive change in society.* For example, during the nineteenth century in the United States, the law of the land made it illegal to harbor or aid runaway slaves. Many people, believing with certainty that all people are equal in the eyes of God and that slavery was a perversion of their faith, helped thousands of fleeing slaves to freedom. They chose to obey the dictates of their conscience and their faith. The main point of obedience is that no earthly power can order you to violate the law of truth and God.[120]

The Church

Christianity teaches that every person who accepts the work of the Messiah on their behalf becomes a member of the *spiritual body of Christ,*[124] commonly known as the Church, or the Universal Church. The word "church" in the New Testament language of Greek is the word *ekklesia,* which literally means "called out." The idea is that Christians are those who have been called out of the world to live for Christ. Our English word church, however, is used in a number of ways: to describe the *building* in which Christians worship; the *worship service* that Christians attend; and also a *group of believers.* When it is used to describe a group of believers it can refer to a *local congregation of believers* that worships together, or to the *entire Christian community worldwide*. In whatever way the word is used, the context determines its meaning. Sometimes, as in this book, the word *Church* is capitalized when it refers to the Christian community worldwide; this makes it easier for the reader to distinguish between the local church and the worldwide Church. The two most common designations for the Christian community worldwide is the *Church*, and the expression the *Body of Christ*.[125] According to the New Testament, the Church is the mystical body of Christ of which He is the head,[126] and is the dwelling place of God's Spirit on earth.[127]

The Purpose of the Church

A major tenet of Christianity is that every believer be actively involved in a local church or community of faith.[128] Its houses of assembly are for corporate worship,[129] the study of the Scriptures,[130] and for the body of Christ to serve one another and share their lives together.[131] But the primary mission of the Church is to do the work of God by being a loving community in the world, and directing people to the Messiah.[132]

Authentic Christian living involves relating to others in love,[133] and not just selfishly living for oneself.[134] Christians are to live out their faith together in loving compassionate communities that transcend all racial and cultural barriers;[135] such love is made possible by the indwelling presence of God's Spirit.[136] The Scriptures teach that believers grow more fully when they grow with others in a community of fellowship.[137] The challenge comes as the Christian community integrates into the general culture at large,[138] because of the temptation to compromise and conform to the ways of the world. Believers are to maintain their spiritual identity and not conform to the standards and values espoused by the world;[139] instead, as they interact with the world, they are to reflect the values and love of Christ.[140]

From the beginning God intended His creation to enjoy an intimate relationship with Him. When humanity fell into sin, it was God's plan that the nation of Israel would be "a light to the nations,"[141] but Israel failed in her calling.[142] Then, according to Scripture, God Himself entered into human history in the person of Jesus Christ. At the time of His dedication in the temple He was declared by Simeon to be "a light of revelation to the Gentiles, and the glory of God's people Israel."[143] Jesus then called twelve disciples, symbolic of the new Israel He was creating,[144] to form the nucleus of God's new people—the Church—which, like Israel of old, was created to be the means to restore humanity to fellowship with its Creator.[145] The

Church is to "declare the wonderful deeds of Him who called them out of darkness into His marvelous light."[146] Thus the Church is entrusted with the responsibility of bringing the message of salvation through the Messiah to the entire world.[123]

The Structure of the Church

There are three titles that have been customarily used by churches to identify their leaders: elders, bishops (or overseers), and pastors.[148] The term *elder* implies that the leader is not a novice; this title originated in the synagogue. The term *bishop* (overseer) describes one who possesses authority and gives oversight, while the term *pastor* suggests an agrarian background, since it comes from the word "shepherd." In the New Testament the words *elder* and *bishop* are used interchangeably,[149] and their office or position is also described by the word *pastor*.[150] The *pastor-bishop-elder* is responsible to the Chief Shepherd—Jesus Christ.[151] The term *deacon* in the New Testament was used of individuals who assisted the bishop or pastor in his duties.[152]

The New Testament does not prescribe a particular pattern for church government, but it does provide some general principles for governing a church. Therefore the Scriptures give a lot of organizational freedom for a variety of operations and ministries.[153] Historically, three basic forms of church government have been used over the centuries:

1. ***Episcopal.*** Our English word "Episcopal" comes from New Testament Greek word *episkopos,* which means, "to look upon" or "care for."[154] Episcopacy calls its chief ministers *bishops* and lesser ones *presbyters* (or priests) and *deacons.* Some within this camp see the function of the bishops as heir to the apostles, or those who had the power to appoint elders.[155] Churches using this type of government are Roman Catholic, Greek Orthodox, Anglican, and Episcopalian.

2. ***Presbyterian.*** Our English word "Presbyterian" comes from the New Testament Greek word *presbuteros,* which literally means "an older man" or "elder."[156] In Presbyterianism, the governing power of a church resides in a group of leaders who form an assembly, synod, or presbytery; thus a plurality of presbyters (or elders) exercises general oversight over the church.[157] Churches using this form of government are Presbyterian, Methodist, and the Reformed Church.

3. ***Congregational.*** Congregationalism tends to place the governing power in the hands of the entire congregation. Such churches are independent

as far as authority and control from the denomination to which they may belong. In part, this type of church government came about as a reaction against churches that placed a priestly class between God and man. Congregationalists stress the priesthood of *all* believers.[158] They also point out that the Scriptures teach that local churches were given the responsibility of protecting themselves against false teachers.[159] Churches using this type of government are Congregational, Baptist, Assemblies of God, Nazarene, and independent churches. Incidentally, some congregations vary slightly from the congregational approach; they elect a board of directors or elders and give them the authority to govern the church.

The Denominations of the Church

In March 2001, the *Washington Post* published the results of a survey conducted by Hartford Seminary's Hartford Institute for Religious Research. This study reported that there are some 325,000 churches in the United States (that is one church for every 900 people). Half of these churches were founded before 1945, and half of them have less than 100 people attending regularly.[160] In addition, there are over 300 different Christian denominations in North America,[161] and an estimated 22,000 denominations throughout the world.[162] A denomination is an association of congregations that express their unity through a common heritage, which generally includes doctrinal and organizational emphases, as well as ethnic, language, and geographical origins. Many denominations have national and international outreach ministries, colleges and seminaries for educating and training, camps and conference grounds for retreats and times of spiritual renewal, and publish various curricula and educational materials.

The Scriptures tell us that the Church is "one,"[163] but unity does not demand uniformity. Since the first century the Church has manifested itself in a myriad of cultures. It exists today in every country of the world, in thousands of different languages and cultural settings, so uniformity is not even a realistic possibility. The New Testament Church was actually quite diverse both in its worship and its structure; therefore, uniformity never has been the ideal.[164]

The challenge for Christian communities today is that they *live in unity* without insisting that worship, structure, or minor theological differences be made uniform. Problems arise when believers make *secondary issues* more important than unity, thus producing divisions within the church. There are, however, other times when division is caused by those in the church who are *not* true believers;[165] generally when this kind of division occurs, it is healthy because the believing community rejects the false teaching of the unbelievers. It should be remembered that Scripture teaches that the church is made up of *sinful people*[166] who are all in the *process* of being transformed into the image of Christ.[167] Though they're in the process of changing, they still frequently stumble and make mistakes.[168] Interestingly enough, regardless of their stumbling and lack of spirituality, the Scriptures still refer to them as *saints*, *holy*, and *sanctified*.[169] Remember, Christians are saints not because of their own behavior, but by virtue of who they are because of their faith in the Messiah.[170] It is Jesus Christ who makes them righteous and holy.

The Sacraments

A sacrament is a religious rite or ceremony instituted or recognized by Jesus Christ. The two principal sacraments of the Church are *Baptism* and the *Lord's Supper*. Both were given a prominent place by Jesus Christ and the early church.[171] That special prominence is continued today in the entire Christian world. Baptism and the Lord's Supper are regarded by the Church as a means appointed by Jesus Christ to bring believers into mutual participation and communion with His death and resurrection.[172] In addition, the Eastern Orthodox Church and the Roman Catholic Church also acknowledge five lesser sacraments: confirmation, penance, extreme unction, holy orders, and matrimony.

1. Baptism. Baptism was a ritual washing with water, which *signified* the believer's being cleansed from sin, the reception of the Holy Spirit, and the individual's dedication to his new life in Christ.[173] From the earliest days of the Church,[174] baptism has been used as the rite of Christian initiation. It consists in going in or under the baptismal water in the name of the Triune God, that is, "in the name of the Father and the Son and the Holy Spirit."[175] The practice of baptism is normally conducted as a public ministry of the church.

The essence of baptism is simple, but it is filled with meaning. It reflects the meaning of the substitutionary death and the resurrection of Christ and the salvation it brings; as a result it portrays the saving work of Christ in accomplishing the believer's regeneration or rebirth[176] and his emergence into new life.[177] In Scripture the believer is described as having participated in the death and resurrection of Jesus Christ, and as such is said to have *died to sin* and been *made alive to God*.[178]

The Christian community essentially views the experience of baptism in two ways: Some churches hold that baptism is the *direct instrument of regeneration* or rebirth; that is, they believe the new birth is actually effectuated by baptism. Thus they believe saving grace is imparted at baptism, and as such they refer to baptism as "baptismal regeneration." Others believe that baptism merely *symbolizes the regeneration* that takes place through union with Christ; that it portrays Christ's death and resurrection in atoning for sin, and its accomplishment in the life of the believer. Therefore, through the external rite of baptism the believer professes his death to sin and resurrection to newness of life;[179] thus baptism for him is an *outward sign* of an *inward reality.*

There are three different methods used by churches for baptizing people. Some *sprinkle* a few drops on the forehead; some *pour* a full pitcher of water over the person's head; and some *immerse* the person's whole body in water. Though some churches focus strongly on the "mode" of baptism, the Scriptures place the strongest emphasis on the "purpose" of baptism.

Some churches also practice *Infant Baptism.* This involves baptizing the children of professing believers. Those who practice infant baptism raise their children with the understanding that through baptism God begins a work of grace in their children's lives to draw them to Himself; thus they believe their children will one day consciously make a confession of faith. Churches that do not practice infant baptism generally practice what is known as *Child Dedication.* This is a ceremony in which parents dedicate their children and themselves to the Lord, promising to raise their children in the ways and the knowledge of God, in the hope that their children will one day consciously place their trust in Christ as their Savior.

2. *The Lord's Supper.* The Lord's Supper, which is also referred to as the *Lord's Table, Communion,* or the *Eucharist* (*eucharisteo* is the Greek word for thanksgiving), was a token meal of *bread and wine*; these were two of the elements used by Jesus in the the Passover Meal He celebrated with His disciples the night before His death. The Lord's Supper pointed to the *sacrifice of His life* on the cross and the *shedding of His blood* to establish a new covenant or agreement between God and His people.[180] During the Passover Meal, which celebrated God's deliverance of the children of Israel from Egypt,[181] Jesus broke bread and poured wine, gave thanks for each, and then gave a portion to each of His disciples to eat and drink, telling them that the bread represented His body and the wine represented His blood.[182] This event is the foundation for Communion; it is a celebration of the person and work of the Messiah on the believer's behalf. In referring to the bread and wine as His own body and His own blood, Jesus in effect was identifying Himself as the true lamb of the Passover whose death would deliver God's people from the bondage of sin.[183]

When believers receive Communion, they're giving thanks to God for the gift of Jesus Christ and are professing their faith in Him. There are slight differences in how various churches view Communion. Some believe the bread and the wine *literally become* the body and the blood of Christ during the priestly blessing, and are ingested as such by those who partake; some believe the body and the blood of Christ *spiritually accompany* the bread and the wine when they are taken; and others see the bread and the wine as merely being *symbolic or representational* of the body and the blood of Christ. The third group of churches focus on remembering and commemorating what Jesus Christ did for them individually and collectively on the cross;[184] as such they emphasize the "remembrance" portion of Paul's words in his letter to the Corinthian church.[185]

Because there is a *constant renewal* in the Lord's Supper of the New Covenant that God made between Himself and the Church,[186] the Christian community is enjoined to celebrate the Lord's Supper regularly.[187] Some celebrate it every week in their worship services, while others celebrate it monthly or quarterly. The Scriptures teach that before Christians partake of Communion, they are to first spiritually examine themselves.[188] Before partaking, they should be sure that they are right with God and right with their fellow man. Self-examination is critical for the believer and his spiritual life, because he drinks or eats judgment unto himself should he partake unworthily.[189] God judges the believer in this life for treating lightly what Christ has done for him. Therefore, if a believer determines that his life does not measure up to God's standards, he needs to make things right with God and others before partaking in Communion.

The Apocalypse

The night before Jesus went to the cross, He met with His disciples to celebrate the Passover with them. At that feast He told them He would be *leaving* them, and this was *very troubling* to them. Everything Jesus told them that evening is recorded in five chapters of John's gospel,[190] and probably the most impacting words He shared that night were these:

> There are many dwelling places in My Father's house; if this were not so, I would tell you plainly. I am leaving you and going there to prepare a place for you, and since I am going to prepare a place for you, I am going to come back and take you to be with Me, that you also may be where I am. Do not be troubled in your heart, but believe in God and believe in Me.[191]

The Scriptures tell us at the end of the age all of humanity will see the Messiah return to this world. Theologians refer to His return as the "Second Coming."[192] Just as He ascended into heaven, so will He come back again to earth.[193] The next time Jesus comes to this world, He will come with great power and in glory.[194] He will destroy His evil adversaries.[195] He will raise the righteous from the dead,[196] and He will gather them together with all of His followers throughout the earth.[197] His return will be an *apokalypsis* (an unveiling) of His presence before the entire world.[198] The gospel of Matthew records these words of Jesus regarding His return:

> Just as lightning flashes from the east to the west, so will My coming be. The sun will be darkened in those days, and the heavenly bodies will be shaken, and all the people of the earth will see My coming on the clouds of the sky, and I shall come with great power and glory.[199]

The Bible says the Messiah of God is now reigning as LORD at God's right hand,[200] and is sharing God's throne.[201] Though His present reign is invisible to the world, when He returns His *apokalypsis* will be visible for everyone to see.[202]

The Book of Revelation records the events of the "last days," the consummation of the age. The Apostle John wrote this book at the end of the first century. John was exiled by the Roman Emperor Domitian about AD 96 to the small Island of Patmos, a rocky little point in the Mediterranean just off the southwestern coastline of present-day Turkey. While he was on the island, the Lord appeared to him in an incredible vision that is referred to as the *Revelation of Jesus Christ*, or the *Apocalypse*—literally, the *unveiling*. John wrote this book to give Christians hope during a time of severe persecution, and it has functioned to sustain that hope ever since.[203] The Book of Revelation tells us of the uncovering of Jesus Christ in His glory and His kingdom, and gives us a prophetic vision of the end of the world and how things ultimately are going to turn out.[204]

A key to understanding the Book of Revelation is found in the nineteenth verse of the first chapter, in which John mentions three things that the book contains: 1) The things which he *had seen*; 2) the things which *are* (chapters 2–3); and 3) the things which *will take place* (chapters 4–22). So John here mentions the *past*, the *present*, and the *future*. Christians are not in full agreement as to how the events that are recorded in Revelation should be interpreted. Some believe the Book of Revelation is a *symbolic description* of the Church Age in which we are now living, while others believe it is a *literal description* of the events that will occur at the end of the age. Though there is disagreement as to how this book should be interpreted, orthodox Christianity is in complete agreement over the three main themes of the book: Christ's return, the resurrection of the body, and the Day of Judgment.

1. ***Christ's return.*** This is one of the most common teachings in the New Testament. One out of every 25 verses deals with the return of Christ; it is mentioned 318 times in 260 chapters. It also occupies a prominent place in the Old Testament in that *most* of the Old Testament prophecies concerning the coming of Christ deal not with His first advent, in which He died as the sin-bearer of the world, but with His second advent in which He is to rule as King.[205]

2. ***The resurrection of the body.*** A second doctrinal point upon which Christians are widely agreed is the resurrection of the body in the last day;[206] specifically the resurrection of the bodies of believers at Christ's second coming.[207]

3. ***The day of judgment.*** The return of Christ and the resurrection of the body are two of the most encouraging things that await the believer, but the idea of judgment is far more sobering. According to Scripture, those who reject the Messiah will experience the Great White Throne Judgment.[208] The sobering fact is that history is ultimately going to come to an end, and its end involves accountability. Christianity teaches that every human being will one day have to answer for what he has done, and he shall be judged either on the basis of his own righteousness (which will *condemn* him), or on the basis of the righteousness of the Messiah (which will *save* him); hence, Jesus Christ is called the "Savior."[209]

The chapters that have led to two different interpretations are Revelation 4–19. Either they are a *symbolic description* of the Church Age, or they are a *literal description* of the final events of human history. In these chapters the Apostle John presents the various judgments God is going to pour out upon the unbelieving world in the last days. They are identified as Seven *Seal* Judgments, Seven *Trumpet* Judgments, and Seven *Bowl* Judgments. As the various judgments are explained, the reader is introduced to various personalities and events that are prophesied to take place during this time of judgment. Because much of the language in the Apocalypse is symbolic, it is important that the reader give very careful attention to detail. Many of the symbols are explained in the text itself, but those that are not are identified in various prophetic passages in the Old Testament (particularly the Book of Daniel). Therefore, to grasp all the meanings of this book, it is necessary to exercise extreme care. Not to do so would be like judging a *complex case* in a court of law after having heard only a small portion of the evidence.

Included in Revelation 4–19 is the Battle of Armageddon, which is identified as the last great war the world is going to fight. The Scriptures state that on what is called "the great day of God,"[210] on the Plains of Megiddo in Israel, the armies of the earth by the millions will clash. In the midst of this unimaginable holocaust, it is said that Jesus Christ will intervene in human history to deliver His people. The text goes on to say that at that point God will bind Satan for one thousand years and throw him into a bottomless pit,[211] and then Jesus will set up His earthly Kingdom where He will rule in peace during that time.[212] This is often referred to as the Millennial Kingdom. After the one-thousand year reign of Christ, Satan will be released for a short time to lead man's final rebellion against God. This is referred to as *the final conflict*, which forever will end humanity's refusal to accept the will of God for their lives.[213]

At the end of time, those who have rejected God will be resurrected from the dead to face the *Great White Throne Judgment*.[214] There is universal agreement among orthodox Christians regarding this final judgment. At the Great White Throne Judgment all of the books will be opened, and those individuals whose names are not found written in the *Book of Life* will be rejected and judged according to their deeds.[215] Then Satan and his angels, and all those who chose his way of life—plus death, sin, and the grave—will all be thrown into the *Lake of Fire*.[216] The Apostle John describes the vision he had of God's judgment of the unrighteous with these words:

> I saw a Great White Throne and Him who was seated on it; from whose presence earth and heaven fled away. And I saw the dead, great and small, standing before the throne, and the books were opened, and finally the Book of Life was opened. Then all the dead were raised and were judged according to all they had ever done. And death and the abode of the dead were thrown into the lake of fire; this is the second death. And if anyone's name was not found written in the Book of Life, He was thrown into the lake of fire.[217]

Following the Great White Throne Judgment, there will be a complete renovation of all creation. At this point the Scriptures say God will make a *new heaven* and a *new earth*.[218] The Bible does not give an exhaustive description of what heaven will be like. As the Apostle Paul says, "No eye has seen, no ear has heard, no mind has conceived of that which God has prepared for those who love Him."[219] In the eternal state God Himself has said that He is going to dwell with man in the new Jerusalem,[220] and that there will no longer be any mourning, crying, tears, death, sin, sorrow, or pain,[221] and that His eternal state will never end.[222] Prior to God's creating everything new, however, there will be the destruction of the present order of creation. The Apostle Peter describes it like this:

> The heavens will disappear with a roar; the elements will be destroyed by fire, and the earth and everything in it will be laid bare. The heavens will be destroyed by fire, and all of its elements will melt with intense heat. And a new heaven and a new earth will appear, the home of righteousness.[223]

CHAPTER 12

SACRED SCRIPTURES
AND ANCIENT WRITINGS

Whereas other books were given for our information,
the Bible was given for our transformation.
— *Anonymous*[1]

The Formation of the Scriptures

In philosophy, knowledge is derived from logic or experience. In religion, however, understanding comes through *revelation*. It is through revelation that God makes known what human beings are supposed to know and do. Our English word "revelation" comes from a Latin word meaning, "to uncover or lay bare"; therefore, revelation is understood to be the uncovering of that which is divine.[2] Those religions which claim to be "revealed religions" believe that their sacred scriptures were directly communicated by God to individuals who wrote them down. Sometimes these revelations happened in a relatively short period of time. The *Qur'an* of Islam, for example, was said to have been completed in a period of about 40 years; the *Guru Granth Sahib* of Sikhism was compiled over a period of 200 years. The revelations of some religions took place over hundreds or thousands of years, as in the case of Hinduism, Judaism, and Christianity.[3] All revealed religions believe their sacred texts are of divine origin and inspiration.

As we know, the sacred text of Christianity is referred to as the *Bible*, which comes from the Greek word *biblos*, meaning book. The Bible is often called the "Word of God," because it is said to be the very words of God Himself;[4]

therefore it is regarded as the ultimate spiritual authority for Christianity.[5] Orthodox Christianity believes the Bible is God's revelation of Himself to humanity, that it is a record of His dealings with various human beings, and that it is the revealed will of the Creator to humanity for instruction and guidance in the ways of life.[6]

The Bible says the process whereby God communicated His revelation in writing is referred to as *inspiration*, which literally means to "breathe in." Therefore, the Word of God was breathed into human writers through the power of the Holy Spirit.[7] Bible scholars tell us that God inspired 40 different writers over a period of 1,500 years to record His personal message to humanity. Likewise, the Scriptures tell us that "men of God spoke as they were moved by the Holy Spirit."[8] In spite of the fact that the writing style, personality, and vocabulary of each biblical writer was unique and distinct, the Scriptures teach that what each of them wrote was God-breathed. Therefore, Christianity teaches that God mysteriously joined with sinful, imperfect human beings to produce His inspired written Word.[9]

Jesus Christ Himself regarded the Old Testament as an *inspired record* of God's self-revelation in history. He repeatedly appealed to the Scriptures as authoritative.[10] The early church also possessed this same attitude toward the Old Testament, and placed the words of the Messiah alongside those of the Old Testament.[11] In addition, the Apostle Paul claimed that his own teaching was inspired by God,[12] as did the Apostle John and his authorship of the Book of Revelation;[13] Paul intended that his letters should be read in the churches.[14] The Apostle Peter told the churches to "remember his words" when he would no longer be with them;[15] in addition, Peter identified Paul's letters with "other Scriptures."[16]

The formation of the Christian New Testament took place over a period of about 300 years. In the first century each of the various books were written and circulated throughout the Christian community. In the second century the rise of heresy served as an impetus to establish a definite body of sacred literature; thus a sifting process began in which *inspired Scripture* was distinguished from Christian literature in general. The three main criteria used to determine which books were inspired by God were these: First, each book had to be authored by one of the apostles, or closely affiliated with the apostles; second, each book had to be accepted by the churches to whom it had been written and circulated; and third, each book had to be consistent in matters of doctrine with what the churches had already believed. The process by which the various books were recognized as Scripture is commonly referred to as the history of the *canon*. In the New Testament language of Greek, the word "canon" meant "a carpenter's rule," and this term was used to identify and describe those books that were "inspired by God," as opposed to those which were measured and found to be of "secondary value" in general church use. Those books were not identified as being canonical in nature.[17] In AD 397, the Council of Carthage gave formal ratification to the 27 books of the Christian canon (New Testament), expressing what had already become the unanimous judgment of the churches.

Both Jews and Christians have canons of Scripture. The Jewish canon (Hebrew Bible) consists of the same books that Christianity identifies as the *Old Testament*. The only difference is that the 39 books of the Christian Old Testament are compressed into 24 books in the Hebrew Bible. The complete Christian canon consists of 66 books. It includes the 39 books of the Jewish canon, and an additional 27 books that make up the *New Testament*. When the books written by Christ's apostles came to be placed alongside the sacred books of the Jews, it became necessary to distinguish between them. The two preeminent covenants of the Bible—God's covenant with Israel mediated by *Moses* (the "Old" Covenant), and the prophesied covenant He established through the *Messiah* (the "New" Covenant[18])—became the two names that delineated the two sets of sacred books.[19] Thus, the early Church adopted the expressions "Old Testament" and "New Testament" to differentiate between these two sets of sacred books.

The Old Testament, or Hebrew Bible, was written in ancient Israel over a period of 1,000 years. This book is seen by many as the most influential work of literature ever written. It is a fascinating compilation in that it explores so many subjects: history and culture; leadership and government; law and anarchy; biography and philosophy; tragedy and romance; violence and heroism; defeat and victory; economics and politics; literature and poetry; intrigue and morality; profundity and stupidity; destruction and rebuilding; parables and sermons; despair and hope.

With regard to the New Testament, virtually all conservative scholars agree that the biographies of Jesus (the gospels) were written and circulated during the lifetime of His contemporaries. Even the most liberal scholars hold that the gospels were written between AD 70 and AD 100. Many scholars argue persuasively that some of the accounts of the life of Christ were written as early as AD 50s. Because the death and resurrection of Jesus in AD 30 is so close to the time in which the gospels were written, this eliminates the possibility for legend to have highly influenced the authors.[20] The entire New Testament was completed prior to AD 100 (within 60 to 70 years of the crucifixion), and the vast majority of it was written within 25 to 40 years of

THE CHRISTIAN BIBLE		
THE OLD TESTAMENT (39 BOOKS)		THE NEW TESTAMENT (27 BOOKS)
PENTATEUCH	PROPHETS	GOSPELS
Genesis	Isaiah	Matthew
Exodus	Jeremiah	Mark
Leviticus	Lamentations	Luke
Numbers	Ezekiel	John
Deuteronomy	Daniel	
	Hosea	EARLY CHURCH
HISTORY	Joel	Acts of the Apostles
Joshua	Amos	LETTERS
Judges	Obadiah	Romans
Ruth	Jonah	1 & 2 Corinthians
1 & 2 Samuel	Micah	Galatians
1 & 2 Kings	Nahum	Ephesians
1 & 2 Chronicles	Habakkuk	Philippians
Ezra	Zephaniah	Colossians
Nehemiah	Haggai	1 & 2 Thessalonians
Esther	Zechariah	1 & 2 Timothy
	Malachi	Titus
POETRY		Philemon
Job		Hebrews
Psalms		James
Proverbs		1 & 2 Peter
Ecclesiastes		1, 2 & 3 John
Song of Songs		Jude
		Revelation

Table 5. The Christian Bible

the resurrection. Table 5 identifies each of the major categories into which each of the Bible's 66 books has been placed.

The Apocryphal Books

The set of books known as the *Apocrypha* were written between the third century BC and the first century AD. It consists of fifteen books that were included in a few ancient Greek translations of the Old Testament. These books are largely Jewish literature and history, and are not directly relevant to Christian doctrine. During the intertestamental period—the 400-year period between the close of the Old Testament and the birth of Jesus—various Jewish scholars had written a number of religious books that they did not consider inspired or authoritative. The Apocrypha were well-known among the Jews two centuries before Christ, and had been included in the *Greek translation* of the Hebrew canon, which was known as the *Septuagint*—Greek was the common language of that era—but the Apocrypha were not included in the *Hebrew canon* as decided upon by the Jewish rabbis in AD 90.[21]

At the end of the fourth century AD, when the bishop of Rome (Damasus) commissioned the biblical scholar *Jerome* to prepare a Latin version of the Scriptures, he asked him to translate the apocryphal books as well. Jerome did so only under protest, because he knew these books were not a part of the Hebrew canon—he recognized them as having only *secondary status*.[22] As a result, Jerome followed the Jewish canon and then added a second category for the apocryphal books. Subsequent copyists, however, frequently failed to state that the Apocrypha were *additional works*.[23] Augustine, who also lived in the fourth century, accepted most of the Apocrypha as Scripture, but he also maintained that they had *secondary status* compared with other Old Testament books.[24]

The Apocryphal books were not officially added to the Old Testament by the Roman Catholic Church until the Council of Trent in 1546, when it decided to make them an integral part of their Scriptures. Up until this time these books were understood to be *deutero-canonical* (secondary canon). During the Protestant Reformation of the sixteenth century, the Reformers returned to the Hebrew rabbinic text, which did not include the *deutero-canonical* books.[25] However, the Apocrypha were always a part of the Eastern Orthodox Scriptures, because Eastern Orthodoxy has always embraced the Greek Septuagint as the official translation of the Bible. Though most theologians do not view the apocryphal books as being *inspired by God* (God-breathed), the vast majority believe they have great value from a cultural and historical viewpoint, because they give understanding to the religious climate during the intertestamental period, showing it to be a time of deep turmoil and religious conflict.[26]

Other Ancient Christian Writings

The ancient writings of Christians whose lives overlapped the lives of the apostles are few in number, not only because of the perishable nature of ancient writing material, but also because this was a period of severe persecution in which many Christian writings were destroyed. The writings that do exist, however, give testimony to the existence of the authoritative writings the early church regarded as *Scripture*, and they contain numerous quotations or references to those writings. Some of the early writings that refer to various New Testament books as Scripture are:[27]

- *Clement of Rome* (AD 95) in his letter to the Corinthians, refers to or quotes from Matthew, Luke, Romans, Corinthians, Hebrews, 1 Timothy and 1 Peter.

- *Polycarp* (about AD 110), a friend of the Apostle John, in his letter to the Philippians, quotes Philippians, and reproduces phrases from nine other letters of Paul and 1 Peter.

- *Ignatius* (AD 110) in his seven letters written during his journey from Antioch to Rome, where he was martyred, quotes from Matthew, 1 Peter, 1 John, and cites nine of Paul's letters.

- *The Didache* (AD 100), or *Teaching of the Twelve*, makes 22 quotations from Matthew with references to Luke, John, Acts, Romans, Thessalonians, and 1 Peter.

- *Irenaeus* (AD 130–200), a pupil of Polycarp, quotes most of the New Testament books as "Scripture," which in his time were known as *The Gospel and the Apostles*, in contradistinction to the Old Testament which was referred to as *The Law and the Prophets*.

- *Tertullian of Carthage* (AD 160–220), lived at a time when the original manuscripts of the apostles were still in existence; he speaks of the Christian Scriptures as the "New Testament." Throughout his writings there are over 1,800 quotations from the New Testament.

- *Origen of Alexandria* (AD 185–254), a Christian scholar of extensive travel and great learning, devoted his life to the study of the Scripture. He wrote so extensively that there were times when he employed as many as twenty copyists. In his extant writings, two-thirds of the entire New Testament can be found in quotations. Origen accepted all 27 books of the New Testament.

- *Eusebius* (AD 264–340), a bishop of Caesarea, and church historian, lived through and was imprisoned during Diocletian's persecution of Christians, which was Rome's final effort to purge the world of Christians and destroy all copies of the Christian Scriptures. For ten years the

Roman army hunted down copies of the Bible and had them burned in public market places. Obviously, to those who were Christians, the question of which books were Scripture was no idle matter. Eusebius also lived into the reign of Constantine, who himself became a convert to Christianity; Eusebius became Constantine's chief religious adviser. One of Constantine's first acts on ascending the throne was to order 50 Bibles for the churches of Constantinople (this city bears his name) prepared under the direction of Eusebius, by skillful copyists, on the finest of vellum. When they were completed, he ordered that they be delivered by royal carriages from Caesarea to Constantinople.

• *The Council of Carthage* (AD 397) gave its formal ratification to the 27 books of the New Testament, as we know them today, expressing what had already become the unanimous judgment of the churches. Hence, the Bible became officially recognized as the Christian Scriptures. Historians tell us that there were some 50 spurious written gospels and a number of letters that false teachers were promulgating during the first, second, and third centuries; thus, it was very important for the early Church to distinguish between what was false and what was true. It has been said that Muhammad got his ideas of Christianity largely from these false sources.[28] The early Church exercised extreme care when distinguishing between genuine and spurious writings.

Textual Accuracy of the Scriptures

When the Old Testament writers finished their scrolls, there were no printing presses to duplicate their writing for the public. Instead they depended on *scribes* to patiently copy the Scriptures by hand, word by word. By the time Jesus was born, the most recent Old Testament book (Malachi) had been copied and recopied over a span of more than 400 years; the books that Moses wrote had been copied in this manner for more than 1,400 years. The copies that were made are called *manuscripts*. These manuscripts are important because historians can collect thousands of them to compare how accurate they are. For example, if a particular manuscript that was copied in Egypt was missing a verse or a phrase, it could be compared with manuscripts copied in Israel in order to find the missing words. Obviously, the more manuscripts available to make such comparisons, the better.[29] Biblical scholars have computed that, on the average, scribes probably incorrectly copied one letter out of every 1,580 letters, and these mistakes were usually corrected when they made new copies.[30]

WHAT ABOUT THE *DA VINCI CODE*?

Many people have become enthralled with the spirited judgments that Dan Brown makes against Christianity in his best-selling novel, *Da Vinci Code*. In it he makes a number of claims that are directly at odds with the teachings of Christianity. What many in society apparently fail to realize is that this novel was written as an intriguing story that was published and marketed as a *fiction book* not to be taken seriously; nevertheless this spellbinding book has captivated the minds of millions of people, and many of them, for some reason, seem to think that it's claims are both credible and disprove the central tenets of the Christian faith. George Barna, president of the *Barna Research Group*, responds accordingly to the claims in this book: "Embracing the information in the novel as factually accurate requires a frontal dismissal of the facts contained in the Bible and in historical documentation and scholarship... [To believe the claims of this book essentially requires that we] rewrite human history and experience in order to support a conspiracy theory that revolves around a two millennia pursuit of a chalice."[31] What contributed to the confusion that surrounded this book was the fact that Brown himself originally claimed that he believed the theories espoused in the book, though he later backed off on a number of these claims. Sadly, his recantations didn't receive the same degree of media attention that his claims were given when the book was first released. Obviously, novelists take great liberties with reality when they write fictional books; therefore it should not come as a surprise to learn that this book is not an accurate, truthful depiction of reality. It is simply fiction.

Bible scholars have found the Bible to be about 99 percent free of *any textual variation* in the copies, with the New Testament containing the least number of variations. Furthermore, the majority of the *copying errors* are most often spelling errors, number errors, word order, punctuation, and very minor word alterations.[32] For example, instead of "Jesus," a variation might be "Jesus Christ." So the amount of textual variation of any concern at all is extremely low. Textual critics believe the degree of textual accuracy for the Bible is greater than that of any other book from the ancient world. The reason for this accuracy is that the number of New Testament manuscripts is much closer in time to the original writings than those of other works from ancient times.[33] (See Table 6.)

The New Testament has far more reliable textual support than do the works of Plato, Aristotle, Herodotus, or Tacitus.[34] The earliest extant manuscripts of these ancient authors date from over a thousand years *after* the works were first written. In contrast, the *Encyclopedia Britannica* says the following regarding the time gap and the abundance of New Testament manuscripts in existence today: "Compared with other ancient manuscripts, the text of the New Testament is dependable and consistent."[35] It should also be noted that the relatively short time gap for the New Testament is unique in the history of religious movements. By contrast, Gautama the Buddha's life and teachings were first written down by Buddhist monks between AD 100 and 400, some 600–900 years after his death; so in the case of Jesus of Nazareth, we're not dealing with long folk traditions or collective mythologies.[36] Additionally, the New Testament documents were public and widely disseminated from earliest times. Therefore it would have been impossible for anyone to have materially changed their contents, just as the Declaration of Independence, for example, as a public document, could not have been privately altered without raising notice and creating public furor. Sir Frederic Kenyon, former Director of the British Museum, comments:

> The interval between the dates of the original composition and the earliest extant evidence (i.e., our oldest manuscripts) becomes so small as to be negligible, and the last foundation for any doubt that the Scriptures have come down to us substantially as they were written has now been removed.[37]

MANUSCRIPT EVIDENCE OF SIGNIFICANT ANCIENT DOCUMENTS		
AUTHOR AND TITLE OF BOOK	**TIME GAP BETWEEN THE ORIGINAL AND THE EARLIEST EXISTENT COPIES**	**NUMBER OF EXTANT COPIES**
Herodotus, *History*	ca. 1,350 years	8
Thucydides, *History*	ca. 1,300 years	8
Plato	ca. 1,300 years	7
Aristotle	ca. 1,400 years	49
Demosthenes	ca. 1,400 years	200
Caesar, *Gallic Wars*	ca. 1,000 years	10
Livy, *History of Rome*	ca. 400 years ca. 1,000 years	1 (partial) 19
Tacitus, *Annals*	ca. 1,000 years	20
Pliny Secundus, *Natural History*	ca. 750 years	7
New Testament (written in Greek)	fragment of a book 50 years books of the NT 100 years most of the NT 150 years complete NT 225 years	5,366 all in Greek

Table 6. Manuscript Evidence of Significant Ancient Documents[38]

Reliability of the New Testament

The New Testament alone has more than *5,366 Greek manuscripts* (Greek was the original language in which the New Testament was written), and many of these manuscripts date from the second and third centuries.[39] In addition to these manuscripts there are more than *15,000 manuscripts in other languages.*[40] Historians tell us that no other piece of ancient literature has anywhere close to the number of ancient manuscripts that are available for the Bible. To help put this manuscript evidence in perspective, no one doubts the reliability of the text of Julius Caesar's *Gallic Wars*, but we only have 10 copies of it and the earliest of those was made 1,000 years after it was written. If someone is to dismiss the New Testament documents by arguing that they are corrupted, then he must also throw out all other ancient documents including the writings of Plato, Socrates, Aristotle, and many others, because none of them come close to approaching the number of manuscripts in existence, nor the reliability, nor the accuracy of the copies that exist of the New Testament documents.[41] Though the "original documents" of the Bible (commonly referred to as "autographs") are no longer available, the evidence is extremely strong that these documents were very carefully preserved.[42] The New Testament has far better textual support than do the works of Plato, Aristotle, Herodotus or Tacticus, whose contents no one seriously questions.[43] See Table 6. When scholars examine the various "copy errors" that have been found in existing manuscripts, in not one instance have any of the errors significantly affected the doctrines of Scripture. Most variants consist in misspellings, as illustrated in the following:

> #ou have won five million dollars.
>
> Y#u have won five million dollars.
>
> Yo# have won five million dollars.
>
> You have won five million dollars.

The foregoing illustrates that one can be sure of the message in spite of the variants because each variant is in a different place, and with each new line we get another confirmation of every other letter in the original message. Incidentally, there are a hundred times more biblical manuscripts than there are lines in the above illustration, and there is a greater percentage of variants in this example than in all the biblical manuscripts combined.[44]

As we saw in chapter eight, in 1947 a phenomenal archaeological discovery was made in some caves in Palestine just northwest of the Dead Sea. Over four hundred scrolls (manuscripts) were found in eleven caves overlooking an

View of Qumran Caves where the *Dead Sea Scrolls* were discovered between 1947 and 1956. Many believe these scrolls represent the greatest archaeological discovery of all time. The diverse collection of documents dates from about 250 BC to AD 68.

ancient religious community known as Qumran. The scrolls have revealed that a commune of monastic farmers flourished in the valley from 150 BC to AD 70. It is believed that they put their cherished leather scrolls in large clay jars and hid them in a number of caves in the surrounding hills when they learned that the Romans were coming to invade the land. These manuscripts included biblical and nonbiblical texts, and date back to the closing centuries BC and first century AD. About one hundred of the manuscripts are biblical texts. All of the Old Testament books except the Book of Esther are represented, and some of them are represented several times. The *Dead Sea Scrolls*, as they are most often called, reduced the gap that separated the original biblical writings from the oldest extant copies by about *one thousand years*. When scholars compared the Dead Sea Scrolls with the manuscripts produced one thousand years later, they found an astonishing reliability in textual transmission. Textual scholars discovered that the two copies of the Book of Isaiah found at Qumran proved to be identical with our standard Hebrew Bible in more than 95 percent of the text; the 5 percent that varied consisted chiefly of obvious slips of the pen and minor variations in spelling.[45]

Writings of First-Century Secular Historians

Many of the events recorded in the New Testament have also been corroborated by the ancient writings of a number of non-Christian first-century Roman historians. One such historian named *Tacitus*, who lived during the reigns of at least six Roman emperors (AD 56–120), is best known for his two books, *Histories* and *Annals*. Within these books he references a number of events that were recorded in the gospels of Matthew, Mark, Luke, and John. The following list shows a remarkable agreement between the gospels and non-Christian historical references:[46]

- Christians were named after their founder, "Christ."[47]

- The governor of Judea, Pontius Pilate, had executed Jesus in Tiberius' reign.[48]

- The gospel message was taken to Rome.[49]

- Christians were persecuted and nailed to crosses.[50]

- Some Christians were persecuted and killed by wild animals.[51]

The non-Christian Roman historian *Seutonius* (born AD 70) refers to both Jesus and to Christians in his writings. Seutonius is best known for his work *Twelve Caesars*, in which he writes about the events surrounding the reigns of twelve Roman emperors, from Julius Caesar to Domitian. He makes the following two references:[52]

- The Emperor Claudius told the Jews at Rome to leave the city because they were blamed for certain disturbances, which were instigated by Christ.[53]

- Christians were being persecuted and tortured by Emperor Nero.[54]

There was also the Jewish historian *Josephus* who lived from AD 37 to about 100. He was a member of the priestly aristocracy of the Jews, and was taken hostage by the Romans in the great Jewish revolt of AD 66–70. He spent the rest of his life in or around Rome as an advisor and historian to three emperors, Vepasian, Titus, and Domitian. For centuries, the works of Josephus were more widely read in Europe than any book other than the Bible. They are invaluable sources of eyewitness testimony to the development of Western civilization, including the foundation and growth of Christianity in the first century. His writings support the historicity of a number of events and people in the New Testament.[55] For example, Josephus names *James* as the "brother of Jesus";[56] he identifies *Pontius Pilate* as the one who condemned Jesus to the cross;[57] he speaks of the ministry of *John the Baptist;*[58] and he mentions *Ananias,* the High Priest.[59] In addition, other non-Christian writings such as the Talmud, Tacitus, and Pliny the Younger (governor of Bithynia in Asia Minor, and author of numerous books near the end of the first century) all lead one to conclude the following about Jesus and His followers:[60]

- Jesus was a Jewish teacher.

- Many people believed that Jesus performed healings and exorcisms.

- The Jewish leaders rejected Jesus.

- Jesus was crucified under Pontius Pilate in the reign of Tiberius.

- Despite Jesus' shameful death, His followers, who believed that He was still alive, spread beyond Palestine so that there were multitudes of them in Rome by AD 64.

- All kinds of people from the cities and countryside—men and women, slave and free—worshipped Jesus as God by the beginning of the second century.

Archaeology and the Scriptures

Archaeology is a science unlike that of physics and chemistry, because archaeologists cannot re-create the processes they study and observe them over and over again. The only evidence archeologists have to work with is the *one and only time* a particular civilization was in existence. Both the Old and New Testaments are filled with *thousands* of references to cities, dates, nations, people, and events that it claims to be historically accurate. Unlike nearly every other religion, Christianity is dependent on the historical reliability of critical events. One can verify the integrity of much of the scriptural record simply by examining the *physical realities* that are recorded in it. If some of these references could be proven to be false, it would then be reasonable to assume that the Scriptures might not be accurate when it addresses *spiritual realities.* For the past several centuries archaeologists have excavated hundreds of sites mentioned in the Bible, and so far no archaeological find has ever run counter to a biblical reference.[61]

The Bible is also unique in its historical emphasis. Other religious books and mythical stories are written in such a way that they are unverifiable; there is no way to examine them or support them with historical evidence.[62] But the Bible is locked into space and time in such a way that the reader can know where and when its events took place.[63] Incidentally, in the last few years archaeologists have confirmed the authenticity of a number of individuals and locations mentioned in Scripture, that critics previously denied ever existed. These include *Pontius Pilate* who conducted the trial of Jesus;[64] *Governor Quirinius* of Syria;[65] and the *Pool of Bethesda*[66] in Jerusalem.[67] Many critics doubted that the town of *Nazareth*[68] ever existed; yet archaeologists recently found a first-century synagogue inscription at Caesarea verifying its existence.[69] Other finds have verified *Herod the Great*[70] and his son *Herod Antipas*.[71] The remains of the *Apostle Peter's house*[72] have been found at Capernaum. Bones with nail scars through the wrists and feet have been uncovered, demonstrating the historicity of the *method of crucifixion* as described in the Bible.[73] The *High Priest Caiaphas' bones*[74] have been discovered in an ossuary (a box used to store bones). In addition, there are hundreds of biblical cities that have been verified in archaeological digs, including Arad, Athens, Berea, Bethany, Bethel, Bethsaida, Caesarea Philippi, Capernaum, Chorazin, Corinth, Cyprus, Dan, Ephesus, Galatia, Gaza, Gezer, Hazor, Hesbon, Joppa, Nineveh, Phillipi, Rome, Shechem, Susa, and Thessalonica.[75]

Abraham's original homeland is mentioned in the Bible as *Ur of the Chaldees*.[76] Critics of the historicity of the Bible once doubted the very existence of that city, but it has long since been excavated and explored. Those numerous critics who claimed that the art of writing was unknown in Moses' day (hence he could not have written the Pentateuch, the first five books of the Old Testament) were proved wrong when great libraries of tablets at Ur and other places revealed beyond question that writing was very common long before the birth of Abraham, let alone Moses.[77]

Archaeology has also confirmed the biblical account of the *walls of Jericho* falling flat.[78] In 1997 two Italian archaeologists, hired by the Palestinian Department of Archaeology, excavated the site of Jericho and discovered piles of mud bricks from the collapsed wall, confirming that the walls were not destroyed by a battering ram, but had just collapsed as the biblical account states. The Scriptures also say the entire city and everything in it was burned;[79] a layer of ash three feet thick with remnants of burnt timbers and debris has been unearthed there.[80]

Although it is not possible to verify every incident in the Bible, the discoveries of archaeology since the 1800s have demonstrated the reliability and plausibility of the biblical narrative. The *Hittites* were once thought to be a biblical legend, until their capital and records were discovered at Bogazkoy, Turkey. Many believed the biblical references to *Solomon's wealth* were greatly exaggerated. Recovered records from the past, however, show that wealth in antiquity was concentrated with the king, and Solomon's prosperity was entirely feasible. It was once claimed there was no Assyrian king named *Sargon*,[81] because his name was not known in any other record. Then Sargon's palace was discovered in Khorsabad, Iraq; his capture of the biblical city of *Ashdod*[82] was recorded on the palace walls. Another king who was in doubt was *Belshazzar*, king of Babylon.[83] According to recorded history, the last king of Babylon was Nabonidus. However, tablets were found showing that Belshazzar was Nabonidus' son and served as co-regent in Babylon.[84]

The discoveries of the creation accounts at Ebla in northern Syria in the 1970s also confirm the *creation story*. The library unearthed at Ebla contains more than 17,000 clay tablets from around 2,300 BC. The creation tablet is strikingly close to the biblical account in the book of Genesis, speaking of

HISTORICAL EVENTS RELATED TO ISRAEL'S EXODUS FROM EGYPT

A very old papyrus written by an Egyptian priest named *Ipuwer* tells of two unique events—a series of plagues and the invasion of a foreign power. The plagues match very well with the biblical record of plagues in Moses' time.[85] The papyrus speaks of the river turning to blood,[86] crops consumed,[87] fire,[88] and darkness.[89] The final plague, which killed Pharaoh's son, is referred to also: "Forsooth, the children of princes are dashed against the walls.... The prison is ruined.... He who places his brother in the ground is everywhere.... It is groaning that is throughout the land, mingled with lamentations."[90] This parallels the biblical account which says, "the Lord struck all the first-born in the land of Egypt, from the first-born of Pharaoh who sat on his throne to the first-born of the captive who was in the dungeon... and there was a great cry in Egypt, for there was no home where there was not someone dead."[91]

Following these disasters, there was an *invasion of a foreign tribe* which came out of the desert.[92] This invasion must have been the Hyksos, who dominated Egypt between the Middle Kingdom and the New Kingdom. The Hyksos have been identified as the Amalekites, whom the Israelites met before they even reached Mount Sinai.[93] They might have reached Egypt within days after the Israelites left. The Egyptians referred to them as Amu, and Arabian historians mention some Amalekite Pharaohs. The names of the first and last Amalekite kings in the Bible correspond with the first and last Hyksos kings.[94] This would indicate that the Hyksos entered Egypt just after the Exodus and remained in power there until King Saul of Israel defeated them and released the Egyptians from bondage. And this would explain the favorable relations that Israel had with Egypt during David and Solomon's time.[95]

one being who created the heavens, moon, stars, and earth. People at Ebla even believed in *creation from nothing*. Christian scholars hold that this discovery demonstrates that the biblical account contains the ancient, less embellished version of the story, and that it transmits the facts without the corruption of the mythological renderings.[96] Hence, the *oldest* archaeological findings confirm the creation story of Genesis.

The destruction of *Sodom and Gomorrah* was thought by critics to be merely a myth until evidence began pouring in to show that all five of the cities mentioned in the biblical account[97] were in fact marketing centers in the area and are geographically situated exactly as the Scriptures say. The biblical description of their demise seems to be no less accurate. There is evidence that the layers of sedimentary rock were molded together by intense heat. Evidence of such burning has been found on the top of Jebel Usdum (Mount Sodom). This is permanent evidence of the great disastrous fire that took place in the long distant past in Sodom.[98]

Another interesting archaeological discovery was at King Saul's fortress at Gibeah. (Saul was Israel's first king.) When archeologists excavated the ruins at Gibeah they discovered that *slingshots* were one of the most important weapons of the day. This is significant not only for David's victory over Goliath,[99] but the statement in the book of Judges that there were 700 expert slingers in Israel who "could sling a stone at a hair and not miss."[100]

In addition, archaeology has confirmed the Assyrian invasion of the Northern Kingdom of Israel in 722 BC. Archaeologists have unearthed 26,000 tablets

---

ARCHEOLOGY AND ROMAN CRUCIFIXION

In 1968 a fascinating discovery was made when an ancient burial site containing thirty-five bodies was unearthed in Jerusalem. Archaeologists determined that most of the bodies had suffered violent deaths in the Jewish uprising against Rome in AD 70. One of the bodies was that of a man named *Yohanan Ben Ha'galgol*. He was about 27 years old, and a seven-inch nail was still driven between his feet. His feet had been turned outward so that the square nail could be hammered through both feet sideways at the heel, just inside the Achilles tendon. This means his legs would have been bowed outward so that he could not use them to support himself on the cross. There was also evidence that spikes had been driven between the two bones of each lower arm. These had caused the upper bones to be worn smooth as the victim repeatedly raised and lowered himself to breathe (breathing is restricted with the arms raised). Victims who were crucified had to lift themselves to free their chest muscles, and when they grew too weak to do so, they would die by suffocation. Yohanan's legs had also been crushed by a blow, consistent with the common practice in Roman crucifixion.[101] Each of these details confirms the description of crucifixion in the New Testament.[102]

found in the palace of Ashurbanipal, the son of Esarhaddon, who had taken the Northern Kingdom into captivity. These tablets tell of the many cruel and violent conquests of the Assyrian empire, confirming the Bible's accuracy each time it refers to an Assyrian king.[103] One of the most interesting finds was King Sennacherib's own record of his siege of Jerusalem. Thousands of his men perished and thousands scattered when he attempted to take the city, thus confirming God's word to Hezekiah, through Isaiah the prophet, that Sennacherib would not be able to conquer it.[104] Since the King of Assyria could not boast about his great victory over Jerusalem, he found a way to make himself sound good without admitting defeat. He wrote: "As to [King] Hezekiah, the Jew, he did not submit to my yoke, I laid siege to 46 of his strong cities, walled forts, and to countless small villages in their vicinity... I drove out of them 200,150 people, young and old, male and female, horses, mules, donkeys, camels, big and small cattle beyond counting and considered them booty. Himself I made a prisoner in Jerusalem, his royal residence, like a bird in a cage."[105]

These are just a few examples of the ways in which archaeology has confirmed the truth of the Scriptures. In every period of biblical history, we find substantial evidence from archaeology to support the accuracy of Scripture. The evidence is compelling. While some critics still continue to doubt the accuracy of the Bible, time and continued research have consistently demonstrated that this ancient text is extraordinarily accurate.

Scientific Accuracy of the Scriptures

Though the Bible was written long before our modern age of science, many of its statements reveal a relatively advanced knowledge of scientific matters.[106] Amazingly, it makes scientifically accurate statements about the earth, the heavens, and the human body that predate such discoveries by thousands of years. It should be noted that these statements were made in the midst of cultures that were basically superstitious in nature, not at all scientific.[107] Following are some of these statements that modern science has confirmed.

The Earth

Many of the physical phenomena mentioned in the Bible not only went against the wisdom of the surrounding cultures at the time, but also predate the earliest scientific discoveries of such phenomena by 2,000–3,000 years:[108]

- *The ocean floor contains deep valleys and towering mountains.*[109] Remember, the people of ancient times thought the ocean floor was "flat, sandy, and bowl-like."[110]

- *The ocean contains underwater springs.*[111] Ancient civilizations believed the ocean was fed only by rain and rivers.[112]

- *Moses wrote, "For six years you are to sow your fields and harvest the crops, but during the seventh year let the land lie unplowed and unused."*[113] Allowing the ground to lie fallow every seventh year was not the custom of nonbiblical cultures. It is a practice that modern science has discovered was considerably ahead of its time.[114]

- *God hangs the earth on nothing.*[115] Until recently, scientists believed that the earth and stars were supported by something; but the truth of the matter is, the earth just hangs or orbits in space.[116]

- *The Bible says, "God draws up the water vapor and then distills it into rain, and the rain pours down from the clouds."*[117] These passages reveal the complete hydrological cycle of evaporation, cloud formation, and precipitation. Not until recently has this hydrological cycle been scientifically determined.[118]

The Heavens

When the Scriptures make statements and facts concerning the heavens, the biblical writers *did not misspeak,* even though common beliefs in the surrounding cultures of their day believed otherwise. Though these biblical statements about the heavens are common assumptions today, they were anything but common in the days when the books of the Bible were penned.[119]

- *Biblical writers did not consider the stars to be near us and fixed in their positions.* The Bible speaks of the heavens as an "expanse," which literally means "spreading out,"[120] and the Book of Jeremiah implies that the heavens cannot be measured.[121]

- *Biblical writers did not consider the heavens to have existed from eternity, but taught that they had a beginning,*[122] a fact that was discovered by astronomers only during the first part of the twentieth century and with much reluctance.[123]

The Body

In the 1840s, one out of every six pregnant woman died from "childbirth fever" after entering a particular hospital in Vienna, Austria. One of the doctors, Dr. Ignaz Semmelweis, noticed that their deaths were not random, but that the dead patients had been examined by doctors who had just autopsied victims of childbirth fever. So Dr. Semmelweis implemented a policy that all doctors must wash their hands after doing autopsies. As a result, the mortality rate among pregnant women dramatically dropped to one in eighty-four. What is significant about this story is that the cleanliness laws set down by God through Moses predated by more than 3,000 years the principles of washing to prevent the spread of disease. Moses wrote:

> The unclean person [someone who has touched a dead person or animal] is to take some of the ashes from the burned purification offering, and place them in a jar and pour fresh water over them.... The person being cleansed must then wash his clothes and bathe with water, and he shall be clean by evening.[124]

Such a statement expresses knowledge that what is unseen to the naked eye—germs and bacteria—is responsible for spreading disease. This knowledge was not discovered until the 1800s. Moreover, washing was not a common practice in the surrounding cultures of Moses' day.[125]

The Bible displays knowledge about scientific matters that have only recently been discovered by the scientific community. One, therefore, has to ask how such things could have been known before science established them as *fact*. Below are a few examples of remarkable compatibility between the Bible and modern science.[126] It should be remembered that the majority of these biblical revelations are more than 3,000 years older than those of science.

- The wind and water cycles.[127]

- The laws of health, sanitation, and sickness.[128]

- The ocean floor containing mountains and valleys.[129]

- The oceans having underwater springs.[130]

- The earth having been created spherical or round.[131]

- The naming and workings of the constellations.[132]

- The laws of agriculture.[133]

- The creation of man from dust (every element of the human body is found in dirt).[134]

- The fact the universe had a beginning.[135]

- The fact the universe is running down (law of entropy).[136]

- The almost infinite extent of the sidereal universe.[137]

- The nearly limitless number of stars.[138]

- The paramount importance of blood in life processes.[139]

Though the list above obviously does not *prove* biblical inspiration, it does provide strong evidence that the Bible indeed is inspired. Obviously the principles are not stated in scripture in the technical jargon of modern science, rather they are given in terms of the basic world of man's everyday experience; as such, they are completely in accord with the most modern scientific facts. It is significant also that *no real mistake* has ever been demonstrated in the Bible, whether it be science, history, or any other subject. Hostile critics have claimed to have found mistakes in the Bible, but conservative Bible scholars have always been able to refute their arguments.

Fulfilled Prophecy and the Scriptures

The Bible's capacity to predict the future is one of the strongest reasons for believing it is trustworthy. The ability to predict future events is called "prophecy." Over one-fourth of the Bible was *prophetic* in nature at the time it was written, and these prophecies stand alone in their graphic detail, accuracy, and scope. The role of the biblical prophet was not only to encourage and teach and warn the people, but also to predict future events in God's divine plan.[140]

The Bible contains hundreds of prophecies that were later fulfilled in the minutest detail. Unlike any other book in the world, *only the Bible* offers specific predictions centuries before they were literally fulfilled.[141] The Bible records both the giving of prophecies and their fulfillment. This amazing feature of Scripture demonstrates that God is all-knowing and has complete control over every event, past and future.[142]

The prophecies of Scripture can be divided into three main groups: 1) Prophecies concerning Israel and those nations which interact with Israel; 2) Prophecies concerning the coming Redeemer of Israel (the Messiah) and the world; and 3) Prophecies concerning those major events that will occur during the last days.[143] Many of the most significant prophecies given in Old Testament times were fulfilled in New Testament times in the life and the work of Jesus Christ. Listed below are several detailed examples of Old Testament prophecies about the Messiah. They foretold that He was to...

- Be of the seed of Abraham—Genesis 12:1–3; 22:18 *and* Matthew 1:1; Galatians 3:16

- Be of the tribe of Judah—Genesis 49:10 *and* Matthew 1:2

- Be a descendent of the house of David—Jeremiah 23:5 *and* Luke 3:23, 31

- Be born in the small town of Bethlehem—Micah 5:2 *and* Matthew 2:1

- Be born of a virgin—Isaiah 7:14 *and* Matthew 1:18, 24–25

- Sojourn in Egypt—Hosea 11:1 *and* Matthew 2:15

- Enter Jerusalem riding a donkey—Zechariah 9:9 *and* Luke 19:35–37

- Be rejected by His own people—Psalm 118:22; Isaiah 53:3 *and* John 1:11; 1 Peter 2:7

- Be betrayed for 30 pieces of silver—Zechariah 11:12 *and* Matthew 26:15

- Be silent before His accusers—Isaiah 53:7 *and* Matthew 27:12–19

- Pray for His persecutors—Isaiah 53:12 *and* Luke 23:34

- Die with malefactors—Isaiah 53:9, 12 *and* Luke 22:37

- Be pierced in His side—Zechariah 12:10 *and* John 19:34

- Be wounded and bruised for our sins—Isaiah 53:5 *and* Matthew 27:26

- Be smitten and spat upon—Isaiah 50:6 *and* Matthew 26:67

- Die a humiliating death—Psalm 22; Isaiah 53 *and* Matthew 27:27ff; Luke 9:22

- Have lots cast for His garments—Psalm 22:18 *and* John 19:23–24

- Be buried in a rich man's tomb—Isaiah 53:9 *and* Matthew 27:57–60

- Not have His body decay after death—Psalm 16:10 *and* Luke 24:5ff; Acts 2:31ff

- Be raised from the dead—Psalm 2:7; 16:10 *and* Acts 2:31; Mark 16:6

The Messiah, Jesus, has already personally fulfilled over 100 prophecies, and those that have not been fulfilled involve the period of His future *second coming*. It is important to understand that these prophecies were written *hundreds of years* before Christ was born. Even the most ardent critics admit that the prophetic books were completed some *400 years* before Christ was born. Remember, it is just as hard to predict an event 200 years in the future, as it is to predict one that is 800 years in the future. Both feats would require nothing less than *divine knowledge*. Therefore, the prophetic character of Scripture gives us good reason to believe it is a book worthy of our trust.[144]

These predictions were not only perfectly fulfilled, but the vast majority of them were clearly beyond human ability to manipulate events in order to fulfill them. For example, as a mere human being, Christ had no control over when, where, or how He would be born, how he would die (considering others were responsible for His death), or whether He would rise from the dead. The best explanation for the exact fulfillment of prophecy made hundreds of years earlier is the existence of a transcendent God who knows all things, including "the end from the beginning."[145]

One of the tests of the false prophets was whether their predictions came to pass.[146] Those whose predictions failed were killed by stoning,[147] a practice that no doubt caused serious pause in any who were not absolutely sure their messages were from God. Incidentally, though there are hundreds of prophecies in Scripture, the prophets are not known to have made a single error.[148] There is no other book—ancient or modern, secular or religious—like the Bible. Bible prophecy is completely different from the vague, erroneous, obscure predictions of psychic readings, astrology, and fortune tellers like Jeane Dixon, Nostradamus, Edgar Cayce, and others, whose specific predictions are wrong the vast majority of the time. Biblical prophecy has a *100 percent success rate*, while psychics, astrologers, and fortunetellers have a *92 percent failure rate*. Jeane Dixon, for example, predicted that Jacqueline Kennedy would not remarry, but she married Aristotle Onassis the very next day![149] Only the Bible manifests this consistent, remarkable prophetic evidence, and it does so on such a tremendous scale that it renders completely absurd any explanation other than divine revelation.[150]

Some people cannot understand how God can predict something that has not yet happened. It's important to understand that God *transcends* time and space. He is beyond it, He exists outside of it, so He is able to see the end from the beginning. Remember, the God of the Bible is *infinite* in every way. The Apostle Paul responded to the greatness of God with these words: "Oh, the depth of the riches both of the wisdom and knowledge of God! How unsearchable are His judgments and unfathomable are His ways! Who has known the mind of the Lord, or has became His counselor?"[151]

CHAPTER 13

THE EARLY YEARS OF CHURCH HISTORY
FIRST THROUGH FIFTEENTH CENTURIES

History is a voice forever sounding across the centuries
the laws of right and wrong.
— *J. A. Froude*[1]

As the largest of the world's religions, Christianity possesses a varied and immensely complex history that dates back nearly two thousand years to the age of its founder, a first-century Jew named *Jesus of Nazareth*. However, the sacred history of Christianity can actually be traced back further, to the time of *Abraham*, the historic figure who lived 2,000 years before Jesus Christ; Jews, Christians, and Muslims all trace the origins of their respective faiths back to Abraham. Yet further still, Christianity can legitimately be traced all the way back to the time of *Creation*.[2]

Over the centuries, Christianity has experienced three significant periods of macrodevelopment: It has gone from a state of *Persecution* under Roman government, to one of *Establishment*, where it enjoyed the full support of the state, and then to one of *Separation* from the state, where it has experienced an autonomous existence in nearly every part of the world. From its very beginning, Christianity has had divisions and schisms within its ranks. There have been individuals within Christendom who have advocated slavery, class distinctions, and racial bigotry; while at the same time there were those who actively spearheaded the eradication of these social inequities. Authentic Christianity is not a perfectionist religion, as some might think, but one that lives with the ambiguities and disappointments of history. This fact does not absolve it from the need to realize the kingdom Jesus envisioned, but it does mean that the perfection of what He preached will only come to full realization at the consummation of human history.[3]

History can be as complex or as simple as we make it. It is easy to trivialize the history of Christianity by dealing with its complex issues in too superficial and cursory a fashion. This chapter and the following one present a general overview rather than a complex untangling of social, political, economic, and religious events. The intention is to provide a historical perspective in which each of the various Christian traditions can be identified. Those who are interested in gaining a more in-depth perspective of each of these traditions will need to read more fully from a variety of different sources.

The First and Second Centuries: The Early Church

Christianity was born into a completely Jewish context, and the earliest followers of Christ did not think of themselves as separate from the Jewish religion and culture. Because the early Church primarily consisted of Jews, Christians saw themselves as a *Jewish sect*, distinguished only by their belief that Jesus was the Messiah.[4] Their worship was modeled on Jewish services and their understanding of what Jesus taught was grounded in the Hebrew Scriptures. The rapid growth of the Christian movement within Judaism caused unrest among Jewish leaders, and as a result they threatened and persecuted the followers of Christ. Peter was imprisoned, Stephen was stoned to death, and James was beheaded by King Herod. Because of the struggles and the tensions that existed within first-century Judaism, the Christian community had to learn not only how they differed from Judaism, but also what they had in common with it. No matter what culture they found themselves in, they had to address these and other questions. As their numbers continued to grow, Christians developed their own religious, philosophical, and political identity.[5]

Christianity was forced to grow and mature in the Hellenistic world of pagan philosophy and ideas. Since the Greek world respected philosophical sophistication, early Christianity was faced with the challenge of making the Christian faith philosophically respectable. As they encountered Greek philosophy, the Christian writers and scholars of the first and second centuries laid the philosophical foundations for what would later become an elaborate Christian theology.[6] Christianity not only learned how to adapt to a culturally and religiously diverse world, it also learned where to borrow, and how to shape its message to fit the climate of the day.[7] In addition, Christianity used the amazing system of Roman roads and sea routes to carry the gospel to every corner of the Mediterranean world. For the first four centuries Christianity's greatest growth occurred in the cities in the Roman Empire and in those places with which Rome had trade or colonial outposts.[8]

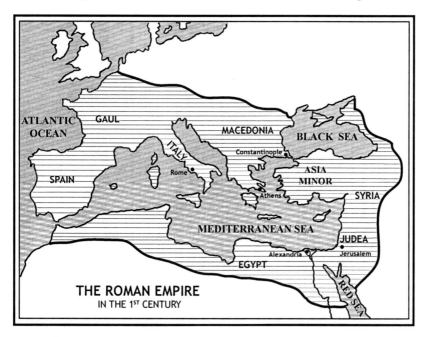

THE ROMAN EMPIRE
IN THE 1ST CENTURY

Persecution in the Early Church

During the first century, the Jews were in a volatile political situation because they were involved in periodic outbreaks of insurrection against Rome. In AD 66 an unprecedented Jewish rebellion took place against the Romans in Jerusalem. It resulted in one of the most savage wars in history: more than one million Jews were killed or sold into slavery. Since a significant part of the early Church was Jewish, this war of national liberation presented a serious problem to those who were Christians. As such, Jewish Christians were caught between the demands of national identity and the words of the gospel. Full of apocalyptic expectation and reminded of Jesus' teachings about the last days,[9] many Jewish Christians fled the city. This act made them *traitors* in the eyes of Jews.[10]

In AD 90, twenty years after the destruction of Jerusalem by Rome, the *Sanhedrin* convened, and many Jews wanted to rid Judaism of any trace of Christianity and condemn those Jews who had accepted Jesus as Messiah. A formal curse against Christians was added to Jewish morning prayer, and

This is a classical reconstruction of the Roman Forum of Antiquity, the center of imperial Rome. This relatively small parcel of land (just five acres) controlled most of the known world for centuries. The victorious generals and emperors would parade down its main street, before finishing at the Temple of Jupiter. The Forum was the scene of public meetings, the location of lawcourts and open-air markets, as well as the center for religious and secular spectacles and ceremonies. Julius Caesar himself moved his residence to the Forum in 45 BC.

Christians were prohibited thereafter from associating with Jews. When Judaism formally severed connections with those who were Christian, in the heat of the controversy some Christian writers disparaged Judaism, arguing that it was a worthless, unnecessary extension to the Christian faith. Christianity therefore developed an identity separate from Judaism, but it was indebted to the Jews for its roots, its Scripture, and for its liturgical forms of worship.[11]

In the Roman Empire religions had to be licensed. Judaism was legal, but when Christians began to see themselves as separate from Jews, and the Jews rejected them, Christians were no longer accepted as members of a legal faith. Because of their illegitimate status and their prophecy that the world would end in fire, they were the obvious scapegoats for the emperor *Nero* when the people accused him of burning Rome in AD 64. To turn the public's hatred away from himself, Nero falsely accused the Christians of having set Rome on fire. He had large numbers of Christians arrested and began a period of bloody persecution of them. According to tradition, the apostles Peter and Paul also suffered martyrdom at this time.[12] While the Roman Empire was basically tolerant of different religions, it persecuted Christians because they were strict monotheists who refused to worship Caesar or honor the Roman city-gods. In an era when everyone in the empire was supposed to worship Caesar or sacrifice to the gods—to insure victory or forestall harm—Christians refused to do so.[13] So Christians found themselves at odds with the normal religious practices of their day, and this led to a ban on all Christian worship practices. Coupled with this was the fact that Christians also refused to serve in the military; this was seen as an act of disloyalty to the state, which was a crime punishable by death. Incidentally, it was not until the fourth century, as a result of Augustine's teaching, that Christians began abandoning the pacifism taught by Jesus[14] and practiced by His followers.[15]

Persecution frequently resulted in Christians moving to less threatening areas within the Roman Empire and thus became a cause for the rapid dissemination of the Christian message.[16] Severe persecution continued to occur sporadically throughout the empire until AD 313, when the emperor Constantine (288–377) converted to Christianity and established it as the primary faith of the empire.[17]

Heresies in the Early Church

Though the early Christian community was small in number, it adapted to new situations, and many were courageous even to the point of death. It has been estimated that the Christian population by the end of the first century numbered about 500,000; by the close of the second century this had risen to nearly 2,000,000.[18] As the Christian church grew it became increasingly complex, and eventually a dominant organizational model emerged in which officers (bishops) were elected by congregations to teach and to supervise.[19] At the outset the church was fairly homogeneous, and their organizational problems were relatively few. But once the Christian community began to attract large numbers from all classes and occupations, controversies and questions arose pertaining to all kinds of issues: discipline, jurisdiction, membership, behavior, and doctrine, to name a few. As time went on, and as questions grew more complex, church leaders from a large region would meet to discuss them.

In the second century, the *Apostolic Fathers* had developed a system for dealing with a few heresies that were being propounded in the church—Marcionism, Docetism, and Montanism. These heresies in large part dealt with the person and work of Jesus Christ and the Holy Spirit. The central figures among the apostolic fathers of the first and second centuries were Clement of Alexandria, Ignatius of Antioch, Polycarp of Smyrna, and Justin Martyr. Each of these was martyred for his faith, with the possible exception of Clement.[20] In addition, there were three other highly acclaimed scholars in the second century: Irenaeus of Lyons, Tertullian of Carthage, and Cyprian of Carthage. To face and resolve the issues of heresy during this era, the church developed *norms*—an agreed upon body or canon of Scripture and creeds. The 27 books of the New Testament had taken the fixed form in which it exists today, and it served as the normative guide for deciding matters of doctrine, practice, and worship.[21] One of the creeds that emerged in the early church was the *Apostles' Creed*. Future creeds and definitive statements came about as church bishops gathered together in a series of meetings called *councils*, where they decided matters of Christian doctrine and practice.[22]

The Third and Fourth Centuries: The Union of Church and State

Toward the end of the third century a priest named Arius taught that Christ was a special creature of God, but that He Himself was not God. This teaching came to be known as *Arianism*, and it gained a very substantial following in the Christian community. At the Council of Nicaea in AD 325, Arius's teachings were condemned as heresy. This council and the Council of Constantinople in AD 383 dealt with matters concerning the divinity of Christ and His place in the Trinity, and from these councils came the *Nicene Creed*.

As noted earlier, the officials of Rome considered the Christian faith to be a banned religion; this policy continued in effect for over two hundred years. The persecution of Christians reached its zenith and became empire-wide under the Roman Emperor Decius in AD 250. Archaeologists have discovered third-century evidence which reveals martyrs' shrines becoming places of pilgrimage, with churches built over their tombs. Toward the end of the third-century popular opinion throughout the empire began to change. A large number of Christians had settled in the Eastern provinces, and despite persecution and anti-Christian propaganda, they began to exert a considerable degree of political and economic influence.[23]

In the first four centuries Christianity grew most vigorously in the cities and the colonial outposts of the Roman Empire. By the end of the third century, it had grown to almost 5 million people. (The entire population of the Roman Empire was about 50 million people at that time.) After the conversion of the emperor Constantine in the fourth century, and the legalizing of Christianity in AD 313, the total number of Christians throughout the empire rose to nearly ten million.[24] Christians constituted about 10 percent of the Latin-speaking population in the West, and approximately 35 percent of the Greek-speaking population in the East.[25]

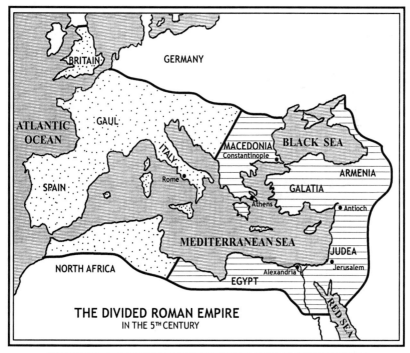

THE EASTERN EMPIRE WAS RULED BY THE *GREEK* CHURCH OF CONSTANTINOPLE.
THE WESTERN EMPIRE WAS RULED BY THE *LATIN* CHURCH OF ROME.

Emperor Constantine Converts to Christianity

After his conversion Constantine became the protector of the Church, and it was the emperor himself who called and presided over the first world council of the church—the Council of Nicaea in AD 325. Early in the fourth century, Constantine established a new capital for the Roman Empire on the site of Byzantium, which would later bear his name—*Constantinople* (present-day Istanbul, Turkey). In AD 330, the city was named the capital of the Christian Empire.

Within seventy years of Constantine's conversion and legalization of Christianity, emperor Theodosius, by proclamation, made Christianity the "official religion of the state." This official recognition had profound implications for Christianity, because now it was not only a legal religion, but it enjoyed the patronage of the state. With this new status, the Church inevitably absorbed the sociolegal structures of the larger culture,[26] and its image became more and more linked to the political stability of the state.

This union of Church and State, bishop and emperor, religion and politics, resulted in an uneasy marriage of convenience. In the centuries that followed there would be a bitter struggle for power and supremacy. This marriage would also discredit the spiritual leaders of the time and transform the Church into an institution that reflected unbending legalism in interpretation and administration. Christianity would become in many ways a mirror image of the empire itself: universal, catholic, orderly, multiracial, and increasingly legalistic. By the fourth century the Church had built up an impressive following, and it began to act like a State Church. It had become the religion of the empire. More and more the Church was administered by *bishops* who were professionally literate and members of the aristocratic, land-owning ruling class; as such they functioned like bureaucrats and acted like imperial governors.[27]

Bridgeman Art Library

Bronze head of Constantine the Great (280–337), the first Roman emperor to convert to Christianity. He helped put an end to institutionalized persecution of Christians in the empire.

The Great Theologians of this Era

By the fourth century Christianity had penetrated as far north as Britain; as far south as Africa; as far west as the Iberian Peninsula; and as far east as Byzantium (Constantinople) and Syria.[28] By the end of the fourth century the churches and bishops of Christendom were centered in five great principalities: Rome, Constantinople, Antioch, Jerusalem, and Alexandria. Their bishops were called *patriarchs*, each with equal authority, and each possessing full control of his own province. After the patriarchs of Jerusalem, Antioch, and Alexandria gradually came to acknowledge the leadership of Constantinople, the struggle for the leadership of all Christendom was between the patriarchs of Rome and Constantinople.[29]

In the fourth century, the simple worship service of the Christian faith grew increasingly more complex and formal.[30] Under Damasus I (366–384), Bishop of Rome, the liturgy became more elaborate and formalized; the vestments worn by the clergy became more colorful; gold and silver ornaments were introduced; and incense and candles became commonly associated with the pomp and pageantry of worship. The Roman language of Latin was taken from the secular world and introduced as the language of liturgy, replacing Greek. Damasus also had his secretary, *Jerome*, translate the Old and New Testaments into Latin; this translation became known as the Latin Vulgate.[31]

Throughout the western part of the Empire no church rivaled that of Rome, and all the churches of the West acknowledged the supremacy of the bishop of Rome. With this acknowledgment the *Papacy* came into existence, and the bishop of Rome came to be called the *Pope*—a title derived from the Latin word papa, meaning "father"—and the church over which the pope ruled as supreme head came to be known as the *Roman Catholic Church*.[32] Most historians identify Leo I (440–461) as the first pope. The West under weak emperors was crumbling, and Leo was the one strong man of the hour. He claimed he was by divine appointment *Primate of all Bishops and Lord of the Whole Church*, and he stated that resistance to his authority was a sure way to hell.[33] The patriarch of Constantinople, however, claimed equal authority with the bishop of Rome, and the struggle for supremacy between these two churches grew.

The greatest scholar of the first three centuries was *Origen of Alexandria*. He was a pupil of Clement, but became far more famous than his teacher. A deep and original thinker, he wrote a number of large scholarly works.

His book *Against Celsus* was a brilliant rebuttal to this critic of the Christian faith and was instrumental in helping the Church come to a better understanding of the person and work of Christ.[34] The three great theologians of the fourth and fifth centuries were Augustine of Hippo, Ambrose of Milan, and Jerome of Rome.

Augustine (354–430) was one of the greatest thinkers and theologians of ancient Christianity, and as bishop of Hippo he was the leading figure in the church of North Africa. He also had a profound and lasting influence on the subsequent development of Western thought and culture. His theological thinking dominated the Middle Ages (500–1500) so much that he has been regarded as the *Father of the Western Church.*[35]

Ambrose (340–397) was a man of great talent and integrity who gave his wealth to the poor and the church.[36] He realized the Church was increasing in wealth due to imperial favor, and in accepting such favor it had become indebted to the emperor and lost its autonomy. He believed if the Church was freed from its links to the State, it could fulfill its prophetic role. He reminded the people that the State was not absolute and that the Church was in need of reform. Ambrose and Augustine both believed the Church was a higher and independent society in comparison to the State.

Jerome (340–420) was another critic of the early Church. He said, "Our walls glitter with gold… yet Christ is dying at our doors in the persons of His poor and hungry." Jerome saw the mission of the church as that of proclaiming the Word of God to the whole world.[37]

One form of resistance to the Roman culture, which had become a part of the Church by the fourth century, was made by a number of highly devoted believers who fled the populated cities for the deserts in order to live a more perfectly religious life. These desert dwellers, often referred to as the Desert Fathers and Mothers, were the seedbed from which a number of *monastic orders* eventually developed.[38] The monastic idea of a celibate life, regular daily prayer, self-denial, and asceticism, and an intense yearning for salvation would leave its mark on later Christianity. In the West, when urban life went into decline after the fifth century, the monastic life provided *missionaries* to Northern Europe. In the East, monasteries became centers of religious life from which bishops were selected. Monasticism was not just the domain of men; from the earliest days there were women ascetics in both the East and the West. Religious orders of women have played an enormous role in the Christian world, especially in Roman Catholic circles.[39]

The Fifth through Fifteenth Centuries: The Middle Ages

The Fall of the Roman Empire

By the end of the fourth century, the political might of the Roman Empire was in a state of decay, and the Germanic barbarian invaders from the north conquered it. Christianity had become the main religion in the empire, so the Roman Church not only survived, but it became the greatest unifying force in Europe during the Middle Ages. It effectively ruled the kingdoms of Europe for a thousand years.[40] During this time the Roman Empire divided into two—the West came under the influence of the *Holy Roman Empire*, and its political rival in the East was ruled by the *Byzantine Empire*. So *Eastern Christendom*, centered in Constantinople, became increasingly separated from *Western Christendom* which was headquartered in Rome. The result was the development of two separate factions within Christendom: Roman Catholicism in the West, and Eastern Orthodoxy in the East. As the split widened, some minor traditions and theological views developed that are unique to both the Eastern and Western churches to this day.[41] Between the fourth and the eleventh centuries, Constantinople was the capital of the Eastern Roman (or Byzantine) Empire. During the feudal Middle Ages, the hundreds of tiny city-states throughout Europe had so little power that the Roman Church became a secular as well as a spiritual power, with the Pope seen as a prince as well as a spiritual leader. By the beginning of the seventh century the Pope was in effect the undisputed ruler of the West.[42]

During this period, a number of circumstances contributed to the growing estrangement that developed between East and West, including linguistic and cultural differences and political events such as the coronation of Charlemagne by Pope Leo II as the *Holy Roman Emperor,* in opposition to the Roman Emperor of Byzantium.[43] While the Pope had no secular authority over the East, he nevertheless claimed that as Peter's successor he had full spiritual authority over all Christendom. However, the patriarch of Constantinople, claiming spiritual descent from the Apostle Paul, made a similar claim.[44] Doctrinal differences, the practice of the Eucharist, the issue of clerical celibacy, and questions regarding the authority of the Pope over all of Christendom were major issues that served to widen the gap between the East and the West.[45]

Although the structures of the empire had vanished in the West, an old Roman sense of order and structure remained alive in the Church. Between the sixth and tenth centuries, the Roman Church gave institutions and laws to barbarian society, and nearly all of Europe and North Africa came under its influence. The Roman Church became a center for learning, with the monks becoming cultural carriers transmitting the written treasures of the past by preserving and copying ancient texts. The evangelizing monks spread the theology of Rome and its law, and popularized its Church liturgy. It was through the growth of western monasticism that the Church's influence spread to even the fringes of the empire. The inspiration behind the development of western monasticism was the monk *Benedict of Nursia*, who founded a monastery of the Benedictine order in 529. He formulated a cohesive and practical rule, which governed the way of life for his followers; they ultimately spread the rule throughout western Europe.[46] This rule of life incorporated a spirit of service and ministry to the wider community, and after its acceptance by Pope Gregory the Benedictine rule was viewed as the norm for monasticism in the West.

The Union of Church and State

The coronation of Charlemagne in 800 by Pope Leo III as the *Holy Roman Emperor* can be seen as a formal recognition that the Church's unity and the political unity of the State were indivisible. Charlemagne decreed that every monastery must have a school for the education of boys in singing, arithmetic, and grammar. With the coronation of Charlemagne, the power of the Church spread quickly, and Christian control of western society became, in theory, complete. Within two centuries, the Church established itself as a form of theocracy that increasingly legislated on every aspect of politics and economics, and especially the everyday lives of individuals.[47]

Bridgeman Art Library

Charlemagne (742–814)—his name in Latin means "Charles the Great." He became king of the Franks in 768, and was crowned "Holy Roman Emperor" by Pope Leo III on Christmas Day in 800. Charlemagne helped define Western Europe and the Middle Ages; his rule is associated with a revival of art, religion, and culture.

By the end of the tenth century the West had spread Christianity into the northern sections of Europe, and the East had evangelized Russia, giving it an eastern form of worship and polity. In time, the Russian Church would come to see itself as an autonomous

"Third Rome," standing as an equal with the patriarchs of ancient Rome and Constantinople. Missionaries from the West then evangelized the Scandinavian countries and the rest of Eastern Europe, which was not under the direct influence of Russia or Constantinople.[48]

With the reemergence of urban life in the Middle Ages, cities took on a more important role in the development of religious life. The rural monastic centers gave way to the preeminence of *Episcopal life* centered around cathedrals. Schools and, eventually, universities were also founded. New religious orders such as the Franciscans, the Dominicans, and others ministered to urban populations. The papacy became increasingly bureaucratic and took to itself more centralized powers of administration and jurisdiction. Intellectual life was robust, partially because of the rediscovery of Greek learning, which came to the West from Islamic sources, influencing Christian thinkers during this period. The theological debates and thinking of the first to the fourth centuries (when Greek philosophy and Christian faith had been in dialogue with each other) were reopened. This blend of Greek philosophy and Christian theology gave rise to a new synthesis of Christian learning called *Scholasticism*,[49] so called because scholars in medieval universities taught it. From this period on, philosophy found its natural home in the university and became less and less exclusively associated with the Church.[50] The most noted scholastics of the eleventh and twelfth centuries were Anselm, Peter Abelard, Bernard of Clairvaux, and Thomas Aquinas.

By the end of the tenth century the Church had taken on an *authoritarian role*, proclaiming the gospel as a divine message to which the world must humbly listen. A great deal of the arable land of Europe passed into the hands of men committed to the discipline of hard work. Abbots and bishops were an innovative elite within society; many of them were aristocrats and themselves were the sons of land magnates. By this time monasticism in the West had become an upper-class movement. Monks who were literate essentially came from these upper classes, while the sons of illiterate peasants usually were kept in lower orders and performed menial tasks.[51]

The darkest period of history for the Papacy was the eleventh and twelfth centuries. During this time *warring princes* often controlled the Church. Pope followed pope in rapid succession, and most of them ended their careers being deposed from office, imprisoned, or murdered. The 200 years between Nicolas I and Gregory VII (858–1085) is referred to by historians as the "Midnight of the Dark Ages"; bribery, corruption, immorality, and bloodshed made it one of the blackest chapters in the history of the Church.[52] This era is often referred to as the Dark Ages, because it was such a *dark time* for the Church spiritually. For example, the church was controlled for a time by three high-ranking, beautiful but utterly unscrupulous women, and the vile tale of their immoralities with popes and nobles is unprintable. Church historians of every stripe have recorded the disgusting behavior of dozens of popes with great indignation.[53]

One of the worst leaders, Pope John XII, was deposed on charges of murder, blasphemy, and gross sensuality. The list goes on and on: Sergius III was said to have had a mistress named Marozia and a number of bastard sons; Marozia had her own illegitimate son appointed pope,[54] and her grandson made the Papal Palace a brothel; Boniface VII murdered Pope John XIV; Benedict VIII bought the Office of Pope with open bribery (this common practice was referred to as "simony"); John XIX also bought the Papacy (he passed all the necessary clerical decrees in one day); Benedict IX was made Pope as a 12-year-old boy through a money bargain with the powerful families that ruled Rome; he surpassed John XII in wickedness by committing murders and adulteries in broad daylight, and some have called him the worst of all the popes. During this period, kings habitually sold Church offices to the highest bidder, regardless of the character of the individual. The result was that there were numerous men who were raised to the position of pope, but who were completely unqualified for giving spiritual leadership of any kind.[55] Such abuses are an embarrassment to the entire Christian community.

The Emergence of Islam

In 600 Islam was founded by *Muhammad*, and it soon began to supplant Christianity across the Middle East and North Africa. In 638 the Muslims captured Jerusalem. The rise of Islam in the seventh century radically changed the geographical face of Christianity. The traditional Christian strongholds of greater Palestine, Egypt, and North Africa fell to Islam, with further Islamic incursions into the Iberian Peninsula in the West.[56] This placed the ancient centers of Christianity under Muslim rule and greatly reduced the Eastern Empire. The occupation of North Africa meant a significant loss to the Western Church. The North African Church had long been an invaluable ally to both popes and emperors, but with Islamic rule it was cut off from the West, making Rome the only religious authority of a barbarian West.

By 700 Christianity had lost nearly half of its territory to the forces of Islam. And by the end of the eighth century, most of the area where Christianity was born had come under the rule of Islam, so that the Orthodox patriarchates of Alexandria, Antioch, and Jerusalem kept only a shadow of their former

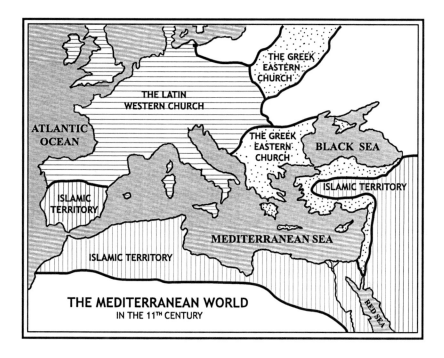

THE MEDITERRANEAN WORLD
IN THE 11ᵀᴴ CENTURY

glory.[57] These were times of acute social turbulence and anarchy that came perilously close to bringing about the collapse of all European civilization.[58] It was not until Charlemagne was crowned Holy Roman Emperor in 800 that stability and unity returned to the Western Empire, along with a new thirst for scholarship.[59]

In response to the advances of Islam, the West conducted a number of Crusades to free the Holy Land and its sacred places from the control of the Muslim Turks. The first Crusade was organized in 1095 by Pope Urban II. Urban ordered red cloth cut up into strips and sewn together into the forms of "crosses"; these red crosses were affixed to the sleeve of every soldier. The Latin word for "cross" is *crux*, which was why these campaigns were called "crusades" and the participants "crusaders."[60] The first Crusade regained the Holy Land, establishing the Kingdom of Jerusalem, ruled by the military leaders who had won the battle. Though the kingdom lasted for about 90 years, it was not a very strong or flourishing kingdom. In 1147, a second Crusade was launched in order to bolster it, but the Muslims ultimately recaptured it in 1187. A third Crusade was launched to retake the kingdom, but this campaign only achieved a face-saving treaty that granted Christians the right to visit the Holy Sepulcher. Most historians say there were nine separate Crusades conducted over a period of 200 years.[61]

Generally speaking, the majority of the Crusades were failures, and those that did succeed were scandalous and disgraceful. By their end in 1291 they had created a level of distrust and hatred between Christians, Muslims, and Jews that have plagued the world to this day.[62] Perhaps the most significant evil perpetuated by the Crusades was the belief that military power could be used to spread the Christian faith; that the sword at times could be more efficient than the word in presenting the gospel. So the Crusades lent support to the idea that the robbery, torture, and murder of those who held different religious beliefs was not only permitted but even approved by Christian teaching.[63] Such teaching is completely contrary to Scripture.

The Great Schism between the East and the West

After one thousand years of existence, the Christian East and the Christian West had begun to manifest some significant differences. Years earlier, when the empire was separated into two parts for purposes of administration, it was only natural that the two areas would tend to grow apart.[64] By the eleventh century the rift between the Eastern and Western churches had reached a point of no return, resulting in what is known as the *Great Schism*. In 1054 an emissary of the Pope went to the Cathedral of the Holy Wisdom in Constantinople and laid on the high altar a bull of excommunication, declaring that the entire Eastern church was cast out and damned for heresy. In return the Patriarch of Constantinople excommunicated the entire Western church.[65]

Once the Roman Crusaders had defeated the Muslims and firmly taken control of Constantinople, they turned their attention to the Orthodox Christians and attempted to convert them to Latin Christianity. When the Greek-speaking eastern Christians refused, the Roman Christians confiscated their Church buildings, imprisoned their clergy, and treated them as though they were of a completely different religion. Though the Islamic conquests were perceived by both Rome and Constantinople with alarm, that was not enough to heal the bitter rift that had emerged between the two Churches. Contemporary Greek historians describe how the drunken soldiers danced on the altars of Orthodox Churches, and how the corpses of men, women, and children were profaned by the conquerors. The Greeks were staggered by the cruelty and sacrilege of the Roman Christians. The conquering of Constantinople was an occasion of plunder and destruction seldom equaled for horror even in modern history. War in the Middle Ages was a brutal and destructive affair. Soldiers and Latin clergy vied in their attempts to seize riches for themselves; even the precious Holy

Altar of St. Sophia was polluted, broken into pieces, and sold. The sack of Constantinople in 1204 dealt the final blow to relations between these two branches of Christendom. The majority of Eastern Christians refused to recognize Western Christians any longer as their brothers and sisters in Christ; they refused to take communion with them; and they refused to pardon and forgive them, considering Latin Christians to be nothing more than *idolaters* who worshiped the Pope.[66]

Therefore, the final blow to the unity of the Eastern and Western Churches was not some heresy, but the drunken Crusaders who conquered Constantinople in 1204 and massacred its Christian population. It was not until their common spirit had been destroyed that differences in doctrine and practice became apparent. In the centuries that followed, the Byzantine and Latin traditions took several different positions. The Christian East was mainly interested in doctrine, whereas the Latin West gave emphasis to morals; the East possessed a particular gift for worship, whereas the West focused more on discipline and order; the East emphasized the divergence of gifts, and the West the need for uniformity and obedience. It became increasingly difficult for the two sides to understand each other, because they often approached problems from completely different perspectives. A study of the relations between East and West throughout the Middle Ages is a sad and sordid business. Both parties willfully persisted in their errors; one side was arrogant, the other unforgiving.[67]

The Papacy at the Time of the Crusades

Just prior to the first Crusade, Gregory VII (1073–1085) was the pontificate of Rome. He was a man of great intellect and a fiery spirit, whose main goals were to reform the clergy and bring absolute power to the papacy. He sought to create a Christian commonwealth under the control of the papacy. During his reign, he decreed that the Roman pontiff alone had the power to depose emperors; that no one could sit in judgment of him; that no one could be regarded as catholic who did not agree with the Roman Church; that he alone could make new laws, call general councils, and authorize canon law; and that all princes should kiss his feet.[68] In the years leading up to Pope Gregory, practically all bishops and priests had paid for their office. As we have seen, kings habitually sold Church offices to the highest bidder, regardless of character. This brought Gregory into a bitter confrontation with the German emperor, Henry IV, and war was the result. Gregory was driven from Rome and died in exile, but he had accomplished his goal of making the papacy independent of imperial power.[69]

The Roman Church reached its greatest political power during the pontificate of Innocent III (1198–1216). He also made extreme claims for papal authority over both the Church and the State. He claimed to be the "Vicar of Christ" and the "Vicar of God," and the "Supreme Sovereign over the Church and the World."[70] To be the "Vicar of Christ" was to be God's ecclesiastical agent in the world. During his reign he was able to raise the papacy to supreme control of the State, and practically all of the kings of Europe obeyed his will. He claimed that Peter was not only given the universal Church to govern, but the entire world. Innocent believed the emperor was given power by the pope, who in turn was given power by God.[71]

It was Innocent III who instituted the *Medieval Inquisition*, a Roman Catholic court, whose business it was to detect and punish heretics. Everyone was encouraged to inform against heretics. Anyone suspected faced the possibility of punishment, without knowing the name of his accuser. The Inquisitor pronounced sentence, and the victim was turned over to civil authorities to be imprisoned for life or burned at the stake. The victim's property was then confiscated and divided between the Church and the State.[72] In 1231, Gregory IX put the Dominican monks in charge of the Inquisition. Its first famous use was against the French Albigensians, who preached against the immoralities of the priesthood and the worship of saints. Historians tell us "their blood flowed like water" for twenty-five years.[73]

Though there were a number of disgraceful popes during the Middle Ages, it should be noted that not all of them were bad. Many were men of character and faith; many allowed for dissenting views; many did their best to represent Christ and His Church; and even some of those whom history identifies as tyrants had noble motives.

Historical Events that Led to the Reformation

From the fourth to the eleventh centuries, the Church in the West had been challenged to survive, to withstand political pressure from outside, and to convert the barbarian tribes of Europe to Christianity. To some the Church had been a remarkable success; most Europeans had become Christians, and the Church had managed to secure autonomy by becoming a powerful political entity as well as the highest spiritual authority in the West. To others, however, the Church had assumed too much power, got involved in the wrong issues, and did not give sufficient attention to spiritual matters. This perception, prominent from the late eleventh century on, markedly increased throughout the Reformation.[74]

From the eleventh to the fourteenth centuries, the Roman Catholic Church found itself involved in intense political struggles. The papacy was being challenged by the emergence of new nationalistic rulers. Many people, especially scholars in universities, believed that the pope ought to surrender all political power, leave politics to kings, and become a strictly spiritual ruler. The response of the church was to exaggerate the papal claims. Popes declared they not only had complete power over Christendom, but power over the entire world as *vicars of Christ*, and that they could step into any situation in which a sin had been committed.[75] The famous nineteenth-century historian, Lord Acton, said, "Power tends to corrupt and absolute power corrupts absolutely." Perhaps that explains why popes did not reform the church along lines that limited their power. It may also explain why so many national leaders become despots when they assume broad political power. Whatever the reasons, the battles between Church and State in the fifteenth and sixteenth centuries were mostly fought over political power. The old authoritarian structures of the medieval papacy were now at odds with the spiritual and intellectual uneasiness of an awakening world. This age of awakening would later come to be known as the *Renaissance*.[76]

In the twelfth and thirteenth centuries the church erected beautiful *cathedrals* in which they displayed valuable relics and major works of religious art. The wealthy were heavy contributors through the purchase of favors and indulgences. The thirteenth century also witnessed the foundations of *universities* throughout Europe. These universities quickly rose in importance and would play a vital role in the intellectual life of the West in the centuries that followed. The thirteenth century also saw the papacy uprooted from Rome and reestablished in Avignon (France) for a period of nearly seventy years. During this time all the popes were French, and were completely under the domination of the French kings. Many of the popes during these years lived lives of luxury and wickedness.[77] The fourteenth century ended with a papacy in turmoil, forced into a schism which saw three rival popes enthroned simultaneously. This period of moral decline, confusion, and conflict led to a schism in the Church. In 1414 the schism ended when the *Council of Constance* held that a general council of the Church, not the pope, was the highest ecclesiastical authority. Then in 1417 the Council elected the Italian cardinal Martin V as the new pope, and the other three popes all gave him their support.[78] By this time, however, the wounds suffered by the papacy were deep and long lasting, and reverence for the papacy would never fully recover among believers.

There were other important developments during this period. By the dawn of the fourteenth century, the Roman Church had founded some 600 Cistercian monasteries or convents. In 1215 St. Francis of Assisi renounced his wealthy life, devoted himself to poverty and charity, and founded the *Franciscans*. At about the same time the Spanish priest Dominic de Guzman founded the *Dominicans*; they emphasized the use of the intellect in matters of faith. Thomas Aquinas became the most famous of the Dominicans. This expansion in Scholastic intellectual theology was located mostly in Northern Europe.[79]

The fourteenth century was characterized by deep social unrest and intellectual upheaval, and Europe was recovering from an outbreak of bubonic plague. The *Black Death* as it was called, moved rapidly across Europe, killing nearly one-half of its population in a very short time. Not surprisingly, this period was characterized by great religious anxiety. Many people believed that the plague was an act of divine punishment, and they were terrified about their own survival and chances for salvation.[80]

During this period much of Europe had developed a great hunger for art and learning. The invention of the printing press, the availability of books, the tremendous influx of Greek manuscripts after the fall of Constantinople to the Muslims (1453), all gave scholars new things to discuss and new ways to discuss them. It is within this labyrinth of issues that we must understand the religious reform movements. One of the central questions concerned religious authority. Where did one turn for the truth? The answers were many: the pope, ecumenical councils, the Bible, tradition, classical antiquity, mystical experience, and one's own conscience.[81] This period is referred to as the *Renaissance*, or "rebirth," and it sparked a period of exploration and discovery that resulted in, among other things, the opening of Asia to the West and the discovery of the Americas. It also threatened the power structure of the Church as people discovered that the "Holy Mother Church" did not have answers to every question.

As people began to question the teachings of Rome, the Catholic Church decided that it had to take drastic action,[82] and in 1478 Pope Sixtus IV, at the request of Ferdinand and Isabella of Spain, issued a papal bull that created the *Spanish Inquisition*. The Inquisition was concerned with Jews who had converted to Christianity either under duress or out of social convenience, and were suspected of still secretly practicing their Jewish faith. But the reach of the Inquisition soon reached further than this, and it brought about a reign of terror throughout Europe, which ultimately was responsible for the impoverishment, exile, and death of thousands of Jews, Muslims, and Christians accused of heresy. Jews were singled out for persecution simply because they were Jews. Jewish children over six years of age were taken from their parents and given a Christian education. Accused heretics were identified by the general population and brought before local tribunals of Inquisition. If they would admit their alleged wrongs and identify other aggressors against the Church, they would be released or given a prison sentence. If they would not admit to heresy or indict others, they were publicly killed or sentenced to life in prison. The Spanish Inquisition was not formally abolished until 1834 by King Bonaparte.

The late Middle Ages was a period of both vitality and decline. Theology, monasticism, the papacy, the arts, and popular piety all flourished as never before. At the same time, however, decadence and corruption had dramatically weakened the Church. Pope Pius II is reputed to have been the father of many illegitimate children; Paul II filled the palace with concubines; Sixtus IV decreed that money would deliver souls from purgatory; Innocent VIII had 16 children by various married women; and Alexander VI, held by many to be the most corrupt of all the Renaissance popes, bought the papacy, had numerous illegitimate children that he appointed to high church offices while they were still children, and had cardinals and others who stood in his way murdered.[83] During this period, the church acquired great wealth. The clergy and monks regularly gathered money from believers through the sale of privileges associated with pilgrimages, relics, and indulgences, and they bought and sold the offices of the Church whenever the need for more money arose. By the end of the Middle Ages it was clear that the popes were without control over either the Church, princes or themselves.

Throughout this difficult period there were calls for reform. In the fourteenth and fifteenth centuries *John Wycliffe* in England and the Czech *Jon Huss* called for both theological and practical reform of the Church. Others looked to the councils of the Church to undertake the cause of reform. Repeated attempts to rid the Church of its corruption, as well as secular control of the Church and its wealth, were ineffective because of the self-interest of those who stood to gain by blocking reform.[84] By the end of the fifteenth century, it was apparent that neither individuals nor councils had succeeded in reforming the Church. To this distress was added the collapse of the Byzantine Empire in 1453 to the Muslim Turks. Constantinople fell after a siege and became the capital of the *Islamic Ottoman Empire*; St. Sophia's Cathedral was turned into a mosque. In time, the Turks would control many of the traditional Byzantine strongholds, including Greece itself, and would maintain that control until their empire collapsed beginning in the nineteenth century.[85] The religious, spiritual, and political traditions of the Byzantine Empire continued to live on to a large extent in the Slavic churches of Serbia, Rumanian, Bulgaria, and Russia.[86]

The flight of Greek scholars from the East to the West during the fifteenth century, as a result of Islamic conquest, gave tremendous impetus to the Renaissance movement in Europe. Many scholars within the Church believed this fresh "new learning" would be a vehicle to help reform the Church. In the end it gave the Christian world many of the intellectual tools that aided the Reformation, including a number of Bible translations and critical writings from the patristic period.[87]

In the middle of the fifteenth century, *Johann Gutenberg* developed a printing press with moveable type. As a result of the invention of the printing press, literacy rates greatly increased, and the Scriptures became widely available to the common person for the first time. Intellectual life became more vibrant and scholars began to challenge old methods like Scholasticism and encourage new reliance on biblical scholarship.[88] People became aware of great discrepancies between what they were reading in Scripture and what was being practiced by the Catholic Church, and an increasingly literate Europe began to seriously question the doctrine and authority of the Church. By the close of the fifteenth century, there were numerous voices throughout Europe calling for urgent reform, and when this did not happen, open dissent led to the Reformation.[89] The Reformation was not an isolated incident of protest, but a series of reform attempts and movements between the fourteenth and seventeenth centuries.

Chapter 14

THE LATER YEARS OF CHURCH HISTORY
SIXTEENTH THROUGH TWENTIETH CENTURIES

We have not formed the right theory of History until we
see History itself as a spiritual drama, moving toward a
significant dénouement and at the same time a process which
has meaning and value as it goes on.
— *Rufus Jones* [1]

The Sixteenth and Seventeenth Centuries:
The Renaissance and The Reformation

The Renaissance

Many factors helped bring about the era of reform in the church, and one
of the most important was the *Renaissance*. As we have seen, when the church
in the East crumbled and Constantinople finally fell to Islamic invaders
(1453), an exodus of Greek-speaking intellectuals went westward. Italy was
geographically close to Constantinople and became a refuge for emigrants
who revitalized interest in the Greek language and its classical culture. The
New Testament had originally been written in *Greek*, but Jerome's *Latin*
translation of the Bible had become the standard of the Roman Church in
the fifth century; this translation was known as the *Vulgate*. It was becoming
increasingly clear to a number of theologians that the Vulgate and other
Latin translations of the Bible were inadequate and unreliable. Access to the
New Testament in its original language of Greek was needed. [2]

Desiderius Erasmus (1466–1536), a Dutch humanist and Catholic advocate of reform produced a critical edition of the Greek New Testament. Erasmus had been educated in classical ideas, studied in Paris, and for a time was a professor at Cambridge in England. He believed the best way to revive the church was by real scholarship that included going back to the original sources—the Hebrew Old Testament, the Greek New Testament, and the early Christian Fathers. Erasmus was the author of a number of books; his literary masterpiece was the *Greek New Testament* that he published in 1516. For the first time, theologians could compare the original Greek text of the New Testament with the later Latin Vulgate translation.[3]

Erasmus not only believed that the Church could be reformed and renewed by the common believer, he also believed that the Christian's inward faith could be deepened through the reading of Scripture. His books had enormous appeal to educated laypeople and underwent numerous editions. His teaching against the corruption of Rome was so effective that all his works were included on Rome's *Index of Forbidden Books* in 1559. Many believe it was his works that laid the foundation for the Reformation.[4] It has been said that "Erasmus laid the golden egg [of the Reformation] and Luther hatched it."[5]

For centuries literacy had been restricted to the clergy in the Church. But at the beginning of the sixteenth century, because of the development of printing, adult literacy was increasing all over Europe. The clerical monopoly on literacy had been broken, and there arose a mood of anticlericalism in which an increasingly articulate laity voiced its contempt for those in religious authority. Those who protested abuses in the Church came to be known as *Protestants*.[6]

The Reformation had begun with a spark, and it soon emerged as a raging fire, fueled by the continued abuses in the Church, such as those associated with Pope Leo X. In 1513, Leo owed 125,000 ducats and was facing bankruptcy. It was during this time that the Vatican was being built in Rome,[7] and a lot of money was required to pay

Desiderius Erasmus (1466–1536), Dutch humanist and Catholic theologian who prepared important new Latin and Greek editions of the New Testament, which raised questions that were highly influential in bringing about the Reformation.

The Basilica of St. Peter's, located at the Vatican in Rome, was built over the traditional burial site of St. Peter. It is the world's largest church—it is some 700 feet long and 450 feet wide. Most of it was built during the Renaissance in the second half of the 15th century, when there was heightened interest throughout Europe in literature, art, and architecture. Raphael and Michelangelo were two of its famous architects. Many of the popes at this time were irreligious men who gave far more attention to their own luxury, the patronage of art and literature, and the building of projects that cost immense sums of money. By using various schemes to exact money from the people, they managed to accumulate vast sums of money in the papal treasury. This caused great dissatisfaction with the papacy in northern Europe, and was one of the important issues that helped launch the Reformation.

for St. Peter's Church, so he implemented the practice of selling *indulgences.* The Roman Catholic doctrine of *purgatory* meant that the souls of the dead went to a place where they could be "purged" for heaven. People were told that by purchasing an indulgence, they could shorten the time they would spend in purgatory, that the souls of the dead could be freed and go straight to heaven.[8] The sale of indulgences was a highly effective way of channeling vast sums of money into the pope's coffers, and the higher the asking price the more people tended to buy them. As the indulgence business grew, so did the abuses associated with this fallacious doctrine.[9]

The increase in learning that was the product of the Renaissance furnished the reformers with the historical background necessary to prove that the Church of their day had departed from the simple faith of the early Church, and had encumbered religious practice with a number of forms, customs, and rituals that had no significant place in the apostolic Church.[10] As people became more and more knowledgeable about what the Scriptures taught, they began to question the doctrines and practices of the Church. Men such as John Wycliffe, Jon Huss, Ulrich Zwingli, Martin Luther, and John Calvin attempted to reform the church from within, but their movements ultimately resulted in schism and a completely new branch of Christianity. This was the start of the *Protestant Reformation*, a movement that is generally considered to have begun officially in 1517 when Martin Luther nailed his *Ninety-Five Theses* to the door of the church in Wittenberg, Germany.[11]

The Reformation

The most significant reform movement before Luther was one associated with two university professors, *John Wycliffe* (1328–1384) in England, and *Jon Huss* (1372–1415) in Bohemia (more recently Czechoslovakia, now the two independent states, the Czech Republic and Slovakia). Wycliffe believed religion had become too much a matter of clerical authority, so he attacked the authority of the pope and extolled the authority of the Bible. He declared that Scripture rather than the Church should be the only rule of faith,[12] arguing that the office and claims of the pope had no support from Scripture. His most courageous work was a translation of the Bible into English. The Catholic Church had for centuries used the Latin translation of the Bible and had discouraged translations into the vernacular. In addition, Rome taught that Scripture was only to be read and interpreted by the Church. Wycliffe, however, believed all Christians should be free to read the Bible for themselves, and to do so meant reading it in their own language.[13]

Bridgeman Art Library

John Wycliffe (1328–1384), English theologian and an early dissident in the Roman Catholic Church during the 14th century. He is credited with helping translate the Bible into English.

When Jon Huss became acquainted with the teachings of Wycliffe, he also began to boldly preach against the hierarchical organization of the Church and the corruption of the clergy. In 1414 the Catholic Church convened a council at Constance; it posthumously condemned Wycliffe and demanded that his remains be dug up and burned. The council then brought Huss to trial for heresy, but he refused to recant unless the council fathers could prove to him, from Scripture, that he was wrong. Though the council could not prove him wrong, they still had him burned at the stake. Many believe the failure of the Council of Constance to implement church reform led directly to the Protestant Reformation.[14]

The Protestant Reformation had the effect of directing the arguments in the Church back to *religious* issues. The four main groups involved in the Reformation—Lutheran, Reformed, Anglican, and Anabaptist—were each united in their opposition to the traditional Roman Catholic positions on the nature of salvation, the sale of indulgences, and the issue of religious authority.[15] The Catholic Church taught that one was saved through a combination of *faith and good works,* that indulgences could procure God's favor, and that the pope was the supreme authority over the Church. The Reformers, on the other hand, shared a strong commitment to the idea that salvation was by *faith alone,* that the authority for Christian faith and life was the *Scripture alone,* and that the sale of indulgences was completely unscriptural. They believed indulgences not only gave Christians a false sense about their salvation, but more importantly, they perverted a right understanding of God. The Reformers argued that to see God as an avenging judge who needed to be appeased, as medieval Catholics sometimes did, was contrary to what Scripture taught. The Reformers believed God was a loving Father who forgave freely.[16]

Martin Luther (1483–1546) was a Catholic monk, scholar, and teacher, who came to believe in his study of Scripture that one is saved by *faith alone;* that good works were useless in procuring salvation. From childhood, he had absorbed the teaching of the Church, yet for years he struggled with issues of guilt, sin, and salvation. Under the influence of the Church, he came to the conclusion that the best way to gain salvation was to flee the world; therefore, he took to a monastery and became a monk. He lived a life of strict asceticism, praying and fasting beyond what the monastic rules required. He kept his cell unheated, even in the cold of winter, and wasted away physically until he was little more than a skeleton. Still he remained oppressed with a terrible sense of his sinfulness and lost condition, and this cast him into deep despair. No matter how hard he tried, he never felt that he had done enough to earn his salvation. Sometime in the later part of 1512, Luther began to study Paul's letter to the Romans, and when he read the seventeenth verse of the first chapter—"the just shall live by faith"—he paused and pondered, and an incredible joy flooded his heart. Luther had learned that man was not saved by *works,* but by *faith.*[17] That day the Holy Spirit set free his guilty conscience.[18] Luther also came to the understanding that salvation is neither a gradual process, nor is it accomplished by the accumulation of merit through righteous action; but that it is a gift from God to anyone who accepts the work of Christ on the Cross, and that this gift is received by faith.[19] So Protestantism was founded on the belief that God deals directly with each individual man and woman, and that salvation is gained by *faith alone*.[20]

While serving as a professor of Scripture at the University of Wittenberg, Germany, Luther grew increasingly appalled at many of the practices that were going on within the Church. So on All Saints' Day in 1517, he publicly criticized the sale of indulgences by attaching his *Ninety-five Theses* to the door of the Castle Church at Wittenberg. There was really nothing unusual about affixing his theses to the door of the church, because the door was commonly used as the university bulletin board. But in posting his theses, in effect he was inviting any doctor of theology to debate him publicly on the value of indulgences.[21] This was the act that became the spark that ignited the Protestant Reformation. Within the next ten years Luther would articulate every major difference he had with the Catholic Church. His underlying principle was a belief in *the human conscience enlightened by the Holy Spirit*. Luther insisted that where human traditions contradict the scriptures—whether they are the product of popes, councils, or anyone else—*Scripture alone* was the authoritative source of religious knowledge.[22]

Luther's theses were quickly printed and disseminated in many languages, and within four weeks they were read all over Western Europe. Soon his views were being debated throughout the Church, and Luther wrote a general answer to those who were opposing him. This book, *Resolutions*, was written very carefully and contained a point-by-point defense of his theses. It was addressed to the pope and it struck hard blows in two tender spots—his power and his purse. Luther's views gained such wide public support that they almost completely stopped the sale of indulgences, thus depleting the pope's coffers. In 1518 Pope Leo X responded by issuing a summons for Luther to appear at the *Diet of Augsburg* to be interviewed. A diet was a national

Bridgeman Art Library

Martin Luther (1483–1546), famed German Catholic theologian and one of the leading figures of the Reformation. He translated the Bible into German, which influenced the translation of the English King James Bible.

meeting of all the princes and leading men in Germany. At the diet, a delegate of the pope, Cajetan, interviewed Luther, and when the discussions became heated, some close friends of Luther tried to persuade him to settle things peaceably by giving in. Luther refused to recant and withdraw his views, which meant that he was now in rebellion against the pope.[23] That evening his friends smuggled him out of Augsburg for his own safety.

On June 15, 1520, Luther was condemned as a heretic by the Church in Rome, and a mandate was issued demanding all the faithful to burn his books. By way of reply, Luther burned the papal document at a public meeting, and the people appeared to be on his side. During this era Germany was divided into some 300 independent states, all loosely under the headship of the Holy Roman Emperor. Although the pope ostensibly exercised control over the churches in Germany, the nationalistic fervor of the German people, and their anti-papal sentiment, reduced his influence in that region. The newly elected emperor of the Holy Roman Empire, Charles V, wanted to see the dispute between the papacy and Luther resolved peaceably, so he summoned Luther to the *Diet of Worms* in 1521. When Luther appeared before the emperor, he said, "Unless I am proved wrong by scriptures or by evident reason, then I am a prisoner in conscience to the word of God. I cannot retract and I will not retract. Here I stand. I cannot do otherwise. God help me."[24] The diet ended with Charles V reluctantly outlawing Luther's writings and condemning him. Though Luther was to have officially been placed under the ban of the empire, punished, and his books burned, the ban was never formally instituted.[25]

Prince Frederick the Wise, a strong territorial ruler and silent defender of Luther, had him seized by friendly hands and taken secretly to the Wartburg Castle for his protection. A majority of the German princes remained sympathetic to Luther, and by 1526 they were granted the right to support either Catholicism or Protestantism in their realms.[26] Soon after Luther went into hiding, he began the huge task of translating the Bible into German, using Erasmus' Greek text as the basis. He completed this massive project in 1534, and in addition he wrote hundreds of hymns, lectures, and liturgies.[27] Luther believed that if people could just read the Scriptures in their own language, they could come to understand and experience the joy, assurance, and freedom of a faith-alone salvation.[28] When his translation was finally published most of the churches in Germany began to conduct their worship services in German rather than Latin. In 1530 at the Diet of Augsburg, Luther's closest friend and co-worker, *Philipp Melanchthon*, was commissioned to draft the Augsburg Confession, which became the official statement of Lutheranism.[29] Because of Luther's great love for music, the singing of hymns by the congregation was another innovation that became an integral part of Protestant worship. Luther said, "After theology, I give to music the highest place and the greatest honor." Of the hundreds of hymns Luther wrote, his most famous was *A Mighty Fortress Is Our God.*

Luther's translation of the Bible into German, his theological writings, and practical leadership made him the primary architect of the Lutheran tradition. He also helped inspire the reformers of a number of other Protestant traditions. By the 1500s the religious map of Europe had been totally changed. Before long Protestantism split into two strands—Lutheran and Reformed. The *Lutheran Movement* took hold in parts of Germany, Scandinavia, and much of the Baltic area. The *Reformed Movement*, initiated by a Swiss reformer named *Ulrich Zwingli* (1484–1531), took root in Switzerland. Though Zwingli was strongly influenced by Luther, he did not hold to all of his views. When Zwingli died the French reformer *John Calvin* (1509–1564), took his place as the leading Reformed theologian. Reformed theology is often referred to as Calvinism. In 1536 Calvin wrote his finest work, *The Institutes of the Christian Religion.*[30]

Besides the classical reformers such as Luther and Calvin, more radical reform movements emerged that attempted to reconstruct a form of Christianity they believed reflected the faith and practices of its early days.[31] The *Anglican Movement* that took place in England developed in a unique way. In order to secure a male heir to the English throne, King Henry VIII sought to remarry. But before he could do that he needed his present marriage to be annulled. When the pope refused, Henry rebelled against Rome, and in 1534 he asserted royal primacy over the church by declaring that the king (not the pope) was to be head of the Church in England.[32] After Henry died a long period of turbulence ensued as English Catholics and Protestants vied for control. When Queen Elizabeth I ascended the throne in 1558, she sought a middle ground between Catholicism and Protestantism. When James I succeeded Elizabeth in 1603, he authorized the making of a new English translation of the Bible. The

King Henry VIII (1491–1547) became king of England in 1509, and helped enact legislation to sever the Church of England from the Roman Catholic Church.

result was the *King James Version*, published in 1611. This translation of the Bible would powerfully shape the English language for centuries to come.

The *Anabaptist Movement* did not believe that it was scriptural to baptize babies, only adults. So they rebaptized one another with a believer baptism. They sought to live in conformity with Scripture, and to restore the Christian faith to its apostolic roots. In order to do this, they declared that the New Testament was the sole norm for Christian living and understood their relationship to Jesus as one of discipleship.[33]

For a period of time Protestantism swept everything before it. This was not only due to the furious, bold attacks on Roman Catholicism by Luther, Zwingli, Calvin, and a host of lesser reformers, but also to the carelessness of the popes and the ongoing corruption of the Roman Church. For a while it seemed like the Catholic Church would collapse in utter ruin. Then the Protestant Reformation began to slow down because more radical reformers began surfacing, and division began setting in among each of the groups advocating reform. But another major cause for the slowing of the Reformation movement was the reform and revitalization of the Roman Church. The Catholic Church, once again, was ready to move forward.

The Counter-Reformation

In 1545 the Roman Church struck back against the Protestant Reformation by convening the Council of Trent in northern Italy. It supported a movement known as the *Counter-Reformation*. This council rejected Protestant theology and sought to reform many of the abuses that had been occurring in the Church. It affirmed the authoritativeness of tradition as well as Scripture, and strengthened the pope's authority and that of the bishops. The Council of Trent (1545–1563) met continuously for 18 years and breathed new life and theological thinking into the Catholic Church. Though some of its policies would later be rescinded, Trent produced some strong theologians who carried the Roman Church out of the Middle Ages and into the light of the Renaissance.[34] Among the many doctrines and practices affirmed by the Council of Trent, six in particular were strongly directed at the reformers.[35]

1. Scripture is *not* the only source of divine revelation.

2. Individuals may *not* interpret the Bible for themselves.

3. The Protestant doctrine of sin and justification is *false*.

4. The chalice (the cup in communion) was *denied* to the laity.

5. The doctrine of *purgatory*, and the use of *relics* and *indulgences* were upheld.

6. Rome published an *Index of books* that church members were forbidden to read.

The Council of Trent strengthened the Roman Catholic Church against the demands of the reformers, and inspired reform that would effectively guide the Church for the next several centuries. Because of its strong centralized model of ecclesiastical authority, the Catholic Church did not foster or accept divisions within itself; one was either a loyal Catholic or one left the church by choice or excommunication.[36] Though the Catholic Church ultimately reached agreement with the Protestants on justification by faith, they refused to compromise on papal authority. This failure to compromise meant that the hard-line Catholic zealots influenced the council to state their doctrinal positions in an anti-Protestant way.

The counterattack on Protestantism was led by the Catholic monk, *Ignatius Loyola*, who in 1534 founded the Society of Jesus, which became known as

the Jesuit Society. Much of Loyola's input at the Council of Trent would become the normative statement of counter-reformation belief for the next four hundred years. Its period of influence was only brought to an end by the *Second Vatican Council* (1962–1965), which breathed a very different spirit.[37] At that council, efforts were made to understand Protestants, and much of the hostile thinking that characterized Trent began to disappear. The primary importance of Scripture was affirmed; lay people were given a greater role in the church; Protestants were recognized as genuine Christians; it was declared permissible to celebrate the liturgy in the vernacular of the people; more congregational participation in worship was encouraged, and the *Index of Forbidden Books* was abolished.[38]

Ignatius Loyola (1491–1556) was the principal founder of the *Society of Jesus* (also known as the Jesuit Society), a religious order of the Catholic Church, whose ambition it was to lead a life of self-denying labor in direct service to the pope in terms of missions. Members of the order are called Jesuits. Loyola was also active in fighting the Protestant Reformation and promoting the Roman Catholic "Counter-Reformation."

Catholicism flourished after the Reformation by reaffirming its differences with Protestantism, and by attending to many of the legitimate complaints about corruption, and eradicating many of the abuses. If Protestants were seeking a simplified Christianity, stripped of splendor and mystery, Catholics responded by emphasizing those very things. Churches were lavishly decorated, especially in Rome, where artists gave Roman Catholicism a glorious baroque flavor; and liturgy was celebrated with pomp and ceremony, often accompanied by elaborate orchestrations of the Mass.[39]

Other Reformation Developments

The Protestant Reformation produced in its wake a host of cultural changes. It shifted religious sensibility away from the old Catholic sense of the iconic and sacramental toward a renewed interest in the *Word of God* enshrined in the scriptures. With that shift, vernacular translations of the Bible became crucial, along with the need for greater literacy. The reformers also put a significant emphasis on music as a vehicle for worship, so that the tradition of vernacular hymnody as well as other musical forms (e.g., the chorale) flourished.[40] The era of reform permanently changed Christianity in the West. Though many lamented the fragmentation of the Church, massive reforms had long been needed, and division was the impelling force that finally brought them about.

The centuries of religious reform overlapped with Europe's exploration and colonization of North and South America. In the aftermath of the great period of Renaissance exploration, Catholic missionary ventures were launched to the New World of the Americas as well as to India and the Orient. Similarly, Protestant churches expanded into the New World as a result of the colonizing impulses of England and Holland in the seventeenth century. Both Catholicism and Protestantism made further incursions into Asia and Africa as a result of colonial expansion that lasted into the twentieth century.[41] Through the missionary efforts of Protestants and Catholics alike, Christianity would become a global religion.

The *Anglican Church* continued to operate with a hierarchical structure, and attempted to find a middle way between Roman Catholicism and Protestantism. There were many, however, within the Anglican Church who sought a more comprehensive reformation. They wanted a Christianity that was purged of anything Roman in practice, liturgy, or doctrine. It was their focus on purity that earned them the nickname *Puritans*. They encouraged direct personal religious experience, sincere moral conduct, and simple worship services. Worship was the area in which Puritans most desired change.

A drawing depicting the landing of the Mayflower in 1620, at the site of what would later become the town of Plymouth, Massachusettes.

In the seventeenth century Puritanism increased greatly in popularity. Because the government and the Church of England were becoming increasingly repressive, many of the Puritans emigrated to America.[42] In 1620 the Pilgrims of Plymouth numbered 102; by 1634 their number had grown to 10,000; and by 1643 they numbered some 18,000. This expansion came through the mass migration of Puritans from England. Over a period of twelve years, in nearly 200 ships, the Pilgrims arrived in Massachusetts Bay. Their social and political program included the building of towns and churches, the founding of free schools, and the creation of Harvard College.[43]

The two main groups of Puritan reformers were the *Presbyterians* and the *Congregationalists*. Presbyterianism is a form of church government that combines some congregational insights (the importance of the local church) with some advantages of the hierarchical model (more centralized authority). Congregationalism is a form of church government that rests on the autonomy and freedom of the local congregation.

The seventeenth century also saw other Protestant groups separate from the Church of England and form their own denominations. Most prominent amongst these were the *Baptists* and the *Quakers*. Both groups shared a common belief in the autonomy of the local congregation. They had Congregationalist roots, but they differed from the Presbyterians and the Congregationalists in that they repudiated infant baptism, and believed baptism was to be done by immersion (not by pouring or sprinkling). The Quakers believed that all people have within them the "Inner Light" as the fundamental source of religious certainty and deep spiritual assurance, and they believed all outward forms of religion should be rejected; i.e., ministers, rituals, church institutions, hymn singing, etc. Although by the end of the seventeenth century the Anglican Church had become the official Church of England,[44] these four dissenting groups—Presbyterians, Congregationalists, Baptists, and Quakers—constituted a sizable minority amounting to about one-tenth of the population of England during the seventeenth century.[45]

The Pilgrim Separatists, Baptists, Quakers, and Puritans did not all agree doctrinally, so when they emigrated to America they often ended up settling in different areas. In the seventeenth century the Pilgrim Separatists founded the *Massachusetts* colony; the Puritan leader Roger Williams founded *Rhode Island* on the principle of religious freedom; *Virginia* was settled by businessmen from London who supported the Church of England and Anglicanism; William Penn and the Quakers founded the *Pennsylvania* colony; the Roman Catholics settled in the *Maryland* area, which was under the control of the Church of England; and the Congregationalists eventually established churches in *Connecticut* and *Massachusetts*. In the eighteenth century Jonathan Edwards would become their greatest preacher.[46]

During the seventeenth and eighteenth centuries, the reverberations of the Reformation were felt throughout the Christian world. Religious reform continued, and Christianity became global in its scope. Many factors contributed to Christian growth and globalization. Catholic missionary orders and Protestant mission societies translated the Bible into a number of languages and planted Christianity in many parts of the world. Asian, African, Hispanic, and American Christians began to build indigenous churches and send out their own missionaries. Colonial settlement on several continents helped contribute to the globalization of Christianity.[47]

The Eighteenth and Nineteenth Centuries: The Age of Enlightenment

Rationalism and the Eighteenth Century

The astronomical discoveries of Copernicus and Galileo in the seventeenth century challenged the beliefs of the common people and resulted in weakening the control exerted on them by the authority of the Church. Much of the challenge from science to religion stems from the radically different approaches each discipline uses. *Science* is predominantly concerned with explaining natural phenomena by the use of empirical methods; i.e., observation, experimentation, and interpretation. On the other hand, *religion* is concerned chiefly with divine revelation and received wisdom. *Copernicus* (1473–1543) was responsible for developing the view that the sun rather than the earth was the center of the universe. *Galileo* (1564–1642) observed the heavens with a telescope and his observations supported Copernicus's view of the solar system. These discoveries challenged the accepted worldview that the earth was the center of the universe, a view the Roman Church had errantly supported.

This new scientific development led to the view that the universe was a closed system of cause and effect. God was considered to be the necessary "first cause" that started the system in the first place, but once He set it in motion, some scientists believed He no longer interfered with its natural processes. Hence the scientific revolution ushered in the *Age of Enlightenment* or *Rationalism*. In everyday language rationalism simply means that everything is judged by "reason."[48] The resultant effect of rationalism was the religion of Deism, which logically argued that the *natural world* sufficiently reveals God, but there is no need for additional *supernatural revelation*. So the enlightened rationalists believed people were now being called out of the darkness of religion (perceived as mystery or superstition) into the enlightened world of reason.[49]

The seventeenth century had been a century of *orthodoxy*, where Protestants and Roman Catholics were both concerned with dogmatic formulation of their positions for the purpose of catechizing their adherents.[50] But cold orthodoxy did not satisfy, and with the rise of *Rationalism* in the eighteenth century the Christian community reacted in a number of ways to this challenge. Some grew defensive, spending their energy denying the legitimacy of the challenge; some tried to defend Christianity by using the skill and tools of post-Enlightenment scholarship; some tried to combine Enlightenment insights with religious impulses and developed a more Deistic religion;[51] some tried to alter or reinterpret Christianity to remove the seeming contradictions and make it more amenable to rational explanation; and still others saw it as an opportunity to adapt to the emergence of a new world.

In the English-speaking Christian churches of the eighteenth century, the Age of Reason became the *age of renewal*. In the United States the Age of Enlightenment undermined religious faith and brought about a serious decline in religious life in the eighteenth century. One of the factors that rejuvenated it was a revival movement known as the *Great Awakening*. This was actually a series of revivals that spread across denominational lines and engendered a spirit of religious cooperation based on shared religious beliefs. The most famous figures of this period were *Jonathan Edwards* (1703–1758) and the English evangelist *George Whitefield* (1714–1770). American Evangelicalism was born in the Great Awakening; it stressed a new birth, and its evangelistic strategy was to elicit a response.[52]

In Germany the age of renewal was fueled by the *Lutheran Pietist Movement*, the central figures of which were *Philip Jacob Spener* (1635–1705), who founded the movement, and *Count von Zinzendorf* (1700–1760), who founded the Moravians.[53] In England the renewal movement was known as the *Methodist or Evangelical Revival*, and its principle figures were *John Wesley* (1703–1791), the founder of Methodism, his brother *Charles Wesley* (1707–1788), and *George Whitefield*, who was also part of the awakening in America. As revival spread throughout England, the nonconformist conscience ultimately brought about sweeping national reform, including the *abolition of slavery* in the British Empire in 1833 (through the efforts John Newton and William Wilberforce), and the ban on the *exploitation of child labor* in 1847 (through the work of the Earl of Shaftesbury).[54]

The Enlightenment of the eighteenth century had gone too far in its effort to eradicate religion and denigrate the role feeling from all of life. As a result there entered a new emphasis on feeling in all phases of life—music, poetry, drama, and the revival of religion of all types.[55] This was known as the Romantic movement. In Germany *Friedrich Schleiermacher* (1768–1834) redefined religion as feeling—man's feeling of dependence on God as he comes to realize how finite he is in comparison with the eternal principle dwelling within the world. In Britain an evangelical revival moved through the Church of England during the early part of the century under the leadership of *John Newton* (1725–1807) and *William Wilberforce* (1759–1833). Meanwhile, the Methodists, Baptists, and other dissenter groups grew rapidly in number. The *Sunday School* movement spread across England like a prairie fire, several *Bible Societies* were founded in Europe and America, as well as dozens of *Missionary Societies*. The modern missionary movement is usually considered to have begun with England's *William Carey* (1761–1834), who pioneered mission activity in India. Catholic missionary efforts received a renewed impetus during the pontificate of *Gregory XVI* (1831–1846), who appointed 195 missionary bishops.[56]

By the end of the eighteenth century, America was an independent nation with a highly diverse religious population. *Denominationalism* was a fact of religious life in the United States. Many churches were allowed to coexist peacefully within the same region. The Baptists, especially under the leadership of *Roger Williams* (1603–1683), had worked very hard to secure freedom of worship for everyone, including Jews. Still, some groups continued to feel the sting of religious persecution well into the nineteenth century, as sectarians and Roman Catholics encountered prejudicial laws and bigoted behavior from some of their neighbors. For the most part, however, Christians in America were free to practice their religion without interference from the government and without hostility from other groups.[57]

The result of Rationalism in the West was a slow, subtle shift toward the *secularization* of society. By the early nineteenth century the Christian Church was under great pressure from the sophisticated ideas of the day, and people began questioning and criticizing churches. Scientific discoveries focused attention on the natural world and suggested that men and women could figure out the problems of their lives for themselves without religion. When millions migrated to the American colonies they found that they had to rely on themselves, and as a result they gloried in self-reliance.[58] By the beginning of the nineteenth century Rationalism had decimated church membership in the United States, leaving a significant portion of its population indifferent toward religion. As a reaction to this indifference, a revival known as the *Second Great Awakening* swept the country. Its two most noted evangelists were Charles Finney (1792–1875) and Dwight L. Moody (1837–1899).

The Scientific Revolution and the Nineteenth Century

If rationalism characterized the eighteenth century, then science characterized the nineteenth century. Although the beginnings of the scientific revolution can be traced back to the sixteenth century, science and the *industrial revolution* did not make its full impact on society until the nineteenth century. The discoveries of rubber, petroleum, and a number of new alloys and synthetic fabrics joined the long list of developments that suddenly changed human existence. All of this speeded up the growth of cities, and people focused on achieving a better way of life. *Materialism* began to impact everything in life, and Sunday increasingly became the workers' day off rather than a day of worship. The publication of Darwin's *On the Origin of Species* (1859) culminated a long period of increasing acceptance of the concept of evolution in the natural sciences. In the hands of its advocates Darwin's teachings were somewhat modified and became widely accepted. In many circles the idea of creative intelligence was banished from the universe, and there was no longer any need for God.[59]

As the scientific revolution and spiritual indifference began making inroads against Christianity during the nineteenth century, the scholarship that had developed in response to rationalism awakened a new spirit of investigation in the Church, and a number of strong theologians surfaced through whom the Scriptures and the doctrines of Christianity would become more widely studied and more intelligently understood. So rationalism, which threatened the overthrow of Christianity, in effect served to develop its strength.[60] The entire Christian community went to work to counter these forces. The Roman Church asserted itself under the leadership of Pius IX (1846–1878), who called the *First Vatican Council* (1870). He condemned almost all the tendencies of the age, and the Council declared the dogma of papal infallibility, which was extended to include all official pronouncements by the pope on matters of faith and morals.[61]

The challenge of rationalism also awakened a new spirit in the Church of England. The *Oxford Movement,* so named because it originated at Oxford University, was developed to move the Church of England away from Protestantism and restore to it the doctrines and practices of the Roman Catholic Church in earlier centuries. The movement published ninety tracts in a short period of time, by several different writers. As the series of tracts progressed, they became more and more Roman Catholic in the principles they set forth, until the bishop of Oxford ordered these publications stopped. Ultimately, its leader *John Henry Newman* (1801–1890), who wrote twenty-nine of the tracts, joined the Catholic Church, and thousands followed him; but the vast majority in the Oxford Movement remained in the Church of England.[62] In later life Newman was made a cardinal for his lifetime contributions to the Church. He has been cited by many theologians as the greatest Catholic figure and the most influential churchman of the nineteenth century. The *Second Vatican Council* (1962–1965) has been called "the Council of Newman" because his ideas made such a profound impact on it. A man of great piety, he wrote, "True religion is a hidden life in the heart."[63] Newman's thoughts and writings show how dissent can help reform a religious tradition.[64]

The industrial revolution of the nineteenth century saw the Church in the West face a brand new world—one of large fast-growing cities, oppressive urban poverty, and constant change. *Dwight L. Moody* and others used new mass evangelism efforts to reach the masses that had come to inhabit the cities. As a result revival spread throughout England and North America.[65] Some Christians sought to change the structures of society in order to alleviate the suffering of the poor, while others formed nondenominational societies to meet these needs. In 1861 William Booth (1829–1912) and his wife, Catherine, began a mission on the eastside of London which he named the *Salvation Army.* This society of evangelism and social work was run with military ranks and discipline, and had spread to more than 50 countries by the time of Booth's death. The Salvation Army was just one of a number of nondenominational organizations that sought to reach out to the workers of the cities. In 1844 the *Young Men's Christian Association* (YMCA) was formed. Its unique mission was to evangelize by combining Bible studies with interests like athletics and education. A sister organization, the YWCA, was organized in 1894. Many other individuals focused on galvanizing their denominations to meet the spiritual and social needs of the masses in the cities.

The rigid structures that existed in the older churches made it difficult for them to respond quickly as urban populations mushroomed. The Methodists and the Baptists were able to respond more quickly than the Catholics and the Anglicans. By holding meetings at informal locations, having local preachers who shared the same needs and concerns as their congregations, and being willing to support the workers in their labor disputes, these denominations were able to spread the gospel message to the masses. By providing everything from soup kitchens and clothing centers to orphanages and schools, they attempted to meet both the spiritual and the physical needs of those they served.[66]

A number of towering individuals led the effort to change their national laws to reflect the values of the gospel more closely. In England, as we have seen, *William Wilberforce* (1759–1833) led the campaign against the slave trade which was finally banned in 1807, and against slavery itself which was abolished throughout the British Empire in 1833. England's *Earl of Shaftesbury* (1801–1885) sought to bring Christian charity to the outcasts of British society; his efforts included reforming laws that affected those with mental illnesses, those who suffered from deplorable housing conditions, the young children who were being exploited by working in mining and chimney sweeping, and the mistreatment of workers by unprincipled employers.[67] Beginning in 1884, Catholic thinkers throughout Europe met each year to discuss social issues and were influential in establishing Catholic trade unions to protect working people against unscrupulous employers.[68]

Bridgeman Art Library

William Wilberforce (1759–1833), British politician who headed the parliamentary campaign against the British slave trade. His efforts eventually led to the *Slavery Abolition Act* of 1833. Wilberforce died just three days after hearing of its passage.

After the middle of the nineteenth century missionary activity spread to make Christianity a truly global enterprise, affecting almost every country on earth. In the West, women were accepted by nearly every missionary society, and by 1900 they far outnumbered the men. One of the greatest missionaries of the nineteenth century was *David Livingstone* (1813–1873) of Scotland. He was a missionary to Africa, and one of the most progressive thinkers of his era. He decried the treatment of blacks by white settlers, and developed several African missions. *James Hudson Taylor* (1832–1905) was a missionary from England who founded the China Inland Mission. He had great respect and love for the native population and adopted their dress and customs so as to fit better into the local culture. He lived to see more than 800 missionaries from many denominations join his efforts. By the time of his death in 1905 over 500,000 Chinese had become adherents to the Christian faith. Among them was Sun Yat-Sen, the first president of the Chinese Republic.[69]

In the United States the restlessness of the nineteenth century produced significant immigrations from Europe and a large movement of people westward. These fertile conditions were ripe for the germination and rapid growth of several movements that did *not* embrace traditional Christian orthodoxy. The three most noteworthy movements birthed in the United States during the nineteenth century were: *Mormonism*, founded in 1830 by Joseph Smith; *Jehovah's Witness*, founded in 1872 by Charles Taze Russell; and *Christian Science*, founded in 1879 by Mary Baker Eddy. Each of these movements departs in varying degrees from the traditional orthodox teaching of Christianity, and are generally referred to as sects or cults of Christianity. All three of these religions take some principles from Christianity and then *blend* in some of their own beliefs that are distinct and divergent from traditional Christian doctrine.

All Christian cults break with historic Christianity and its confessions, and believe their founder brought God's "final revelation" to humanity. In addition, all Christian cults make Christ out to be something far less than God. They maintain that salvation is obtained by following certain rules and regulations; as such, they believe in salvation by works. Also, they all have additional sacred texts that take precedence over the Bible. Some of the other unique elements of these three cults are as follows:

- *Mormonism*—Mormons believe in such things as eternal progression, and the ability of humans to become gods. They do not believe God the Father is the eternal, self-existent, all-powerful God of the universe; instead, he is nothing more than a man who became a god. Mormons believe God the Father was created by another god who existed before

Him, and that god was created by a god before him, ad infinitum. They believe that all faithful Mormons will also one day become gods. This belief in polytheism means that Mormonism is not in the tradition of monotheistic religions. According to the Mormon faith, Jesus and Satan (Lucifer) are actually "spirit brothers," and all human beings were first born in heaven as siblings to them both, before being born naturally on earth. Mormons believe Jesus was born naturally on this earth as a result of sexual intercourse between God the Father and Mary (so much for the "virgin" Mary), and that he grew up, got married, and had several human children himself. Mormonism believes obedience and good works are a necessary condition for salvation, and that salvation by "grace alone" (traditional Christian orthodoxy) is a fallacious doctrine originated by Satan and promulgated by man. There are some 14,000,000 adherents of the Mormon religion in the world today.

- **Jehovah's Witnesses**—They believe in "one God" (Jehovah) and "no Trinity." They teach that Jesus was Michael the archangel who became a human being when he came to this world, and that Jesus was only a perfect man, not God in the flesh. They do not believe Jesus rose from the dead in his physical body, but that he was simply raised a spirit; when Jesus returned to heaven after the resurrection, he then became Michael the archangel again. Jehovah's Witnesses do not believe the existence of hell or eternal punishment; they believe that all non-Witnesses are simply annihilated immediately upon death, without suffering in an afterlife. Only Jehovah's Witnesses will experience an afterlife, and only a select group of them (144,000) are actually admitted into heaven; the rest will live on a new and improved earth, which Jehovah will establish in the millennium. Salvation is achieved by being a Witness and testifying for Jehovah; therefore, salvation is not based on a relationship with God (Christ), rather it is based on being faithful to the requirements of the institution of Jehovah's Witnesses. This is why Jehovah's Witnesses are so fervent in their efforts at door-to-door witnessing. There are some 15,000,000 adherents of this religion in the world today.

- **Christian Science**—The following doctrines are referenced out of the primary Christian Science work, *Science and Health with Key to the Scriptures,* by Mary Baker Eddy. This work, together with the Bible, is called the Pastor of Christian Science, but the only way to interpret the Bible is to do so spiritually with Eddy's divinely inspired book. Mary Baker Eddy is highly regarded as a "revelator of God's word." Christian Science teaches that God is the infinite Universal Principle; that God is Mind, the only intelligence in the universe. They believe the life of God and the life of man are the same, so in essence man is God. Therefore this belief system is nothing more than pantheism, which is the belief that all is God (Ultimate Reality). Because the Divine Mind fills all reality, the individual should seek to harmonize his mind with it so that he can become one with it. Christian Science does not believe that Jesus is the Christ, or that he is God; he was simply a human being who possessed the "divine idea" of the Christ. Christian Science also believes that matter, sin, and sickness are only illusions; that is, they are not truly real—and neither is the devil. The sacrifice of Jesus was not sufficient to cleanse from sin; true healings are the result of true belief. Death is merely a transition for the mind, which keeps on living so it can continue to correct the wrong thinking about sickness and death. There are some 500,000 Christian Science adherents in the world today; the majority of whom live in the United States.

The Twentieth Century: The Age of Modernism

Developments within Christianity

At the dawn of the twentieth century *Protestantism* had developed into a number of new denominations. This happened because the largest denominations—the Lutherans, Anglicans, Congregationalists, Presbyterians, Baptists, and Methodists—all experienced factional disputes and renewal movements, and would experience more in the second half of the century. The Methodist Church in the United States, for example, spawned various denominations, including the Disciples of Christ, the Wesleyan Church, the African Methodist Episcopal Church, and influenced a number of others. As Protestant denominations proliferated, in many ways their differences became less important, and members of most denominations were willing to cooperate with other denominations on a number of issues, including social action.[70]

In the early years of the twentieth century *Liberal Theology* was at its height in Europe and America. Liberal Protestants and Catholic Modernists sought to focus religion on man and the present, rather than on God and eternity. The liberal theologians lost sight of the traditional orthodox Christian belief that Christ's message was one of atonement, not just one of acting and serving in the here and now. As liberal Christianity began to accommodate itself to contemporary culture, it began to regard Jesus as just another wise teacher—not the God of creation. In doing so, the liberal church essentially just reflected society's values in sanctified form. The most dramatic liberal theologian of the twentieth century was the missionary doctor, *Albert Schweitzer* (1875–1965), who attempted to rewrite Christian doctrine. The defenders of orthodoxy in both the Catholic and the Protestant traditions, however, fought back; while the pope fought liberal theology in the Vatican, Protestants fought this battle in their denominations and churches.[71]

Looking back on the twentieth century, it is easy to see a series of shifts that have taken place in the Christian world. After a long period of persecution, Christianity is experiencing a tremendous rebirth in *Eastern Europe* since the fall of Marxist communism. This new openness was signaled when the Soviet government passed a law granting freedom of religion in 1990. *Western Europe* still reflects the secularized values of its inherited past with a continuing erosion of spirituality. The traditional Catholicism of *Central* and *Latin America* is being invigorated by "liberation theology"; as a result significant numbers of Catholics are joining Protestant churches. Christianity is showing exceptional strength in places such as *Africa*, parts of *India* that have a historic Christian presence, and newly independent countries such as Indonesia.[72] The new churches across the continents of Asia, Africa, and South America became self-governing and grew so rapidly in the twentieth century that soon they were more numerous and dynamic than the European churches. In fact, Europe was the one continent where Christian churches declined. The church in the *United States* remains vibrant, active, disunited, and vastly influential, and continues to be the single greatest source of funding for evangelization and ministry around the world. The vast majority of Americans still claim Christianity as their religious faith, and 30–35 percent of the population can be found in church on weekends.[73]

Prominent Orthodox Christians of the Twentieth Century

Some of the most prominent orthodox Christian thinkers and figures of the twentieth century in the West were these: the English journalist and Roman Catholic *G. K. Chesterson* (1874–1936) who believed the modern world had lost the balanced framework of value provided by Christian orthodoxy; the English Anglican academic *C. S. Lewis* (1898–1963) whom many have acclaimed the twentieth century's

Pope John Paul II Cultural Center, Washington, D.C.

Pope John Paul II

most influential critic of modern secular beliefs; the American Catholic Nobel prize-winning poet and critic *T. S. Eliot* (1888–1963) who expressed deep concern over the state of modern culture; the German Lutheran *Dietrich Bonhoffer* (1906–1945) who fought for religious freedom and suffered martyrdom by the Nazis; the Macedonian-born Catholic *Mother Teresa* (1910–1997) who founded a new order called the Missionaries of Charity and established a home for the destitute and the dying in the gutters of Calcutta, India; the American Nobel prize-winning Baptist *Martin Luther King, Jr.* (1929–1968) who fought against the evils of racism and segregation and died by an assassin's bullet; the Roman pontiff *John XXIII* (1881–1963) who spent considerable energies helping the poor, defending human rights, abolishing anti-Semitism in the Catholic Church, healing divisions between the Roman Catholic Church and other Christian communities, and convening the Second Vatican Council, considered by many a watershed in the history of the Catholic Church; the American Protestant philosopher *Francis Schaeffer* (1912–1984) who produced a number of wide-ranging, biblically-based critiques on the moral and spiritual decline of society; the British Anglican theologian and preacher *John R. W. Stott* (1921–present) who has been one of the strongest and most articulate voices for Christian orthodoxy; the Roman pontiff *John Paul II* (1920–2005) who was a champion of human freedom and an advocate of compassion for the poor and the helpless; and one of the most recognized religious figures of the twentieth century, the American evangelist *Billy Graham* (1918–present) who has been a spiritual advisor to multiple U. S. presidents, and has shared the message of Christ with an estimated 210 million people in 185 countries, and hundreds of millions more via television and radio.

Billy Graham

Billy Graham Evangelistic Association

Issues of Growth

The twentieth century has witnessed massive changes unlike any other age in history. It has provided us with a quantum leap on technological and intellectual levels that has no parallel. The current increase in the world's population staggers the imagination. There are 90 million more people on earth today than just one year ago! That's 250,000 more than yesterday! Over 10,000 more than one hour ago! It took from Adam to 1830 for the world's population to reach one billion people; it took only 100 years to add a second billion, 30 years to add a third, 15 years to add a fourth, 12 years to add a fifth, and only 9 years to add a sixth billion.[74] The world's population today is approaching seven billion! In 1800 nearly 97 percent of the world's population lived in rural areas; today more than 55 percent live in larger towns and cities. Thus one of the greatest challenges for modern missions in the twenty-first century is in the cities, where violence, oppression, and poverty plague human life.[75]

The Christian community numbered 1.4 billion people in 1980, which represented 32.8 percent of the world's population. By 1993 the number had grown to 1.9 billion or 33.5 percent. In 2002 the number rose to more than 2.1 billion or 34 percent. It had been projected there would be as many as 2.4 billion Christians in the world by 2006, or roughly 35 percent of the world's population (statistics for 2006 were not yet available). That represents a growth rate of over 100,000 people per day.[76] The most significant areas of Christian growth in the world today are Latin America, Africa, South Asia, East Asia, and the countries of the former Soviet Union.

In 1980 there were 1,720,000 individual churches in the world, and these churches were a part of 20,800 different groups or denominations within Christendom. The number of churches grew to just over 2,000,000 by 1993, and reached 2,200,000 by 2003; this number was projected to grow to approximately 2,400,000 by 2006 (statistics for 2006 were not yet available).[77] Another phenomenon of the last 25 years is the tremendous increase in missionary activity by non-Western countries; they are now more actively engaged in spreading the Christian faith outside their own lands than are the Western nations.[78] In addition, there has been significant growth in the number of Christian service organizations in the world. In 1980 there were 17,500 organizations; by 1993, the number had risen to 22,000, and totaled 25,000 in 2003; they were projected to reach 27,000 by 2006 (statistics for 2006 were not yet available).[79]

In 1800, a part or the entire Bible had been translated into some 70 languages. By 1900 the complete Bible had been translated into over 100 languages, and substantial parts of it into 400 other languages.[80] By 1997 the Bible had been translated into 349 languages, and another 841 languages had the complete New Testament; 933 other languages had at least one book of the Bible.[81] In 2004 the *International Bible Society* reported that the Bible had been translated and printed into approximately 2,500 languages.[82] In 2005 *Wycliffe Bible Translators* reported that there were an additional 1,500 translation projects currently underway in 70 different countries;[83] thus raising the total number of languages or people groups possessing all or a part of the Bible to more than 4,000. It is interesting to note that over 3,500 of these translations into new languages took place in the past 100 years. The number of remaining people groups and languages targeted for future translation has been estimated at about 2,000.

As the Church moves into the twenty-first century, it faces a brand new set of challenges. On one hand, it is experiencing astonishing growth in most areas of the world; broadcasting and publishing organizations are bringing the gospel message to all but the most remote and restricted regions; many spiritual and social ministries are thriving; and the Bible has been translated into the languages of nearly 97 percent of the world's population, with millions of copies being freely and widely distributed. Yet many challenges abound. Many Christians are "biblically illiterate," with only a vague understanding of their Christian faith and its essential doctrines. This is true even in the United States, which is flooded with churches. The global Church has grown to encompass more than one-third of the world's population (2.4 billion people), yet the pattern of growth is very uneven. In Africa, parts of Latin America, and much of Asia the global Church is growing at a tremendous rate. Yet in Europe, long the bastion of the Christian faith, the story is quite different. Attendance at church services in Europe fell so dramatically in the second half of the twentieth century that it is now estimated that less than 10 percent of the population are regular churchgoers.[84]

Differences in Buildings, Décor, and Worship

1. Roman Catholic churches. Most churches in the Roman Catholic tradition are built in the shape of a cross. In these churches, the altar is often placed at the crossing where the horizontal and vertical parts of the cross meet. Because the entire Catholic Mass centers on the Eucharist, or the Lord's Supper, the Communion altar is placed at the center or focal point. Catholic churches also include a "crucifix," a cross with the figure of Jesus on it.[85]

2. Eastern Orthodox churches. The Greek and Russian Orthodox churches are similar in many ways to Catholic churches, with a few minor differences. For example, the altar is behind a screen that has holy doors on it; these doors are opened and closed during various parts of the service. In addition, Eastern Orthodox churches use more incense than their Roman Catholic counterparts. The purpose of the incense is to remind the congregation that, just as smoke filters through the air, God's presence filters through all aspects of their lives.[86]

3. Protestant churches. Early Protestant churches were a reaction against what the reformers considered Catholic excesses. The churches' designs and ornamentation (or lack thereof) also reflect Protestant ideas of the relationship between God and humanity—it is direct; it does not use interceders or icons; it only focuses on faith. Most Protestant churches prefer the plain symbol of the cross, representative of the *risen* Christ, rather than the crucifix, with its image of a *crucified* Christ. Because Protestant churches focus on the sermon, their architectural emphasis is on the pulpit, where the minister preaches, rather than on the altar, which would contain the elements for the celebration of Communion. Protestant churches, depending on the denomination, usually celebrate the Lord's Table either weekly or monthly. Because early Protestants rejected the symbols of wealth, which included gold, fine clothes, and jewels worn by church officials, many Protestant churches are sparsely decorated in comparison to Roman Catholic and Eastern Orthodox churches.[87]

Conclusion

Christianity seems so complex in its history and practice one can forget that, at its core, it is based on a very simple premise. Christianity asserts that human beings exist in a state of *alienation* from God because of sin, and this condition has been healed through the life and saving work of a single person, Jesus the Messiah, the incarnate Christ. Christianity, then, has at its heart not an idea but a *person.* The goal for believers is to reflect the qualities that Jesus preached: to live out an ethic based on selfless love; to care for the poor and the dispossessed; and to forgive those who wrong us. The complex historical evolution of Christian caregiving institutions (hospitals, orphanages, leprosaria, schools for the poor, etc.) must be seen as obedient submission to the command of Jesus to "love one's neighbor as oneself."[88] Some believe the early successes of Christianity in the Roman Empire can be partially explained by the strong commitment of early Christian communities to provide such aids at a time when social services were rudimentary or nonexistent.[89] Christian missionaries have done far more than bring the gospel to the peoples of the world, though that is their primary mission. In many countries they brought modern medicine, education, hospitals, schools, and agriculture, and gave thousands of people groups a written language for the first time. They fed the hungry, enhanced the status of women, gave shelter to children by building orphanages, and they decried and helped abolish or diminish the nefarious practices of slavery and the opium trade.[90] As Christianity enters the third millennium, the Church continues to prepare itself to extend the message and the love of God to all humanity.

EPILOGUE

The important thing is not to stop questioning. One cannot help but be in awe when he contemplates the mysteries of eternity, of life, of the marvelous structure of reality. It is enough if one tries merely to comprehend a little of this mystery every day. Never lose a holy curiosity.
— *Albert Einstein*[1]

The Christian encounter with people of other beliefs has brought both enrichment and conflict. The Christian faith was born into a world every bit as pluralistic in ideology and behavior as our own. In the first century, Christians were newcomers in the Greco-Roman world, with no history or land of their own. In many countries, Christians today are identified with a history which, at several points, has served to obscure the gospel message from the gaze of the non-Christian; a history that includes inquisitions and bloody crusades, social intolerance, and intellectual bigotry, the improper use of biblical passages to justify colonial expansionism, slavery, sexism, and a host of other evils.[2] Much has been written since the Age of Enlightenment to expose the betrayals of the gospel by the Church.

The Christian community should not be ashamed to confess its sins and those of its forebears, an expectation that the gospel demands. To identify the truth of the gospel with the moral superiority of Christians is to turn the gospel on its head. The truth of the matter is that the Messiah has stooped to pitch His tent with a flawed and faithless people. Any sharing of the gospel message with a pluralistic world has to begin with the humble acknowledgment of betrayals of the gospel by the Church itself.[3]

In his book, *Hypocrisy: Moral Fraud & Other Vices*, James Spiegel quotes an ardent atheist who had difficulty separating Christianity from many of the atrocities committed by individuals who were identified as Christians:

> Christianity… has generated savage wars of religion and supported innumerable "just wars"; has tortured and burned multitudes of heretics and witches in the name of God; has motivated and authorized the persecution of the Jews; has validated systematic racism; and has tolerated the Western capitalist "rape of the earth", the misuse of nuclear energy, and the basic injustice of the North-South division into rich and poor nations.[4]

Though this scathing indictment against Christianity has considerable merit, in truth, the accusation is misdirected. The question this statement should evoke is this: "Is it really Christianity that is to blame, or is it misguided Christians?" Surely the religion that calls on its adherents to "turn the other cheek"[5] and "love one another,"[6] that says "God is no respecter of persons,"[7] and was also founded by a Jew[8] cannot be blamed for the injustices described above.

The Christian religion is not properly represented by events such as the Crusades, the Inquisition, or the Salem Witch Trials. Though these things happened in the name of Christianity, it does not mean that this is the behavior espoused by the Christian faith. Instead, Christianity professes conversion by love not by torture. Therefore, those who used coercive means did so against the teaching of Scripture.[9] Because people in the Christian Church have committed a number of atrocities, many outside the church are skeptical of Christianity and often see it as reactionary and violent. But an objective look at church history will show that the *Crusades*, for example, happened at a time when the papacy was a political institution corrupted by power and greed. As is frequently demonstrated in history, when anyone comes into complete political and military control, abuse almost always follows.[10] Some people would say religion is the source of most of the world's wars, but the truth of the matter is that economic motivations and imperialist ambitions are the source of far more wars than religion ever was. In fact, religious reasons were often cited just to cover up motives of greed and desire for power.[11]

Church history is vital to our understanding of the institution of the Christian Church, and much can be gleaned from it. The *Inquisition* was a Roman Catholic invention intended to root out all sorts of heresies; it used torture to force confessions out of people. Thousands were killed mercilessly and unjustly. Protestants have their own sordid history and the *Salem Witch Trials* here in America are but one example; they allowed their paranoia and ignorance to overtake reason and scripture. As a result, many people were killed because they were falsely accused and convicted of being witches.[12] Events like the Crusades, the Inquisition, and the Salem Witch Trials took advantage of the religion of Christianity, because these behaviors are completely contrary to the teachings of Christ. Understanding Christian doctrine in light of church history helps us to separate falsehood and fiction from facts and doctrine of true Christianity.

The brutal atrocities perpetrated by Christians and the vicious persecution of them has generated a tremendous amount of interest in recent years. Statistician David B. Barrett presents some grim facts about the martyrdom of Christians over the centuries.[13] More than 43,000,000 Christians have been killed for their faith since the crucifixion of Christ. From the crucifixion of Jesus to 1990, there have been 420 incidents of martyrdom in which large groups of Christians were killed. In 56 of these cases over 100,000 were killed; in 20 cases more than 500,000 were killed; and in 12 cases over 1,000,000 were killed. The bulk of these incidents occurred in two periods; the first was between the years 1000 and 1500, and the second was a much shorter period, between 1900 and 2000. Over half of all Christians ever martyred—26,000,000—were killed during the twentieth century.[14]

Rabbi Daniel Lapin is the author of a number of books including *America's Real War*, and is the founder and president of *Toward Tradition*, a Jewish educational organization dedicated to promoting those traditional Judeo-Christian values that, he says, have been "the blueprint for the building of America."[15] Lapin, an orthodox Jew, is an outspoken supporter of Christianity. He recently made these comments on the contributions Christianity has made to American culture:

> America has provided the most tranquil, prosperous haven that Jewish people have enjoyed in the last 2,000 years. No other culture has even come close. No other country has even resembled the graciousness and hospitality that Jews have found in this country from day one.... This is not in spite of America being a Christian nation (a nation predominantly made up of Christian people and shaped by Judeo-Christian values), it is because America is a Christian nation.... I believe it to be a truism to say that Judaism's safety belt in America is

America's Bible belt. I also believe the religious freedom Jews enjoy in this country is guaranteed only by America remaining a Christian nation.[16]

Lapin believes the most important battle being waged in America today is the struggle between *barbarism* and Western civilization (i.e., traditional Judeo-Christian values). He defines barbarism as the world of the jungle, or the world of the untamed human desires and instincts. Lapin says it is in the world of barbarism that the darkest fantasies of uncivilized man reside, and that it is this dark world that brought down the Greek and Roman Empires. Therefore the most significant war being waged in twenty-first century America, according to Lapin, is the war between the *secular* fundamentalists, who are committed to seeing Judeo-Christian values abolished, and the *traditional* fundamentalists, who are committed to seeing these values restored. Should secularism prevail, as it is in Europe, it will mean the fall of Western civilization as we know it. The one force fighting for her survival, says Lapin, is the religion of Christianity.[17] These are astounding statements about Christianity to be made by an orthodox Jew.

As we have seen, religion is the major influence on any culture, and it is clearly a beneficial influence. For instance, it was reported in the June 27, 2002 edition of the *Washington Times* that "Americans who help religious congregations not only give more time and money than people working for secular causes, but provide 75 percent of the secular charity as well."[18] This suggests that those individuals who serve in religious organizations are far more generous with their time and money than those involved in secular causes, and they even generate three-fourths of all secular charity giving as well.

Therefore, one could deduce that America is a generous nation because it is, in large part, a Christian nation. This finding is also supported when one examines two of the most diverse regions of the country, the northeast and the south. In the northeast, a much lower percentage of people attend church regularly than any other region of the country. The highest percentage of regular church attendance is in the south. Bearing this in mind, it is interesting to note that the *least generous* section of the country is the northeast, and the *most generous* is the south.[19] This is even more astounding when one remembers that the northeastern section of the country has far more wealth than its southern counterpart. We'll have to leave it to the political pundits to do with this information what they will, but there is a pretty significant message here.

Part of what it means to be an adherent of a particular religion is to own *all of the history* of that religion—both the good and the bad—and not lie about it or deny it.[20] Just because someone may have had an ancestor who was a horse thief does not mean he should abandon his family. Well, being a part of a religion is like being a part of a family. Christianity is not false because one of its members commits some serious sin or transgression, any more than the science of mathematics is false because some math teacher miscalculates; neither discipline is a failure because one of its adherents does something wrong. The truth of the matter is there are bad mathematicians, bad accountants, bad doctors, bad teachers, bad ballplayers, bad electricians, bad senators, bad everything. In addition, there are a number of bad Christians.

It should also be remembered that the history of Christianity is not just a history of failure; it also has a long history of helping millions of people, establishing orphanages, building shelters, schools, and hospitals, helping famine-ravaged countries, liberating slaves and women, and seeking to aid the downtrodden. If anyone wishes to condemn Christianity because of the failures of some of its adherents, to be consistent, they must also applaud Christianity for its successes. As the author of this book, I want to encourage you to look at the entire history of Christianity—the good and the bad—yet even more important, look at what the Bible actually teaches, in particular the New Testament from which Christianity is derived. Do not believe or disbelieve in Christianity because of the actions of some of its adherents; instead believe in Christianity because of *who Jesus is* and *what He did.*

BIBLIOGRAPHY

Adherents.com Online at: http://www.adherents.com/adh_predom.html

Allison, Gregg R. *Getting Deep: Understand What You Believe About God and Why*. Nashville, TN: Broadman & Holman Publishers, 2002.

Anders, Max. *New Christian's Handbook*. Nashville, TN: Thomas Nelson Publishers, 1999.

Archer, Gleason L., editor. *Encyclopedia of Bible Difficulties*. Grand Rapids, MI: Zondervan Publishing House, 1982.

Arizona Republic. "Universe's Star Tally: 70 Sextillion." August 6, 2003. (Originally appeared in the *Los Angeles Times* in early August.)

Arizona Republic. December 9, 2003, A10—Article on human DNA.

Asimov, Isaac, editor. *Isaac Asimov's Book of Facts*. New York: Random House, 1997.

Asimov, Isaac. "In the Game of Energy and Thermodynamics You Cannot Break Even," *Smithsonian Institute Journal*. June 1970.

Barfield, Kenny. *Why the Bible is Number One*. Grand Rapids, MI: Baker Book House, 1988.

Barna, George, Pres. of *The Barna Research Group, Ltd*. (1957 Eastman Ave., Ste B, Ventura, CA 93003).

Barnett, Lincoln Kinnear. *The Universe and Dr. Einstein*. New York: William Morrow, 1968.

Barrett, David B. *Our Globe and How to Reach It*. Birmingham, AL: New Hope, 1990.

Batten, Don, editor. *The Revised & Expanded Answers Book*. Green Forest, AR: Master Books, 2002.

Baxter, Batsell Barrett. *I Believe Because....* Grand Rapids, MI: Baker Book House, 1971.

Berlitz, Charles. *Native Tongues*. New York: Grosset & Dunlap Publishers, 1982.

Bethell, Tom. "Agnostic Evolutionists," *Harper's Magazine*. February 1985.

Bickel, Bruce and Stan Jantz. *Guide to Cults, Religions, & Spiritual Beliefs*. Eugene, OR: Harvest House Publishers, 2002.

Bimson, John N., editor. *Baker Encyclopedia of Bible Places*. Grand Rapids, MI: Baker Book House, 1995.

Bloom, Allan. *The Closing of the American Mind*. New York: Simon & Schuster, 1987.

Boice, James Montgomery. *Foundations of the Christian Faith*. Downers Grove, IL: InterVarsity Press, 1986.

Brown, Walter. Online at: http://www.creationscience.com/onlinebook/LifeSciences.html

Bruce, Frederick Fyvie. *The New Testament Documents: Are They Reliable?* Downer's Grove, IL: InterVarsity Press, 1972.

Cairney, William. "Biomedical Prescience 1: Hebrew Dietary Laws." *Evidence for Faith*. John W. Montgomery, ed. Dallas, TX: Word Publishing, 1991.

Carm.org. Online at: http://www.carm.org/evidence/rewritten.htm

Carson, D. A. *Telling the Truth*. Grand Rapids, MI: Zondervan Publishing House, 2000.

Chittick, Donald E. *The Controversy: Roots of the Creation-Evolution Conflict*. Newberg, OR: Creation Compass, 1984.

___. *The Puzzle of Ancient Man*. Newberg, OR: Creation Compass, 1998.

Christian Answers.net. Online at: http://www.christiananswers.net

Collier's Encyclopedia. New York: Collier's, 1996.

Collins, Michael. *The Story of Christianity*. New York: DK Publishing, Inc., 1999.

Colon, Peter. "Archaeology Confirms the Walls Fell Flat," *Israel My Glory*. Jan/Feb 2004, Vol. 62, No. 1. Westville, NJ: The Friends of Israel Gospel Ministry, Inc.

Colson, Charles. *Answers to Your Kids' Questions*. Wheaton, IL: Tyndale House Publishers, 2000.

___. *How Now Shall We Live?* Wheaton, IL: Tyndale House Publishers, Inc., 1999.

Comparative Religion.com. Online at: http://www.comparativereligion. com/salvation.html# Christianity

Corduan, Winfried. *Neighboring Faiths*. Downers Grove, IL: InterVarsity Press, 1998.

CreationMoments.com, Online at: http://creationmoments.com/resources/ article.asp?art_id=58

Darwin, Charles. *On the Origin of Species*. London: John Murray, 1859.

Davies, Paul C. *The Edge of Infinity: Where the Universe Came From and How It Will End*. New York: Simon & Schuster, 1982.

"Death of Spontaneous Generation," Encyclopedia Britannica Online at: http://members.eb.com/bol/topic?eu=119731&sctn=29

Denton, Michael. *Evolution: A Theory in Crisis*. Bethesda, MD: Adler & Adler, 1986.

Dobshansky, Theodosius. *Evolution*. Vol. 29, 1975.

"Does God Exist," online at http://www.doesgodexist.org/phamplets/mansproof. html

Douglas, J. D., editor. *The New Bible Dictionary*. Grand Rapids, MI: William B. Eerdmans Publishing Company, 1977.

Dowley, Tim, editor. *Eerdmans' Handbook to the History of Christianity*. Grand Rapids, MI: William B. Eerdmans Publishing Company, 1977.

Edersheim, Alfred. *The Life and Times of Jesus the Messiah*. Grand Rapids, MI: William B. Eerdmans Publishing Company, 1962.

Edwards, Linda. *A Brief Guide to Beliefs, Ideas, Theologies, Mysteries, and Movements*. Louisville, KY and London: Westminster John Knox Press, 2001.

Eerdmans' Handbook to The World's Religions. Grand Rapids, MI: William B. Eerdmans Publishing Company, 1994.

Eldredge, Niles. "Missing, Believed Nonexistent," *Manchester Guardian* (The Washington Post Weekly). November 1978, Vol. 119, No. 22, 26.

Elwell, Walter A., editor. *Evangelical Dictionary of Theology*. Grand Rapids, MI: Baker Book House, 1992.

Etinger, Judah. *Foolish Faith*. Green Forest, AR: Master Books, Inc., 2003.

Forward, Martin. *Religion: A Beginner's Guide*. Oxford: Oneworld Publications, 2001.

"Francis Crick," Encyclopedia Britannica Online at: http://members.eb.com/ bol/topic?eu= 28338&sctn=1

Gamkrelidze, Thomas V. and V. V. Ivanov. "The Early History of Indo-European Languages," *Scientific American*. March 1990.

Geisler, Norman L. and Joseph Holden. *Living Loud: Defending Your Faith*. Nashville, TN: Broadman & Holman Publishers, 2002.

Geisler, Norman L. and Ron Brooks. *When Skeptics Ask: A Handbook on Christian Evidences*. Grand Rapids, MI: Baker Book House, 2001.

Geisler, Norman L. and William E. Nix. *General Introduction to the Bible*. Chicago: Moody Press, 1986.

Gellman, Marc and Thomas Hartman. *Religion for Dummies*. New York: Wiley Publishing, Inc., 2002.

Gibbons, Ann. "Calibrating the Mitochondrial Clock," *Science*. Vol. 279, No. 5347, January 2, 1998.

Gish, Duane. Institute for Creation Research Online at: http://www.icr.org/pubs/imp/imp-004.htm

Gitt, Werner. *The Wonder of Man*. Bielefeld, Germany: Christliche Literatur-Verbreitung, 1999.

Gould, Stephen J. "Evolution's Erratic Pace," *Natural History*. Vol. 86, No. 5, May 1977.

Grasse, Pierre. *Evolution du Vivant*. New York: Academic Press, 1977.

Grasse, Pierre-Paul. *Evolution of Living Organisms*. New York: Academic Press, 1977.

Grunlan, Stephen A. and Marvin K. Mayers. *Cultural Anthropology*. Grand Rapids, MI: Zondervan Publishing House, 1988.

Halley, Henry H. *Halley's Bible Handbook*. Grand Rapids, MI: Zondervan Publishing House, 1965.

Halverson, Dean C., editor. *The Compact Guide to World Religions*. Minneapolis, MN: Bethany House Publishers, 1996.

Hancock, Graham. *Fingerprints of the Gods*. New York: Crown Trade Paperbacks, 1995.

Helm, Thomas E. *The Christian Religion*. Englewood Cliffs, NJ: Prentice Hall, 1991.

Hiebert, Paul G. *Anthropological Insights for Missionaries*. Grand Rapids, MI: Baker Book House, 2003.

___. *Missiological Implications of Epistemological Shifts*. Harrisburg, PA: Trinity Press International, 1999.

Hitching, Francis. "Was Darwin Wrong?" *Life*. April 1982.

Holmes, John. "Neanderthals Linked to West Europeans," *Insight*. September 11, 1989.

Hopfe, Lewis M. and Mark R. Woodward. *Religions of the World*. Upper Saddle River, NJ: Prentice Hall, 2001.

Hoyle, Fred. *The Intelligent Universe*. New York: Holt, Rinehart, and Winston, 1983.

Hume, Robert E. *The World's Living Religions*. New York: Charles Scribner's Sons, 1959.

Hurlbut, Jesse Lyman. *The Story of the Christian Church*. Grand Rapids, MI: Zondervan Publishing House, 1970.

International Bible Society Online at: http://www.ibs.org

James, William. *The Varieties of Religious Experience*. New York: Longman, 1902.

Jastrow, Robert. "Genesis Revealed," *Science Digest*. Special Winter Issue, 1979.

___. *God and the Astronomers*. 2nd ed. New York and London: W. W. Norton & Company, 1992.

Jauncey, James H. *Why We Believe*. Cincinnati, OH: Standard Publishing, 1969.

Keels, Steve. *Survival Guide*. Nashville, TN: Broadman & Holman Publishers, 2002.

Kitts, David B. "Paleontology and Evolutionary Theory," *Evolution*. Vol. 28, Sept. 1974.

Kole, Andre and Jerry MacGregor. *Mind Games*. Eugene, OR: Harvest House, 1998.

Kole, Andre. *Miracle and Magic*. Eugene, OR: Harvest House, 1984.

Kuiper, B. K. *The Church in History*. Grand Rapids, MI: William B. Eerdmans Publishing Company, 1978.

Lapin, Rabbi Daniel. President of *"Toward Tradition,"* P. O. Box 58, Mercer Island, WA 98040; (206) 236-3046.

Larson, Muriel. *God's Fantastic Creation*. Chicago: Moody Press, 1975.

Lewis, C. S. *Mere Christianity*. New York: The Macmillan Company, 1960.

Libby, William F. *Radiocarbon Dating*. Chicago: University of Chicago Press, 1955.

Losch, Richard R. *The Many Faces of Faith*. Grand Rapids, MI: William B. Eerdmans Publishing Company, 2001.

MacDonald, William. *Believer's Bible Commentary*. Nashville, TN: Thomas Nelson Publishers, 1995.

Margulis, Lynn, as quoted by Charles Mann, "Lynn Margulis: Science's Unruly Earth Mother," *Science*. Vol. 252, April 19, 1991.

Martin, Jobe. *The Evolution of a Creationist*. Rockwell, TX: Biblical Discipleship Publishers, 1996.

McDermott, Gerald R. *Can Evangelicals Learn From World Religions?* Downers Grove, IL: InterVarsity Press, 2000.

McDowell, Josh. *The New Evidence.* Nashville, TN: Thomas Nelson Publishers, 1999.

McDowell, Josh and Don Stewart. *Handbook of Today's Religions.* Nashville, TN: Thomas Nelson Publishers, 1983.

McLaren, Brian D. *A New Kind of Christian.* San Francisco, CA: Jossey-Bass, 2001.

Morris, Henry. Institute for Creation Research Online at: http://www.icr.org/pubs/ imp/imp-003.htm

Morris, Henry M. *Many Infallible Proofs.* Green Forest, AR: Master Books, 2002.

___. *Science and the Bible.* Chicago: Moody Press, 1986.

Morris, John D. *The Geology Book.* Green Forest, AR: Master Books, 2000.

Nash, Ronald H. *Faith & Reason.* Grand Rapids, MI: Zondervan Publishing House, 1988.

___. *Worldviews in Conflict.* Grand Rapids, MI: Zondervan Publishing House, 1992.

Natur Magazine (German). July 1989, 57-59.

Noebel, David A. President of *Summit Ministries.* P. O. Box 207, Manitou Springs, CO 80829; (719) 685-9103.

Overbye, Dennis. *Lonely Hearts of the Cosmos.* New York: Harper Collins Publishers, 1991.

Pache, Rene. *The Inspiration and Authority of Scripture.* Chicago: Moody Press, 1969.

Packer, James I., editor. *The Bible Almanac.* Nashville, TN: Thomas Nelson Publishers, 1980.

Patton, Robert. "OOPARTS," *Omni.* September 1982.

Pritchard, James B. *Ancient Near East Texts.* Princeton, NJ: The Princeton University Press, 1950.

Prochnow, Herbert V. *The Toastmaster's Treasure Chest.* New York: Harper & Row, 1988.

Ramachandra, Vinoth. *Faiths in Conflict?* Downers Grove, IL: InterVarsity Press, 1999.

Raup, David M. "Conficts Between Darwin and Paleontology," *Field Museum of Natural History.* Vol. 50, No. 1, January 1979.

Rehwinkel, Alfred M. *The Wonders of Creation.* Grand Rapids, MI: Baker Book House, 1974.

Reid, David R. *Big Flood* (Study No. XIX-4 1991/92). Post Office Box 2268, Westerly, RI 02891.

Renwick and Harman. *The Story of the Church*. Leicester, England: Inter Varsity Press, 1985.

Rhoads, David. Israel in Revolution, AD 6–74: *A Political History Based on the Writing of Josephus*. Philadelphia, PA: Fortress Press, 1976.

Roetzel, Calvin J. *The World That Shaped the New Testament*. Atlanta, GA: John Knox Press, 1985.

Runzo, Joseph. *Global Philosophy of Religion: A Short Introduction*. Oxford: Oneworld Publications, 2001

Sagan, Carl. *Broca's Brain*. New York: Random, 1979.

___. *Cosmos*. New York: Random House, 1980.

Schaeffer, Francis A. *Escape From Reason*. Downers Grove, IL: InterVarsity Press, 1968.

Smith, John Maynard. *Evolution Now: A Century after Darwin*. San Francisco, CA: Freeman, 1982.

Smith, Jonathan Z., editor. *Dictionary of Religion*. San Francisco, CA: HarperCollins Publishers, 1995.

Spiegel, James S. *Hypocrisy: Moral Fraud & Other Vices*. Grand Rapids, MI: Baker Books, 1999.

Stanley, Steven M. *The Evolutionary Timetable*. New York: Basic Books, Inc., 1981.

Stansfield, William D. *Science of Evolution*. New York: Macmillan Publishing Company, 1977.

Stott, John R. W. *Basic Christianity*. Grand Rapids, MI: William B. Eerdmans Publishing Company, 1957.

Strobel, Lee. *The Case for a Creator*. Grand Rapids, MI: Zondervan Publishing House, 2004.

Sunderland, Luther D. *Darwin's Enigma*, 4th ed. Green Forest, AR, 1988.

Tacitus. *The Annals of Imperial Rome*. rev. ed., Michael Grant, translator, London and New York: Penguin Books, 1989.

Taylor, Richard. *Metaphysics*. 2nd ed. Englewood Cliffs, N.J.: Prentice-Hall, 1974.

Templeton, Sir John. *The Humble Approach: Scientists Discover God*. Philadelphia, PA: Templeton Foundation, 1998.

Tierney, John, Lynda Wright, and Karen Springen. "The Search for Adam and Eve," *Newsweek*. January 11, 1988.

Unger, Merrill F., editor. *Unger's Bible Dictionary*. Chicago: Moody Press, 1979.

Vos, Howard F. *Exploring Church History*. Nashville, TN: Thomas Nelson Publishers, 1994.

Walker, Williston. *A History of the Christian Church*. New York: Charles Scribner's Sons, 1970.

Walvoord, John F. and Roy B. Zuck. *The Bible Knowledge Commentary (New Testament)*. Wheaton, IL: Victor Books, 1983.

Ward, Keith. *Christianity: A Short Introduction*. Oxford: Oneworld Publications, 2000.

Washington Times. Article *"Faith and Philanthropy Linked"* in the June 27, 2002 Edition, page A09 (www.washtimes.com).

Watson, James D. *DNA: The Secret of Life*. New York: Alfred A. Knopf, 2003.

Weaver, Mary Jo. *Introduction to Christianity*. Belmont, CA: Wadsworth Publishing Company, 1991.

Wikipedia Encyclopedia Online at: http://en.wikipedia.org/wiki/Pantheism

Wilkins, Michael. *Jesus Under Fire: Modern Scholarship Reinvents the Historical Jesus*. Grand Rapids, MI: Zondervan Publishing House, 1996.

Wilkinson, Bruce and Kenneth Boa. *The Wilkinson & Boa Bible Handbook*. Nashville, TN: Thomas Nelson Publishers, 2002.

Willis, Tom. "Lucy Goes to College," *Christian Science Association (CSA) News*. February, 1987.

Woodruff, David S. "Evolution: The Paleobiological View," *Science*. Vol. 208, May 16, 1980.

Woods, Ralph L. *The World Treasury of Religious Quotations*. New York: Garland Books, 1966.

World Book Encyclopedia. Chicago: World Book, Inc., 2002.

Wycliffe Bible Translators Online at: http://www.wycliffe.net

Zondervan Handbook to the Bible. Grand Rapids, MI: Zondervan Publishing House, 1999.

GLOSSARY

Abraham. Oldest "patriarch" of the Jewish and Christian faiths, who according to the biblical record, lived about 2000 BC, and migrated from the lower Mesopotamian city of Ur (present-day Iraq) to Canaan.

agape. Greek word for "love" in the Christian New Testament, meaning God's love for humans and the selfless love that should bind them. Contrasted with Greek *eros*, meaning the type of love characterized by longing and desire.

Age of Reason. Historically, a designation used for the eighteenth century in the Western world, when the philosophy of rationalism, stressing the powers of the human mind and reason, was a dominant force.

agnosticism. The view that there is insufficient evidence on which to make any decisions about the existence of God.

alienation. The estrangement of oneself from God.

Allah. Arabic word for God deriving from the word *Illah*, meaning "the One deserving all worship." Allah is the supreme and only God of Islam.

allegory. Type of interpretation of scriptures that minimizes the literal meaning of a text in favor of a symbolic or hidden spiritual meaning.

angel. From the Greek word meaning "messenger." A type of spiritual being who becomes involved in human affairs; common to Judaism and Christianity. A leader among the angels is sometimes called an archangel (e.g., Michael, Gabriel).

Anglicanism. The theological movement and churches originating directly or indirectly from the Church of England.

Animism. Religious belief and practice relating to spiritual beings that sees natural objects as possessing spiritual life and values.

Anti-Semitism. Literally means "opposed to Semites." It is usually applied specifically to the hatred of Jews, which may take the form of discrimination or outright persecution.

apocalypse. From the Greek word meaning "revelation." A symbolic type of literature common in Judiasm and Christianity that foretells a dramatic end of the world, a judgment by God, rewards for believers, and punishment for the wicked.

Apocrypha. Fourteen Judeo-Hellenistic books that are included in the Greek Septuagint, but are not considered canonical by Protestants because they fail to meet the necessary standards of reliability and inspiration, which are met by the rest of the Hebrew Scriptures. Eleven are accepted as secondary canon by the Roman Catholic Church, and are thus present in the Latin Vulgate Old Testament. From the Greek, meaning "to hide" or "to cover."

apostle. "One sent" with a message; a messenger. The first twelve disciples or followers of Christ;[1] any Christian sent forth as a messenger of Christ.

Apostolic age. The early period of the Christian church from approximately AD 30 to 90, when the apostles of Jesus were still alive.

Arianism. Fourth-century AD belief that Christ was a created human, not co-eternal with God. Rejected by the church as heresy in the Nicene Creed phrases "begotten not made," and "of one substance with the Father."

Armageddon. The place of the final great struggle between the forces of good and evil.[2]

asceticism. Practices of self-restraint such as fasting and celibacy undertaken to attain closeness to the divine.

atheism. The belief that there is no God or ultimate reality.

atonement (Christianity). In orthodox Christianity, the biblical doctrine referring to the substitutionary death and sacrifice of Jesus Christ on behalf of mankind, effecting salvation and making possible the reconciliation of the human race to God.

atonement (Judaism). Reconciliation with God. In biblical teaching sacrifice was the outward form of atonement. After the destruction of the Temple in AD 70, the only means of atonement were prayer, repentance, fasting, charity, and self-restitution.

baptism. Literally means "to be dipped." Christian initiatory ritual and a sacrament. Some see baptism as washing away the original sin inherited from Adam and Eve, others as an initiation into the Church. Baptism symbolizes the believer's identification with Christ's death and resurrection, in dying to sin and being raised to new life. Some baptize infants, others do not.

Buddha. The "Enlightened One" Siddhartha Gautama, called the Buddha (563?–483? BC), was the first man to discover the Way of Truth (dharma) and teach it to humankind.

Buddhism. One of the five major religions of the world. Oriented around preserving, propagating, and studying the practices and teachings of Buddha, with the goal of reaching enlightenment.

Calvinism. Major Protestant Reformation teaching of John Calvin (1509–1564) of Geneva. Emphasizes God's calling believers to salvation rather than human choice, or divine predestination.

canon. The official sacred texts of a religion.

catechism. A manual of Christian doctrine, usually in the form of question and answer, for the use of religious instruction.

Christ. Greek word for "Messiah"; in Hebrew it stands for "Anointed One." The Messiah is the Jewish term for an anointed one of God. Christians believe that Jesus was the expected Messiah.

Christmas. Christian holy day, December 25, celebrating the birth of Jesus Christ in Bethlehem, just southwest of Jerusalem.

circumcision. Removal of the male foreskin as a sign of the covenant in the Hebrew Bible and Christian Old Testament.[3] It signified membership within the Hebrew community.

Confucianism. A Chinese religion of optimistic humanism founded on the teachings of Confucius.

Conservative Judaism. One of the three main types of modern Judaism, along with Orthodox and Reform. Founded in the nineteenth century.

cosmos. The orderly, harmonious, complex, systematic universe. This term is frequently used as a synonym for the universe; it includes everything that exists in all creation, both seen and unseen.

Council of Trent. Roman Catholic meetings held from 1545 to 1563 to reform the church and oppose new Protestant teachings.

covenant. A pact between two parties. In Judaism, the covenant is a major theological concept referring to the eternal bond between God and the people of Israel that calls for the nation's obedience to the divine commandments and instruction (Torah). The first covenant is with *Noah* (covenant of the rainbow[4]); the second with *Abraham* (circumcision[5]); the third with *Moses* on Mount Sinai (Ten Commandments[6]). For

Christianity, God made a new covenant (thus, "New Testament") with the followers of Jesus the night before He went to the cross, superseding the old covenant (thus, "Old Testament") with Moses at Sinai.

creation ex nihilo. The Christian view that God created all things "out of nothing" and is thus the ultimate cause and source of meaning for the whole created order.

creed. A formal summary of the Christian faith, held in common by Christians. The most important creeds are those generally known as the Apostles' Creed and the Nicene Creed.

Crusades. A number of military attempts in the eleventh, twelfth, and thirteenth centuries by late-medieval Western kingdoms (France, England, and Germany) and the papal states of Italy to reclaim for Christendom the Holy Lands from Muslim rule. The Crusaders succeeded temporarily by occupying Jerusalem but were driven out by Saladin in 1187. Subsequent attempts failed, and Crusaders were finally driven from Palestine at the close of the thirteenth century.

Darwinism. The theory propounded by Charles Darwin (1809–1882) that all things now living have emerged through a process of evolution and natural selection from primitive life-forms to more complex life-forms. The relation of this theory to biblical accounts of God as Creator has been a major source of controversy, because it contradicts the teaching of Scripture.

Deism. The belief that God created the world and is transcendent but has no continuing involvement with the world.

demon. In Christianity, an evil spirit that works contrary to the divine will.[7]

denomination. A sectarian branch of Protestant Christianity whose congregations are united by a single administrative body; for example, Baptists, Presbyterians, Episcopalians, Methodists, etc.

doctrine. Statements of the basic beliefs of a religion.

Easter. The yearly Christian festival celebrating the raising of Jesus Christ from the dead three days after His crucifixion. It is preceded by Good Friday. Theologically it celebrates the victory of Christ over death and evil as well as Christian hope.

Eastern Orthodox Church. Consisting of mainly Greek or Slav Christians, including the ancient Eastern Patriarchates. They are in communion with the Patriarchate of Constantinople, which conforms to the creeds of the great ecumenical councils. The Eastern Orthodox Church is strong in Russia, Eastern Europe, and the Balkan states; it rejects the pope, reveres icons, and allows no women priests.

Elohim. Frequent Hebrew term for "God" in the Hebrew Bible and Christian Old Testament. Though the term is plural it is used to designate the one God of Israel. It is also a synonym for "Yahweh," the self-revealed name of the God of Israel.

Enlightenment (history). Eighteenth-century intellectual movement that stressed the applicability of reason and science to the improvement of society and humankind in general.

epistemology. The study of knowledge or how we know; the science of the validity of knowledge.

eschatology. Beliefs concerning the endings or last things: death, heaven, hell, judgment, resurrection, reincarnation, end of the known world.

eternal. That which exists without beginning, end, or change; not simply of endless duration, but the absence of time.

ethics. The study of human values and moral conduct; the study of right and wrong.

Eucharist. One of the terms used in Christian theology to describe the sharing and giving of the bread and cup at the Last Supper before Christ's death. Performed in memory of Christ's body broken for the world and His blood shed for the sins of the world. Other expressions used to describe this sacrament are Communion, Lord's Table, and Lord's Supper.

Evangelical. Protestant Christian tradition of enthusiastic preaching, literal authority of the Bible, salvation by faith in Christ, conversion (born again) experience.

Exodus. The escape of the ancient Hebrews from slavery in Egypt, around 1400 BC, led by Moses to the Promised Land, now Israel.

faith. Attitude of belief in, trust, and commitment to a divine being or a religious teaching. It can also refer to the beliefs of a religion, "the faith," which is passed on from teachers to believers.

false prophets. Those who claim to speak for God but whose predictions fail to come to pass, or who preach the wrong god(s).

fundamentalism. The doctrine that the Bible is directly inspired by God and therefore inerrant and infallible on all matters of doctrine and history.

Galilee and Judea. The northern and southern regions of Israel during the time of Christ.

Gnosticism. An early religious cult that held God is good, matter is evil, and man is saved by knowledge (gnosis) of special hidden truths.

God. In Greek it is the word *Theos*. The supreme being who is Creator and Ruler of the universe. The study of God is referred to as "Theology."

Good Friday. Traditional day of Jesus Christ's crucifixion.

gospel. In Christianity, the "Good News" that God has raised Jesus from the dead and in so doing has begun the transformation of the world. Also one of the four founding texts telling of Jesus' life: Matthew, Mark, Luke, John.

grace. In Greek it is the word *charis*. Unmerited favor. God's grace is extended to sinful humanity in providing salvation and forgiveness through Jesus Christ that is not deserved, and withholding the judgment that is deserved.[8]

Hanukkah. Jewish holy day commemorating the Jewish rebellion led by Judas Maccabees against Syrian oppressors in 167 BC. The family and supporters of Judas Maccabee were the forerunners of the Zealots in fighting a holy war against alien rulers.

Hebrew. A Jewish person. Also the language of the Jewish nation. In the early Church period, the term referred to Hebrew or Aramaic-speaking Christians.[9]

Hellenization. The civilization that spread from Greece through much of the ancient world from 333 BC (Alexander the Great) to 63 BC. As a result, many elements of Greek culture (names, language, philosophy, athletics, architecture, etc.) penetrated the Near East and also Europe.

heresy. A religious belief that contradicts the official teachings of a church. Such a belief is thus regarded as spurious and potentially dangerous for faith.

Hinduism. A syncretistic body of religious, philosophical, and social doctrines native to India. Most religious expressions of Hinduism emphasize pantheism, reincarnation, karma, and nirvana.

Holy Spirit. The third person of the Trinity. God the Father, God the Son, and God the Holy Spirit constitute the eternal Godhead in Christianity. The Spirit inspired biblical writers, makes known the saving work of Jesus Christ, and as God is present in and with the church.

humanism. The belief that the dignity of man is the highest value in the universe.

immanent. God's immanence is His presence within the universe. (See transcendent.)

immortality. In religious thought, the doctrine that man will live forever.

inerrancy. The term used to describe the Bible as being wholly without error in all that it affirms in the original autographs (writings).

infallible. The term used to describe the Bible as being absolutely correct and perfectly reliable in all that it teaches.

infinite. Without limits or boundaries.

inspiration. When used in Christian thought, inspiration refers to the teaching that the Bible is "God-breathed." It is, therefore, accurate in all it addresses. The authors of the Bible were inspired of God; that is, they wrote under the divine guidance of God.

Islam. Literally, "submission to the will of Allah." Religion founded by Muhammad about AD 600.

Jehovah. A name for God in Jewish and Christian tradition.

Jerusalem. Capital city of Israel founded by King David about 1000 BC.

Judaism. The religion that developed from the religion of ancient Israel, and has been practiced ever since by the Jews. It is an ethical monotheism based on the revelation of God to Moses on Mt. Sinai and His giving of the Law. The three main branches of Judaism are: 1. *Orthodox*: strict adherence to Torah laws, such as not allowing women rabbis; 2. *Conservative*: Moderate tradition acknowledging importance of Torah laws but allowing some modifications for new conditions, such as women rabbis; 3. *Reform*: Liberal openness to new ideas such as women rabbis and local language in services, and a more liberal interpretation of the dietary laws.

Judas. One of Jesus' twelve disciples. Judas betrayed Jesus to the authorities.

karma. In Hinduism and Buddhism, the law of cause and effect on a moral plane. Often refers to the debt accumulated against a soul as a result of one's actions during life or lives on earth.

Kingdom of God or Kingdom of Heaven. God's sovereign reign and rule in the individual and in the world. The main theme of Jesus' teaching.[10] The fullness of the kingdom is in the future tense,[11] although it has also come in the person of Jesus Himself.[12] Christian reign of God where God's will is done and his power is evident, both in the present and future.

liberation theology. A movement that developed in Latin America in the late 1960s, stressing the role of political action with goals of political liberation from poverty and oppression.

Lutheranism. The founding principles of the Protestant Reformation. Martin Luther, a German priest/professor began to teach in 1517 that all have direct access to God (priesthood of all believers), justification by faith (not by works alone), and the sole authority of the Bible. Also a later Protestant denomination.

manuscript. A document or a copy of an original writing (autograph).

martyr. The Greek word means "witness." A general term for persons who endure persecution, usually leading to death, for the sake of their religious witness.

materialism. The belief that all of reality is material, and that no spiritual entities, such as the soul or God, exist.

Messiah. "Anointed One." In Greek it is the word *Christos*, from which we get our word "Christ." The Messiah was the redeemer figure descended from the royal dynasty of David who would restore the united kingdom of Israel and Judah, bringing in an age of peace and justice. The concept of Messiah has been taken to mean a time of radical new beginnings, a new heaven and earth, after divine judgment. The title was applied to Jesus by His followers.

miracle. A general term for special events that seem inexplicable by normal (rational) means. Miracle reports are frequent in Jewish and Christian scriptures and early traditions, while in Islam, the only miracle associated with Muhammad is said to be the reception and transmission of the Qur'an.

modernity. A term that designates the post-Enlightenment period in Europe and America, in which people relied on scientific culture and its potential to fill the void that accompanied a decline in religion.

monasticism. The religious practice of monks and nuns, usually celibate, who live in a community according to a life of prayer, work, study, meditation, and service to others.

monotheism. The belief in one God. The term is applied particularly to three religions: Judaism, Christianity, and Islam.

Moses. Leader of the Hebrews who took them out of slavery in Egypt about 1400 BC, received the Ten Commandments at Mt. Sinai, and led the Hebrews to the Promised Land.

Muhammad. Founder of Islam. Born in AD 570, and died in AD 632.

naturalism. The belief that the universe is all there is; everything operates by natural law; therefore it precludes any supernatural intervention in the natural order.

Ninety-five Theses. The lists of topics for debate about Roman Catholic doctrine that Martin Luther nailed to the cathedral door in Wittenberg, Germany in 1517. Beginning of Protestant Reformation.

omnipotent. All-powerful. When designating an attribute of God, it means God has the power to do anything He desires; naturally, it would only include those things that would be in agreement with His own essence and character. For example, He would not commit sin, because that would be a violation of His holiness.

omnipresent. Everywhere present. When designating an attribute of God, it refers to the doctrine that everything is immediately in the presence of God, not that God is somehow intrinsically a part of everything, which would be pantheism. God transcends creation, He is not creation itself; but He is present everywhere in creation.

omniscient. All-knowing. When designating an attribute of God, it refers to God's complete and perfect knowledge; that is, He knows everything there is to know.

orthodox. From the Greek for "correct opinion/outlook," as opposed to that which is heretical or spurious. Historically, the term orthodox has come to denote the traditional, classical, or mainstream, such as rabbinic Judaism, Roman Catholic, or Orthodox Christian churches.

pantheism. The worldview that denies God's transcendence and identifies God with His immanence in the universe; therefore it holds that God is one in essence with the created world.

Passover. A Jewish festival commemorating God's protection and deliverance of the Jews as a people when He brought judgment against their cruel Egyptian captors. This incident occurred about 1400 BC, when Moses led the Jews out of the land of Egypt.

Pentateuch. The Greek word used to describe the Torah. It was a Jewish designation for the first five books of the Hebrew Scriptures (Old Testament).

philosophy. Literally, "love of wisdom." Careful thought about the fundamental nature of the world, the grounds for human knowledge, and the evaluation of human conduct.

Pilate, Pontius. The Roman Procurator of Judea (approximately AD 26–36) who condemned Jesus to crucifixion.

Plato. Ancient Greek philosopher (fourth century BC), student of Socrates, and teacher of Aristotle, who identified reality with the nonmaterial world of ideas ("the ideal world"), which played a central role in subsequent philosophy and religion.

pluralism (religious). A situation in which no single worldview or religion is dominant. Religious pluralism believes there is good in all religions, that people need to be open and tolerant of all views.

polytheism. The belief in many gods, such as Vishu and Shiva in Hinduism.

pragmatism. The philosophy which makes practical consequences the criterion for truth.

Protestant Church. Term for people who "protested" against the corruption and power of the Roman Catholic Church. A general term for the Christians who broke away from Roman papacy at the Reformation. The Catholic monk, Martin Luther, was a central figure in this movement. Protestants emphasize the sole authority of the Bible, justification by faith, and the priesthood of all believers—that all believers have direct access to God. Denominations include Presbyterians, Baptists, Methodists, Lutherans, Anglicans/Episcopalians, Quakers, and numerous other groups.

rabbi. A teacher of the Jewish law or an ordained Jew who is the spiritual leader of a congregation.

rationalism. A general term for the belief that everything is actually or potentially understandable by human reason.

Reformation. The Protestant Christian movements (and the period itself) in the sixteenth century which opposed Roman Catholicism in the interest of reforming Christianity to what was considered its earliest known form (found in the New Testament).

reincarnation. The successive rebirths of a soul into this life, as it progresses toward perfection or salvation. Referred to as *samsara* in Hinduism.

relativism. The modern position that affirms that everything is relative to the particularities of the given situation, and that no absolutes exist.

religion. Religion consists of a strong belief that there is an *unseen order* in the universe that controls human destiny, and that our supreme good lies in harmoniously adjusting ourselves unto it. The term is often used interchangeably with faith or belief system.

Renaissance. Name usually given to the "rebirth" of classical knowledge that erupted in fifteenth-century Europe and provided background for the Protestant Reformation.

repentance. A term used especially in Protestant Christianity to indicate the subjective state of sorrow, regret, and concern over sin, on the way to salvation. In Greek, the word translated as repentance means to change one's mind or purpose, and it involves a change for the better.

Roman Catholic Church. The Christian Church headed by the pope, bishop of Rome. Roman Catholics believe in the authority of the pope; in addition to the Scriptures, they give significant emphasis to tradition; they center the entire Catholic Mass on the Eucharist; and they require that priests be male and celibate.

Sabbath. Jewish weekly day of rest. The seventh day of the week in Judaism begins at sundown Friday and ends at sundown Saturday.

sacrament. An outward sign established by God to convey an inward or spiritual grace. Although Roman Catholic theology and church practice recognize seven sacraments (Eucharist, baptism, confirmation, marriage, ordination, penance, and unction), Protestant theologians generally argue that only two (Eucharist and baptism) are found in the New Testament itself.

sanctification. The process whereby a Christian believer is made holy, becoming like Jesus Christ.

Satan. Hebrew for "adversary," refers to the archangel Lucifer who rebelled against God and was banished from God's presence.

scholasticism. Philosophical study as practiced by Christian thinkers in medieval universities. The scholastics typically relied upon ancient authorities as sources of dogma and engaged in elaborate disputations over their proper interpretation.

sect. A small religious group that has split away from an established religion. The early Jewish Christian groups in Jerusalem around AD 35 would have been considered sects of Judaism at the time. A sect may eventually differentiate itself into a new denomination.

secular. A term that describes culture without any religious influence; it denotes the absence of religion, or the essence of irreligion.

secular humanism. That branch of philosophical humanism that denies specifically the existence of God.

secularism. The ideology of the secular world without reference to religious thinking.

Septuagint. The Greek translation of the Old Testament, dating from the third century BC, that was used during the time of Christ. The abbreviation LXX ("seventy" in Roman numerals) is generally used to refer to this text, because it was a translation of the Hebrew Scriptures into Greek by seventy Jewish scholars in Alexandria, Egypt (the intellectual center of the world in that day). The Greek translation was needed because many Jews only spoke Greek as a result of the hellenization of much of the ancient world.

Sermon on the Mount. Christ's teaching on the Kingdom of God in chapters 5–7 of Matthew's Gospel.

shaman. A medicine man, witch doctor, diviner; used in polytheistic religions.

sin. An action that breaks divine law. It also refers to the state of rebellion against God that results in self-rule in a person's life rather than God-rule.

Sinai. A mountain range in the Negev desert south of Israel.

soul. The active principle present in living things.

synagogue. A Jewish center of worship and teaching. The synagogue evolved after the destruction of the Temple by Babylon in the sixth century BC, when the Jewish people were exiled in Babylon.

syncretism. The religious practice of selecting religious beliefs, symbols, or practices from different sources and combining them.

Tanakh. The complete Jewish holy scriptures, including Torah, Prophets, and Writings.

Taoism. A mystical Chinese religion founded by Lao-tzu in 570 BC.

telos / teleological. Greek term for the "end," completion, purpose, or goal of any thing or activity.

Testament. Latin for "Covenant." The Old and New Testaments are the Old and New Covenants.

theism. The worldview that affirms the existence of a personal, infinite Creator of the world, who is immanent in the world, unlimited in power and in love.

theology. Derived from two Greek words meaning "study of God." A general term for discussions pertaining to God and religious matters. A person who engages formally in theological studies is called a theologian.

Torah. The Pentateuch, the first five books of the Hebrew Scriptures (Christian Old Testament).

transcendent. That which is more than our experience or goes beyond the world. Theists say God is transcendent because He exists outside of or beyond space, mass, and time. (See immanent.)

Trinity. The Christian belief that God is a unity composed of three persons: Father, Son, and Holy Spirit. Though God is composed of *three persons*, He is regarded as *one in essence*. Just as a human being is body, soul, and spirit—he is one person—so God is three persons, yet He is one. It should be noted that Christianity does not believe in "three gods," as Muhammad assumed when writing the Qur'an; he apparently thought the essence of Christianity was that God the Father and His wife Mary cohabitated and bore a child named Jesus. Obviously, this is not what Christianity believes.

universal. That which is true at all times and all places. The general concept or idea of a thing, as opposed to a particular instance or example.

Vatican II. The second general council (Vatican I was in 1868) of Roman Catholic bishops called in 1962 by Pope John XXII for the purpose of reforming Church practice to make it more accessible to a modern world. The most important changes resulting from Vatican II included the translation of the liturgy into the vernacular of the people (using the local languages that people spoke rather than Latin) and greater involvement of the laity in local matters of governance, worship, and church practice.

Vulgate. The Latin translation of the Bible, largely deriving from Jerome (AD 347–420), on which medieval theology was largely based. In the Reformation, its inaccuracies were recognized.

Yahweh. The personal name of the God of Israel; it is based on sacred Hebrew tetragram YHWH (without vowels). Considered by some Jews to be too sacred to speak, it is replaced by the Hebrew word *Adonai*.

NOTES

Introduction

1. Gerald R. McDermott, *Can Evangelicals Learn From World Religions?* (Downers Grove, IL: InterVarsity Press, 2000), 7.

2. David B. Barrett, *Our Globe and How to Reach It* (Birmingham, AL: New Hope, 1990).

3. Linda Edwards, *A Brief Guide to Beliefs, Ideas, Theologies, Mysteries, and Movements* (Louisville, KY and London: Westminster John Knox Press, 2001), 1.

Chapter One

1. Joseph Runzo, *Global Philosophy of Religion: A Short Introduction* (Oxford: Oneworld Publications, 2001), 216.

2. http://www.adherents.com/adh_predom.html.

3. Josh McDowell and Don Stewart, *Handbook of Today's Religions* (Nashville, TN: Thomas Nelson Publishers, 1983), 11.

4. Vinoth Ramachandra, *Faiths in Conflict?* (Downers Grove, IL: InterVarsity Press, 1999), 143.

5. Ramachandra, 141.

6. William James, *The Varieties of Religious Experience* (New York: Longman, 1902), 53.

7. Winfried Corduan, *Neighboring Faiths* (Downers Grove, IL: InterVarsity Press, 1998), 21.

8. Runzo, 19.

9. Runzo, 22.

10. Marc Gellman and Thomas Hartman, *Religion for Dummies* (New York: Wiley Publishing, Inc., 2002), 28.

11. Stephan A. Grunlan and Marvin K. Mayers, *Cultural Anthropology* (Grand Rapids, MI: Zondervan Publishing House, 1988), 228.

12. Corduan, 22.

13. Grunlan, 226.

14. Corduan, 22, 24.

15. Corduan, 25.

16. *World Book Encyclopedia*. Chicago: World Book, Inc., 2002, Vol. 20, 434.

17. Charles Berlitz, *Native Tongues* (New York: Grosset & Dunlap, 1982), 7.

18. Corduan, 33.

19. Corduan, 33.

20. Corduan, 34.

21. Robert E. Hume, *The World's Living Religions* (New York: Charles Scribner's Sons, 1959), 3.

22. Hume, 4.

23. Runzo, 217.

24. Runzo, 217.

[25] Luke 6:38; Luke 22:24–26;
      Galatians 6:7; Philippians 2:3–4.
[26] Gellman, 33.
[27] Gellman, 33–37.
[28] Gellman, 38.
[29] Greg R. Allison, *Getting Deep:
      Understand What You Believe
      About God and Why* (Nashville,
      TN: Broadman Publishers, 2002),
      124–125.
[30] Allison, 133–134; also cf. I
      Corinthians 15:24, 26.

Chapter Two

[1]   Ralph L. Woods, *The World Treasury
      of Religious Quotations* (New York:
      Garland Books, 1966), 839.
[2]   Ronald H. Nash, *Faith & Reason*
      (Grand Rapids, MI: Zondervan
      Publishing House, 1988), 16–17.
[3]   Nash, *Faith*, 24.
[4]   Nash, *Faith*, 18.
[5]   Charles Colson, *How Now Shall We
      Live?* (Wheaton, IL: Tyndale House,
      1999), 477.
[6]   Martin Forward, *Religion: A
      Beginner's Guide* (Oxford: Oneworld
      Publications, 2001), 121.
[7]   http://www.adherents.com online.
[8]   Gellman, 47.
[9]   Isaiah 55:8.
[10] Luke 15:11–32.
[11] Edwards, 77.
[12] Genesis 1:26.
[13] Dean C. Halverson, ed., *The
      Compact Guide to World Religions*
      (Minneapolis, MN: Bethany House,
      1996), 14–15.
[14] Colson, *How Shall We Live*, 16.
[15] Galatians 6:7; Deutereonomy
      28:1, 15; Isaiah 1:18–20; Jeremiah
      18:1–12.
[16] Proverbs 1:7; 9:10–12; 16:1–9;
      Matthew 7:24–27.
[17] http://www.adherents.com online.
[18] Deutereonomy 6:4.
[19] Halverson, 14.
[20] Norman Geisler and Joseph Holden,
      Living Loud: Defending your Faith
      (Nashville, TN: Broadman &
      Holman Publishers, 2002), 80.
[21] Corduan, 29.
[22] Corduan, 30.
[23] Corduan, 29.
[24] http://en.wikipedia.org/wiki/
      Pantheism.
[25] Geisler & Holden, 72.
[26] Allison, 101–102.
[27] Geisler & Holden, 72.
[28] Ronald H. Nash, *Worldviews
      in Conflict* (Grand Rapids, MI:
      Zondervan Publishing House,
      1992), 132.
[29] Nash, *Worldviews*, 135.
[30] Geisler & Holden, 72.
[31] Nash, *Worldviews*, 116.
[32] Forward, 3.
[33] Lewis M. Hopfe and Mark R.
      Woodward, *Religions of the World*
      (Upper Saddle River, NJ: Prentice
      Hall, 2001), 10.
[34] Forward, 13.
[35] Colson, *How Shall We Live*, 19.
[36] Colson, *How Shall We Live*, 20.
[37] Nash, *Worldviews*, 120.
[38] Nash, *Worldviews*, 121.
[39] Donald E. Chittick, *The Controversy:
      Roots of the Creation-Evolution
      Conflict* (Newberg, OR: Creation
      Compass, 1984), 85.
[40] Chittick, *Controversy*, 92.
[41] Nash, *Worldviews*, 128.
[42] Carl Sagan, *Cosmos* (New York:
      Random, 1980), 4.
[43] Colson, *How Shall We Live*, 52.
[44] Carl Sagan, *Broca's Brain* (New
      York: Random, 1979), 287.
[45] Forward, 20–21.
[46] Ramachandra, 141.
[47] Ramachandra, 141.
[48] Ramachandra, 142.
[49] Halverson, 185.
[50] Halverson, 185.
[51] Forward, x.
[52] Allan Bloom, *The Closing of the
      American Mind* (New York: Simon
      & Schuster, 1987), 25.

53 *Eerdmans' Handbook to The World's Religions* (Grand Rapids, MI: Eerdmans Publishing, 1994), 407.

54 Brian D. McLaren, *A New Kind of Christian* (San Francisco, CA: Jossey-Bass, 2001), 126.

55 Edwards, 12.

56 McLaren, 14–19.

57 McLaren, 14–19.

58 D. A. Carson, *Telling the Truth* (Grand Rapids, MI: Zondervan, Publishing House, 2000), 371.

59 Paul G. Hiebert, *Missiological Implications of Epistemological Shifts* (Harrisburg, PA: Trinity Press, 1999), 51–53.

60 Carson, 142.

61 Carson, 187.

62 Carson, 207–208.

63 Runzo, 30.

64 McDermott, 42.

65 Carson, 402.

66 Matthew 11:2–5; John 20:30–31; Acts 2:22; 17:11; 17:30–31; 2 Corinthians 12:12; Hebrews 2:4

67 James 3:17; Isaiah 1:18–20; 1 Peter 3:15

68 Nash, *Worldviews*, 57–59.

69 Geisler & Holden, 74–75.

70 Geisler & Holden, 74–75.

71 *Eerdmans'*, 410.

72 Judah Etinger, *Foolish Faith* (Green Forest, AR: Master Books, 2003), 14.

73 Carson, 402.

Chapter Three

1 Woods, 898.

2 Etinger, 151.

3 Donald E. Chittick, *The Puzzle of Ancient Man* (Newberg, OR: Creation Compass, 1998), 138.

4 Chittick, *Puzzle*, 138–139.

5 Chittick, *Puzzle*, 140.

6 Chittick, *Puzzle*, 146.

7 Chittick, *Puzzle*, 147.

8 Paul G. Hiebert, *Anthropological Insights for Missionaries* (Grand Rapids, MI: Baker Book House, 2003), 27.

9 Gellman, 78.

10 Sir John Templeton, *The Humble Approach: Scientists Discover God* (Philadelphia, PA: Templeton Foundation, 1998), 115.

11 Heibert, *Mission*, 104.

12 Francis Hitching, "Was Darwin Wrong?" *Life* (April, 1982), 48.

13 Lee Strobel, *The Case for a Creator* (Grand Rapids, MI: Zondervan Publishing House, 2004), 31.

14 Chittick, *Controversy*, 62.

15 Chittick, *Controversy*, 51.

16 Chittick, *Controversy*, 54.

17 Chittick, *Controversy*, 17.

18 Chittick, *Controversy*, 54.

19 Chittick, *Controversy*, 59.

20 Edwards, 45–46.

21 Francis A. Schaeffer, *Escape From Reason* (Downers Grove, IL: InterVarsity, 1968), 30–31.

22 Geisler & Holden, 65.

23 Theodosius Dobshansky, *Evolution* (Vol. 29, 1975), 376–387.

24 Pierre Grasse, *Evolution du Vivant* (New York: Academic Press, 1977), without page.

25 Etinger, 39; Professor Louis Bounour as quoted in *The Advocate* (March 8, 1984), 17.

26 Etinger, 37–38.

27 Etinger, 38, from *Nature* (Vol. 290, March 12, 1981), 82.

28 Etinger, 10, from John Boslough *Stephen Hawking's Universe* (New York: Quill, 1985), without page.

29 *Collier's Encyclopedia* (New York: Collier's, 1996), Vol. 8, 678.

30 *World Book Encyclopedia*, Vol. 6, 2002, 146.

31 Edwards, 52.

32 Edwards, 53.

33 Chittick, *Controversy*, 32.

34 Chittick, *Controversy*, 47.

35 Henry Morris (Institute for Creation Research), http://www.icr.org/pubs/imp/imp-003.htm.

36 Morris.

37 Duane Gish (Institute for Creation Research), http://www.icr.org/pubs/imp/imp-004.htm.

38 Isaac Asimov, "In the Game of Energy and Thermodynamics You Cannot Break Even," *Smithsonian Institute Journal* (June 1970), 6.

39 Steve Keels, *Survival Guide* (Nashville, TN: Broadman & Holman Publishers, 2002), 8.

40 Gish.

41 Halverson, 188.

42 Etinger, 152.

43 Etinger, 154.

44 Etinger, 155.

45 Walter Brown, http://www.creationscience.com/onlinebook/LifeSciences.html.

46 Steven M. Stanley, *The Evolutionary Timetable* (New York: Basic Books, Inc., 1981), 73.

47 Pierre-Paul Grasse, *Evolution of Living Organisms* (New York: Academic Press, 1977), 88.

48 David B. Kitts, "Paleontology and Evolutionary Theory," *Evolution* (Vol. 28, September 1974), 467.

49 Lynn Margulis, as quoted by Charles Mann, "Lynn Margulis: Science's Unruly Earth Mother," *Science* (Vol. 252, April 19, 1991), 379.

50 David S. Woodruff, "Evolution: The Paleobiological View," *Science* (Vol. 208, May 16, 1980), 716.

51 Tom Bethell, "Agnostic Evolutionists," *Harper's Magazine* (February 1985), 49–61.

52 Sagan, *Cosmos*, 4.

53 Lincoln Kinnear Barnett, *The Universe and Dr. Einstein* (New York: William Morrow, 1968), 114.

54 Colson, *How Shall We Live*, 58.

55 Colson, *How Shall We Live*, 59.

56 Don Batten, ed., *The Revised & Expanded Answers Book* (Green Forest, AR: Master Books, 2002), 23.

57 Colson, *How Shall We Live*, 58.

58 Paul C. Davies, *The Edge of Infinity: Where the Universe Came From and How it Will End* (New York: Simon & Schuster, 1982), 169.

59 Gish, ICR Online.

60 Stephen J. Gould, "Evolution's Erratic Pace," *Natural History* (Vol. 86, No. 5, May 1977), 12–14.

61 John Maynard Smith, *Evolution Now: A Century After Darwin* (San Francisco, CA: Freeman, 1982), 140.

62 Niles Eldredge, "Missing, Believed Nonexistent," *Manchester Guardian* (The Washington Post Weekly, Vol. 119, No. 22, November 26, 1978), p. 1.

63 Charles Darwin, *On the Origin of Species* (London: John Murray, 1859), 280.

64 Batten, 26.

65 Luther D. Sunderland, *Darwin's Enigma*, 4th ed. (Green Forest, AR: Master Books, 1988), 89.

66 Norman Geisler and Ron Brooks, *When Skeptics Ask: A Handbook on Christian Evidences* (Grand Rapids, MI: Baker, 2001), 229.

67 Geisler & Brooks, 229.

68 Colson, *How Shall We Live*, 73.

69 Colson, *How Shall We Live*, 73.

70 Michael Denton, *Evolution: A Theory in Crisis* (Bethesda, MD: Adler & Adler, 1986), 185.

71 David M. Raup, "Conflicts Between Darwin and Paleontology," *Field Museum of Natural History* (Vol. 50, No. 1, January 1979), 25.

72 Fred Hoyle, *The Intelligent Universe* (New York: Holt, Rinehart, and Winston, 1983), 11.

73 Colson, *How Shall We Live*, 74.

74 Chittick, *Puzzle*, 47, 162–170.

75 Robert Jastrow, "Genesis Revealed," *Science Digest* (Special Winter Issue, 1979), 40.

76 Geisler & Brooks, 223–224.

77 Geisler & Brooks, 223–224.

78 Chittick, *Puzzle*, 89–90.

79 John Holmes, "Neanderthals Linked to West Europeans," *Insight* (Sept. 11, 1989), 56.

80 Chittick, *Puzzle*, 90.

81 Chittick, *Puzzle*, 159.

82 Geisler & Holden, 60–61.

83 Tom Willis, "Lucy Goes to College," *CSA News* (Feb., 1987), 2.

84 Chittick, *Puzzle*, 91.

85 Geisler & Holden, 58.

Chapter Four

1 Strobel, 273.

2 John D. Morris, *The Geology Book* (Green Forest, AR: Master Books, 2000), 52–53.

3 Batten, 75–77.

4 Batten, 78.

5 Batten, 85.

6 Batten, 86.

7 John Morris, *Geology,* 49.

8 Batten, 79.

9 John Morris, *Geology,* 52.

10 John Morris, *Geology,* 54–55.

11 John Morris, *Geology,* 55.

12 John Morris, *Geology,* 55.

13 John Morris, *Geology,* 56.

14 John Morris, *Geology,* 56.

15 John Morris, *Geology,* 57.

16 John Morris, *Geology,* 57.

17 Batten, 86–88.

18 Batten, 87.

19 Batten, 87.

20 William D. Stansfield, *Science of Evolution* (New York: Macmillan Publishing Co., 1977), 84.

21 Batten, 152.

22 Josh McDowell, *The New Evidence* (Nashville, TN: Thomas Nelson Publishers, 1999), 104; *Zondervan Handbook to the Bible* (Grand Rapids, MI: Zondervan Publishing House, 1999), 123.

23 Genesis 6–9.

24 Matthew 24:37–39; Luke 17:26–27; Psalm 29:1–11; 104:5–9; Isaiah 54:9; Hebrews 11:7; 1 Peter 3:19–20; and 2 Peter 2:5; 3:3–6.

25 Geisler & Brooks, 182.

26 McDowell, *Evidence*, 105.

27 Gleason L. Archer, ed., *Encyclopedia of Bible Difficulties* (Grand Rapids, MI: Zondervan Publishing House, 1982), 84.

28 Archer, 84.

29 Genesis 7:2–3, 15.

30 Genesis 8:17.

31 Archer, 84.

32 Genesis 1:6–8.

33 Jobe Martin, *The Evolution of a Creationist* (Rockwell, TX: Biblical Discipleship, 1996), 126.

34 Henry M. Morris, *Science and the Bible* (Chicago: Moody Press, 1986), 82.

35 Morris, *Science*, 83.

36 Genesis 2:5.

37 Morris, *Science*, 83.

38 Genesis 1:10.

39 Morris, *Science*, 84.

40 Martin, 128.

41 Martin, 128.

42 Martin, 128–129.

43 Genesis 7:11–12.

44 John Morris, *Geology,* 62–66.

45 John Morris, *Geology,* 65.

46 John Morris, *Geology,* 66.

47 Batten, 156.

48 John Morris, *Geology,* 66–67.

49 Batten, 155–156.

50 Archer, 82.

51 Archer, 82–83.

52 Archer, 83.

53 John Morris, *Geology,* 38.

54 John Morris, *Geology,* 38.

55 David R. Reid, *Big Flood,* Study No. XIX-4 1991/92 (PO Box 2268, Westerly, RI 02891), 4.

56 Martin, 129.

57 Genesis 1:30.

58 Martin, 130.

59 Martin, 130.

60 Martin, 133.

61 Martin, 134–135.

62 Martin, 133.

63 Martin, 135.

64 Martin, 135.

65 Martin, 135.

66 Genesis 5:5, 27.
67 Martin, 136.
68 Psalm 90:10.
69 Martin, 136.
70 William F. Libby, *Radiocarbon Dating* (Chicago: University of Chicago Press, 1955), 7; Martin, 136–137.
71 Martin, 144.
72 Martin, 146.
73 Martin, 144–146.
74 Martin, 146–147.
75 Martin, 142.
76 Genesis 7:19–23.
77 Genesis 6:14–16.
78 Genesis 6:19–20.
79 Genesis 7:20.
80 Genesis 7:11.
81 Genesis 7:24–8:14.
82 2 Peter 3:7, 12; 2 Thessalonians 1:7; Daniel 7:9–10
83 Matthew 24:37–39; 2 Peter 2:5; 3:3–7; also Hebrews 11:7 and Isaiah 54:9.
84 Geisler & Holden, 55.
85 Geisler & Holden, 65–66.
86 Robert Jastrow, *God and the Astronomers*, 2nd ed. (New York: W. W. Norton, 1992), 107.

Chapter Five

1   Woods, 373.
2   Nash, *Faith*, 122.
3   Geisler & Holden, 43, 220–221.
4   Geisler & Holden, 220–221.
5   Henry M. Morris, *Many Infallible Proofs* (Green Forest, AR: Master Books, 2002), 117.
6   "Does God Exist," http://www.doesgodexist.org/phamplets/mansproof.html.
7   "Universe's Star Tally: 70 Sextillion," *Arizona Republic* (Aug. 6, 2003), no page, (originally published in *Los Angeles Times*, Aug., 2003).
8   http://www.doesgodexist.org.
9   Gellman, 44–45.
10 Morris, *Proofs*, 109–110.
11 Morris, *Proofs*, 110.
12 Geisler & Brooks, 219.
13 Geisler & Brooks, 217.
14 Geisler & Brooks, 217.
15 Edwards, 23.
16 Genesis 1:1.
17 Colossians 1:17.
18 Nash, *Faith*, 125.
19 Nash, *Faith*, 125.
20 Jastrow, *Astronomers*, 111.
21 Jastrow, *Astronomers*, 15, 18.
22 http://www.doesgodexist.org.
23 http://www.doesgodexist.org.
24 http://www.doesgodexist.org.
25 Batsell Barrett Baxter, *I Believe Because…* (Grand Rapids, MI: Baker Book House, 1971), 55.
26 Keith Ward, *Christianity: A Short Introduction* (Oxford, Oneworld, 2000), 8.
27 Ward, 8.
28 Gellman, 45.
29 Richard Taylor, *Metaphysics*, 2nd. ed. (Englewood Cliffs, NJ: Prentice-Hall, 1974), 115.
30 Taylor, 115.
31 http://creationmoments.com/resources/article.asp?art_id=58.
32 Geisler & Holden, 45.
33 Woods, 372.
34 *DeLegibus, Lib. XI, 4th Century BC*; Woods, 372.
35 Geisler & Holden, 45.
36 Geisler & Brooks, 22.
37 Etinger, 30–31.
38 Muncaster, 20.
39 Edwards, 24.
40 Nash, *Faith*, 142.
41 Edwards, 24–25.
42 Psalm 19:1–4; Romans 1:18–20.
43 Ward, 8.
44 Baxter, 45; Genesis 1:1.
45 God.
46 Gellman, 46–47.
47 Geisler & Holden, 48; also see James 4:12.
48 Allison, 6.
49 Geisler & Holden, 49.
50 Geisler & Holden, 49.
51 Geisler & Brooks, 23–24.

52 James H. Jauncey, *Why We Believe* (Cincinnati, OH: Standard Publishing, 1969), 14.
53 Baxter, 45.
54 Halverson, 189.
55 C. S. Lewis, *Mere Christianity* (New York: The Macmillan Company, 1960), 3–4.
56 Baxter, 52.
57 Allison, 6.
58 Bruce Bickel and Stan Jantz, *Guide to Cults, Religions, & Spiritual Beliefs* (Eugene, OR: Harvest House, 2002), 29.
59 Halverson, 192; also see Romans 1:19–20; 2:14–15; Psalm 8:1, 3; 19:1–4; Isaiah 40:12–14, 26; Acts 14:15–17; 17:24–25.
60 Ecclesiastes 3:11.
61 Romans 2:14–15.
62 Halverson, 189.
63 Halverson, 190.
64 Morris, *Proofs*, 109.
65 Exodus 1–15.
66 Keels, 12.
67 Halverson, 194.
68 Halverson, 194.
69 Allison, 15.
70 Nash, *Faith*, 56.
71 Edwards, 18.
72 Etinger, 157.
73 Etinger, 158.
74 Etinger, 158.
75 Woods, 372.

Chapter Six

1 Woods, 576.
2 Werner Gitt, *The Wonder of Man* (Bielefeld, Germany: Christliche Literatur-Verbreitung, 1999), 8.
3 "Death of Spontaneous Generation," *Encyclopedia Britannica Online,* http://members.eb.com/bol/topic?eu=119731&sctn=29.
4 Etinger, 48.
5 Etinger, 41.
6 Hoyle, 11.
7 "Francis Crick," *Encyclopedia Britannica Online,* http://members.eb.com/bol/topic?eu=28338&sctn=1.
8 Etinger, 78.
9 Gitt, 13.
10 *World Book*, Vol. 6, 462.
11 Gitt, 15.
12 *World Book*, Vol. 6, 462.
13 Muriel Larson, *God's Fantastic Creation* (Chicago: Moody Press, 1975), 174.
14 Gitt, 19.
15 Gitt, 21–28.
16 Gitt, 30–31.
17 Gitt, 31.
18 *World Book*, Vol. 4, 548.
19 Gitt, 31.
20 *Collier's Encyclopedia*, Vol. 11, 1996, 743.
21 Gitt, 49.
22 Alfred M. Rehwinkel, *The Wonders of Creation* (Grand Rapids, MI: Baker Book House, 1974), 246–247.
23 Gitt, 54.
24 Leviticus 17:11.
25 Larson, 164.
26 Gitt, 57.
27 *World Book*, Vol. 2, 408.
28 *World Book*, Vol. 2, 410.
29 Gitt, 57.
30 Gitt, 57.
31 *World Book*, Vol. 2, 410.
32 Larson, 168.
33 Rehwinkel, 244.
34 Rehwinkel, 245.
35 Larson, 167.
36 Rehwinkel, 245.
37 Gitt, 57.
38 Larson, 167.
39 Rehwinkel, 245.
40 *World Book*, Vol. 2, 410.
41 Gitt, 57.
42 *World Book*, Vol. 2, 410.
43 *World Book*, Vol. 2, 410.
44 Larson, 165.
45 Gitt, 62–63.
46 Larson, 165.
47 Gitt, 62–63.
48 Gitt, 58.
49 Gitt, 58–59.
50 Gitt, 58–59.
51 *World Book*, Vol. 2, 411.
52 *World Book*, Vol. 2, 411.

53 Rehwinkel, 248.
54 Gitt, 67.
55 *World Book*, Vol. 11, 312.
56 Gitt, 67.
57 *World Book*, Vol. 2, 550a.
58 Larson, 175.
59 Gitt, 81.
60 *World Book*, Vol. 2, 550a–550b.
61 Gitt, 81–82.
62 Gitt, 82.
63 Collier's, Vol. 4, 464.
64 *World Book*, Vol. 2, 552.
65 Collier's, Vol. 4, 464.
66 Gitt, 82.
67 James D. Watson, *DNA: The Secret of Life* (New York: Alfred A. Knopf, 2003), 166.
68 Gitt, 77.
69 Larson, 170.
70 Watson, 165.
71 Gitt, 77.
72 Gitt, 78.
73 "DNA," *Arizona Republic* (Dec. 9, 2003), A10.
74 Colson, *How Shall We Live*, 73.
75 Colson, *How Shall We Live*, 79.
76 Chittick, *Puzzle*, 47.
77 John Tierney, Lynda Wright & Karen Springen, "The Search for Adam and Eve," *Newsweek* (Jan. 11, 1988), 46–52.
78 Chittick, *Puzzle*, 166.
79 Ann Gibbons, "Calilbrating the Mitochondrial Clock," *Science* (Jan. 2, 1998, Vol. 279, No. 5347), 29.
80 Rehwinkel, 239.
81 Larson, 163.
82 Rehwinkel, 240–241.
83 Elmore, 59–60.

Chapter Seven

1 Woods, 437.
2 Mary Jo Weaver, *Introduction to Christianity* (Belmont, CA: Wadsworth Publishing Company, 1991), 5.
3 2 Timothy 3:16; 2 Peter 1:20–21; Exodus 20:1ff; 24:3–4; Leviticus 27:34; Num. 36:13; Deuteronomy 1:1–3; Psalm 119:1ff; Isaiah 1:1–3; Jeremiah 1:1–3; Ezekiel 1:1–3; Hosea 1:1; Joel 1:1; Jonah 1:1; Micah 1:1; Zephaniah 1:1; Haggai 1:1; Zechariah 1:1; Malachi 1:1.
4 Thomas E. Helm, *The Christian Religion* (Englewood Cliffs, NJ: Prentice Hall, 1991), 14.
5 Genesis 1:6, 9,11, 14, 20, 24, 26; John 1:1–3, 14.
6 Weaver, 7.
7 Genesis 1:1; Isaiah 40:27; John 1:1–3.
8 Colossians 1:17.
9 Max Anders, *New Christian's Handbook* (Nashville, TN: Thomas Nelson Publishers, 1999), 18.
10 Genesis 1:26–27.
11 John 19:30; Acts 7:59.
12 John 4:24.
13 Anders, 98.
14 Romans 2:15; Ecclesiastes 3:11.
15 Anders, 98.
16 Galatians 5:22–23.
17 Anders, 99.
18 Chittick, *Controversy*, 74.
19 Genesis 1:27.
20 Anders, 99.
21 Genesis 1:27.
22 Allison, 41.
23 Deuteronomy 6:5; Matthew 22:37.
24 Psalm 8:4–6.
25 Genesis 1:26; 2:15.
26 Helm, 25.
27 Genesis 2:8.
28 Genesis 3.
29 Genesis 2:17; 3:16–19; Romans 8:20–22.
30 Weaver, 9–10.
31 *Natur* (German, July 1989), 57–59.
32 Gitt, 113.
33 Genesis 3:16.
34 Genesis 3:14–19; Romans 8:20–22.
35 Genesis 2:3.
36 Genesis 2:17; 3:19; 5:5.
37 John Morris, *Geology*, 61.
38 James 1:13–15.

39 Luke 10:18; 1 Timothy 3:6; 1 Peter 5:8; 2 Peter 2:4; 1 John 3:8; Jude 1:6; Revelation 12; e.g., Isaiah 14;12–15; Ezekiel 28:12– 15.
40 Geisler & Holden, 85.
41 Genesis 3:1–13.
42 Helm, 28.
43 Isaiah 53:6; Romans 5:15–25; 7:14–25.
44 Psalm 14:1–3; 51:5; Romans 3:9, 23.
45 Anders, 99.
46 Anders, 100.
47 2 Corinthians 3:18; Romans 8:28–29; Galatians 4:19.
48 Genesis 1:26.
49 John 3:3; 2 Corinthians 5:17; Galatians 6:15.
50 Weaver, 10–11.
51 Isaiah 30:15; Jeremiah 15:7; Ezekiel 18:30–32.
52 Matthew 3:2; Mark 6:12; Luke 13:3; 24:47; 2 Peter 3:9.
53 Chittick, *Controversy*, 74–75.
54 1 Corinthians 2:14.
55 Chittick, *Controversy*, 76–78.
56 Genesis 4:20–22.
57 Chittick, *Puzzle*, 7.
58 Genesis 3:7.
59 Genesis 3:8.
60 Genesis 3:21.
61 James M. Boice, *Foundations of the Christian Faith* (Downers Grove, IL: InterVarsity Press, 1986), 603.
62 Genesis 4:4; 8:20–21; 15:8–21.
63 Genesis 4:10; Leviticus 17:11.
64 Leviticus 4:13–35; Hebrews 9:22.
65 Genesis 2:17.
66 Anders, 76–77.
67 Genesis 2:17.
68 Genesis 2:17; Romans 6:23.
69 Merrill F. Unger, ed., *Unger's Bible Dictionary* (Chicago: Moody Press, 1979), 942–946.
70 Eerdmans', 30.
71 Exodus 23:15, Deuteronomy 16:16– 17.
72 Unger, 942–943.
73 Genesis 6:5.
74 Genesis 6:3–8, 17.
75 Genesis 7:1–9.
76 Genesis 8:4.
77 Genesis 9:1.
78 Genesis 11:1–4.
79 Genesis 11:6–9.
80 Genesis 10–11.
81 Morris, *Science*, 94.
82 Thomas V. Gamkrelidze and V. V. Ivanov, "The Early History of Indo-European Languages," *Scientific American* (Mar. 1990), 110.
83 Graham Hancock, *Fingerprints of the Gods* (New York: Crown Trade Paperbacks, 1995), 135.
84 Robert Patton, "OOPARTS," *Omni* (Sept. 1982), 54.
85 Chittick, *Puzzle*, 95.
86 Joshua 24:2.
87 Genesis 12:1–7.
88 Corduan, 48.
89 Genesis 12:1–3.
90 http://www.comparativereligion.com/salvation.html#Christianity.
91 Genesis 2:24.
92 Genesis 21:14.
93 Genesis 21:18.
94 Unger, 540.
95 Israel.
96 Exodus, 3:13–15; Deuteronomy 10:14–15; Psalm 24:1; 47:7–9; 95:3ff; Jeremiah 10:10–13.
97 Deuteronomy 4:35; 6:4; Isaiah 43:10; 45:5–6, 18, 21, 22.
98 Ramachandra, 95–96.
99 Isaiah 43:8–13.
100 Exodus 19:4–6; Deuteronomy 4:5–8.
101 Ramachandra, 96.
102 Joshua 24:14.
103 Exodus 7:13; 7:22; 8:15; 8:19; 8:32; 9:7; 9:34.
104 Exodus 12.
105 Exodus 12:7.
106 Exodus 12:13.
107 Bruce Wilkinson and Kenneth Boa, *The Wilkinson & Boa Bible Handbook* (Nashville, TN: Thomas Nelson Publishers, 2002), xvii.
108 Exodus 8:1; 9:1; 10:3.

[109] Exodus 14.
[110] Exodus 1:7–11; 12:37.
[111] William MacDonald, *Believer's Bible Commentary* (Nashville, TN: Thomas Nelson Publishers, 1995), 98.
[112] Corduan, 48.
[113] Exodus chapters 19 and following.
[114] Corduan, 48–49.
[115] Exodus 19:5.
[116] http://comparativereligion.com.
[117] Deuteronomy 7:1.
[118] Num. 13–14.
[119] Exodus 20:3.
[120] Jeremiah 7:1–11, 22–23.
[121] http://comparativereligion.com.
[122] Deuteronomy 34.
[123] Joshua 1–12.
[124] Joshua 13–21.
[125] Henry H. Halley, *Halley's Bible Handbook* (Grand Rapids, MI: Zondervan Publishing House, 1965), 168.
[126] Wilkinson, xvii.
[127] Psalm 106:39–43; Deuteronomy 12:31.
[128] Judges 2:2; 10:6–7; 2 Kings 17:17; Isaiah 57:3–6; Jeremiah 7:31; Ezekiel 16:20–21.
[129] James I. Packer, ed., *The Bible Almanac* (Nashville, TN: Thomas Nelson Publishers, 1980), 139.
[130] Exodus 23:20–33; Deuteronomy 7:1–11.
[131] Psalm 106:34–39.
[132] Deuteronomy 20:17–18; Num. 33:55; Joshua 23:12–13.
[133] Hosea 12:19.
[134] Isaiah 42:8; Psalm 115:3–8; 135:15– 18; Exodus 20:3; Psalm 29:2; Acts 12:23.
[135] Psalm 14:1; Isaiah 29:16; Jeremiah 10:1–11.
[136] Corduan, 49.
[137] 1 Chronicles 6:27.
[138] 1 Samuel 8:10–22.

Chapter Eight

[1] Woods, 437.
[2] 1 Samuel 9:15–17.

[3] Packer, 33.
[4] 1 Samuel 18:5–9; 19:8–10.
[5] 1 Samuel 16.
[6] Packer, 34.
[7] Deuteronomy 12:1–14; 2 Samuel 6:12.
[8] 2 Samuel 12–18.
[9] Matthew 1:1–17; Luke 3:23–38.
[10] 1 Kings 2:12.
[11] 1 Kings 9:4–7; 11:11.
[12] 1 Kings 11:1–4.
[13] 1 Kings 11:1–3.
[14] 1 Kings 11:43; 12:20.
[15] Matthew 15:19–20.
[16] 1 Kings 6–8.
[17] Gellman, 295.
[18] John N. Bimson, ed., *Baker Encyclopedia of Bible Places* (Grand Rapids, MI: Baker Book House, 1995), 169.
[19] J. D. Douglas, ed., *The New Bible Dictionary* (Grand Rapids, MI: Eerdmans, 1977), 698.
[20] 2 Kings 8:16–27; 16:1–20; 21:1–26.
[21] 1 Kings 11:4–6; 15:3; 2 Kings 14:3.
[22] 1 Kings 22:43; 15:3–4.
[23] 2 Kings 18:3–4; 22:2; 23:5–8.
[24] 1 Kings 12–22; 2 Kings 1–25.
[25] Edwards, 175.
[26] 1 Kings 16:29–18:46; e.g., Deuteronomy 13:1–5.
[27] 1 Kings 21.
[28] 2 Kings 1–13.
[29] 2 Kings 4:38–5:19.
[30] 2 Chronicles 36:16; Nehemiah 9:26, 30; Jeremiah 7:25–26; Micah 6:3; Isaiah 5:4; Matthew 23:37; Romans 11:3; 1 Kings 19:10.
[31] Corduan, 50.
[32] Unger, 514.
[33] Wilkinson, xviii.
[34] Wilkinson, xix.
[35] Edwards, 175.
[36] Halley, 402.
[37] Halley, 403.
[38] Halley, 403–404.
[39] John 10:22.
[40] Corduan, 51.
[41] Packer, 64.

42 John 2:13, 20.

43 Packer, 64.

44 Leviticus 16.

45 Mark 13:2–3.

46 Corduan, 51.

47 Weaver, 23.

48 Calvin J. Roetzel, *The World That Shaped the New Testament* (Atlanta, GA: John Knox Press, 1985), 30.

49 Weaver, 24.

50 Weaver, 24.

51 Weaver, 24.

52 Edwards, 175.

53 Roetzel, 28.

54 Weaver, 25.

55 Roetzel, 43.

56 Corduan, 52–53.

57 Weaver, 24–25.

58 Roetzel, 35.

59 Isaiah 42:7; 61:1.

60 Mark 6:34.

61 David Rhoads, *Israel in Revolution, AD 6–74: A Political History Based on the Writing of Josephus* (Philadelphia, PA: Fortress Press, 1976), 33.

62 Mark 7:1–23.

63 Roetzel, 45.

64 Roetzel, 64–66.

65 Roetzel, 66–67.

66 Roetzel, 77.

67 Halley, 412.

68 Halverson, 122.

69 Ramachandra, 99.

70 Genesis 12:3.

71 Bickel, 52.

72 Weaver, 23.

73 Unger, 718–719.

74 Weaver, 22.

75 Weaver, 22–23.

Chapter Nine

1 Isaiah 53:3, 5, 6, 10, 11.

2 Weaver, 32.

3 Weaver, 33.

4 Luke 2:1–11.

5 Matthew 1:18–21; Luke 1:26–35.

6 MacDonald, 1371.

7 Matthew 1:1–17; Luke 3:23–38.

8 Luke 2:41–47.

9 Matthew 13:55.

10 Edwards, 192.

11 Isaiah 53.

12 Isaiah 7:14; Matthew 1:21–23.

13 Genesis 49:10; Luke 3:23, 33.

14 Isaiah 53:3; John 1:10–11; 7:5.

15 Zechariah 9:9; Matthew 21:4ff.

16 Isaiah 53:7; Matt 27:12–14.

17 Isaiah 52:14; Matthew 27:26.

18 Psalm 22:16; Matthew 27:31.

19 Psalm 34:20; John 19:32–36.

20 Psalm 22:18; John 19:23ff)

21 Micah 5:2; Luke 2:4–7.

22 Hosea 11;1; Matthew 2:14–15.

23 Psalm 41:9; Luke 22:3–4.

24 Zechariah 11:12; Matthew 26:14–15.

25 Psalm 22:7–8; Matthew 27:31.

26 Isaiah 50:6; Matthew 27:30.

27 Isaiah 53:12; Matthew 27:38.

28 Isaiah 53:9; Matthew 27:57–60.

29 Psalm 16:10; Acts 2:31.

30 Unger, 718.

31 Unger, 718; also see Genesis 3:15; 9:27; 12:3; 22:18; 49:8, 10; Deuteronomy 18:18; 2 Samuel 7:11–16; 23:5; Psalms 2, 16, 22, 40, 110; Isaiah 2, 7, 9, 11, 40, 42, 49, 53; Jeremiah 23:5, 6; Daniel 7:27; Zechariah 12:10–14; Haggai 2:9; Malachi 3:1; 4:5, 6. For a complete list of the messianic passages found in rabbinic writings, see Alfred Edersheim, *The Life and Times of Jesus the Messiah.* (Grand Rapids, MI: Eerdmans Publishing, 1962), Appendix IX.

32 Genesis 49:10; Luke 3:23, 33.

33 Luke 3:3–9.

34 Isaiah 40:3; Malachi 3:1.

35 John 1:19–34.

36 Matthew 3:1–17.

37 Matthew 3:5.

38 Matthew 3:13–17; John 1:19–23.

39 John 1:29; 1 Peter 1:18–19.

40 Matthew 10:1–4; Luke 6:12–16.

41 Matthew 17:1–13; Mark 9:2–10; Luke 9:18–20.

42 Matthew 16:21–23; Mark 9:30–32; Luke 18:31–34.

43   Luke 24:45–48; John 12:16.
44   Matthew 11:20–24; 24:12.
45   Mark 2:17; Matthew 15:17–20.
46   Matthew 7:15–16; 12:35; 5:21.
47   Mark 1:15; Luke 5:32.
48   Luke 19:1–10.
49   Luke 11:4; 18:9–14.
50   John 12:31; 2 Corinthians 4:4;
     Ephesians 2:2; 6:12; 1 John 5:19.
51   Revelation 20:10–15.
52   John 14:2–3; Revelation 21:1–8.
53   Ephesians 6:10–17.
54   Roetzel, 97.
55   Unger, 632; also see Acts 1:6;
     2 Samuel 7:16; Isaiah 11:1–12;
     32;1–20; 65:17–66:24; Jeremiah
     33:14–22; Daniel 7:13–14; Micah
     4:1–3; Zechariah 9:9–10; 14.
56   Acts 1:6.
57   MacDonald, 1737; also see Matthew
     19:13–14; Luke 17:20–21; Romans
     14:17.
58   Mark 4:35–41; 6:35–51.
59   Matthew 8:1–17; 9:1–8.
60   Luke 8:26–39; 9:37–45.
61   Luke 7:11–17; Matthew 8:18–26.
62   Matthew 5–7.
63   Matthew 9:1–8; 9:18–22; Luke
     8:43–48.
64   Luke 5:20–26; 7:48–50.
65   John 2.
66   John 5.
67   John 6.
68   John 6.
69   John 9.
70   John 11.
71   Matthew 10:1; Acts 2:22; Hebrews
     2:3–4.
72   Halverson, 265.
73   Exodus 4–14.
74   I Kings 18.
75   John 2:1–11.
76   Luke 7:20–22.
77   John 3:2.
78   John 20:30–31.
79   Acts 2:22–24.
80   Acts 2:41.
81   Matthew 10:1; 2 Corinthians 12:12.
82   Acts 2:4.
83   Acts 3:1–10.
84   Acts 20:9–12.
85   Acts 5:12.
86   Suras 3:184; 17:103; 23:45.
87   Suras 2:118; 4:153; 6:8, 9, 37.
88   Halverson, 265.
89   Acts 17:11; 1 Thessalonians 5:21;
     1 John 4:1; Jeremiah 29:8–9.
90   Exodus 4:1–9; 1 Samuel 3:1–20; I
     Kings 18:36–39; Matthew 11:2–5;
     Mark 16:20; Luke 10:13; John 2:11;
     2:23; 3:2; 4:48; 6:14, 30; 9:1–38;
     10:25; 10:37–38; 20:30–31; Acts
     2:22; 4:1–33; Romans 15:17–21;
     1 Corinthians 2:4–5; 9:1–2;
     14:20–22; 2 Corinthians 12:12;
     1 Thessalonians 1:5; 2 Thessalonians
     2:9; Hebrews 2:4.
91   Jeremiah 32:36–41; 33:14–26;
     Isaiah 11:6–9; 54:11–15; 59:20–21;
     Ezekiel 16:59–63; 36:22–32.
92   Exodus 19:5; Deuteronomy
     28:1–2, 15.
93   Romans 8:3–4.
94   Jeremiah 31:31–37; Hebrews 8:8–13;
     9:11–15; 10:1–10.
95   Galatians 3:24.
96   Jeremiah 31:31–34; Ezekiel 36:22–
     27; 37:14; 39:29; Joel 2:28; Hebrews
     8:8–12.
97   Genesis 12:1–3.
98   Genesis 15:6.
99   Exodus 6:6–7.
100 Deuteronomy 28:1–14.
101 Deuteronomy 28:15–68.
102 Douglas, 266.
103 Galatians 5:22–23.
104 1 Corinthians 11:31–32; Galatians
     6:10; Hebrews 12:5–11.
105 John 14:16–21; Romans 8:9, 14–16.
106 Galatians 5:16–18.
107 Galatians 5:16, 22–23.
108 Genesis 1:26; Romans 8:26–27;
     2 Corinthians 3:17–18.
109 John 14:26; 15:26; 16:8–13.
110 1 Samuel 10:6–7; 16:13–14; 19:20;
     Psalm 51:10–12.
111 Matthew 26:28; Mark 14:24; Luke
     22:20; 1 Corinthians 11:25.

112 Genesis 2:17; Romans 6:23.
113 Hebrews 10:1–4, 11.
114 Hebrews 9:11–14; 10:10–18; 1 Peter 2:24.
115 Hebrews 8:13.
116 Hebrews 9:12; 10:12, 14, 18.
117 1 Corinthians 15:1–3.
118 John 1:11.
119 John 1:12.
120 John 3:16–18.
121 Hebrews 11:6.
122 Ephesians 2:8–9.
123 Matthew 22:36–39; John 1:12; Romans 8:14–16; 1 John 5:1.
124 Mark 16:16; John 3:18, 36; 8:24; 8:42–45; 10:26–28.
125 John 3:16–21; 20:30–31.
126 Romans 10:9–10.
127 Luke 9:47; Psalm 77:6; Proverbs 23:6–7; Isaiah 6:10.
128 James 2:19–20.
129 Romans 6:17–18.
130 James 4:6; Ephesians 2:8–9; Acts 16:14; Jeremiah 24:7.
131 Isaiah 2:12; 13:11; Romans 2:5; Hebrews 3:8–11; Jam. 4:6.
132 John 1:12.
133 Romans 6:4; 2 Corinthians 5:17; John 13:34–35; 1 John 3:7–11; 4:7–8.
134 John 3:3; 2 Corinthians 5:17; Galatians 5:22.
135 Luke 4:40–42; 5:15, 26; 6:17–19.
136 Matthew 14:13–21; Mark 6:30–44; Luke 9:10–17; John 6:5–13.
137 John 6:15.
138 Weaver, 26.
139 Luke 14:1.
140 Matthew 19:1–3; Luke 11:53–54.
141 John 11:41–45.
142 John 11:46–53.
143 Matthew 23:1–39; Luke 20–45–47.
144 Matthew 21:33–44; 22:1–14; Mark 12:1–12; Luke 20:9–47.
145 Matthew 23:2, 3, 13, 27, 29, 30, 31, 37.
146 Jeremiah 26:8ff
147 Romans 10:2–3.
148 John 8:37.
149 Matthew 15:19.
150 Mark 11:27–34.
151 Mark 3:6.
152 John 10:30–33; John 5:10–18; Matthew 26:63–67.
153 Mark 15:10.
154 Matthew 26:14–15.
155 Matthew 26:59–68; 28:11–15; Mark 14:55–65; Luke 22:65–71.
156 Matthew 27:11–26; John 18:33–38.
157 Luke 23:6–16.
158 Matthew 27:11–31; Mark 15:2–20; Luke 23:2–25; John 18:28–19:15.
159 Matthew 27:32–56.
160 Ramachandra, 88.
161 John 10:15, 17–18.
162 Matthew 26:53–54.
163 Isaiah 52:13–53:12.
164 Matthew 16:21–23; 17:22–23; 20:18–19.
165 Hebrews 12:2.
166 John 4:22.
167 Genesis 12:3; 27:29.
168 Romans 11:33–35; Isaiah 40:13–26.
169 Romans 11:11–36.
170 Matthew 26:56; Mark 14:66–72; John 20:19.
171 Luke 24:1–11.
172 John 20:24–28.
173 Acts 2:1–41.
174 Nash, *Faith*, 147–149.
175 I Corinthians 15:1–8; Ephesians 2:19–22; Romans 10:9–10.
176 Romans 4:25; 1 Corinthians 15:12–19.
177 Hebrews 2:3–4; Matthew 12:40–41.
178 John 1:1–3, 14; Romans 1:4.
179 John 11:25–26.
180 Matthew 27:62–66.
181 John 19:23.
182 Geisler & Holden, 136–137.
183 Matthew, Mark, and John
184 Ramachandra, 92.
185 Acts 1:3.
186 Geisler & Holden, 137.
187 John 20:1.
188 Matthew 28:1.
189 Luke 24:10.
190 Luke 23:55.

[191] Luke 24:34.
[192] Luke 24:13–32.
[193] John 20:24.
[194] John 20:26–29.
[195] John 21:1–24.
[196] Matthew 28:16–20.
[197] 1 Corinthians 15:6.
[198] 1 Corinthians 15:7.
[199] Acts 1:4–12.
[200] 1 Corinthians 15:7; 9:1.
[201] Geisler & Holden, 137.
[202] Mark 3:20–21; John 7:5.
[203] Acts 1:14.
[204] 1 Corinthians 15:7.
[205] Galatians 1:19.
[206] Galatians 2:9.
[207] Acts 15:13.
[208] Unger, 553.
[209] Acts 1:3.
[210] John 14:16–18, 26–29; 15:26–27; 16:6–7; Acts 1:4–5.
[211] Acts 1:8.
[212] Acts 1:9–11.
[213] Acts 1:8; Matthew 28:20.
[214] Galatians 1:12.
[215] Ephesians 2:20; 1 Corinthians 3:10–11; Jude 3:20.
[216] Acts 2:43; 4:29–33; 2 Corinthians 12:12.
[217] Acts 2:14–41.
[218] Acts 2:44–46; 5:32–34.
[219] Acts 5:17–32.
[220] Acts 8:1.
[221] Acts 9:4.
[222] Acts 9:20–25.
[223] Acts 14:8–19.
[224] Acts 15:40–18:22.
[225] Acts 18:23–21:16.
[226] Acts 22:1–21.
[227] Acts 28:17–20; 30–31.
[228] Packer, 43.
[229] Anders, 78–79.
[230] Weaver, 29.

Chapter Ten

[1] Woods, 363.
[2] Genesis 1:1; Psalm 90:2.
[3] Genesis 1:3, 5, 9, 11, 14, 20, 24; Psalm 33:9; 148:5; John 1:1ff
[4] Psalm 103:19; Daniel 4:17, 1 Timothy 6:15; Isaiah 14:24, 27; Isaiah 43:10–13.
[5] Walter A. Elwell, ed., *Evangelical Dictionary of Theology* (Grand Rapids, MI: Baker Book House, 1992), 461.
[6] Isaiah 42:8.
[7] Gellman, 47.
[8] Isaiah 40:25.
[9] Isaiah 55:8.
[10] Woods, 362.
[11] Psalm 145:3; Romans 11:33.
[12] 1 Corinthians 1:21a.
[13] Elwell, 460; also see Romans 1:20.
[14] Psalm 19: 1–4.
[15] Romans 1:19–20.
[16] Elwell, 460.
[17] Elwell, 451.
[18] Genesis 21:3; 1 Kings 8:27; Psalm 90:1–2; Isaiah 57;15; Micah 5:2; John 1:1–2; 1 Timothy 1:17; Revelation 1:8; 21:6; 22:13.
[19] Genesis 1:1.
[20] Ephesians 1:11.
[21] John 4:24; 1 Timothy 6:16.
[22] Exodus 20:4–5.
[23] John 4:24.
[24] Allison, 36.
[25] Isaiah 6:3; also see Revelation 4:8.
[26] Jam. 1:13; 1 John 1:5; 3:5; 2 Corinthians 5:21; Hebrews 7:26.
[27] Deuteronomy 10:17; Psalm 5:4; 92:15; Acts 10:34; Romans 2:11.
[28] Micah 6:8; 1 Peter 1:14–17.
[29] Psalm 33:11; Malachi 3:6; Hebrews 13:8; Num. 23:29.
[30] Titus 1:2; Hebrews 6:18; Jam. 1:17.
[31] Genesis 1:1; John 1:1–3; Isaiah 44:24; Col 1:16–17; Hebrews 1:10.
[32] Genesis 18:14; Jeremiah 32:17, 27; Matthew 19:26.
[33] Genesis 1:1–27; Psalm 33:6.
[34] Keels, 43.
[35] Isaiah 40:15.
[36] Genesis 17:1–2; 35:11–12.
[37] Ephesians 1:11.

38 1 Samuel 16:7; 1 Chronicles 28:9;
Psalm 139:1–4; Proberbs 5:21; Isaiah
66:18; Jeremiah 23:24; Matthew
9:4; John 2:24; 16:30; Romans
11:33; Colossians 2:3; 1 John 3:20.

39 Matthew 10:30.

40 Keels, 36.

41 Psalm 147:4; Isaiah 40:26.

42 *Arizona Republic,* August 6, 2003.

43 Isaac Asimov, ed., *Isaac Asimov's
Book of Facts* (New York: Random
House, 1997), 293.

44 Hebrews 4:13.

45 Ephesians 1:11.

46 Psalm 139:7–12; Jeremiah 23:23–24.

47 John 3:16; Romans 5:8; 6:23; 8:7–8;
1 John 4:8, 16.

48 1 John 4:10.

49 Luke 18:27; John 3:16; Romans
6:23.

50 John 1:12; 3:16.

51 Unger, 1041.

52 Psalm 50:1; 66:7; 93:1–2; 103:19;
Isaiah 40:15, 17; 43:10–13; Matthew
6:13; Revelation 19:16.

53 Elwell, 1039; also see Ephesians 1:11;
Acts 2:23.

54 Unger, 1041.

55 Colossians 1:17.

56 Psalm 139:1–4.

57 Psalm 145:8–9.

58 Genesis 1–3.

59 John 14:1–21ff

60 Matthew 5:45; 6:26–32.

61 2 Chronicles 7:13–15; Psalm
4:3; 50:15; 91:15; Jeremiah 33:3;
Hebrews 4:15–16.

62 Psalm 66:18; Proberbs 1:28–29;
Isaiah 59:1–2; Galatians 6:7–8; Jam.
4:3.

63 2 Chronicles 20:6; Isaiah 14:24–27;
43:13; 46:11; Jeremiah 29:10–14;
Daniel 4:34–37.

64 Deuteronomy 6:4; Isaiah 44:6; 45:5;
Mark 12:29; John 10:30; Galatians
3:20; Ephesians 4:6; Jam. 2:19.

65 Matthew 28:19.

66 2 Corinthians 13:14.

67 Ephesians 4:4–6.

68 1 Peter 1:2.

69 Elwell, 262.

70 Gellman, 51.

71 Genesis 1:1, 26.

72 Elwell, 465.

73 Genesis 1:26; 3:22; 11:7; Isaiah 6:8.

74 Elwell, 262.

75 Genesis 1:26.

76 Genesis 6:3; 1 Samuel 16:13–14;
Nehemiah 9:20; Job 33:4; Psalm
51:11; 139:7; Isaiah 11:2; 30:1;
40:13; 42:1; 44:3; 59:21; 61:1; 63:10;
Ezekiel 36:27; 37:14; Joel 2:28–29;
Zechariah 4:6.

77 Isaiah 48:16.

78 John 15:26; Matthew 28:19; John
14:23, 26; 2 Corinthians 13:14;
Ephesians 5:4–6; 1 Peter 1:2.

79 Morris, *Science,* 22–24.

80 Morris, *Science,* 22.

81 John 5:18; 10:30–33; 14:8–10; John
17:5; Philippians 2:5–6.

82 John 5:19–23, 30; 10:29–33; 12:49;
14:28; John 17:5; 1 Corinthians
11:3.

83 Geisler & Holden, 124.

84 Romans 13:1–7.

85 Hebrews 10:30–31.

86 Deuteronomy 28:1, 15; John 14:15;
2 Corinthians 9:8; Galatians 6:7;
Ephesians 3:20.

87 John 3:16–17; Philippians 2:5–11.

88 Geisler & Holden, 126.

89 John 1:1–3, 14.

90 John F. Walvoord and Roy B. Zuck.
*The Bible Knowledge Commentary
(New Testament)* (Wheaton, IL:
Victor Books, 1983), 271.

91 Romans 11:36; 1 Corinthians 8:6;
Colossians 1:16; Hebrews 1:2.

92 1 John 1:1.

93 Luke 24:48; John 15:27; Acts 1:8;
2:32; 4:20; 1 John 1:1–4.

94 John 10:30; Matthew 26:63–66.

95 John R. W. Stott, *Basic Christianity*
(Grand Rapids, MI: Eerdmans
Publishing, 1957), 27.

96 Matthew 11:17; John 8:19; 14:7.

97 John 12:45; 14:9.

98 John 12:44; 14:1.
99 John 15:23.
100 Mark 9:37.
101 John 5:23.
102 John 14:8–10.
103 Matthew 16:16; John 20:28.
104 Nash, *Faith*, 147.
105 Lewis, 55–56.
106 John 5:16, 18; 7:1; 7:19; 8:37, 40; 10:33; 11:53; Matthew 26:4; 26:63–66; John 18:2–12; 19:6–7, 16.
107 John 1:14.
108 John 20:28.
109 Colossians 1:15.
110 Colossians 2:9.
111 Luke 1:76.
112 Hebrews 1:3.
113 Hebrews 1:8.
114 Titus 2:13.
115 2 Peter 1:1.
116 Mark 14:61–64.
117 1 Timothy 4:10.
118 Philippians 2:6.
119 1 John 5:20.
120 Luke 1:26–35.
121 Matthew 3:17; 17:5.
122 Luke 4:1–41.
123 Matthew 14:25–33.
124 John 11:27.
125 Geisler & Holden, 120–121.
126 Genesis 1:1; Isaiah 40:22, 28 *and* John 1:3; Colossians 1:15–17.
127 Isaiah 41:4; 44:6 *and* Revelation 1:17; 22:12–13.
128 Isaiah 43:10; 45:22 *and* John 1:1; 20:28; Titus 2:13; Hebrews 1:8.
129 Isaiah 45:21; 43:3, 11 *and* Acts 4:12; Romans 10:9.
130 Psalm 23;1 *and* John 10:11.
131 Exodusus 3:14; Isaiah 43:10 *and* John 8:24, 58; 13:19.
132 Jeremiah 31:34 *and* Mark 2:7, 10.
133 Daniel 6 *and* Acts 7:59.
134 Psalm 34:3; Isaiah 45:23 *and* Philippians 2:10.
135 Psalm 148:2 *and* Hebrews 1:6.
136 Exodusus 34:14 *and* Matthew 14:31–33.
137 Malachi 3:6 *and* Hebrews 13:8.
138 Deuteronomy 33:27 *and* John 8:58; Hebrews 13:8.
139 Psalm 139:1–6; 1 John 3:20 *and* John 2:24–25; John 4:16–19.
140 Psalm 139:7–12 *and* Matthew 18:20.
141 Psalm 139:13–24 *and* Colossians 2:10; Matthew 28:18.
142 John 9:16–41.
143 John 9:40–41.
144 Isaiah 6:9–10; Jeremiah 5:20–21; Matthew 13:10–16; Acts 16:14.
145 Ramachandra, 110.
146 Geisler & Holden, 128.
147 Ramachandra, 111.
148 Matthew 3:16–17; 28:19; John 14:16–17; 15:26.
149 1 Corinthians 2:10; 12:11.
150 1 Corinthians 2:11; 12:11; Hebrews 9:14.
151 Genesis 1:2; Job 26;13; John 3:3, 8.
152 Isaiah 6:3–10; Acts 28:25–27; 2 Corinthians 13:14.
153 John 15:26; 16:15; 14:26; Philippians 1:19; Acts 11:17.
154 Genesis 1:3, 6, 9, 11, 14, 20, 24.
155 Genesis 2:7.
156 Elwell, 521; also see Job 33:4; Genesis 6:17; 7:15.
157 Num. 11:17, 25; 2 Samuel 23:2; Isaiah 40:13–14; John 14:16–17, 26; 15:26; 16:7–8, 13–14.
158 Genesis 1:2 Job 26:13; Psalm 104:30.
159 2 Peter 1:21; 2 Samuel 23:2; Acts 1:16.
160 1 Kings 8:12; Judges 14:6ff; 1 Samuel 11:6.
161 Isaiah 37:6; 38:1; 44:6, 24; 45:18; Ezekiel 36:22.
162 Boice, 380.
163 Exodus 17:7; Psalm 95:7; Hebrews 3:7–11.
164 Matthew 12:28; 1 Corinthians 12:9–11.
165 Isaiah 6:3; Matthew 28:19; Acts 28:25; Romans 9:1; Revelation 1:4.
166 Ezekiel 36:22, 24, 26, 27; also cf. Isaiah 44:3; Joel 2:28–29.

167 1 Samuel 10:6, 10; 11:6; 16:13–14; 18:12; Psalm 51:11.
168 John 14:1–3, 16–18; 16:7; Acts 1–2.
169 Joel 2:28–29.
170 Zechariah 10:2; Matthew 23:1–7, 23–37; Mark 6:34; Luke 11:46.
171 John 14:26; 15:26; 16:8, 13; 1 Corinthians 2:12; 1 John 2:27.
172 Luke 4:17–18; Isaiah 61:1; Jeremiah 31:31–34.
173 Elwell, 527.
174 Matthew 4:1–11; 12:18; Luke 4:18; John 14:10.
175 Isaiah 61:1–2; Luke 4:18–19.
176 John 7:38; 14:16–17, 26; 15:26; 16:7.
177 John 16:13.
178 John 15:26–27.
179 Acts 13:2; 15:28; 16:6–7; 20:28.
180 John 15:26; 16:13–14.
181 Boice, 381.
182 Acts 16:14; 1 Corinthians 2:14; 1 Thessalonians 1:5; 1 Peter 1:23.
183 James 4:6; Ephesians 2:8.
184 John 16:9–11.
185 John 1:12; 3:3–8, 36; Romans 8:14–16; 2 Corinthians 5:17; Galatians 3:26; Titus 3:5; 1 John 3:1; 5:1.
186 1 Corinthians 12:13; Galatians 3:27; Ephesians 2:19; 4:5.
187 Romans 8:9.
188 John 7:37–39; 14:17; 1 Corinthians 6:19–20; John 17:23; Colossians 1:27.
189 Romans 8:16.
190 Ephesians 1:22–23; 2:22.
191 John 14:26; 15:26; 16:13.
192 John 14:26; 15:26; Acts 9:31; 2 Corinthians 1:4; 7:6.
193 John 16:13; Matthew 24–25; Mark 13; Romans 11; 1 Corinthians 15; Book of Revelation
194 Matthew 27:66.
195 Ephesians 1:13; 2 Corinthians 1:22 ; 2 Timothy 2:19; Matthew 28:20.
196 Ephesians 1:14.
197 Ephesians 1:11, 18; 1 Peter 1:4.
198 Walvoord, 619.
199 Ezekiel 36:27.
200 Galatians 5:16–17–24; Ephesians 5:17–18.
201 Romans 5:5; Ephesians 2:22; 3:17; 4:11–16.
202 1 Corinthians 12:11; Ephesians 4:11–16; 1 Peter 4:10; Romans 12:6–8.
203 2 Corinthians 3:18.
204 Genesis 1:26; 9:6.
205 2 Corinthians 3:18; 5:17–21.
206 Romans 12:2; 2 Corinthians 10:5; Ephesians 4:23; Hebrews 4:12; Jam. 1:22–27; 2 Peter 3:18.
207 Galatians 5:22–23; John 15:1–5.
208 Elwell, 462–463.

Chapter Eleven

1   Woods, 49.
2   1 John 2:22–23; 4:1–3; 5:1, 10–12, 20.
3   Mark 16:15; Acts 13:32–33; 1 Corinthians 1:18–31; Colossians 4:3; 2 Timothy 4:2.
4   1 Corinthians 11:24–26.
5   Jonathan Z. Smith, ed., *Dictionary of Religion* (San Francisco, CA: HarperCollins, 1995), 250.
6   Romans 3:24; 4:3–16; Ephesians 2:8–9.
7   Genesis 2:17; Romans 6:23; 1 Peter 2:24.
8   John 3:16; Romans 5:8; 1 John 3:16; 4:10.
9   John 1:12; 3:16.
10 Acts 2:38.
11 Ephesians 2:8–9.
12 James 2:19.
13 Hebrews 9:27; Revelation 20:11.
14 Romans 3:28; Ephesians 2:9; 2 Timothy 1:9; Titus 3:5.
15 John 3:16–19; Acts 4:12; 10:43.
16 Ephesians 2:1, 4–9; Philippians 2:6–8.
17 2 Peter 3:9.
18 http://comparativereligion.com.
19 Charles Colson, *Answers to Your Kids' Questions* (Wheaton, IL: Tyndale House Publishers, 2000).

20   Matthew 25:40; Ephesians 2:10;
     Titus 2:14; 3:14.
21   Smith, Jonathan Z., 251.
22   Matthew 22:37–40; Mark 12:29–31.
23   Elwell, 659.
24   1 John 4:8, 16.
25   Elwell, 657.
26   Isaiah 43:4, 10; 54:10; 63:9;
     Jeremiah 31:3; Romans 5:8; 1 John
     3:1; 4:9–10.
27   John 3:16; 1 John 3:16.
28   Romans 8:7.
29   Romans 5:6–11; 2 Corinthians
     5:14–21; 1 John 4:10, 19.
30   John 3:16; Ephesians 2:4–5; 1 John
     4:9–10.
31   Romans 5:5.
32   Galatians 5:22; 1 John 4:7–8, 12–19.
33   Leviticus 19:18.
34   John 13:34–35; 15:12; 1 John 4:16.
35   Elwell, 659.
36   John 13:35.
37   Gellman, 200.
38   1 Corinthians 13:1–3, 13.
39   Deuteronomy 10:18; Jeremiah 22:3;
     Jam. 1:27.
40   Luke 10:27–37; 1 John 3:17.
41   1 Corinthians 4:7; Jam. 1:17.
42   Ephesians 5:20; 1 Thessalonians
     5:18.
43   Philippians 2:5–11; Hebrews 12:2–3.
44   Matthew 28:20.
45   Romans 8:28.
46   Romans 8:28–32; 2 Corinthians
     3:18; 12:7–10; Galatians 4:19;
     Philippians 3:21; Colossians 3:10.
47   Philippians 1:6; Hebrews 13:5.
48   Romans 5:3–4; Jam. 1:2–4; 1 Peter
     1:6–7; 4:12; 5:10.
49   Unger, 613.
50   Psalm 5:11.
51   Psalm 16:11.
52   Psalm 30:5.
53   Psalm 35:9.
54   Psalm 51:12.
55   Psalm 71:23.
56   Psalm 126:5.
57   Luke 2:10–11; Philippians 4:4.

58   Romans 14:17; 15:13; Galatians
     5:22.
59   Gellman, 187.
60   John 16:33.
61   James 5:11.
62   Job 2:9–10.
63   Hosea 11:8; 2 Peter 3:9.
64   Matthew 18:21–35; 1 Corinthians
     13:4; Galatians 5:22;
     1 Thessalonians 5:14.
65   Matthew 5:5.
66   Gellman, 183.
67   Matthew 23:12; Philippians 2:5–11;
     Jam. 4:6; 1 Peter 5:5.
68   Gellman, 185.
69   Gellman, 185.
70   Proberbs 13:34.
71   Romans 8:24–25; 2 Corinthians
     1:10.
72   Romans 15:4.
73   Douglas, 535.
74   Hebrews 6:19.
75   Romans 15:13; Hebrews 11:1.
76   1 Corinthians 15:19.
77   Hebrews 13:14.
78   1 John 3:2–3.
79   James 1:2; 1 Peter 1:6.
80   Galatians 5:17–21; 1 Peter 2:11.
81   Romans 1:24–28; Hebrews 13:4.
82   1 Corinthians 7:9.
83   Matthew 5:27–28.
84   Galatians 5:16–23.
85   Matthew 5:8; Galatians 6:7–9.
86   Matthew 18:6; Romans 14:13;
     1 Corinthians 8:12–13.
87   Gellman, 194–195.
88   Ephesians 4:30–32.
89   Matthew 5:22–24; Romans
     12:17–19.
90   Romans 8:1; 1 Corinthians 3:12–15.
91   Psalm 51:12; Matthew 6:15;
     Galatians 5:16–25.
92   Psalm 32:1–5; Hebrews 12:5–11.
93   Psalm 51:17; Matthew 6:14; 1 John
     1:9.
94   Psalm 51:17.
95   Ephesians 4:32; Colossians 3:13.
96   Matthew 6:12; 18:21–35.
97   Deuteronomy 32:35; Hebrews 10:30.

98 Matthew 16:27; Romans 2:5–6;
Colossians 3:25; Revelation 20:12.

99 Unger, 377.

100 Matthew 18:21–35; 1 John 4:19.

101 John 15:4–5; Galatians 5:22.

102 Luke 23:34.

103 Gellman, 204.

104 Deuteronomy 28:1–14.

105 Deuteronomy 28:15–68.

106 Ezekiel 36:26–27; Jeremiah 31:33;
32:40.

107 1 John 1:6–2:6.

108 Acts 6:7; Romans 6:17; 1 Peter 1:22.

109 John 6:29; 1 John 3:23.

110 John 3:18, 36; 1 Peter 2:8; 4:17.

111 Romans 7:1–8:4.

112 Douglas, 904.

113 Romans 3:28; 5:1; Ephesians 2:9.

114 Ephesians 6:1.

115 Hebrews 13:17.

116 Romans 13:1–7; 1 Peter 2:13–15;
Titus 3:1.

117 Matthew 22:21.

118 Gellman, 205–206.

119 Acts 5:29.

120 Gellman, 208.

121 John 8:31–32; 2 Corinthians 3:17;
Galatians 5:1.

122 Galatians 6:7.

123 John 8:31–32.

124 John 1:12; 1 Corinthians 12:13.

125 Matthew 16:18; Romans 12:4–5;
1 Corinthians 10:32; 12:12–13; 15:9;
Galatians 1:13; Ephesians 1:22–23;
4:4, 12; 5:30; Colossians 1:18, 24;
1 Timothy 3:15.

126 Ephesians 1:22–23.

127 Ephesians 2:21–22.

128 Hebrews 10:25.

129 Acts 2:42; 20:7; 1 Corinthians 16:2;
Hebrews 10:25; 13:15; Psalm 96.

130 Acts 2:42; Ephesians 4:11–15;
Colossians 1:28; 1 Timothy 4:13;
2 Timothy 2:15; 3:16; 1 Peter 2:2.

131 Acts 2:42; 4:32, 34; 1 Corinthians
12: 4–7, 25; Ephesians 4:1–3, 11–16;
Philippians 2:1–5; 1 Thessalonians
5:11; Hebrews 10:24–25.

132 Matthew 5:13–16; 28:19–20;
1 Corinthians 1:18–21;
2 Corinthians 5:18–20; 1 Peter 3:15.

133 John 13:34.

134 Philippians 2:3–4.

135 Romans 3:22; 1 Corinthians 12:13;
Galatians 3:28; Colossians 3:11;
1 John 3:16–18; 4:7–8, 20.

136 Romans 5:5; Galatians 5:16, 22.

137 Acts 2:42; Ephesians 4:11–16;
Hebrews 3:13; 10:24–25.

138 Gellman, 219.

139 Romans 12:2.

140 Matthew 5:13–16; John 13:34–35;
17:15–18.

141 Isaiah 42:5–8.

142 Isaiah 65:2–7; John 1:11; Romans
11:21.

143 Luke 2:32.

144 Matthew 19:28.

145 Acts 1:8; Matthew 28:18–20.

146 1 Peter 2:9.

147 Elwell, 233.

148 Acts 20:17–28; Ephesians 4:11;
1 Timothy 3:1–7; Titus 1:5, 7;
1 Peter 5:1–2.

149 Titus 1:5–9; Acts 20:17, 28.

150 Ephesians 4:11.

151 1 Peter 5:1–4.

152 Acts 6:1–6; 1 Timothy 3:8–13.

153 1 Corinthians 12:5–6.

154 1 Timothy 3:2; Titus 1:7.

155 Titus 1:5; Acts 14:23.

156 Acts 14:23; 15:4; 1 Timothy 5:17;
Titus 1:5.

157 1 Thessalonians 5:12–13; Hebrews
13:17.

158 1 Peter 2:9.

159 Galatians; 2 Corinthians 10–13;
2 John

160 WashingtonPost.com online.

161 ForMinistry.com online.

162 Elwell, 231.

163 Ephesians 4:4.

164 Elwell, 232.

165 1 Corinthians 1:10; 11:18–19;
Ephesians 4:3; Jude 1:18–19; John
17:23.

166 Philippians 3:12a; 1 John 1:8.

[167] 2 Corinthians 3:18; Ephesians 4:13; Philippians 1:6; Colossians 1:28; 1 John 3:2.

[168] 1 John 1:8–10; 2:1.

[169] Romans 1:7; 1 Corinthians 1:2; 6:11; 2 Corinthians 1:1; Ephesians 1:1; Philippians 1:1; Colossians 1:2; Hebrews 3:1; 10:10, 14; 1 Peter 2:5.

[170] Romans 8:1; Hebrews 10:10.

[171] Matthew 26:26–29; 28:19–20; Luke 3:21; John 1:26–34; Acts 2:41; 8:12; 1 Corinthians 11:23–26.

[172] Elwell, 965.

[173] Eerdman's, 359.

[174] Acts 2:41.

[175] Matthew 28:19.

[176] John 3:5.

[177] Romans 6:3–4.

[178] Romans 6:3–11; 2 Corinthians 5:14; Colossians 3:1.

[179] Romans 6:3–5.

[180] Eerdman's, 359.

[181] Matthew 26:17; John 13:1; Exodus 12–13.

[182] 1 Corinthians 11:23–32; Matthew 26:26–29; Luke 22:14–23; Mark 14:22–25.

[183] Mark 14:12; John 1:29; 1 Corinthians 5:7; 1 Peter 1:19.

[184] Gellman, 123.

[185] 1 Corinthians 11:24–25.

[186] Elwell, 653.

[187] 1 Corinthians 11:23–32; Matthew 26:26–29; Luke 22:14–23; Mark 14:22–25.

[188] 1 Corinthians 11:27–34.

[189] 1 Corinthians 11:29.

[190] John 13–17.

[191] John 14:1–3.

[192] Hebrews 9:28.

[193] Acts 1:11; Matthew 24:3; Zechariah 14:4.

[194] Matthew 24:27.

[195] 2 Thessalonians 2:8.

[196] 1 Corinthians 15:23.

[197] Matthew 24:31; 2 Thessalonians 2:1.

[198] 1 Peter 4:13.

[199] Matthew 24:27–30.

[200] Hebrews 1:3; 12:2; 1 Corinthians 15:25.

[201] Revelation 3:21.

[202] 1 Corinthians 1:7; 2 Thessalonians 1:7; 1 Peter 1:7, 13.

[203] Weaver, 30.

[204] Wilkinson, xx.

[205] Boice, 705.

[206] John 5:29.

[207] Boice, 708.

[208] Revelation 20:11.

[209] Luke 2:11; Acts 5:31; 1 Tim 1:1; 2 Tim 1:10; Titus 1:4; 2 Peter 1:1; 1 John 4:14.

[210] Revelation 16:12–16.

[211] Revelation 20:1–3.

[212] Revelation 20:4–5.

[213] Wilkinson, xxi.

[214] Revelation 20:11.

[215] Revelation 20:12.

[216] Revelation 20:13–15.

[217] Revelation 20:11–14.

[218] Revelation 21.

[219] 1 Corinthians 2:9.

[220] Revelation 21:3.

[221] Revelation 21:4.

[222] Revelation 22:5.

[223] 1 Peter 3:10–13.

Chapter Twelve

[1] Woods, 68.

[2] Gellman, 86.

[3] Edwards, 125.

[4] Hebrews 1:1.

[5] Bickel, 31.

[6] Halley, 22.

[7] 2 Timothy 3:16.

[8] 2 Peter 1:21.

[9] Wilkinson, xxiii.

[10] Matthew 19:4; 22:29.

[11] Elwell, 136.

[12] 1 Corinthians 2:7–13; 14:37; 1 Thessalonians 2:13.

[13] Revelation 1:2.

[14] Colossians 4:16; 1 Thessalonians 5:27; 2 Thessalonians 2:15.

[15] 2 Peter 1:15; 3:1–2.

[16] 2 Peter 3:15–16.

[17] Elwell, 140.

18 Jeremiah 31:31; 2 Corinthians 3:6;
    Hebrews 9:15.
19 Unger, 1085–1086.
20 Etinger, 159.
21 Edwards, 131–132.
22 MacDonald, 16.
23 Gellman, 253–254.
24 Geisler & Brooks, 155–156.
25 Edwards, 131–132.
26 Gellman, 255.
27 Halley, 742–747.
28 Halley, 747.
29 Geisler & Holden, 107.
30 Rene Pache, *The Inspiration and
    Authority of Scripture* (Chicago:
    Moody Press, 1969), 190.
31 George Barna, Pres. of *The Barna
    Research Group, Ltd.* (1957 Eastman
    Ave., Ste B, Ventura, CA 93003).
32 Norman L. Geisler and William E.
    Nix, *General Introduction to the
    Bible* (Chicago: Moody Press, 1986),
    chapter 22.
33 Halverson, 259; and http://www.
    carm.org/evidence/rewritten.htm.
34 Frederick Fyvie Bruce, *The New
    Testament Documents: Are They
    Reliable?* (Downer's Grove, IL:
    InterVarsity Press, 1972), 13ff.
35 Encyclopedia Britannica Online,
    http://members.eb.com/bol/
    topic?eu=119712&sctn=9.
36 Ramachandra, 91.
37 Bruce, 20.
38 Halverson, 259; and http://www.
    carm.org/evidence/rewritten.htm.
39 Geisler & Brooks, 159–160.
40 Geisler & Holden, 108.
41 http://www.carm.org/evidence/
    rewritten.htm.
42 Geisler & Holden, 108.
43 Bruce, 13ff.
44 Halverson, 260.
45 Geisler & Brooks, 159–160.
46 Tacitus. *The Annals of Imperial Rome,*
    rev. ed., Michael Grant, translator
    (New York: Penguin Books, 365.
47 Acts 11:26; 26:28.
48 Luke 3:1; 23:24–25.
49 Acts 28:16.
50 John 15:20.
51 Hebrews 11.
52 Geisler & Holden, 109–110.
53 Acts 18:2.
54 Acts 26:28.
55 Geisler & Holden, 110.
56 Matthew 13:55; Acts 15:13.
57 Luke 23:24–25.
58 John 1.
59 Acts 23:2.
60 Michael Wilkins, *Jesus under Fire:
    Modern Scholarship Reinvents the
    Historical Jesus* (Grand Rapids, MI:
    Zondervan Publishing House, 1996.
61 Keels, 15.
62 Wilkinson, xxiii.
63 For example, see Jeremiah 1:1–3;
    Ezekiel 1:1–3; Luke 3:1–2.
64 John 18:28–19:22.
65 Luke 2:2.
66 John 5:2.
67 Geisler & Holden, 112.
68 Matthew 2:23; 10:47.
69 http://www.carm.org/evidence/
    rewritten.htm
70 Matthew 2:1.
71 Matthew 2:19, 22; 14:1.
72 Mark 1:29.
73 John 19; 20:24–29.
74 Matthew 26:57.
75 http://www.carm.org/evidence/
    rewritten.htm
76 Genesis 11:31.
77 Morris, *Science*, 94–95.
78 Joshua 6:20.
79 Joshua 6:24.
80 Peter Colon, "Archaeology Confirms
    the Walls Fell Flat," *Israel My Glory*
    (Jan./Feb. 2004, Vol. 62, No. 1), 16.
81 Isaiah 20:1.
82 Isaiah 20:1.
83 Daniel 5.
84 Christian Answers; http://www.
    christiananswers.net.
85 Exodus 7–12.
86 Exodus 7:20.
87 Exodus 9:25.
88 Exodus 9:23–24.

[89] Exodus 10:22.

[90] Papyrus 4:3; 6:13; 2:13; 3:14.

[91] Geisler & Brooks, 192; also see Exodus 12:29–30.

[92] Papyrus 3:1.

[93] Exodus 17:8–16.

[94] Agag I and II; also see Numbers 24:7; 1 Samuel 15:8.

[95] Geisler & Brooks, 192–193.

[96] Geisler & Brooks, 182.

[97] Genesis 14.

[98] Geisler & Brooks, 187.

[99] 1 Samuel 17.

[100] Geisler & Brooks, 196; see also Judges 20:16.

[101] John 19:31–32.

[102] Geisler & Brooks, 207.

[103] Geisler & Brooks, 198–199.

[104] Isaiah 36–37.

[105] James B. Pritchard, *Ancient Near East Texts* (Princeton, NJ: The Princeton University Press, 1950), 288.

[106] Etinger, 92.

[107] Halverson, 260.

[108] Halverson, 261–262.

[109] See 2 Samuel 22:16; Job 38:16; Psalm 18:15; Jonah 2:6.

[110] Kenny Barfield, *Why the Bible is Number One* (Grand Rapids, MI: Baker Book House, 1988), 170.

[111] See Genesis 7:11; Job 38:16; Proverbs 8:28.

[112] Barfield, 171.

[113] Exodus 23:10–11.

[114] William Cairney, "Biomedical Prescience 1: Hebrew Dietary Laws." *Evidence for Faith,* John W. Montgomery, ed. (Dallas, TX: Word Publishing, 1991), 134.

[115] See Job 26:7.

[116] Etinger, 95.

[117] See Job 36:27–29; also Job 26:8; Ecclesiastes 1:67.

[118] Etinger, 95.

[119] Halverson, 262.

[120] Genesis 1:8, 14–17.

[121] Jeremiah 31:37.

[122] Genesis 1:1.

[123] Dennis Overbye, *Lonely Hearts of the Cosmos* (New York: Harper Collins, 1991), 39; Jastrow, *Astronomers,* 112–113.

[124] Halverson, 261; also Numbers 19:17, 19.

[125] Halverson, 261.

[126] Geisler & Holden, 114–115.

[127] Job 36:27–29; Ecclesiastes 1:6–7.

[128] Leviticus 12–15; Numbers 19.

[129] Job 38:16; Psalm 18:15; Jonah 2:6.

[130] Genesis 7:11; Proverbs 8:28.

[131] Isaiah 40:22.

[132] Job 9:9; 38:31.

[133] Exodus 23:10–11.

[134] Genesis 2:7.

[135] Genesis 1:1.

[136] Psalm 102:22–27; Romans 8:20–22.

[137] Isaiah 55:9.

[138] Genesis 15:5; Jeremiah 33:22.

[139] Leviticus 17:11.

[140] Geisler & Holden, 115.

[141] Halverson, 262.

[142] Halverson, 262; also see Isaiah 46:9–10; Isaiah 48:3–5; 2 Peter 1:19–21.

[143] Elwell, 886–887.

[144] Geisler & Holden, 115–116.

[145] Halverson, 263; also see Isaiah 46:10.

[146] Deuteronomy 18:22.

[147] Deuteronomy 18:20.

[148] Halverson, 264.

[149] Andre Kole and Jerry MacGregor, *Mind Games* (Eugene, OR: Harvest House, 1998), 37–52; Andre Kole, *Miracle and Magic* (Eugene, OR: Harvest House, 1984), 69–70.

[150] See Christiananswers.net online.

[151] Romans 11:33–34.

Chapter Thirteen

[1] Woods, 437.

[2] Helm, 1.

[3] Smith, Jonathan Z., 251–253.

[4] Edwards, 307.

[5] Weaver, 44–45.

[6] Weaver, 46.

[7] Acts 17:16–34.

8 Smith, Jonathan Z., 243.

9 Matthew 24:15–21.

10 Weaver, 45.

11 Weaver, 46.

12 B. K. Kuiper, *The Church in History* (Grand Rapids, MI: Eerdmans Publishing, 1978), 8.

13 Weaver, 49.

14 Matthew 5:9; 5:38–42 26:52; Luke 6:27–35.

15 http://www.adherents.com online.

16 http://www.adherents.com online.

17 Richard R. Losch, *The Many Faces of Faith* (Grand Rapids, MI: Eerdmans Publishing, 2001), 70.

18 http://www.adherents.com online.

19 Weaver, 41.

20 Edwards, 309.

21 Weaver, 42.

22 Weaver, 47.

23 http://www.adherents.com online.

24 http://www.adherents.com online.

25 Weaver, 50.

26 Smith, Jonathan Z., 243.

27 http://www.adherents.com online.

28 Smith, Jonathan Z., 244.

29 Halley, 769.

30 Smith, Jonathan Z., 244.

31 http://www.adherents.com online.

32 Kuiper, 41–42.

33 Halley, 770.

34 Kuiper, 18.

35 Edwards, 325.

36 Williston Walker, *A History of the Christian Church* (New York: Charles Scribner's Sons, 1970), 129.

37 http://www.adherents.com online.

38 Smith, Jonathan Z., 245.

39 Smith, Jonathan Z., 246.

40 Packer, 23.

41 Losch, 70.

42 Losch, 70–71.

43 Edwards, 332.

44 Losch, 71.

45 Edwards, 332.

46 Walker, 127–128.

47 http://www.adherents.com online.

48 Smith, Jonathan Z., 247.

49 Smith, Jonathan Z., 247.

50 Edwards, 341.

51 http://www.adherents.com online.

52 Halley, 774.

53 Renwick and Harman, *The Story of the Church* (Leicester, England: Inter Varsity Press, 1985), 86–87.

54 John XI)

55 Halley, 774–784.

56 Smith, Jonathan Z., 246.

57 Edwards, 333.

58 Edwards, 339.

59 Edwards, 340.

60 Kuiper, 120.

61 Kuiper, 121.

62 Losch, 71–72.

63 http://www.adherents.com online.

64 Kuiper, 89.

65 Losch, 71.

66 http://www.adherents.com online.

67 http://www.adherents.com online.

68 http://www.adherents.com online.

69 Halley, 775.

70 Halley, 776.

71 http://www.adherents.com online.

72 Halley, 776–777.

73 Kuiper, 142.

74 Weaver, 84.

75 Weaver, 84.

76 Weaver, 89.

77 Kuiper, 136–137.

78 Edwards, 385.

79 Edwards, 344.

80 Weaver, 85.

81 Weaver, 86.

82 Losch, 72.

83 Halley, 779.

84 Smith, Jonathan Z., 247.

85 Smith, Jonathan Z., 247.

86 Edwards, 333.

87 Smith, Jonathan Z., 247–248.

88 Weaver, 83.

89 Edwards, 346.

Chapter Fourteen

1 Woods, 437.

2 Edwards, 346.

3 Edwards, 347.

4 Edwards, 347.

5 Kuiper, 151.

6   Edwards, 347.

7   Kuiper, 149.

8   Edwards, 348.

9   Kuiper, 158–160.

10   Kuiper, 149.

11   Losch, 72.

12   Kuiper, 143.

13   Weaver, 87.

14   Weaver, 88–89.

15   Weaver, 94.

16   Weaver, 94.

17   Kuiper, 162–163.

18   John 8:32; Acts 16:14; Galatians 5:1.

19   John 1:12; 3:16; Romans 6:23.

20   Edwards, 346.

21   Kuiper, 164.

22   Edwards, 349.

23   Kuiper, 170–171.

24   Edwards, 349.

25   Michael Collins, *The Story of Christianity* (New York: DK Publishing, 1999), 134.

26   *Collin's*, 135.

27   Edwards, 349.

28   Weaver, 95.

29   Collins, 135.

30   Edwards, 349.

31   Smith, Jonathan Z., 248.

32   Weaver, 100.

33   Weaver, 101.

34   Losch, 73.

35   Weaver, 103–104.

36   Weaver, 109.

37   Edwards, 351–352.

38   Weaver, 104.

39   Weaver, 109–110.

40   Smith, Jonathan Z., 248.

41   Smith, Jonathan Z., 248.

42   Edwards. 355–356.

43   Edwards. 363.

44   Weaver, 114.

45   Kuiper, 256.

46   Edwards. 363–367.

47   Weaver, 109.

48   Timothy Dowley, ed., *Eerdmans' Handbook to the History of Christianity* (Grand Rapids, MI: Eerdmans Publishing, 1977), 480.

49   Weaver, 115.

50   Howard F. Vos, *Exploring Church History* (Nashville, TN: Thomas Nelson Publishers, 1994), 111.

51   Weaver, 115.

52   Weaver, 119.

53   Dowley, 442.

54   Edwards. 358–359.

55   Vos, 118.

56   Collins, 183.

57   Weaver, 123.

58   Weaver, 129.

59   Vos, 120.

60   Jesse Lyman Hurlbut, *The Story of the Christian Church* (Grand Rapids, MI: Zondervan Publishing House, 1970), 140.

61   Vos, 121.

62   Kuiper, 304.

63   Collins, 181.

64   Edwards, 388.

65   Vos, 121.

66   Collins, 190.

67   Collins, 180.

68   Collins, 192–193.

69   Collins, 194–195.

70   Collins, 200–201.

71   Collins, 200.

72   Smith, Jonathan Z., 250.

73   Collins, 226.

74   Heibert, *Anthro*, 288.

75   Heibert, *Anthro*, 289.

76   Eerdman's, 383.

77   Eerdman's, 384, 386.

78   Eerdman's, 385.

79   Eerdman's, 385.

80   Collins, 196.

81   Collins, 229.

82   International Bible Society, http://www.ibs.org.

83   Wycliffe Bible Translators, http://www.wycliffe.net.

84   Collins, 226.

85   Gellman, 316.

86   Gellman, 318.

87   Gellman, 318–319.

88   Matthew 22:39.

89   Smith, Jonathan Z., 251.

90   Collins, 197.

Epilogue

[1] Herbert V. Prochnow, *The Toastmaster's Treasure Chest* (New York: Harper & Row, 1988), 93.

[2] Ramachandra, 167.

[3] Ramachandra, 168.

[4] James S. Spiegel, *Hypocrisy: Moral Fraud & Other Vices* (Grand Rapids, MI: Baker Book House, 1999), 129.

[5] Luke 6:29.

[6] Romans 13:8.

[7] Acts 10:34.

[8] Matthew 1:1–16.

[9] Matthew 5:43–44; Romans 16:19; Colossians 4:5–6; 1 Timothy 3:7.

[10] http://www.Carm.org.

[11] Gellman, 71–72.

[12] http://www.Carm.org.

[13] Barrett.

[14] Barrett.

[15] Rabbi Daniel Lapin, Pres. of *Toward Tradition* (PO Box 58, Mercer Island, WA 98040; 206-236-3046).

[16] Lapin.

[17] Lapin.

[18] *Washington Times* (June 27, 2002). www.washtimes.com.

[19] David A. Noebel, Pres. of *Summit Ministries* (PO Box 207, Manitou Springs, CO 80829; 719-685-9103).

[20] Gellman, 71–72.

Glossary

[1] Matthew 10:2–5; Acts 1:13–14.

[2] Revelation 16:16.

[3] Genesis 17:9–14.

[4] Genesis 6:18; 9:8.

[5] Genesis 17:2.

[6] Exodus 20–23.

[7] Mark 1:34, 39.

[8] Romans 3:24; Ephesians 1:7; Titus 2:11.

[9] Acts 6:1.

[10] Matthew 6:33; Mark 1:15.

[11] Luke 13:29.

[12] Luke 10:9; 17:21.

INDEX

Printed in the United States
202266BV00001B/82-1026/P